INCLUSIVE CITIES

About the Authors

Prof. Kalpana Markandey has been Faculty at Osmania University since 1979. She has published 10 books and about 40 research papers. She has also prepared two digital atlases. Prof. Markandey has guided 11 research projects and brought out 15 technical bulletins. She has attended about 70 international and National Seminars, Conferences, Workshops and Symposia, many of which she has organized. She has been instrumental in starting M.Sc Geoinformatics course in Geography Department, Osmania University, Hyderabad, India. She is former Head, Department of Geography, Osmania University, Hyderabad and also former Chairperson Board of studies of the same department. She has guided a number of M.Phils and Ph.Ds and is the member of a large number of Professional Bodies. She has given lectures on about 35 topics for Educational Multimedia Country-Wide classroom of UGC as Subject Expert apart from being a resource person for various other programmes. She is also on the advisory board of various national committees. Prof. Markandey's area of interest is Urban Geography.

Dr. B. Srinagesh, working as Associate Professor, has an experience of 14 years in teaching as well as research. He has 19 papers to his credit. His area of specialization is urban and regional geography. He has three major research projects to his credit and one minor research project. He has been actively involved in many International and National Conferences as Organizing Secretary. He has done 10 programmes in collaboration with UGC-EMMRC, Hyderabad. At present he is holding the post of Additional Controller of Examination, Osmania University, Hyderabad. He is a visiting faculty to reputed institutions in Hyderabad.

INCLUSIVE CITIES

Kalpana Markandey
and
B. Srinagesh

CONCEPT PUBLISHING COMPANY PVT. LTD.
NEW DELHI-110059

ISBN-13 : 978-81-8069-953-5

First Published 2014

Published and Printed by

Concept
Since 1974

Concept Publishing Company Pvt. Ltd.
A/15-16, Commercial Block, Mohan Garden
New Delhi-110059 (India)
T: 25351460, 25351794, *F*: 091-11-25357109
E: publishing@conceptpub.com, W: www.conceptpub.com
Editorial Office: H-13, Bali Nagar, New Delhi-110 015, India.

Cataloging in Publication Data—*Courtesy:* D.K. Agencies (P) Ltd. <docinfo@dkagencies.com>

Markandey, Kalpana, 1956-
Inclusive cities / Kalpana Markandey and B. Srinagesh.
p. cm.
Includes bibliographical references (p.) and index.
ISBN 9788180699535

1. Housing policy—India—Hyderabad. 2. Urbanization—India—Hyderabad. 3. Cities and towns—India—Hyderabad—Growth. I. Srinagesh, B., joint author. II. Title.

DDC 333.33709542 23

Preface

An inclusive city seeks to bring the poor and the lower income groups into the mainstream of cities. The problem of houselessness in the shadow of opulence is not new to urban areas, but the city of Hyderabad has witnessed an unprecedented increase of the housing stock of the more affluent in the past twenty years, which glares in the face of housing shortage and street dwellers on the other side. The city has witnessed an unprecedented phenomenon 'the gated communities', which have increased multifold in the recent past, occupying prime land in the city. The gated communities are a kind of representation of plural society having a fair mix of caste and religious groups. The community is thus **inclusive** in terms of caste and religious groups. The element of **exclusivity** of these communities comes when the income, educational attainment and occupation of the people is taken into consideration. This book seeks to analyze the housing situation in Hyderabad from a multipronged perspective.

Informality and attendant vulnerability have been associated with urban housing especially of the lower - middle and lower income groups. Risks associated with respectable housing reflect on the productivity of the people. We can cater to affordable housing through policies and incentives that will lessen the gap between price and affordability. Rental housing also needs to be encouraged for those who cannot pay for a house even in the face of incentives. The perceptions of people on various count like satisfaction with regard to rent, spaciousness of accommodation, accommodation size, source of credit for building house, reason for change of house in the recent past, satisfaction or otherwise with regard to neighbourhood, prevalence of Human Dignity, Equity, Social Justice, Solidarity, Free Choice, Free Movement, Civic Participation by Residents etc have been measured. The satisfaction or otherwise of residents on an array of variables related to the house and neighbourhood has been examined. Housing Finance and Governmental Housing Schemes have also been examined for their merits or otherwise. The perception of inclusivity by residents stratified by income, religion, caste, occupation and education has also been examined.

The recommendations that flow out from this study are that land meant for housing the underprivileged should be subsidized and funds at low rates of interest should be provided for construction purpose. Home loan rates should be lowered as also the Income Tax exemption limit on home loan interest repayment.

Development of integrated township in the area which can also house information technology firms can be taken up. The development of the township can be undertaken, in the private public partnership. The poor can be provided access to safe drinking water and drainage. Also pollution control and personal safety in slums can help the poor. This will cut down the health costs of the less privileged. They can also be given a sense of belongingness by encouraging labour intensive work routines and providing support for small-scale family enterprises and the informal sector. Inclusiveness in housing can be brought about by providing reasonably priced housing and also by guarding rental housing and ensuring that people are not displaced due to reasons beyond their control. This is apart from providing a well knit society, more so that which is assorted from the religious, cultural and caste point of view, giving a multi - cultural touch to the society, which will be healthy, tolerant and nationalistic.

Hyderabad

Kalpana Markandey
B. Srinagesh

Acknowledgements

This book is the outcome of a Major Research Project funded by UGC entitled 'Inclusive Cities'. We are immensely indebted to the Commission for funding the project. We are grateful to the Osmania University authorities to permit us to carry out this project from the Department of Geography. We are thankful to all the Governmental agencies and organizations that have provided data for this work. We are grateful to the respondents in the sample households who spared their precious time to answer questions in the rather elaborate questionnaire. We are thankful to the staff that worked on the project specially Mrs. D. Sri Usha, Mr. V. Vijay Kumar, Dr. Kavita Toran and Mrs. G. Swapna Reddy and the entire team of Field Assistants who worked tirelessly for the project. But for their hard work we could not have acquired the huge mass of primary data. We are thankful to Ms. J. Lavanya for helping with proof reading and other Secreterial assistance.

Hyderabad

Kalpana Markandey
B. Srinagesh

Contents

List of Figures

List of Tables

1

Introduction

Context

Globalization, the spread of outsourcing and related culture, has immeasurably transformed the economy and society of many cities of the developing countries. This transformation has manifested itself in the form of an expansion of the tertiary sector of the economy and modernization of societies in cities which are frontrunners in the Information Technology arena. Hyderabad has been one such city in India, which has witnessed this revolutionary change in its economy and society in the past two decades.

While the pros include a vibrant economy, new improved infrastructure, structures which vie with international standards, a world class work culture and gender inclusivity apart from others, the cons manifest themselves in the form of erosion of traditional values and belief systems, the widening chasms between the haves and have-nots, disposable income etc.—factors which have made their presence felt of late.

The role of international players in shaping the destinies of cities and countries at large has set in motion the competitive ecological forces where the players who are advantageously placed and can strike the right chords, usually head the symphony or call the shots. These enrapturing tendencies are found in the infrastructure arena, housing markets, educational fields, banking and health care among a motley of activity types. The result is that a certain section of these activities find themselves catapulted to the world class standards, of course at a handsome price tag, while the other end of the spectrum is steeped in disarray and the twain are in absolute disharmony. This is where one finds that a certain section of these services cater to an exclusive genre of clientele. The rest of the population finds itself excluded from this 'exclusive club'.

Globalization has, in fact, widened the chasm between the haves and the have-nots leading to the exclusion of a large majority of the population from the mainstream society. It has created an identity crisis between 'we' and 'they' and it is 'they' who are perceptibly excluded in the midst of all the wealth[1]. The Human Development Report, 1999, notes that the income gap between the world's richest and the world's poorest has increased from 60 to 1 in 1990 to 74 to 1 in 1997[2]. This profound gap manifests itself several fold in the urban areas and is clearly evident in social exclusion and locational marginalization of groups within the city. Research shows that decreasing inequality can have as much impact on reducing poverty as increasing economic growth[3]. More inclusive urban governance is the key for cities to not only make human rights more effective, but also to make growth more equitable. Habitat's Global Campaign on Urban Governance promotes a vision of the "Inclusive City," a place where everyone can participate in and benefit from the opportunities cities offer. At the heart of the "Inclusive City" are three inter-related ideas that contribute to the realization of full citizenship: respect for human rights, good urban governance and equitable growth[4].

Social inclusiveness is an important goal for municipal governance: it is just, it is democratic and it is productive. As the world globalizes, diversity is going to be more, not less important. And the successful governance of diversity will distinguish the most accomplished and creative cities from all the rest[5].

The problem of houselessness in the shadow of opulence is not new to urban areas, but the city of Hyderabad has witnessed an unprecedented increase of the housing stock of the more well-to-do in the past twenty years, which glares in the face of housing shortage and street dwellers on the other side. The present study seeks to analyze the housing situation in Hyderabad in order to see what are factors prompting the inordinate growth in the housing stock of one type and an increase in unfulfilled demand from the other side of the spectrum.

The rate of increase of housing stock has not kept pace with the rate of increase of demand and the gap has been widening with the passage of time. Factors on the demand front include—(a) first generation migrants. They seek accommodation in various places depending on their educational level, placement in society as manifested in their occupations, etc., (b) Demand could also be created due to obsolescence. For every addition in the housing stock at a given point in time, there is also a deletion consequent on dilapidation and ageing. Fresh demand for housing is thus created by people who already had housing earlier, (c) Demand is also created by people who move up vertically in the socio-economic ladder, though this might be a nominal figure, and (d) All this is notwithstanding the existing compounded shortage.

Supply could be generated—(a) out of the people's own resources, (b) own resources plus loan or assistance (from banks, LIC, Housing boards etc), (c) in the absence of own resources or credibility to raise loans, on external assistance. It is a combined mix of the above factors that are responsible for the present housing scenario in Hyderabad, which has brought in more of 'Exclusivity' on the urban front.

Inclusiveness in housing can be brought about by creating direct benefits like eliminating houselessness, by providing reasonably priced housing and also by protecting rental housing and ensuring that people are not displaced due to reasons beyond their control. This is apart from providing a well knit society, more so that which is heterogeneous from the religious, cultural and caste point of view, giving a multi-cultural touch to the society, which will be strong, open-minded and patriotic.

Everyone is entitled to the full realization of their fundamental human rights. The Human Development Report, 2000 building on the theories of Nobel Laureate, Amartya Sen, characterizes these rights into seven core freedoms: freedom from discrimination—for equality; freedom from want—for a decent standard of living; freedom for the realization of one's human potential; freedom from fear—with no threats to personal security; freedom from injustice; freedom of participation, expression and association; and freedom for decent work—without exploitation[6].A city that is committed to the full realization of these freedoms is on the path to becoming an Inclusive City.

Human rights, however, must be realized within a society. The quality of urban governance—the way individuals and institutions, public and private, plan and manage the common affairs of the city—therefore is crucial. New roles and relationships between national government, city government, the private sector and civil society are required to address the challenges posed by an urbanizing and globalizing world. This is one of the central messages of the State of the World's Cities report, 2001 "a country's global success rests on local shoulders. For the good of all citizens, city and state must become political partners rather than competitors."[7] Cities that are committed to realizing human rights and to practicing good urban governance are more likely to ensure that economic growth is equitable.

According to Saskia Sassen, the top fifth of people in the richest countries produce 86 per cent of the world's GDP; the bottom fifth just 1 per cent. According to him "The urban glamour zone has fine restaurants, state of the art buildings, state of the art residences. It has it all: beautiful streets, private security, world class culture... The urban war zone, for me, is a part of the city that has been neglected in terms of basic public services, such as garbage collection... It's a zone where you have a sense of surplus population, a sense of who needs these people. And also a sense that these people have been robbed of something."[8]

Studies on urban disparities, urban economy and urban polity abound. Poverty in India is viewed as an aspect of social inequality and stratification. Slum housing is viewed as a commodity of exchange in the housing market where the trade off in the exchange value was seen as far greater than the use value by the slum dwellers[9]. The marginalization and sometimes deprivation in some of the pockets of the city cannot be overstated and demands an intensive study with a firm theoretical and methodological base. The concept of 'Inclusive Cities' encompassing the entire gamut of participants and viewed at from all perspectives has to be infused in the urban studies in India which are more compartmentalized and many a times outright empirical, without a firm theoretical grounding.

This study combines the traditional tools of the Geographers like maps with the modern Geoinformatic tools in carrying out this application oriented study of the housing or shelter problem in Hyderabad. The concepts from Society, Economy and Polity are knit into the structure of this study thus making it thoroughly interdisciplinary in nature. It is of as much use to the theoretician as to the practitioner and will also provide effective inputs into the planning policy at the local—Municipal level, regional—State level and also at the National Policy making level. The digital maps generated out of this study will be of interest and use to the technocrats, students and researchers.

Objectives

1. To view the change in the housing situation in Hyderabad in the past 20 years and relate it with the total population and land use scenario.
2. To observe the location of high, middle and low class residential areas and the changes and shifts in their location.
3. To identify gaps in adequate housing within the city and the social ramifications thereof.
4. To look for polarization in the housing market and allied ancillary facilities—schools, parks and playgrounds, shopping and service areas, religious places, etc.
5. To look for housing blight in a 'city-centre-suburban context'.
6. To look for the negative impact of blight on the economic and social health and the quality of life in many city neighbourhoods.
7. The perceptions of people with regard to rating of localities for residential preference will be studied.
8. The perceptions of people so far as amenities are concerned can also be studied. This could aid in the housing programme as a co-ordination of amenities with housing within the framework of income levels could be aimed at.
9. Perception with regard to house type will also be studied.

Methodology

A multi-stage stratified sampling frame is adopted for collecting primary data for this study. Table 1.1 and 1.2 gives the framework within which the sample has been collected. Primary data has been collected for a total of 1463 household in Hyderabad. A multi-stage stratified sampling frame is adopted for collecting data by means of a structured questionnaire where 10 per cent of localities in every ward chosen and 1 per cent households in sample localities are chosen. A structured questionnaire is administered to each one of the sample households to measure and consequently analyze and map their views.

Information was educed from the residents about a variety of issues besides the housing and neighbourhood conditions in the city and lacunae if any. This has helped in arriving at the perceptions of the people with regard to desirable locations, requirements of amenities, and economic capabilities. It is hoped that this exercise will enlighten all those who are involved in the housing scenario which include among others, the state, the civic authorities, private providers and the consumers, who span all categories of users, in making diligent decisions on their respective fronts.

Data and information with regard to the housing stock has also been collected from secondary sources like the Municipal Corporation of Hyderabad (now GHMC), Hyderabad Urban Development Authority (HUDA now HMDA), A.P. Housing Board, A.P State Housing Corporation Limited (APSHCL), Housing Finance Corporation and so on. Data with regard to the demographic variables is collected from the Census of India. Besides, this, the study is supplemented and complemented by archival data from newspapers and internet sources. Satellite Data has also been made use of in this study. This includes IRS 1D PAN and IRS 1D LISS of 2002, IRS LISS III Data of 2006, 2009 and IRS P6 Data of 2009 besides map data available from Google. GPS data has been made use of for georeferencing. Survey of India Toposheets have also been made use of.

The base map for the city and its extended extent has been done involving digitization, editing and rectification of base maps. The following base maps have been prepared for linking with the attribute data (Fig.1.1) in the GIS environment.

- Hyderabad City Map
- Hyderabad Urban Agglomeration Map
- Hyderabad City Locality Map
- Hyderabad Constituency Map
- Hyderabad Ward and Block Maps

The land use picture has been culled out (Fig. 1.2a and b) from the latest Imagery of the city. It is in an interactive mode where the Area Of Interest (AOI) has been placed on the satellite image of Hyderabad and animated. The AOI gradually fades into the image picture thus highlighting the land use profile in each one of the units.

Table 1.1: Multistage Stratified Probability Sampling Frame for MCH Units

Ward	*No of Localities*	*10% Sample*	*Name of the sample localities*	*1% sample household*
1	16	2	Ashok Nagar	22
1	16	2	Chikkadpally	31
2	11	1	Amberpet	22
3	8	1	Himayat Nagar	53
4	6	1	Sultan Bazar	14
5	8	1	Abids N and S	23
6	6	1	Khairatabad (E and W)	89
7	6	1	Ameerpet	51
8	15	2	Banjara Hills	118
8	15	2	Jubilee Hills	58
9	13	1	Langhar house (N and S)	20
10	9	1	Vijaynagar colony	27
11	3	1	Red Hills	28
12	6	1	Mehdipatnam	22
13	18	2	Sabzimandi	9
13	18	2	Karwan	3
14	4	1	Gosha mahal	20
15	3	1	Gowliguda Chaman	17
16	13	1	Saidabad Colony	30
17	10	1	Sarrornagar (E and W)	47
18	24	2	Barkas	16
18	24	2	Aliabad(S)	10
19	16	2	Devi bagh	18
19	16	2	Doodh Bowli	4
20	7	1	Hussain Alam	13
21	3	1	Gulzar House	14
22	6	1	Patther Gatti	5
23	6	1	Moghal pura	10
24	7	1	Begumpet	32
25	1	1	Ramgopalpet	16
26	1	1	General Bazar	8
27	1	1	Old Bhoiguda	10
28	1	1	Rani Gunj	12
29	5	1	Padmarao Nagar	10
30	1	1	Monda Market	9
31	1	1	Shivaji Nagar	20
32	1	1	Regimental Bazar	21
33	5	1	West Marredpally	30
33			Erukula Basti (Slum)	12
34	4	1	Warasiguda	31
35	9	1	Lalapet	30

Table 1.2: Multistage Stratified Probability Sampling Frame for Urban Agglomeration Units other than MCH

Sl. No.	*Direction*	*No.of Units*	*20% of Units*	*Name of Sample Localities*	*No.of Households*	*Sample Chosen*
1	North	4	1	Secunderabad (Cantonment Board)		30
2	North			Qutubullapur (M)	52188	30
3	North			Malkajgiri (M)	42291	30
4	North			Alwal (M+OG)	19478	29
5	East	4	1	Lal Bahadur Nagar (M+OG)	62290	20
6	East			Gaddiannaram (CT)	12053	30
7	East			Uppal Kalan (M+OG)	26275	40
8	East			Kapra (M)	36240	30
9	West	4	1	Serilingampally (M)	3611	39
10	West			Ramachandrapuram (CT)	32642	50
11	West			Patancheru (CT)	11678	30
12	West			Kukatpally	9282	30
13	South	3	1	Rajendranagar (M+OG)	30730	20
14	South			Shamshabad		10
15	South			Nadergul		10
					Total	**400**
					Grand Total (MCH & Non-MCH area)	**1463**

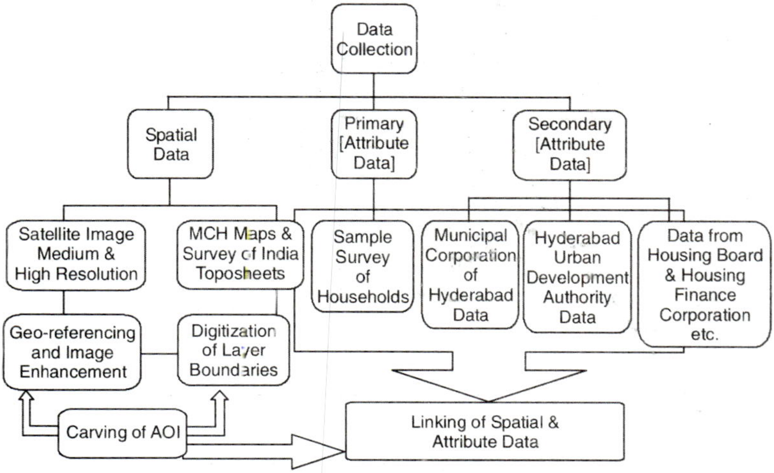

Fig. 1.1: Methodology

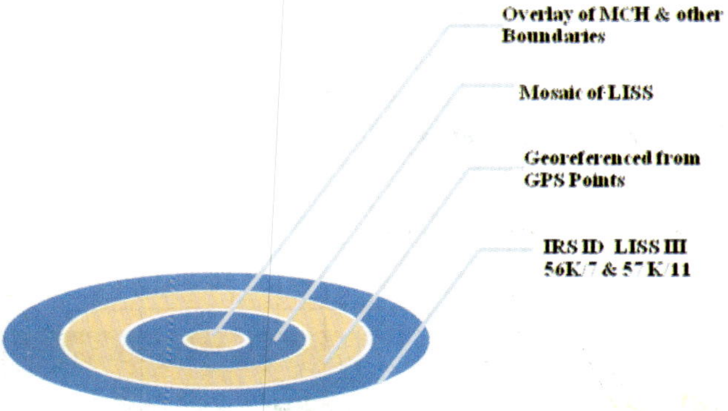

Fig. 1.2(a): Methodology for Satellite Data Processing

The satellite imagery has been projected, transformed and rectified. The study has made use of 50 true GPS points to rectify the web based satellite data pertaining to Hyderabad. The AOI of varying categories like Zonal Boundaries, Municipal boundaries, etc. have been superimposed on these satellite imagery (Fig. 1.3 and 1.4). City ward map, locality map as well as the constituency maps has also been prepared to link attribute data at appropriate places (Fig. 1.5, 1.6 and 1.7).

Study Area

Hyderabad is the sixth largest and one of the fastest growing cities in India. The urban agglomeration area under the jurisdiction of Hyderabad Urban Development Authority (HUDA) has increased stupendously

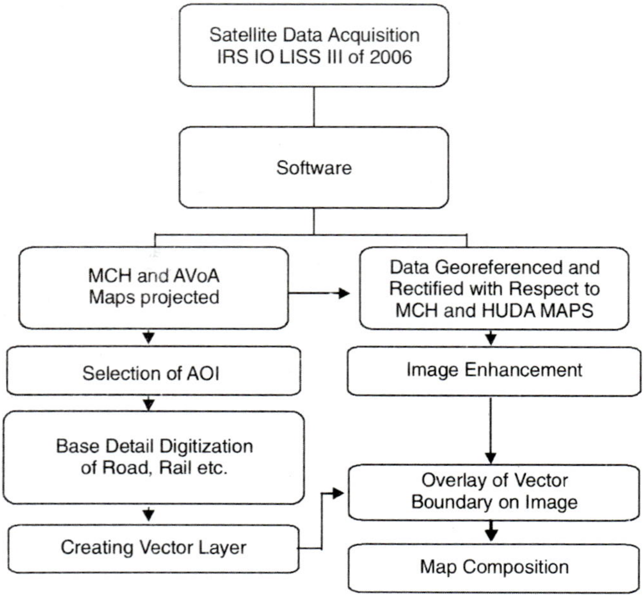

Fig. 1.2 (b): Methodology for Satellite Data Processing

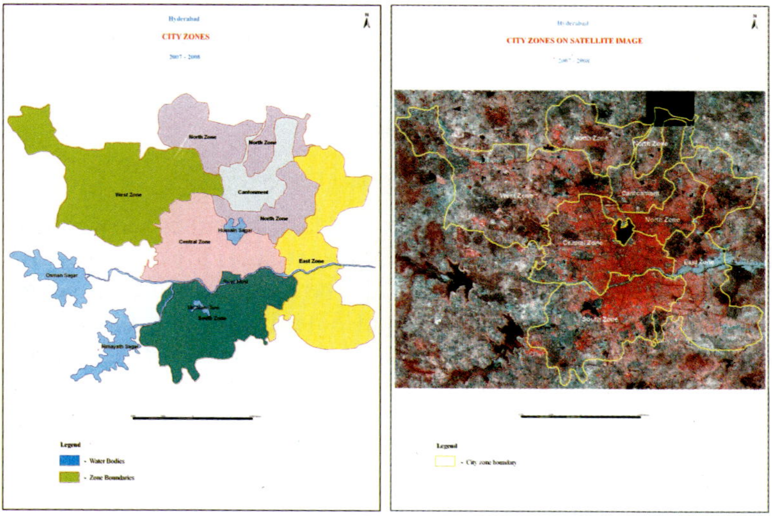

Fig. 1.3: City zones on Satellite Image (2007-2008)

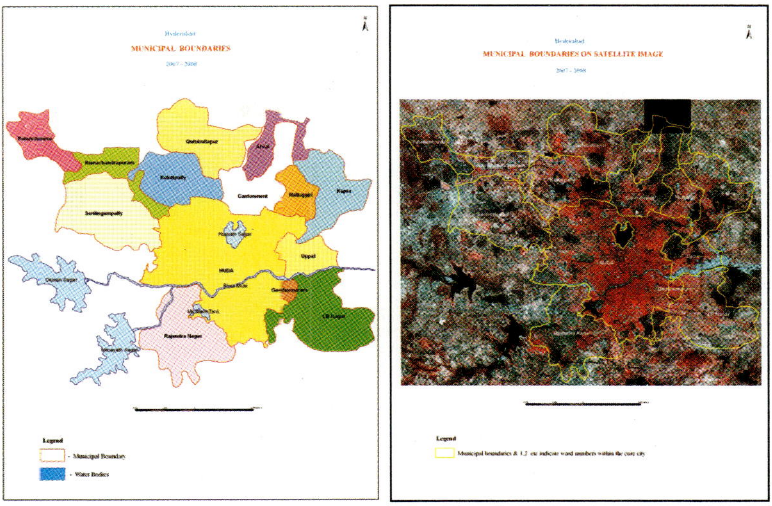

Fig. 1.4: Municipal boundaries on Satellite Image (2007-2008)

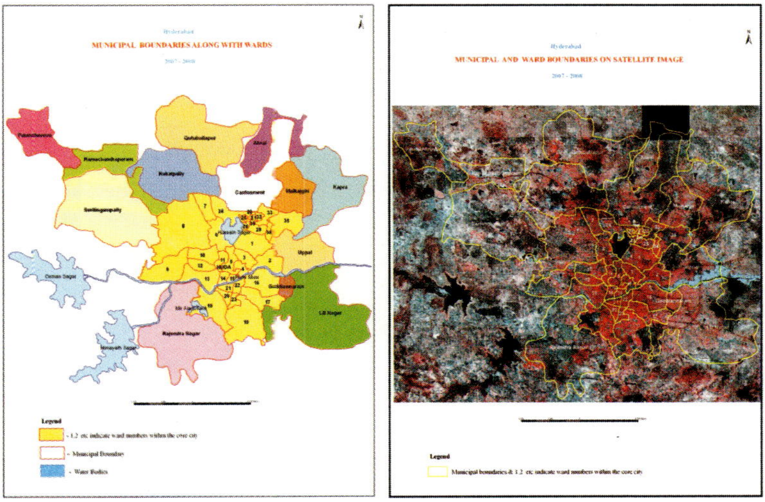

Fig. 1.5: Wards of Hyderabad and Peripheral Municipalities on Satellite Image (2007-2008)

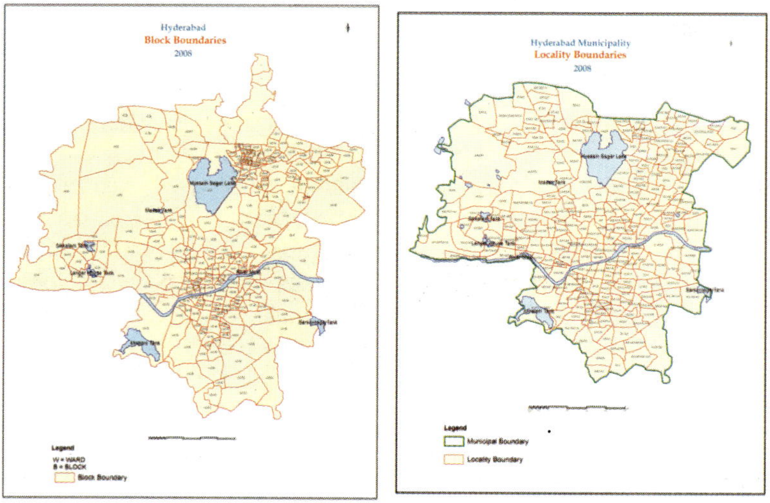

Fig. 1.6: Block Boundaries and Locality Boundaries, 2006

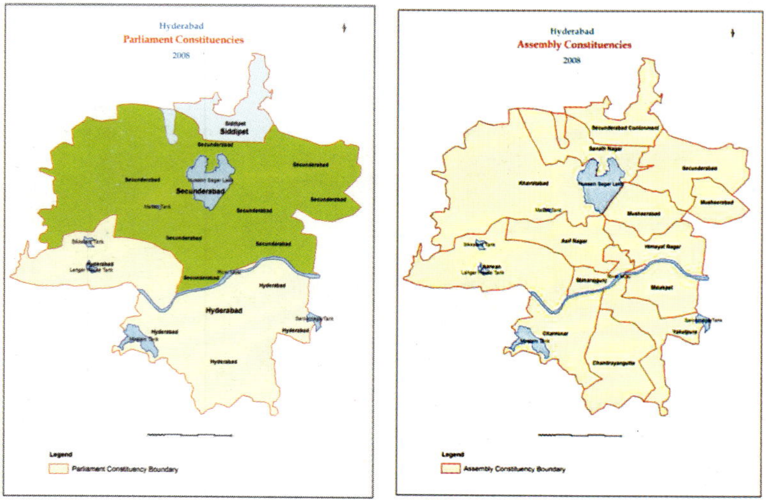

Fig. 1.7: Assembly Constituencies and Parliamentary Constituencies, 2006

in size, from 245 sq.kms in 1971 to 1865 sq.kms in 2001. During the same period, its population increased from 1.8 million to 6.14 million. The Municipal Corporation of Hyderabad (MCH), which lies at the centre of the Hyderabad Urban Agglomeration area is spread over

172 square kilometres and has a population of 3.61 million according to the 2001 census. The fallout of rapid urbanization and industrial growth has been changes in land use, burgeoning rural-urban migration, increasing pressure on infrastructure and environmental degradation. The resultant problems that the urban areas face are: growing number of slums and homelessness, social exclusion or social segregation and poverty and marginalization. Globalization, along with liberalization, has cast its shadow on Hyderabad in a way where it has come to resemble International cities in certain pockets—especially where there is a concentration of the Information Technology sector. Information and Capital have been the catalysts (Fig.1.8) which have spurred this process of mega urbanization and this is particularly evident in the western part of the city. The well developed national and regional rail-road network along with excellent domestic and international air link to all the major destinations made it a key growth centre within and outside the State. The emergence of new economy has catapulted Hyderabad to a prime position in India. In a fast globalizing world, it is essential for Hyderabad to offer world-class services to attract global investments. The global companies consider not only the investment climate and economic potential of cities while making investment but also the quality of services offered by cities. In this context, Hyderabad has one of the best world-class services comparable to other cities. However, the city is experiencing severe strain on its infrastructure.

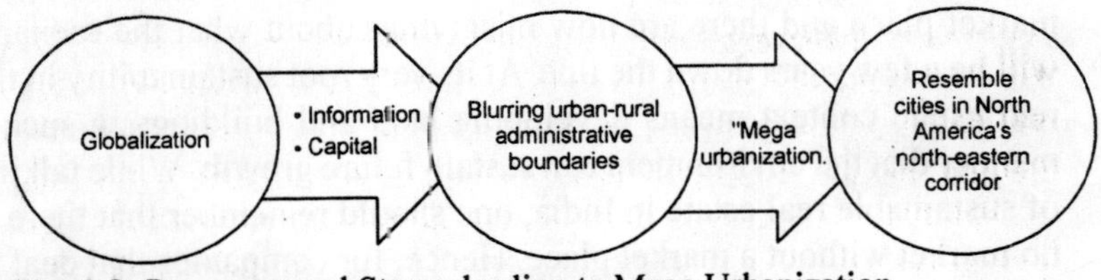

Fig. 1.8: Processes and Stages leading to Mega Urbanization

Hyderabad has witnessed a lot of change in terms of economy thus affecting the entire lifestyle, culture and the social structure of the people residing here. The change is evident with the rise of different IT and ITEs that cater to the needs of countries at the international level. Many famous IT companies have turned towards this city which otherwise did not know of globalization. Migration at both levels from rural to urban and from urban to urban area has left no space in the existing land and forced the city to expand in all directions. To accommodate the extra population the government has made various strategies and plans to circumvent disarray in city in a long run. To ensure this several municipalities have been merged with the Municipal Corporation of Hyderabad (MCH) in 2007 and this is named as Greater Hyderabad Municipal Corporation (GHMC). The GHMC presently has an area of 625 sq. kms but is poised for an expansion where it will encompass 800 sq. kms. This will be done with a proposed merger of 52 surrounding Gram Panchayats into GHMC and is intended for all-round development and better infrastructure especially in Gram Panchayats like Shamshabad which houses the International Airport. The 52 Gram Panchayats are in 10 mandals and include Shamshabad, Almasguda, Boduppal, Meerpet, Kokapet, Nizampet, Medchal, Badangpet, Bandlaguda Zagir, Peerzadiguda, Poppalguda, Kompally, Gundla Pochampally, Satamrai, Utupally, Tondupally, Jilelaguda, Jalpally, Kothapet, Nadergul, Pahadisharif, Balapur, Sardarnagar, Peeramcheruvu, Bachupally, Doolapally, Bahadurpally, Pragatinagar, Injapur, Kuntlur, Manganur, Thattu Annaram, Rampally, Nagaram and Dammaiguda. Hyderabad is the sixth largest city in terms of area after Kolkatta, Delhi, Mumbai, Chennai and Bangalore. With the addition of these villages it will emerge as a 'giant global player' (*Times of India*, October 6, 2010).

Rapid urbanization is fast compromising the urban real estate market place and there are now misgivings about what the scenario will be a few years down the line. At its very root sustainability in the real estate context means developing land and buildings in such a manner that the environment can sustain future growth. While talking of sustainable real estate in India, one should remember that there is no market without a market place. Hence, for companies that deal in real estate in any capacity, environmental sustainability is not a concept too distant from business sustainability. In other words, there is no difference between sustaining the environment and maintaining the market place for indefinite business activity.

Urbanization has caused the residential conditions in most of India's larger cities to decline rapidly. There is a general shortage of infrastructure, increased air, water and noise pollution and spots of illegal and unorganised structures. Given this depressing scenario, it has now been established that townships are the most suitable residential solution. If planned and executed properly, townships are definitely the answer to the growing housing woes brought on by rapid and lopsided urbanization. They are efficient vehicles of social integration while offering the necessary infrastructure. (Anuj Puri, DC, Nov 21, 2008)

Globalization at the national level leads to economic restructuring and global linkages of select regions in the nation, select cities in these regions and select geographical segments within these cities. Since a marked change has taken place in the income levels of the people of Hyderabad as a result it has led to the change in their settlement, attitude, perception and culture. The way of dressing is modern as they have to move in an ambience where different cultures mingle. It is mostly influenced by western culture. Usage of English language is prevalent as it is the lingua-Franca of the world. Eating habits of the people of Hyderabad have also changed to a large extent.

The city is deficient in service delivery, it has lowest rating in terms of parameters like GDP, Literacy rate, School dropout rate, Child mortality rate, Sewerage, transportation, etc. but yet there is potential for growth as it is establishing itself as a technology hub through initiation of various reforms. Table 1.3 gives an inter city comparison, where Hyderabad is compared with the four major cities of the country i.e. Mumbai, Delhi, Chennai and Kolkata. The comparison has been made in terms of economic, educational, housing, health, water, sanitation and transport factors. A look at the economic factors reveals that the GDP per capita in Hyderabad is less than that of the other cities at Rs. 23,000 and the population below poverty line is second in the 5- city comparison, where it ranks after Mumbai with 23 per cent of the population below poverty line in terms of economic disparity it ranks after Chennai with 37 per cent of the households being of the low and lower middle income. On education front Hyderabad has 79 per cent of the population that is literate, which compares very unfavourably with the other cities under consideration. This figure is complemented by that of the percentage of school dropouts where Hyderabad ranks highest compared with other four cities.

It ranks third after Kolkata and Delhi, with regard to the slum population where 37 per cent of the population resides in slums. The infant mortality rate is high, at 6.9 per cent, when compared with the other major cities. The daily supply of drinking water facility is almost the same as that of Delhi. The household water connections in just about 36 per cent of the households in Hyderabad compares adversely

Table 1.3: Hyderabad in National Scenario—Comparison with other Major Cities of India

Category	*Variable*	*Hyderabad*	*Mumbai*	*Delhi*	*Chennai*	*Kolkata*
Economic	GDP per capita (in Rupees)	23000	43000	39000	34000	33000
	% Population below poverty line 2001	23	27	8	20	6
	Economic disparity (% of low and lower middle income households, 2002)	37	27	18	42	32
Education	Literacy Rate (in %) (2001)	79	87	83	80	81
	Dropout Rate (in %) (2001)	66	42	52	46	42
Housing	% Population living in slums (2001)	37	55	35	40	31
Health	Child mortality rate (in %) (2001)	6.90	NA	2.60	3.70	1.60
Water	Piped water supply per day (in hours)	2	NA	2	1	NA
	Per capita availability in lpcd of potable water	110	168	180	106	173
	Household water connections (in %)	36	58	51.30	NA	23
Sanitation	Sewerage connections (UA) (in %)	41	NA	55	55	NA
Transport	Average commute time (in Minutes)	60	30	45	NA	NA
	Public transport utilization rate (in %)	44	NA	62	36	NA
	%area covered by roads	6	10	18	10	12
	Vehicle density	723	242	NA	293	NA

NA: Not available
Source: HUDA, 2003.

with the scenario in Mumbai where the figure is 58 per cent, Delhi with 57 per cent. The average commuting time in Hyderabad is much more than that in other cities. It is 60 minutes, whereas in Delhi it takes 45 minutes and in Mumbai 30 minutes, which reflects on the infrastructure facilities of the cities. The rate of public transport utilization is only 44 per cent in Hyderabad, while Delhi has the highest percentage at 62. The area covered by roads is 6 per cent, but the vehicle density is four fold, which is the highest compared with the other major citi.

Table 1.4 gives an insight into trends and comparison between Hyderabad and other emerging international cities. In economic terms, Hyderabad has the lowest per capita income and the highest unemployment rate. When other factors like education, housing, health, water and sanitation are considered Hyderabad, quite dismally, has the least facilities when compared to other international cities. However, the positive aspect is seen in public transport utilization rate, which is 44 per cent is above all the other cities.

In Hyderabad, a large part of the society which can afford high standard of living is happy. This era of globalization has all the more widened the gap between those who could afford and who could not. The very fact that GHMC came in to existence tells that the city has expanded in all directions which forced the people—mostly the have-nots—to live in the periphery of the city. At first glance, it might seem unusual to address housing as a basic human right. Insecure and inadequate shelter, however, threatens physical and mental health and the overall quality of life, in other words, human dignity. This idea is mirrored in relevant international legislation, such as the Universal Declaration and the International Covenant on Economic, Social and Cultural Rights.

Government policies play an integral role in bridging inequalities. But in their excitement to push rapid global economic integration, governments strengthen the processes of exclusion through fragmentation of employment, housing and social services. There is a yawning gap between words and actions. According to UN figures, one billion urban inhabitants live in inadequate housing, mostly in slums and squatter settlements in developing countries. As many civil society organizations and experts have pointed out, there is one big culprit: corporate globalization and its negative effects on the life of the poor. As Miloon Kothari, UN Special Rapporteur on the subject puts it, "the deepening inequalities of income and opportunities

Table 1.4: Comparison between Hyderabad and other Emerging International Cities

Category	*Variable*	*Hyderabad*	*Hanoi*	*Bangkok*	*Jakarta*	*Johannesburg*
Economic	Per capita income (USD)	511	3510	15053	7269	2900
	% Population below poverty line 2001	23	1.80	NA	NA	25
	Unemployment rate (%) (1998)	22	10.30	2.20	16.80	26.40
Education	Literacy Rate (%) (2001)	79	92	97	98	93
	Dropout Rate (%) (2001)	66	7.4	NA	NA	NA
Health	Child mortality rate (%) (2001)	6.9	4.2	3.3	2.4	5.5
Water	% Household access to water	81	100	NA	91	84.5
Sanitation	Per capita availability in lpcd of potable water	106	NA	NA	77	261
	Household water connections (%)	64	70	99	50.3	50
	Sewerage connections (UA) (%)	41	50	100	64.8	84
Transport	Average commute time (in minutes)	60	15	60	NA	50
	Public transport utilization rate (%)	44	2	28	NA	33.4

NA = Not available

Source: HUDA, 2003.

between and within nations have lead to an increase in the number or people without adequate and secure housing. The human rights of people and communities to housing, water and sanitation (...) continue to erode as the process of privatisation deepens and accelerates". (Choike.Org)

An increase in inequality in cities leads to issues of internal security. This pushes the rich to live in enclaves that are well protected. The city gets segmented between the rich and the poor. Segregation may not be total, but some segments of the city would have a concentration of the rich and others of the poor. The Habitat International Coalition, a network of NGOs has identified 14 constituent elements of the human right to housing.

These elements are:

- security of tenure;
- public goods and services;
- environmental goods and services (water, considered an essential prerequisite to the right to housing);
- affordability;
- habitability;
- accessibility;
- location;
- cultural appropriateness;
- freedom from dispossession;
- information, capacity and capacity-building;
- participation and self-expression;
- resettlement;
- safe environment; and
- security and privacy.

The question arises how many people in Hyderabad are able to get these facilities after the establishment of big companies?

In this city the bigger part of the society which could not or cannot make big in the race finds it in formidable to keep pace with the new changes. This can be attributed to many factors like lack of education, lack of awareness, poverty and so on. If this large chunk of society is neglected there are chances of the youth getting frustrated and indulging in all sorts of illegal activities. The crime rate may also escalate in due course of time. To curb this government has to take precautionary measures by providing non-skilled employments and regulate self-employed schemes on which already many non-governmental organizations (NGOs) are working. Another very important aspect cannot be overlooked while speaking of housing that is gender. It is seen that when addressing housing as a human right, it is impossible to adopt a gender neutral approach. Women, either by law or by action, are excluded from or discriminated against in virtually every aspect of housing. It is necessary to take positive action to ensure their right to inheritance and the ownership of land and other property, credit, natural resources and appropriate technology, as well as to guarantee their right to security of tenure and to enter into contracts.

Along with this strategy of economic growth, the city would also need to consider a strategy to alleviate the living conditions of the urban poor. The number of slums and slum population in Hyderabad has been increasing rapidly with the growing population of the city. The number of notified slums increased from 106 in 1962 to 1476 in 2009. The population residing in these slums increased from 1 lakh in 1962 to 20.9 lakhs in 2009. Thus 686 new slums have emerged in the past fifteen years. Thus one finds houselessness in the shadow of affluence, an unprecedented increase of the housing stock of the well-to-do in the past twenty years, housing shortage in general and increase in unfulfilled demand from middle and lower income groups.

A country is considered to be a developed one if it keeps pace with the rest of the world or is sometimes ahead of the world. So is the case with Hyderabad wherein it has grown big at international level thus making its people's standard of living relatively high. At the same time it is confronted with other related problems which are inevitable. So she has to take care of every stratum in the society and move forward.

Demography

As mentioned earlier, Hyderabad consists of MCH and 12 Peripheral municipalities, Secunderabad Cantonment and Osmania University. The population growth is more than 50 per cent during 1981-1991 and 27 per cent in 1991-2001. The population increased from 4.3 million in 1991 to 5.7 million in 2001.Table 1.5 gives us an insight into the population trends in the Hyderabad Urban Agglomeration (HUA) area. The MCH covers an area of 172 sq. km and the population has increased from 21 lakhs in 1981 to 36.3 lakhs in 2001.

The surrounding municipalities covers an area of 419 sq.km and the population has increased from 3.8 lakhs to 17 lakhs. The area under HUA is about 778 sq. km and the population has increased from 27.1 lakhs in 1981 to 57.5 in 2001. In HUDA, which covers an area of 1905 sq.km, the population has increased from almost 3 million in 1981 to 6.3 million in 2001. Hyderabad Urban Area (HUA) has grown faster than Mumbai, Kolkata and Chennai between the years 1991-2001. The population of Hyderabad has grown rapidly and it is amongst the most densely populated cities and this requires long term planning and significant investments for improved service delivery.

The Hyderabad Urban Development Authority (HUDA) had announced as many as 22 satellite townships around the ORR 3 years back. However, except at Tellapur and Srinagar the others have remained on paper. Townships were planned at Medchal, Goudavelli, Dommata, Pochampally, Bowrampet, Aliyapur, Sultanpur, Kharanur, Paatighanpur, Edulanagulapalli, Kollur, Balapur, Nadargul, Thorrur, Munaganuru, Kuntluru, Korremul, Rampalli, Cheryala, Dharmaram, and Shamirpet. Even HMDA officials are not sure whether the remaining townships will come into being or not. Major reasons for the projects not taking off are real estate slump, large land acquisitions and widespread agitations by farmers. (*Deccan Chronicle*, November 11, 2008) The plans of the HMDA to develop 20 satellite townships around Hyderabad have been hampered by the economic recession (slow down in real estate). It is also facing problems with large-scale acquisition of land for satellite townships.

Most of the growth has taken place away from the city core, which is visible from Fig.1.9 for 1981-2001. The period from 1981-91 to 1991-2001, however, has witnessed a fall in the rate of increase in all the three categories that constitute the city i.e. MCH, 10 surrounding municipalities and Secunderabad Cantonment. Yet, one finds all the surrounding municipalities barring one have a rate of increase which is upwards of 50 per cent and in the range of 56 per cent to 103 per cent during 1991-2001. This compares with a rate lower than 20 per cent in the core city (i.e. the MCH area).

Growth in the peripheral areas is because of residential settlements and expensive real estate. Residential growth creates a demand for better infrastructure in surrounding municipalities. The reason for such high percentage of growth is areas near to the city and proximity to employment.

Table 1.5: Hyderabad: Population Trend, 1981-2001

Component	*Area (sq.km)*	*Population (lakhs)*			*Density (2001)*
		1981	*1991*	*2001*	*(P/SQ.KM)*
MCH	172	21.0	30.5	36.3	21048
Surrounding Municipalities	419	3.8	9.9	17	4102
Others	187	2.3	3.2	4	2147
HUA	778	27.1	43.6	57.5	7393
HUDA	1905	29.9	46.7	63.8	3351

Source: HUDA 2003.

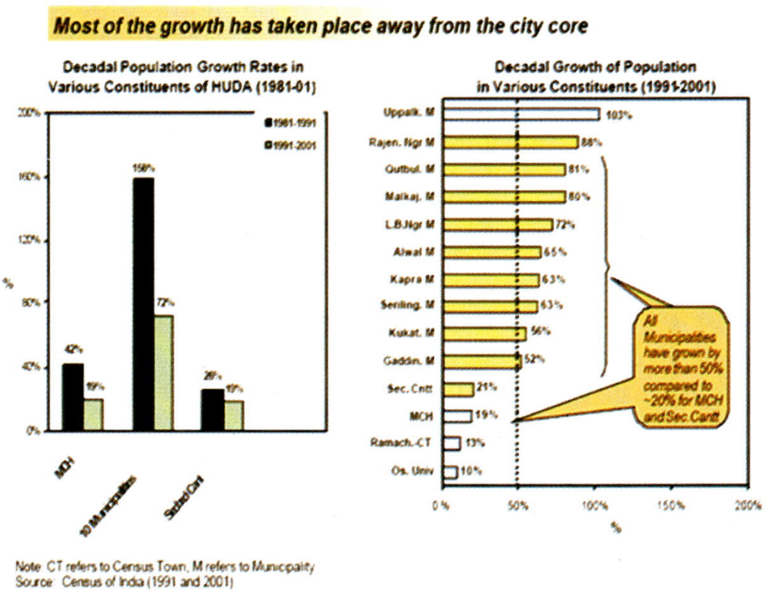

Fig. 1.9: Decadal Population Growth Rates in Various Constituents of HUDA (1981-01) and Decadal Growth of Population in Various Constituents (1991-2001)

Source: HUDA.

One of the key reasons for inadequate service delivery outcomes in HUA is absence of effective coordination mechanism among the agencies which are involved in orderly spatial development, so there is an urgent need to integrate the spatial and functional service delivery system for achieving better service outcomes (Fig.1.10).

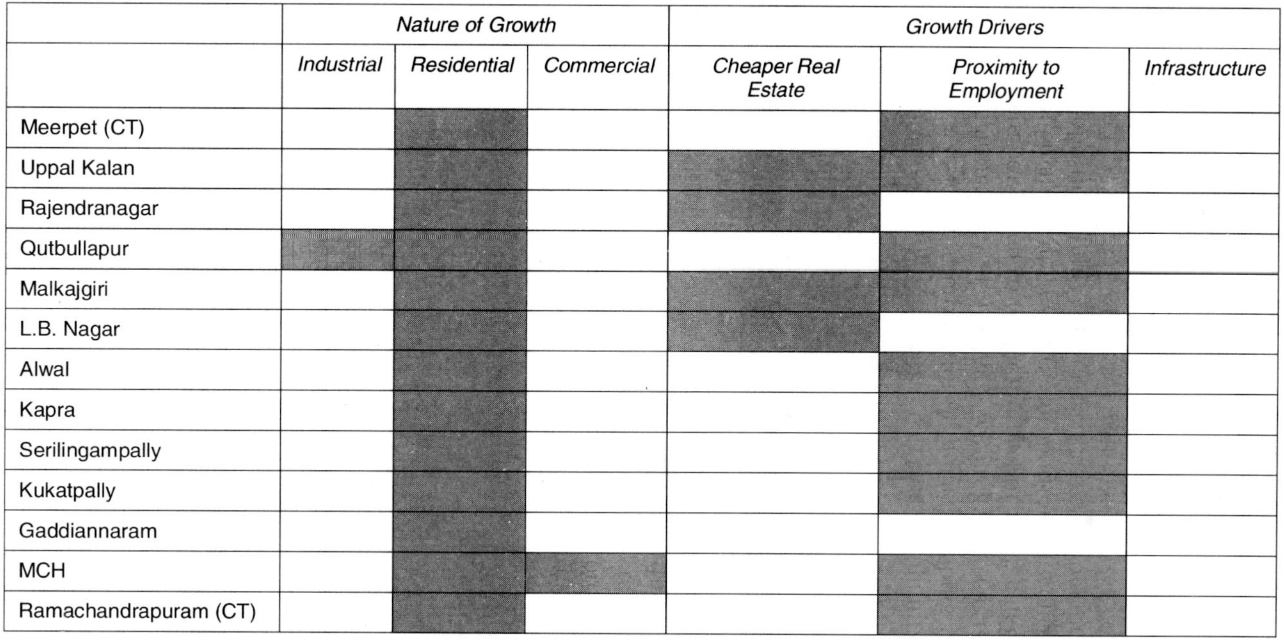

Fig. 1.10: Growth and Growth Drivers in Hyderabad

Source: HUDA, 2003.

It has been found that while Uppal Kalan, Rajendranagar, Malkajgiri and L.B. Nagar have the benefit of having cheaper real estate values; it is Uppal Kalan and Malkajgiri, which have a greater advantage by way of the additional gain by proximity to work place.

Table 1.6 gives the components of population growth. Population increase is on account of natural increase, migration and jurisdictional increase. It is apparent from this table that natural increase is the largest causative factor so far as the growth of Hyderabad is concerned. It can be surmised from Table 1.7 that while the annual exponential growth rate of Hyderabad has been the highest during 1981-1991, it has tapered off after that and is expected to fall slightly up to 2011. It may, however, be mentioned, that this fall is a statistical illusion as the rate of growth at the later point in time has been calculated on an already existing high base of population and portrays a relative picture rather than an absolute one. The HUA has experienced high growth in population and the same trend is expected to continue over the next two decades (Fig.1.11). It is expected to emerge as fourth largest UA in 2021 in the country overtaking Chennai and Bangalore. Most of the growth has taken away from the city. This has serious implications for service delivery for both core city and peripheral areas since the traffic and population flow occurs between them. This calls for integrated planning with equal provision of services to all the areas and all the sections of the populations.

Table 1.6: Components of Population Growth (Hyderabad Urban Area)

Composition/Year	*Population Increase during*			
	1981-1991 (in Lakhs)	*Percent of total*	*1991-2001 (in Lakhs)*	*Percent of total*
Natural Increase	8.7	59	9.0	70
In migration	3.7	25	3.1	24
Jurisdictional Change	2.4	16	0.8	6
Total Change	**14.8**	**100**	**12.9**	**100**

Source: HUDA.

Though a majority of the people surveyed (83%) belong to the Hindu religion Fig. 1.12 yet there are marked regional variations with regard to the distribution of different religious groups in Hyderabad and the surrounding municipalities which form part of GHMC.

Table 1.7: Hyderabad Urban Agglomeration: Annual Growth Rates

Year	*Population (in Lakhs)*	*Annual Exponential Growth Rate (%)*
1981	27.1	
1991	43.6	6.4
2001	57.5	3.2
2005 (Estimated)	65.4	3.4
2011 (Projected)	77.2	3.0

Source: HUDA: 2003.

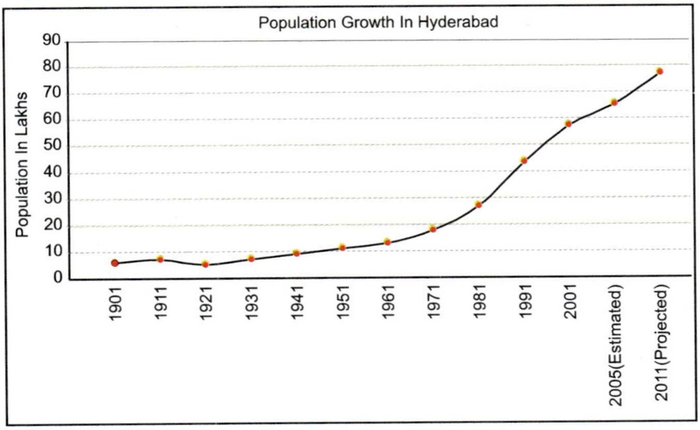

Fig. 1.11: Population Growth in Hyderabad

Source: Census of India and Hyderabad Urban Development Authority (HUDA).

A glance at Fig 1.13 and Fig. 1.14 reveals that while some of the localities in the city have the extreme ascendancy of a single religion, as for example, according to the sample Padmaraonagar, Warasiguda and Malkajgiri have 100 per cent of the people who are Hindus and Patthergatti and Moghalpura have 100 per cent of people who are Muslims. Dominance of the Muslims is also witnessed in Aliyabad and Gulzar house where more than 50 per cent of the population is Muslim. Though other localities in the city have a predominance of Hindu population yet mixed localities are not to be ruled out for instance Abids North and Sultan Bazaar have a mix of Hindu, Muslim, Christian and Parsi population, infact the Parsi component of the population is witnessed only in the Abids. The Christian population is found in 20 out of the 48 localities, though areas of relative

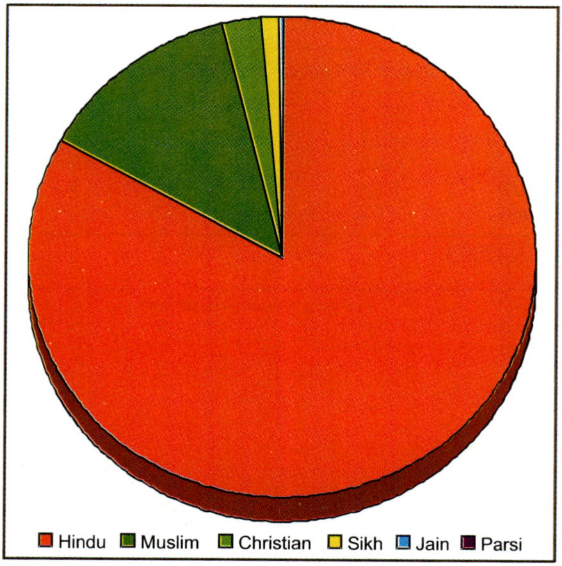

Fig. 1.12: Religious Composition of Hyderabad (2007-2008)

domination are North Abids-Sultan bazaar, Saidabad colony, Ranigunj, West Marredpally-Erukula basti and Vijaynagar Colony in central city locations besides Kapra in the peripheral areas. Sikh population finds relative dominance in Ameerpet followed by Hussaini Alam, Vijaynagar Colony, Kukatpally and Red hills in that order. The Jain population is confined to select pockets which are close to the main commercial areas of Hyderabad (Goshamahal and Khairtabad) and Secunderabad (Shivajinagar) their proportion of the total city population is, however, minuscule (Fig.1.12) and other interesting feature witnessed from Fig 1.12 mapping is that most of the localities with mixed religious groups are found in central city locations. The peripheral municipalities show a preponderance of Hindus with most of them barring one having Hindu population of more than 90 per cent.

Notwithstanding these variations, the perceptions of the people with regard to the presence of places of religious importance is marked by different filters, which could also be impacted by overload of information in some parts and lack of it or distorted information in other parts. Keeping this in mind the respondents were quizzed with regard to the presence of religious places in different localities of the

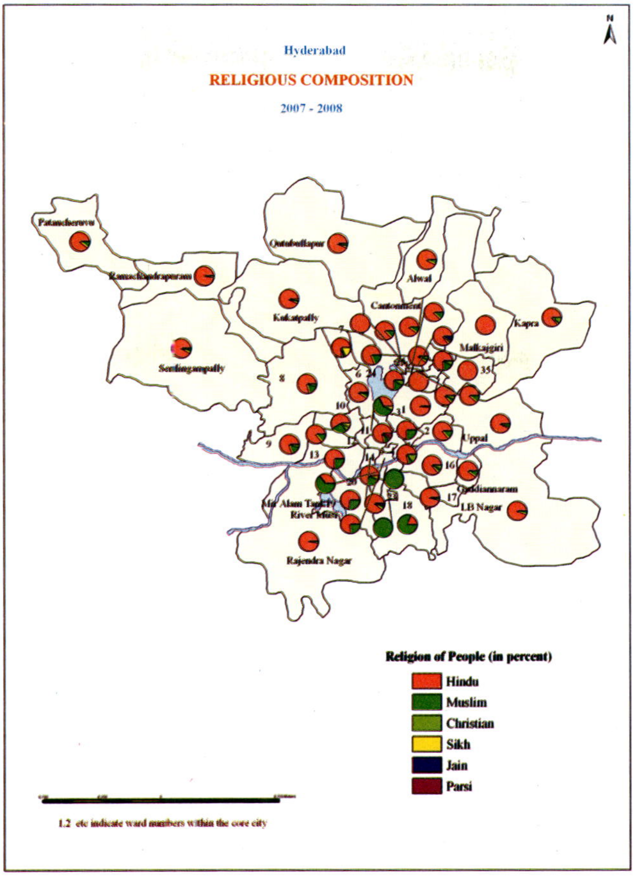

Fig. 1.13: Religious Composition of Hyderabad (2007-2008)

city. This data has been mapped on the basis of religious places in a GIS environment (Figs. 1.15, 1.16 and 1.17).

It has emerged from Fig. 1.15 that most of the people (>85%) perceive that temples are found in the localities were they reside. In other words, it emerges from this map that large parts of the city are perceived to have temples in an ample measure. 75 to 100 per cent of the residents in most parts of North Hyderabad, Secunderabad and peripheral Municipalities perceive that temples exist in their locality. Even in South Hyderabad people in 50 per cent of the localities have a perception level of 75 to 100 per cent so far as location of temple in their locality is concerned. However, in Aliyabad less than 25 per

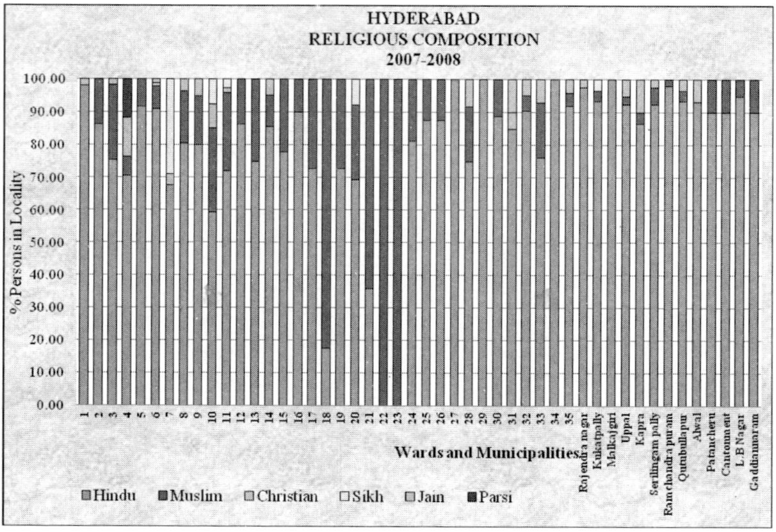

Fig. 1.14: Religious Composition of Hyderabad (2007-2008)—(Bar Graph)

cent of the people perceive that a temple exists in their locality while in Gulzar house the figure stands at 25–50 per cent. This is notwithstanding the fact that in the 3 peripheral municipalities to the south of the Musi 75 per cent 200 per cent of the people perceive that a temple persist in their locality. Also in Kapra municipality only 25-50 per cent of the people perceive that existence of a temple in their locality. This can also be correlated with a relatively lower population in Kapra compared to other peripheral Municipalities. The picture presented by Fig. 1.16 showing the perception of people with regard to the location of Mosques in the city is quite distinct from that presented by Fig. 1.15. Mosques are perceived to exist in a larger measure (by 75 to 100% of the residents) in Aliyabad, Gulzar House, Patthergatti, Regimental bazaar and Warasiguda in central city locations and Ramchandrapuram, Serilingampally and Secunderabad Cantonment in the peripheral areas. A smaller measure of their existence marks places in a latitudinal belt to the North of Musi as well as similar sections to the North of Hussainsagar apart from Kukatpally Qutubullapur Municipalities as also Lalapet. Quite surprisingly Hussainialam to the South of river Musi also displays a picture where relatively less number of people perceive the existence

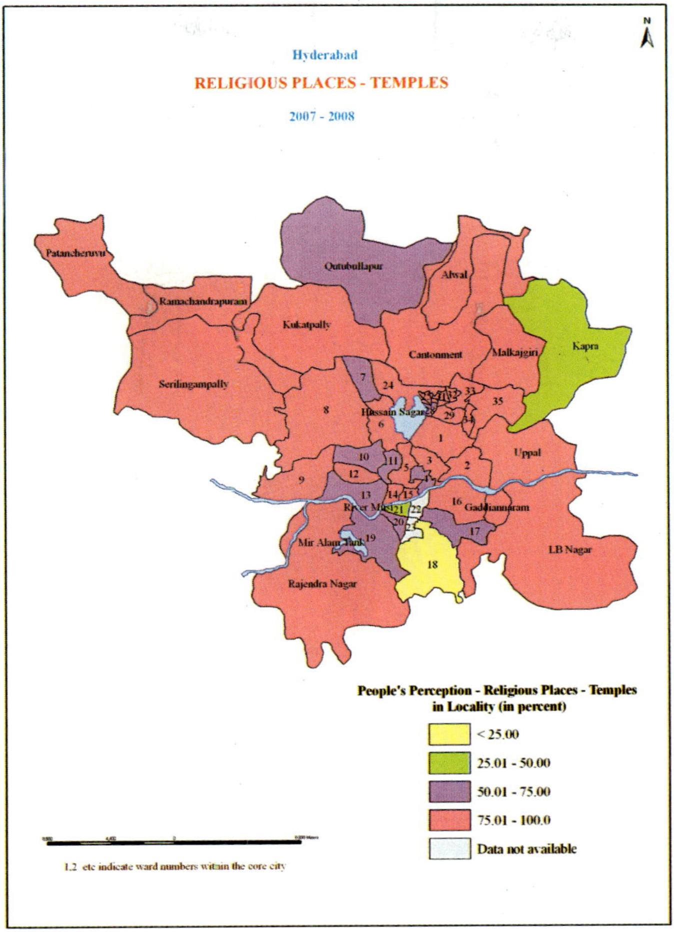

Fig. 1.15: Hyderabad: Religious Places—Temples

of mosques in their locality. Fig. 1.17 pertaining to perception of people conveys that 75–100 per cent in Secunderabad Cantonment, Warasiguda, Banjara hills and Jubille hills, Serilingampally and Ramchandrapuram perceive the existence of Churches in their locality. The highs on this count are clearly marked in the Northern part of the study area. There is distinct North-South divide on this count and Southern areas are perceived to have less number of churches. These are also the areas where the Christian population is not present in noticeable numbers.

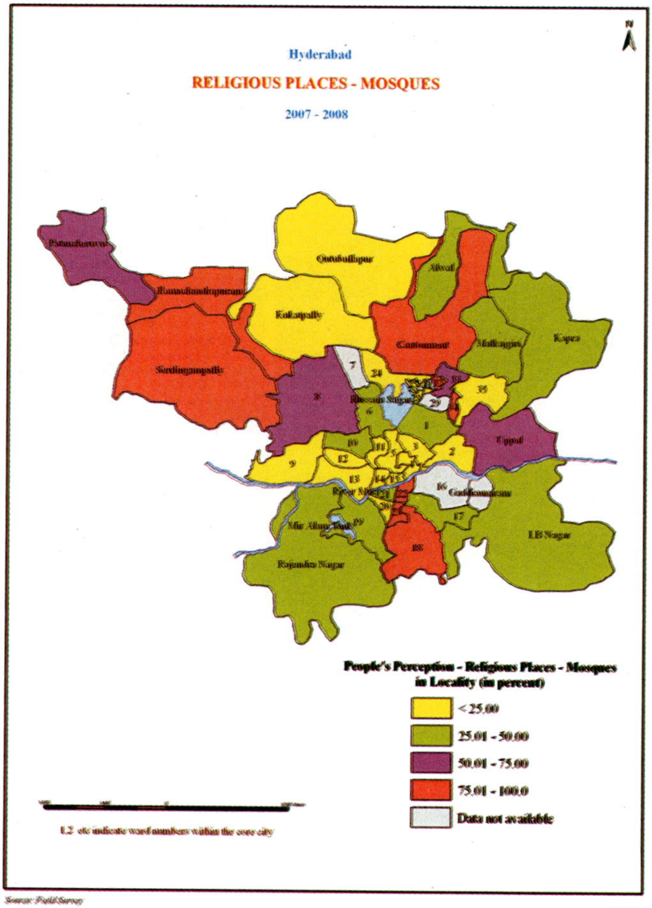

Source: Field Survey

Fig. 1.16: Hyderabad: Religious Places—Mosques.

So far as presence of "other" religious places apart from those mentioned above is concerned, it is found that people in 56 per cent of the localities are not aware of the existence of religious places other than those belonging to Hindus, Muslims, and Christians. All such cases incidentally fall in the central city. The awareness and citation of other religious places is more in the northern part of the city in the relatively posh Banjara hills and Jubilee hills area along with Serilingampally which houses the IT hub of Madhapur and industrial enclaves of Ramchandrapuram and Patancheru in the north-west and Kapra in the north-east.

Figs. 1.19, 1.20, 1.21, and 1.22 give an insight into the caste composition of the population of Hyderabad. It may be pertinent to mention here that about 5 per cent of the population did not consider necessary to mention their caste. A kaleidoscope of castes spans the city horizon, Fig 1.19 conveys that while Scheduled Caste (SC) and Scheduled Tribe (ST) population are confined to smaller numbers it is the Open Category (OC) and the Backward Caste (BC) who dominate the city scape.

A glance at Fig. 1.20 showing the details of the castes leads one to infer that the miscellaneous category among the OCs and BCs is dominant in most of the wards and peripheral municipalities. In such cases the people have not specifically mentioned their caste but have mentioned their category that they belong to. While some of the wards/ municipalities display a miscellany of castes others show lesser number of castes. For instance ward 1 and 3 show 14 caste categories and thus display the highest heterogeneity. They are represented by Ashoknagar-Chikkadpally and Himayathnagar localities. Other localities with larger representation of castes are Lunger Houz (ward 9), Mehdipatnam (ward 12), West Marredpally-Erukula basti (ward 33), Malkajgiri, Uppal, Qutubullapur and Alwal all with 9 caste categories, Ameerpet (ward 7), Regimental Bazaar (ward 32) and Rajendranagar with 8 caste categories each. Wards which show a lesser number of castes are those which have predominantly Muslim population this include Gulzar houz, Aliyabad etc.

Open Category (OC) population is highest in Malkajgiri (68.97%) followed by Sultan Bazaar-Abids North, Goshamahal, Hussaini Alam, Gulzar House, Alwal, Rajendranagar, Ashoknagar-Chikkadpally, Banjara-Jubilee hills, Vijaynagar Colony, Mehdipatnam, Barkas, Devibagh, General Bazaar, Kukatpally and Qutubullapur in that order.

It is evident from Fig 1.20 and Fig. 1.21 that among the OC category the largest group is the miscellaneous category which includes a motley of castes like Kayasth, Maratha, Lingayath besides others. The single community which dominates in terms of numbers is that of Reddys (landlord cum farming community). They are found mainly in Sarrornagar, Ameerpet, Raajendranagar, Vijaynagar colony, Abids-Sultan Bazaar, Ashoknagar-Chikkadpally, Ranigunj, Doodhbowli and Qutubullapur, etc. Brahmin community follows Reddy community so far as numbers are concerned. The main areas where they dominate are Padmaraonagar, Ranigunj, Doodhbowli-Devibagh, Ashoknagar-Chikkadpally. Some wards are marked by the

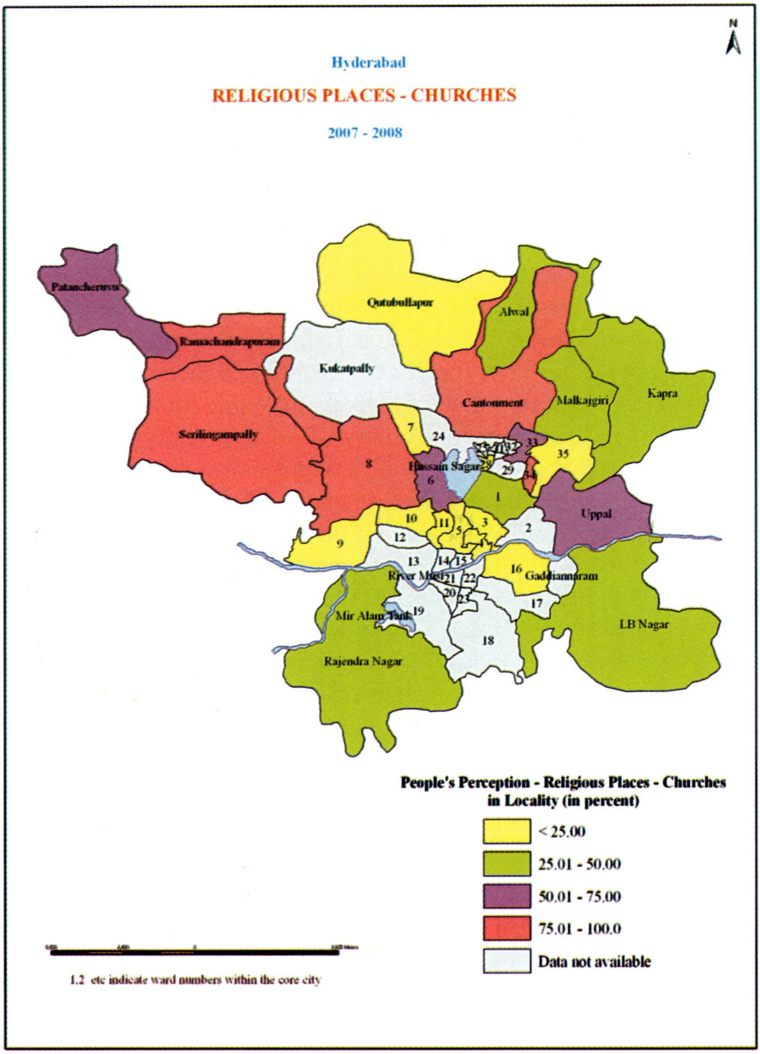

Source: Field Survey

Fig. 1.17: Hyderabad: Religious Places—Churches

absence of this community. The Vaishya community which is known as Komati Community (business community) is again confine to select pockets and is more preponderant in Old Bhoiguda, Barkas-Aliyabad and Shivajinagar with few exceptions they are mostly confine to central city locations. Kapu/Telaga/Naidu castes which are farming

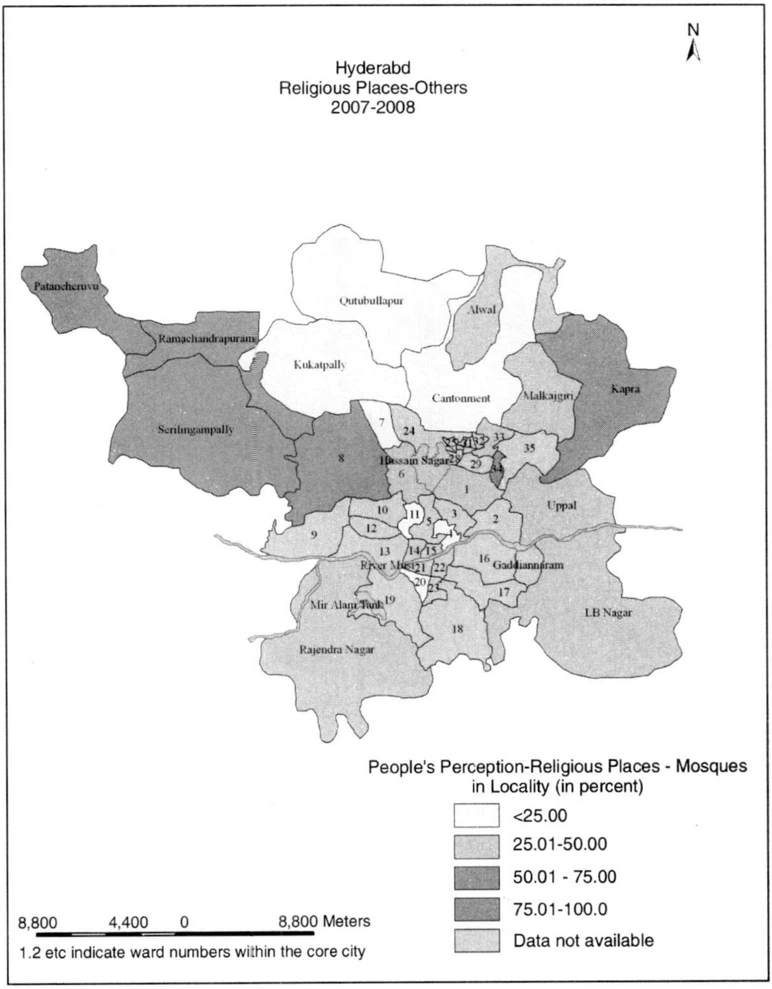

Fig. 1.18: Hyderabad: Religious Places—Others

Communities are not numerical strength to reckon with in the city though in terms of financial viability they stand their stead. They are found in a sizeable measure in Vijaynagar colony and Goshamahal, apart from that their presence is very limited in Gowliguda, Redhills, Banjara-Jubilee hills, Shivajinagar, Malkajgiri, Alwal, Qutbullapur, L.B.Nagar, etc. Similarly, Kamma also known as Choudary Community is found in a minuscule proportion in the city. They are basically landlords and constitute fewer than 2 per cent of the

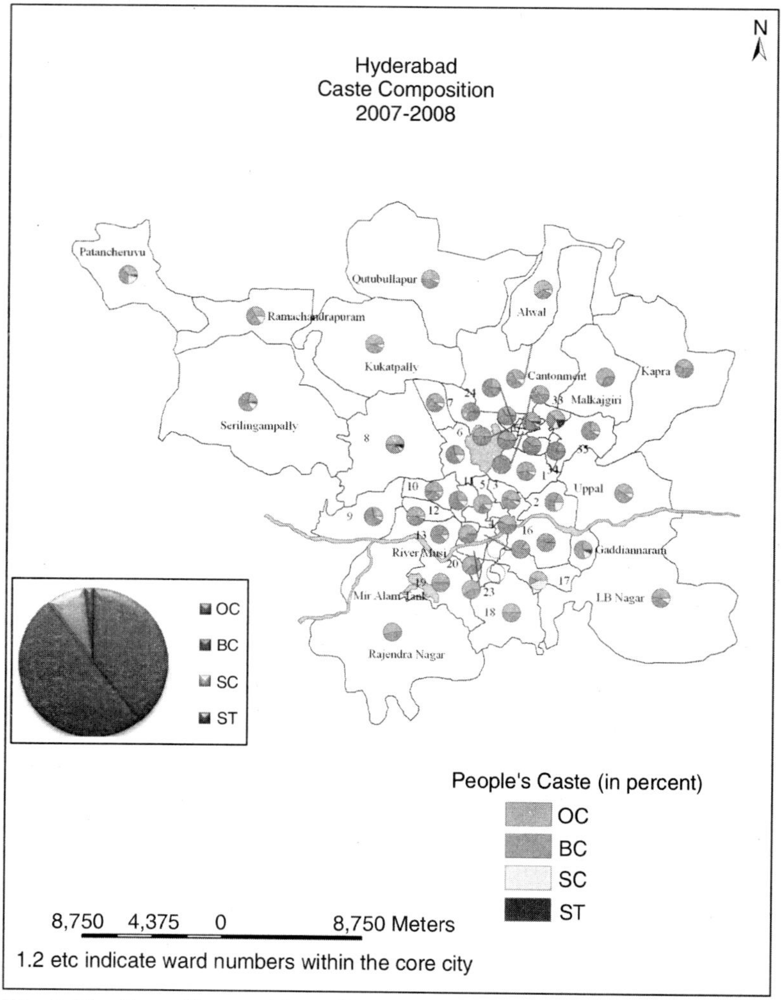

Fig. 1.19: Caste Composition of Hyderabad (2007-2008)

population in the city which is spread over about 25 per cent of the localities. A glance at the attribute table of this variable reveals that they are by and large into business and well paid jobs. They reside mainly in Malkajgiri, Mehdipatnam, Vijaynagar colony, Qutbullapur, L.B.Nagar, Kapra, Kukatpally, Himayathnagar, Khairtabad and Banjara-Jubilee hills though there numbers are very diminutive in each of these localities. Other Communities like Marwadi (business

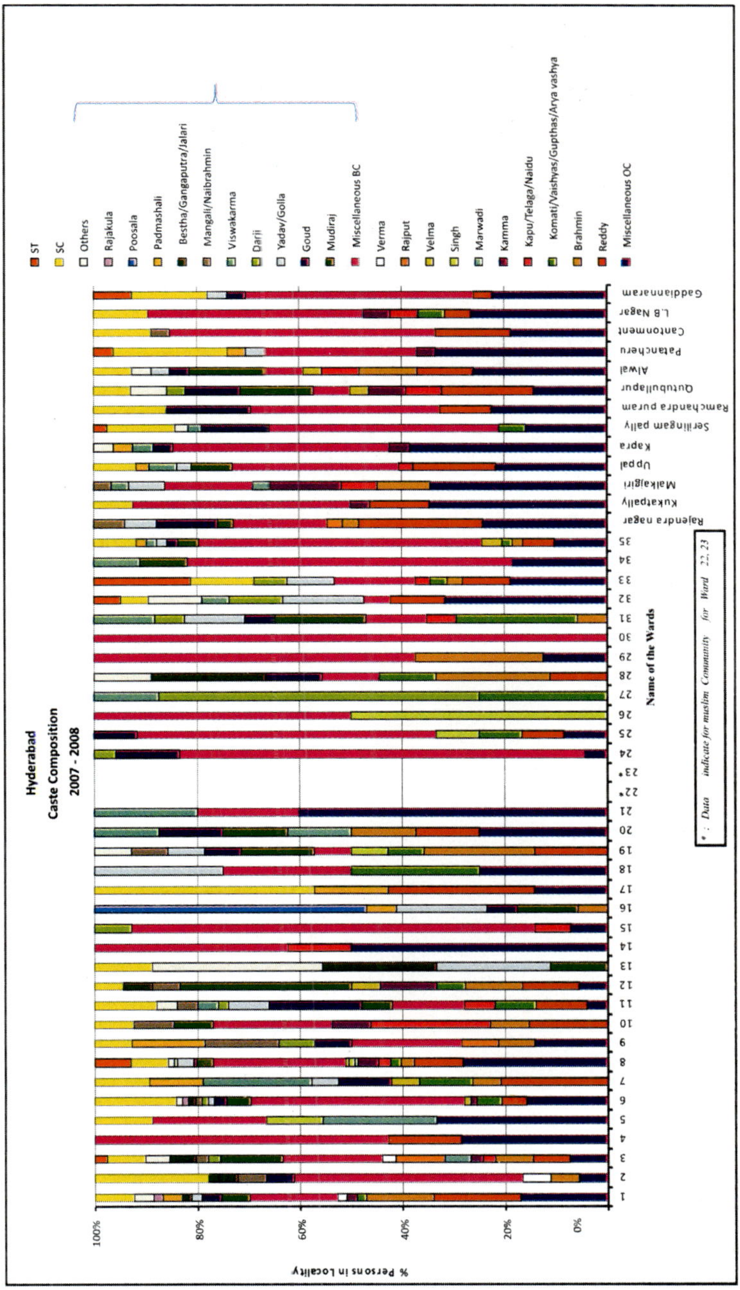

Fig. 1.20: Caste Composition of Hyderabad—(2007-2008)

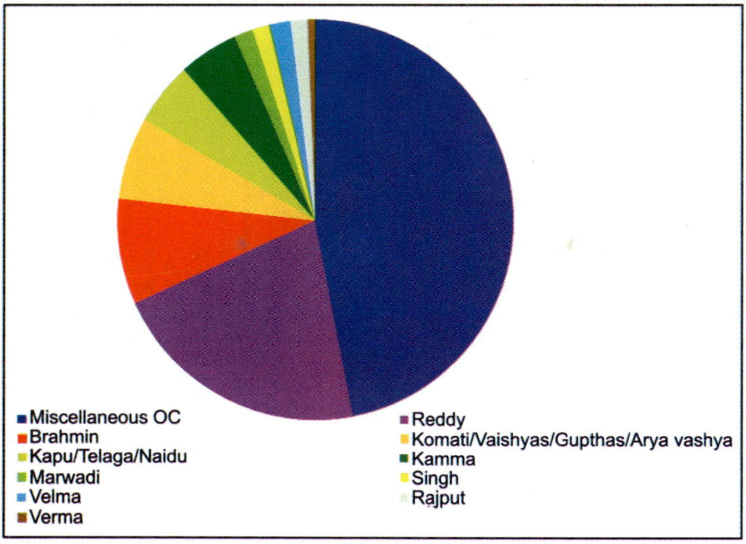

Fig. 1.21: Other Castes Composition of Hyderabad—(2007-2008)

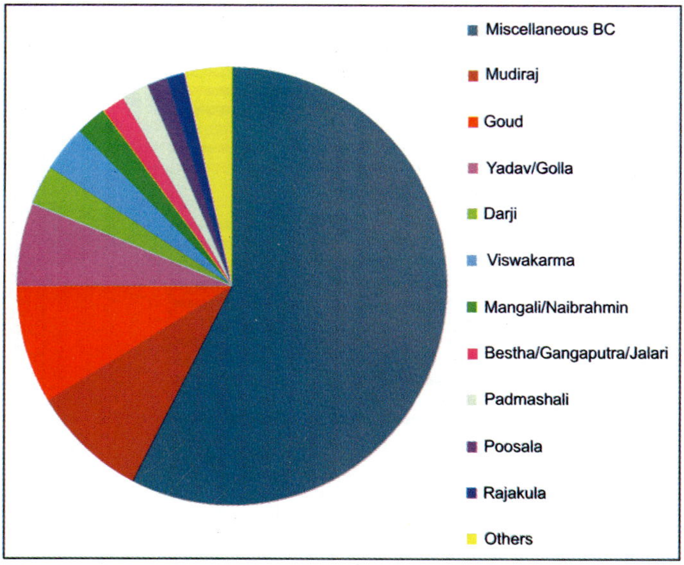

Fig. 1.22: Backward Caste Composition of Hyderabad—(2007-2008)

community), Thakurs/Singhs (landlords), Rajputs, Velmas (landlords) and Vermas are found in vary small proportions in different localities of the city. It may be noted that the Marvadis are concentrated in Abids-Koti area and also found in a fair presence in Himayathnagar, Hussainialam and Uppal. All of which are business areas.

The Backward Caste (BC) population has relatively higher concentration in a larger number of localities 56 per cent of localities report a BC population of more than 50 per cent, in addition to the fact that 50.6 per cent of the total population surveyed revealed that they belong to backward caste. Fig 1.19 further conveys that the BC population is present in a fair measure in all parts of the city however their preponderance in Secunderabad part of the core city cannot be ruled out. Most of them engage in business and private jobs and some are present or former railway employees.

Fig 1.20 conveys that BC population dominates in Monda market, Sabzimandi, Saidabad colony and Begumpet which have close to 90 per cent of the population in the BC category. Other localities which have a sizeable BC component are Gowliguda Chaman with close to 80 per cent, Redhills with close to 60 per cent, Amberpet with close to 60 per cent, Sultan bazaar—North Abids which have 50 per cent, Khairtabad with about 60 per cent, Lunger houz with 64 per cent, Ameerpet with 46 per cent, Ramgopalpet with 67 per cent, Ranigunj with 56 per cent, Padmarao nagar with 62 per cent, Shivaji nagar -65 per cent, West Marredpally -72 per cent, Lalapet -68 per cent and Kapra with 58 per cent BC approximately.

Among the BC categories most have not specified their proper castes and this category of miscellaneous BC groups dominates in maximum number of localities (Fig. 1.20 and Fig. 1.22). They invariably include Kummari (potters), MunurKapu (farming community), Vaddera (stone cutter), Balija (engaged in peripheral works in temples) and Sagara (masons) Mahendra (basket-maker), Nakash (stone carver), Gandla (oil presser), Kuruma (sheep rearer), Vanjari, Vamsharaj (story tellers and mat makers), Boyas (dealing in forest produce) etc. The largest single caste among the BCs is Mudiraj (who originally extract forest produce), they are employed in an assortment of services in the city. The main area where they reside is Mehdipatnam, followed by Shivaji nagar, Doodhbowli and Devibagh in that order. They are closely followed by the Gouds (toddy tappers) who dominate in Redhills area, Ramchandrapuram, Serilingampally in that order. They are however found in almost 44 per cent of the localities in the city though in a smaller measure. The Yadav/Golla Community (sheep and cattle rearers) is found in almost 40 per cent of the localities in the city. The places where they dominate are Mehdipatnam, Barkas, Saidabad Colony and Regimental Bazaar. Most of them engage in business (43%) including the traditional milk business and some of them are employed (37%). Other Backward Communities like Darji (tailors), Vishwakarma (artisans like Goldsmith, Carpenters, Blacksmith, etc.). Mangali, Naibrahmins (barbers), are mostly found scattered in small proportions in select localities of the city. The Bestha/Gangaputra/Jalari castes (fishing community) are dominant only in Ranigunj and Karwan areas and have a spotty presence in 4 to 5 other localities in the city. Similarly, Padmashali Community (weaver) also have a very scanty and sparse spread in the city. The Poosala Community is found only in Saidabad colony, they are itinerant, pin sellers and most likely migrated from the neighbouring districts. The Rajakula/Chakali (Washerman) community is found in a very microscopic proportion in places far and in between.

Fifty-four per cent of the localities have the presence of Scheduled Caste (SC) population. Scheduled Caste (SC) population seems to be more in the South-eastern and North-western part of the city. It could be attributed to the caste specific migration from adjacent rural areas. It is also noticed that about 77 per cent of the peripheral municipalities have a noticeable SC component of the population. Based on the master table 27 per cent of the SC population are migrants who have come to the city in the past ten years. The highest figure is found in Saroornagar followed by Amberpet both of them in the eastern part of the city and most likely recipients of immigrant streams from neighbouring districts. Patancheru and Ramchandrapuram which are peripheral industrial enclaves on the Bombay highway and Khairtabad, Serlingampally, Gaddiannaram also have a high proportion of the SC population.

It is also observed that ST population in the city is quite low and confined to select pockets. The highest proportion is in Erukala basti which is a slum occupied by tribal population followed by Gaddiannaram, Banjara-Jubilee hills, Regimental Bazaar, Patancheru, Serilingampally and Himayathnagar, etc. In the vicinity of most of these localities construction activity is going on and many of the members of the tribal families are engaged in this activity.

Women own just about 13 per cent of the surveyed houses and of these 45 per cent belong to the BC Community, this compares with a BC population of 40 per cent in the total samples comprising all religions and castes. The proportion of women owners compares favourably in this particular social category. In the Open Caste Community 30 per cent of the women own houses compared to a similar proportion of this category in the total population; in the SC and ST population, however, the proportion of women owners is much more compared to the proportion of these categories in the total population. So is also the case with regard to Christian women who own a substantial proportion of houses keeping in view their numbers compared to the proportion of this community in the total population, so is also the case with the Parsi population. (Table 1.8). The picture presented by women house owners in the Muslim, Sikh and Jain community presents a downside where their numbers are much less keeping in view the proportion of these communities in the total population. In fact in the Jain Community there are no women household owners.

A fleeting glance at the graphs (Fig. 1.23 and Fig. 1.24) and map (Fig. 1.25) pertaining to the mother tongue of the people in the different wards and municipalities of Hyderabad reveals that while there is a diversity of languages spoken in the core of the city, the

Table 1.8: Hyderabad: Women House Owners: 2007-2008

Social Groups	*Sub-Category*	*Total Population*		*Women house owners*	
		Number	*Percent*	*Number*	*Percent*
Hindu	OC	452	30.87	58	30.05
	BC	587	40.09	87	45.08
	SC	96	6.56	17	8.81
	ST	23	1.57	5	2.59
Muslim		189	12.91	14	7.25
Christian		33	2.25	8	4.15
Sikh		15	1.02	1	0.52
Jain		4	0.27	0	0.00
Parsi		2	0.14	1	0.52
Data not available		63	4.30	2	1.04
Total (Sample Size)		**1464**	**99.98**	**193**	**100.01**

Source: Field Survey 2007-2008.

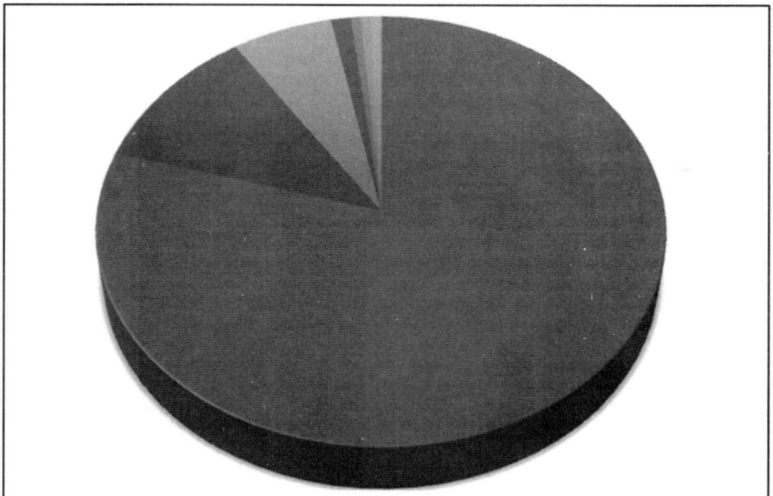

Fig. 1.23: Mother Tongue in Hyderabad (2007-2008) (Pie Graph)

peripheral areas exhibit homogeneity with regard to the languages spoken. Most of the people have Telugu as their mother tongue in the peripheral municipalities and other languages find a diminutive presence. With very few exceptions, the Secunderabad part of the twin cities also shows an ascendancy of Telugu. Hindi as the mother tongue seems to be more dominant in the commercial areas like Monda Market and General Bazaar in Secunderabad and Sultan Bazaar and Abids in Hyderabad which have a large Marwadi population. This is apart from Gosha Mahal, which is close to the CBD of Hyderabad, Hussaini Alam which has a sizeable Kayasth population in the old city part of Hyderabad and Langar House, which has some retired defence personnel. The old city of Hyderabad comprising Pathergatti, Moghalpura, Barkas, Aliabad and also Gulzar House report Urdu as the mother tongue of a majority of the people. It may also be pertinent to note here that the maximum numbers of languages/language groups (6) are reported in the Banjara-Jubilee Hills area, which is a high class and hence a cosmopolitan area of the city, followed by Sultan Bazar-Abids area which is the CBD of Hyderabad, Himayatnagar and Marredpally. Marathi has also been reported significantly from Sultan Bazaar, Himayat Nagar, Vijay Nagar Colony, Mehdipatnam, Sabzi Mandi, Karwan and Gulzar House in Hyderabad and

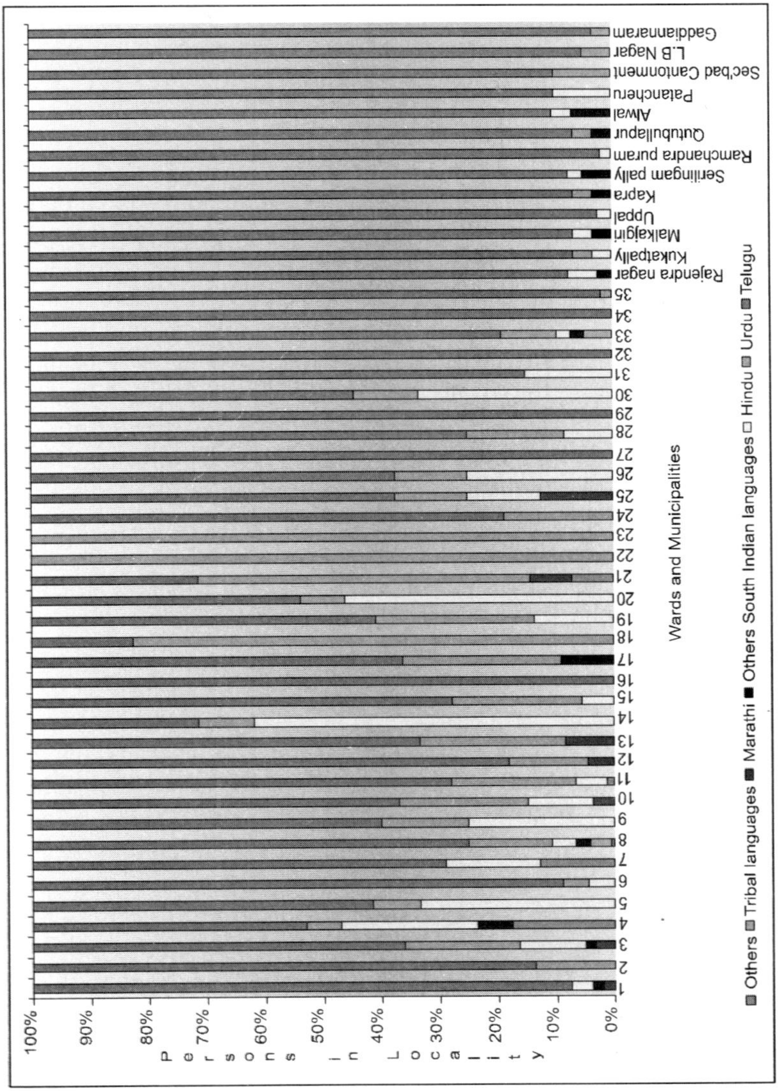

Fig. 1.24 Mother Tongue in Hyderabad (2007-2008) (Bar Graph)

Ramgopalpet in Secunderabad, quite significantly none of the peripheral localities report Marathi as mother tongue. Notably enough, these localities also lack the 'Others' category which has a miscellany of languages like Bengali, Oriya, Punjabi, Gujarati, etc. and which are found only in such localities as Himayat Nagar, Sultan Bazaar, Ameerpet and Gulzar House in central locations in the city. Other South Indian Languages like Tamil, Kannada and Malayalam are spoken in select parts of the city. It may also be observed that Tamil as a mother tongue finds presence in Abids, Ameerpet, Saroornagar, Marredpally, Alwal-Malkajgiri-Kapra in a continuous stretch on the north eastern periphery of the city and Serilingampally in the west. Most of these areas have the old settled Tamil families, who were employed either with the railways as in the north eastern part of the city or are now with other government organizations like research labs, etc. Kannada and Malayalam are reported only in select localities like Chikkadpally, Himayat Nagar, and Banjara-Jubilee Hills areas in the core city of Hyderabad and Alwal, Qutbullapur and Rajendra Nagar in the peripheral municipalities. It is also noteworthy that Tribal Languages like Yerakala and Lambadi are spoken in Yerakala Basti and Banjara Hills respectively. These areas have a large tribal population some among whom initially came in as construction workers and subsequently took up government jobs or got into business.

Economy

Hyderabad is not only the administrative capital but also the economic and financial capital of Andhra Pradesh. It is the largest contributor to the state's GDP, state taxes and excise revenues. It has a large population and has the potential to power the state's future economic growth. Over the past couple of decades, the economy of Hyderabad has shifted from the purely secondary and tertiary sectors to a combination of the secondary tertiary, quaternary and quinary sectors. However, the old city has suffered a decline and the peripheral areas are playing a dominant role in growth and employment generation.

The urban economic profile is undergoing a transformation in recent years with service industry playing a major role in the economic development of Hyderabad. Manufacturing sector includes pharmaceuticals, electronic goods and other industrial products. Pharma industry is also dominant in manufacturing sector and is playing an

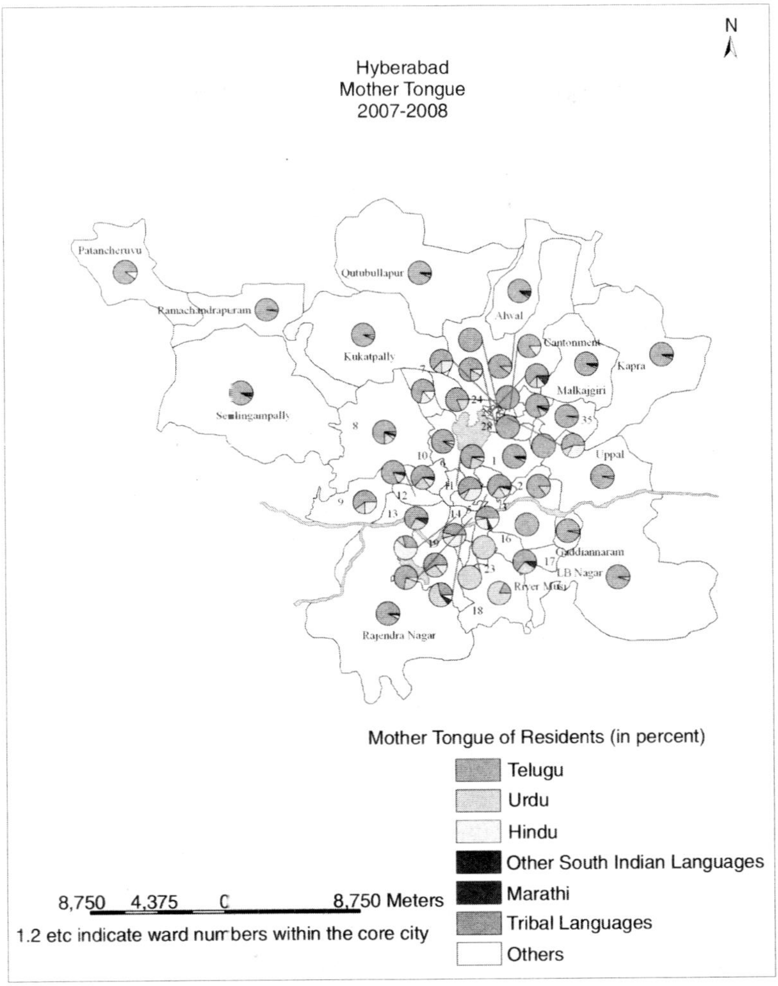

Source: Field Survey

Fig. 1.25: Mother Tongue of Hyderabad (2007-2008) (Map)

increasing role in even the exports and this will continue in the future. Hyderabad is called "Bulk Drug" capital due to the presence of large number of bulk drug units and accounts for 30-35 per cent of the total production in the country. The service sector has increased in the recent years with a significant proportion of new jobs. Of late, it has emerged as the single largest employer and it contributed more than 50 per cent of the total city's work force.

Locational Aspects of Growth

The increased economic growth of the city has been responsible for the growth of the surrounding areas. The economic activities, mainly manufacturing and associated facilities are concentrated in Ramachandrapuram, Patancheru, Balanagar, Uppal, Cherlapalli, etc, which lie on the periphery of the city.

The economy of Hyderabad is witnessing a change from traditional manufacturing towards a knowledge-based economy. This is mainly because of government policies to promote knowledge sector and tourism. IT and IT enabled services along with Biotechnology and Medical Sciences and industrial technologies are gaining momentum in the state.

Spatial Growth and Planning

Fig. 1.26 conveys that while upto 1981 the city has expanded towards the north east and the north west, subsequent growth has been in all

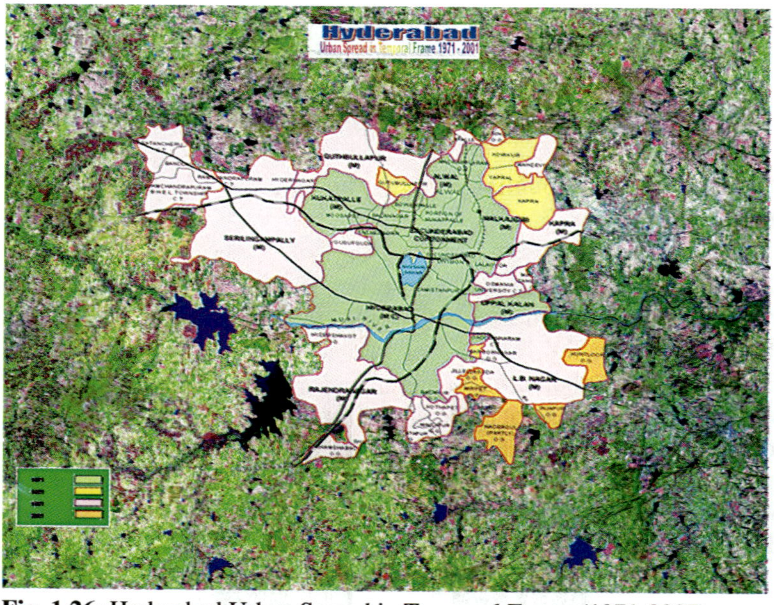

Fig. 1.26: Hyderabad Urban Spread in Temporal Frame (1971-2007)

Source: HUDA and Google.

the directions. The city however has expanded in a tentacle like fashion, with major extensions along the main highways leading to Mumbai, Bengaluru, Vijayawada and Warangal.

After Andhra Pradesh was formed, the city experienced haphazard growth and irregular pattern of circulation. To address the negative effects the first Development Plan was prepared in 1975 for an area of 172.6 sq.km. The important feature of this plan was to provide a frame work for balanced growth and development.

In 1975 the Hyderabad Urban Development Authority (HUDA) was constituted with the responsibility of planning, controlling and monitoring the developmental activities within Hyderabad Development Area including MCH. The Master plan was prepared for peripheral development and to bring a balanced development between rural and metropolitan environment.

Hyderabad Urban Development Authority (HUDA) revised its Master Plan in 2003 with the aim of making Hyderabad a truly world class city with sound and evenhanded planning. It advocates clustering of developed areas, promotes corridor development and underlines the need for an environmentally sustainable planning through appropriate planning for services and industrial areas.

In August 2008, the Hyderabad Metropolitan Development Authority (HMDA) was setup which replaced the HUDA. It has a jurisdiction over 6,856 square kilometres of area and has made Hyderabad the second largest metropolitan area of the country after Delhi in terms of area. This area which was formed after merging the surrounding municipalities with the capital city has a population of almost 7.8 million.

Unauthorized layouts are increasing in areas surrounding the twin cities but the HUDA has failed to curb their spread. The terrain under HUDA was increased from 3,000 to 6,000 villages after the government decided to form the HMDA for planned growth in the outskirts. However, mushrooming of unauthorized layouts has only increased after this. HUDA has not taken action on realtors who had developed more than 400 unauthorized layouts in and around the city except putting names in the black list. Lack of coordination between HUDA and the panchayats of surrounding areas is also contributing to the problem. (K. Srinivasa Rao, *Deccan Chronicle*, October, 20, 2007)

Hyderabad Urban Development Authority (HUDA) prepared a final overall map consolidating the maps of all 18 zones; the revised master plan draft of HUDA-2020 is set to be official. It covers about

2000 square km for sustainable development going on for 3 years. It has some commendable features but for the twin cities to benefit, it should be implemented properly. The new revised master plan takes into account to eliminate future land use changes by including multiple land use zones, surplus demarcation of residential zones, and at the same time giving importance to healthy and peaceful living. Given the present scenario, with changes in even recreation, bio-conservation, water bodies, mushrooming of apartment complexes, commercial complexes without parking space, requires setbacks that lead to enormous burden on the civic infrastructure and existing road space. One needs to be more sceptical about these master plans. The recent shifting of book stalls from Koti tells that such encroachments/violations would not be viewed lightly anymore. Those who violate building norms must be penalized. (*The Hindu*, November,18, 2006)

Hyderabad Urban Development Authority (HUDA) and MCH issued warning notices to builders and property buyers that if constructions or usage of the buildings deviated from the sanctioned plan and permitted purpose, stern action including cancellation of permission, demolition of buildings, disconnection of electricity and water supply besides prosecution as per law by local bodies would be initiated. It delegated certain development control powers to 12 municipalities. (M.L.Melly Maitreyi, *The Hindu*, November 25, 2006)

- Technical approval of HUDA is necessary for all layouts and sub-division permission,
- Approval of residential buildings above G+2 floors,
- Approval in plot area exceeding 1000 sq.m.,
- Approval in all non-residential buildings in the jurisdiction of 12 municipalities (i.e. Malkajgiri, Kukatpally, L.B.Nagar, Ramchandrapuram, Kapra, Rajendranagar, Keesara, Serilingampally, Qutubullapur, Gaddiannaram, Patancheru and Alwal).

Shamshabad and later other nodes may emerge as next focus of development as has happened to HITEC city. With only little more than a year away for all the major infrastructure projects to take shape, including the Elevated Expressway Corridor from Mehdipatnam to Shamshabad by then, not many layouts that have mushroomed in the surroundings of Shamshabad and within and outside HADA limits have infrastructure amenities in place like proper roads, drainage, electricity, drinking water to get the final approval. This approval is required for construction to meet housing demand for the projected growth in future. As of today, there are three approved layouts in HADA area where the price in approved layouts is at least three times more than that in the unauthorized layouts. There is a need to be more cautious in dealing strictly with illegal layouts and prevent the proposed New City to be turned into a conglomeration of slums. (M.L.Maitreyi, *The Hindu*, October 28, 2006)

Maytas Housing Pvt. Limited (formerly known as Satyam Homes Pvt. Limited) took up illegal construction in Rama Raja Nagar Colony. They have constructed apartments in the common area, including public road and in the area meant for public amenities. (*Deccan Chronicle*, January 10, 2009)

Residents of Rama Raja Nagar Colony near Suchitra have alleged that the Maytas Housing Pvt Ltd undertook illegal constructions in the area against rules. According to them the developers encroached upon the internal roads and also constructed shops and parking sheds and apartments in the common area, including the public road, and in the area meant for public amenities in the residential colony. Though complaints were lodged with the Basheerabad police station neither the Qutubullapur municipality nor the HUDA authorities reacted and did not even entertain the complaint. They purchased land measuring 8 acres 29 guntas in 1970 and obtained permission for housing projects but later constructed commercial complexes. The group obtained permission to construct 535 flats in 36 blocks but constructed only 23 blocks. (*Deccan Chronicle*, January 10, 2009)

Shamshabad features high on the list of emerging corridors in India. By definition, these emerging corridors are extensions of tier I and tier II cities that stand to gain from the existing pool and benefits from pre-planned infrastructure. That it made it to the top in the India list exemplifies the strength of the physical and social infrastructure, real estate development in the adjoining markets and the nature of economic activity present with the broader location; by national standards.

Corridors are rated according to 3 broad parameters: Sustainability, Momentum and Economic environment. On the basis of a multi variable analysis these corridors will have limited exposure to risk and will bring assured returns due to demand dynamics and readiness of infrastructure. Therefore, the long term sustainable corridors would emerge as preferred choice for investment from the risk minimization perspective. Hence, even from a global view, this area has been earmarked as one to watch out for. Since, all along the new airport in Shamshabad there is development in terms of houses etc, the gaps would get filled up with Shamshabad becoming very much part of the city and not the outskirts. (*Times of India*, March 16, 2008)

Shamshabad airport—the multi-million dollar project, has been built in an area of around 5,500 acres with the longest runway among Indian airports. This project also envisages plenty of real estate developments within the airport like hotels, convention centres, shopping malls/entertainment complexes, Free trade zones etc. besides a lot of business activity near or inside the airport. Hence, it is witnessing many related investments in the area of hospitality, education, IT, ITES, Biotech parks, business parks, SEZ's and housing. The fab-city investment alone is around $ 3 billion and the project spans over 1500 acres being developed by a consortium of firms including both AMD & Intel. Govt of Andhra Pradesh has allotted 5,000 acres for Software and Hardware parks near Shamshabad ensuring a multitude of investments into these parks. Other related investments in Shamshabad are:

1. The Mucherla IT park—located around 14 kms from the new airport has 850 acres, where 20 acres have been allotted to Dell. Infosys is setting up a 550 acre campus, the biggest software facility in India.
2. Amusement park—Asia's biggest amusement park being developed close to Shamshabad airport is to attract thousands of tourists every day.
3. Apparel park—spread over 176 acres of prime industrial land completes with banks, post offices, exhibition halls and shopping complexes is a conglomeration of several garment making units.
4. Videocon project—the country's largest consumer electronics manufacturer plans to pump Rs. 500 crore into manufacturing facility in next 3-4 years.
5. Astra Micro Wave Products Ltd.
6. International University—100 acres.
7. AP Housing Board Township—proposed 125 acres township

with Malaysian collaboration. In addition HUDA plans to auction a mega venture of 350 acres and develop a 600 acres Township at Maheshwaram mandal.

8. Nova Park—3000 acres of land has been allotted near the hardware park for the proposed NOVA Park.

The ORR coupled with the Express highway and MMTS railway connectivity will lead straight to the IT hub of Gachibowli and Madhapur. For the area, it will mean a giant leap into the future. (Ajit Nair, *Times of India*, March 16, 2008)

The completion of the first phase of the ORR has given a fillip to real estate activity on the city outskirts. The connectivity provided by the ORR will be a major incentive for real estate investment. The 1st phase of the project (22 km) linked Gachibowli and Shamshabad and is likely to spur real estate deals in surrounding areas such as AP Police Academy, Chilkur and Tellapur. The government invested Rs. 500 crore on the 1st phase taken up in January 2006. For the completion of 140 km 2nd phase, it is likely to spend Rs. 2500 crore in next 3 years. It will provide connectivity to Narsingi, Kollur, Patancheru, Medchal, Shameerpet, Yapral, Peddamberpet, and surrounding areas. Several realty majors such as PBEL (constructing 2000 apartments) Aliens Group, Sri Lakshmi Venkateshwara Estates (constructing 120 villas near Yapral), Satyavani Green Homes, Lanco hills, Manjeera projects have taken up mega projects in and around the ORR.

Several IT and business establishments are also going to come up in Pocharam and surrounding areas. The ORR will make Hyderabad an International city. The main benefits of the ORR are that it relieves congestion on the metropolitan area and the inner ring road, provides orbital linkage to radial arterial roads, creates options for development of satellite townships, provides linkage to the proposed MRTS and bus system, provides quick access to the International Airport and connects various new urban nodes outside the city.

Lack of coordination among HUDA, the GHMC and the revenue authorities has proved a boon for land grabbers within the corporation. HUDA officials say they can demolish illegal constructions only if the GHMC and the revenue authorities support them. They could not prevent land grabbing even at Saroornagar tank bund which was recently developed by HUDA. Illegal land transactions with fake documents are rampant in other lake bed areas in the city as well. HUDA issued a notification in May, 2000, listing 169 lakes with an extension of more than 10 hectares. Some NGOs say thousands of acres of land near lakes had already been encroached upon. As per their surveys, land at Durgam, Medikuta, Gangaram, Nallagandla and Ambar Lakes situated in Lingampally and Serilingampally areas respectively were grabbed by realtors. The intervention of the government is called for here as these encroachments deplete the ground water resources too. (*Deccan Chronicle*, February 17, 2008).

Over 20000 encroachments dot the 250 odd lakes in and around the city. The officials prefer to turn a blind eye to the illegal construction activities. The problem has been further compounded with the HUDA failing to demarcate the Full Tank Level (FTL), the dry area that submerges during rains. Sources said nearly 200 lakes in Hyderabad and Ranga Reddy district do not have the FTL markings and at the same time the land dealings are continuing. Lack of co-ordination between the HUDA, GHMC, District Town and Country Planning Department, Pollution Control Board and the Industries Department officials led to shrinkage of lake area. The lakebed land sold like hot cakes between 2002 and 2004 when a drought like situation prevailed in the state and the real estate market sky-rocketed. Musi riverbed and its FTL area alone has over 10000 permanent and temporary encroachments followed by Hussainsagar, Himayathsagar and Osmansagar. *Pucca* structures have come up in the FTL areas of Safilguda, Saroornagar lake, Durgam Ceruvu, Medikunta Cheruvu, Chandanagar, Pedda Cheruvu at Serilingampally, Nallagandla Cheruvu, Gowlidoddi Cheruvu, and so on. The MGBComplex (Asia's biggest bus terminal) at Imlibun was constructed by filling up the Musi riverbed area. Several colonies have mushroomed in the tank beds with municipal authorities blindly giving permission for construction activities. (*Deccan Chronicle*, August 22, 2008)

HUDA is also contemplating entrusting the task of surveying lakes and tanks in the twin cities and surrounding municipalities to the EPTRI (Environment Protection Training and Research Institute). There are about 300 to 400 lakes and tanks falling in HUDA limits and a majority of them are encroached by land sharks and majorities are polluted. (*The New Indian Express*, S. Bachan Jeet Singh, December 5, 2006)

Interestingly enough the realtors are developing artificial lakes to create the right ambience for their projects. Several villa projects are coming up near existing lakes and in some spots, estate companies are developing artificial lakes to create the right ambience for villa owners. Several firms are developing the existing natural lakes with the support of HUDA. Landmark builders is constructing 58 villas in the Stepping Meadows integrated homes project near Nallakunta Lake in Tumukunta village. PBEL has taken up the task of rejuvenating the Peerancheruvu lake adjacent to its residential project near the AP Police Academy. City based architect says 'lakes need to be developed in such a way that micro-climate conditions are created. There is also a need to conserve the heritage and environmental aspects in and around the lakes. Aliens group is developing Tellapur Lake, which is adjacent to its Aliens Space Station-1 project and Lanco group has sought the government's assistance in developing the lake located near its project at Manikoda. (K.Srinivasa Rao, *Deccan Chronicle*, Nov 14, 2008)

The number of migratory birds as well as many common avians has also dwindled in number because of all the commercial activity in the city and real estate boom on its outskirts. The Hussain Sagar Lake had a 'rock island' where 100's of migratory birds used to flock. But sadly with concrete structures dotting the lake, despite the High Court's ban on permanent structures by the lakeside, their natural habitats have been destroyed. Areas like Gachibowli, Kondapur, Shamirpet once used to be a haven for bird watchers. Now these areas in the city outskirts have also been attacked by concrete giants, which are enough to scare away the winged guests. The expansion of the city has also led to excessive tree felling as a result tree-dwelling birds have also dwindled in number (Sulogna Mehta, *Deccan Chronicle*).

Slums

More than one fifth of the population of Hyderabad dwells in the slums and their number has been escalating with the passage of time. These notified slums are besides the squatters and other poverty neighbourhoods. Though they contribute to the city economy immeasurably, the slum dwellers suffer from many insufficiencies and it becomes imperative to bring them into the mainstream of the city.

The number of people living Below Poverty Line (BPL) is 540,000 of which 430,000 live in MCH area. The percentage of BPL population is highest in Qutubullapur with 36.58 per cent. Rajendernagar follows with 23.66 per cent. Uppal, Serilingampally and LB Nagar have a very low percentage at 3-4 per cent (HUDA). Slum population includes Hindus, Muslims, and Christians having migrated from neighbouring districts. Telugu and Urdu are the main languages spoken followed by Marathi and Kannada.

Slums are scattered across the city and surrounding municipalities with high population densities and the number of people is estimated around two million (Table 1.9). Half of the slums are on private lands and rest on public land. Poverty has visible gender dimension too. Female-headed households constitute the poorest of the poor, as poverty among women is higher. There are around 1500 slums in and around Hyderabad constituting HUDA.

Table 1.9: Slums of Hyderabad (MCH Area) 1962–2009

Year	*No. of Slums*	*Increase in No.*	*Growth Rate of no. of Slums*	*Population (in Lakhs)*
1962	106	—	—	1.20
1972	282	176	9.07	3.00
1979	455	173	6.71	4.08
1986	662	207	5.29	8.59
1994	811	149	2.53	12.59
2009	1479	668	8.2	20.39

Source: GHMC manuscript document.

Sixty per cent of the slum population resides in Qutubullapur, Alwal and Rajendernagar. The total number of slums in HUDA in 2003 was 1631 out of which 1142 fall under MCH area. The highest number of slums is in Kukatpally i.e., about 81 and the total population in these slums is only 19,585 which is 6.74 per cent of the slum population of the HUDA area. In Qutubullapur on the other hand, the number of slums is 77 with a population of 1, 38,360 and constitute 61.27 per cent of the total slum population. Rajendernagar has 38 slums with a population of 84284 constituting 58.8 per cent of the total slum population.

Literacy rate in slums was found to be between 60-80 per cent. Female literacy varied from 52-73 per cent. Alwal has the highest literacy rate among the slums with 80.29 per cent and a female literacy rate of about 72.38 per cent. Rajendernagar has least literacy rate with 60.15 per cent.

Slums are located on Government, Municipal, private and unclaimed lands. 55 per cent of the slums are on private lands, 30 per cent on government land, only 9 per cent on own land, 3 per cent on MCH land and the rest 6 per cent on MCH, AP Housing Board and Endowment land (Fig. 1.27).

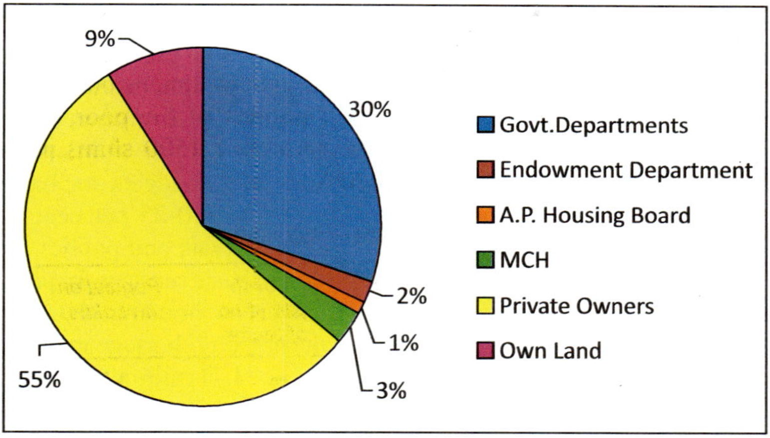

Fig. 1.27: Status of Land in Slums of Hyderabad

Source: Hyderabad- City Development Plan.

The environmental conditions are very poor and basic amenities like protected water supply, street lights, drainage are not provided. The prevalent diseases are gastro-enteritis, dysentery, liver enlargement, malnutrition, ringworm, scabies and other skin diseases. To overcome health hazards 64 primary health centres were established but such facilities are not available in surrounding Municipalities.

Basic infrastructure provided in the slum areas indicates the quality of life in slums. Roads, sewer lines, storm water drains, community latrines, streetlights, drinking water supply, schools, electricity etc. were proposed in slum improvement projects. One-third of the slums have individual connections and the rest depend upon public taps. Basic infrastructure facilities in the slum are minimal and inadequate and need to be strengthened.

The government has planned to make India slum-free in five years through a new scheme, Rajiv Awas Yojana (RAY)—beginning in 2009, though officials are skeptical about the same. The respective state governments have been given the onus of devising and putting through the ropes a plan of action. In the preparatory phase of RAY, each state is supposed to prepare its plan of action based on

Geographic Information System (GIS)-enabled mapping for the cities identified to be made slum-free. The states will later extend the programme to make the entire state free of slums. Unlike previous schemes, RAY seeks to provide property rights to slum dwellers.

The programme seeks to tackle shortage of urban land and housing that keep shelter out of the reach of the poor. According to a National Sample Survey Office (NSSO) report, around 57 per cent of slums come up on public land, owned mostly by local bodies and state government, 24 per cent along drains and around 12 per cent along railway tracks.

The states will also be required to continue three reforms under the JNNURM (Jawharlal Nehru National Urban Renewal Mission) including internal earmarking within local body budgets for basic services to the urban poor, earmarking at least 20-25 per cent of developed land in all housing projects (both private and public) for economically weaker sections and provision of basic services for poor.

A technical group on estimation of urban housing shortage constituted by MoHUPA had estimated the housing shortage in urban areas at the beginning of the Eleventh Plan at 24.71 million, of which 98 per cent pertained to the economically weaker sections and low income groups. The total shortage of dwelling units is expected to rise to 26.53 million by the end of Eleventh Plan. The officials said the existing schemes for affordable housing and interest subsidy for urban housing will be dovetailed into RAY. The scheme requires each state setting up a Rajiv Awas Yojana Mission Authority (RAYMA) to take decisions regarding land use and town planning.http://in.news.yahoo.com/43/20100802/818/tnl-india-cannot-be-made-slum-free-in-fi.html

The GHMC has taken it upon itself to make Hyderabad slum free and towards this end they plan to either shift or remodel slums. Also, slums lacking basic facilities will be provided those facilities. Plans are afoot to develop, remodel and relocate 290 slums in the coming year under Rajiv Awas Yojana (RAY) of the central government. 1470 slums in the city will be taken up under this project over the coming five years. Once, they have adequate infrastructure they will be denotified as slums. They are short of basic facilities like sewer lines, water supply, roads and sanitation. Slums are categorized into three categories for purposes of development.

(a) The big slums will be provided all facilities like roads, sewer lines, water supply and housing marked as 'Gap Filling'.

This effort will be taken up in 192 slums and weaker section colonies.

(b) Slums which have minimum facilities will be remodelled by providing houses, roads etc. Infrastructure will be provided in 28 slums and 70 slums will be remodelled.

(c) Identified slums from the core of the city will be relocated to the periphery in planned layouts. (*Times of India*, January 23, 2011)

While the slums signify one end of the urban spectrum (Fig. 1.28, 1.29, 1.30, 1.31, 1.32 and 1.33) the other is signified by the exclusive enclaves of the ultra rich sometimes manifesting themselves in the form of 'Gated Communities' which are physically and emotionally isolated from mainstream society. The present study will probe this entire gamut of localities in order to gauge the conditions in each one of them as also the perceptions of the residents inhabiting them. Perceptions in any case translate as expressions of requirement or otherwise of facilities and amenities in the city, their use, strain on them, besides a whole horde of related issues. It will also look at governmental schemes towards social and financial inclusion, besides viewing the supply chain with regard to housing. The bond between infrastructure and housing will also be looked at from a multi-pronged

Fig. 1.28: Shadow under the Lamp: Slums in Close Vicinity of Plush Government Offices

Fig. 1.29: Urban Spectrum

Fig. 1.30: Slums in Basheerbagh

Fig. 1.31: Housing Blight Alongside Modern Structures

Fig. 1.32: Housing Blight

Fig. 1.33: Juxtaposition of Poverty and Plenty

angle. The concept of inclusivity in housing will be viewed from the perspective of different income, educational, occupational, religious and caste groups to ascertain their individual viewpoints.

References

1. Sheela Patel, Director, Society for the Promotion of Area Resource Centres (SPARC), quoted in the *TV*-Evideo series, Life II, "City Life," *Programme* 1, 2001.
2. United Nations Development Programme, "*Human Development Report*," Oxford University Press, New York, 1999, p. 2.
3. UNCHS, *Global Report on Human Settlements 2001*, Earthscan Press, London, 2001, p. xxviii and pp. 15-23.
4. UNDP, *Human Development Report 2000*, Oxford University Press, New York, 2000, pp. 31-41.
5. Richard Stren, "Thinking About Urban Inclusiveness," paper prepared for the 18th Session of the Commission on Human Settlements,

entitled, "Bridging the Divided City: A Dialogue on Social Inclusion in Cities," 14 February 2001. See http://www.unchs.org/govern/

6. UNDP, *Human Development Report 2000*, Oxford University Press, New York, 2000, pp. 31-41.
7. UNCHS, *State of the World's Cities 2001*, Nairobi, 2001, p. 109.
8. Saskia Sassen, Professor of Sociology, University of Chicago, quoted in the TV-E video series, Life II, "City Life," *Programme 1*, 2001.
9. D'souza Alfred and Singh "*The Indian City*" Manoher Publishers, New Delhi 1978.

2

Housing Market

The land market in Hyderabad like that of any other city of its ilk in the country is apt to change very rapidly—it can at best be called 'volatile with periodic up and down swings,' which have become the order of the day. While the general tendency has been towards an upswing in the land market in Hyderabad, in the post globalization era, the impact of various factors like the overall stability of the economy, the ranking of the city in terms of its economic potential, the skewed nature or otherwise of income distribution in the city, the type of origin area of migrants, the attitudes of people towards the different investment options, all these and many more have an impact on the urban land market. Short term influences on the land market like elections, political stability or lack of it have an impact on the urban land market and add to its buoyancy, stability or vicissitude.

The factors that have acted as catalysts of the growth of Hyderabad are new International Airport at Shamshabad, Metro rail on the anvil, 160 km Outer Ring Road, > 30 IT SEZs, new IT units, real estate projects with international stakeholders. All these have imposed an immense amount of pressure on the land market of Hyderabad (*Deccan Chronicle*, September 29, 2008).

Telangana issue has not affected property deals in the twin cities according to the land registration records. Till the first half of December 2006, the Registration Department had received 34,186 documents for registration out of which 16,858 properties were processed for sale in the twin cities alone. (M. Sai Gopal, *The Hindu*, December 16, 2006)

Developers/builders believe that the upward march in prices will pause and correct itself, not because of the 'T' factor. Crash of the booming real estate was expected during the bye polls but nothing of that sort has apparently happened. Those who brewed hopes of a real estate price crash now sport frowns. The rising prices of cement, steel and construction material would continue to be the deciding factor in fixing the property values. Since, the election process began not even a single flat was sold in Nizampet and Kukatpally. Hyderabad is too hot a property to be affected by political upheavals. Property prices continue to be high as Telangana factor fails to impact it. Several buyers had postponed their plans to purchase plots and flats anticipating that rates would come down if TRS won the by-poll elections. (*The Hindu*, December 16, 2006).

However, "with real estate prices falling in the last two years due to global recession and meltdown, the leaders from this district (*Rangareddy*) cutting across party lines see no reason why they shouldn't jump on to the Telangana bandwagon."(Mahesh, K., 2009) A reality twist is thus found for demand for a new state of Telangana. While a slump in land prices has been a consequence of the global meltdown, it has set in motion a trail of political processes which have strong national and local bearing. (*Sunday Times of India*, December 27, 2009)

The number of real estate transactions in Hyderabad have come down by 50 to 60 per cent compared to last year as no liquidity in market. The prices of residential space are down by 30 to 40 per cent. The prices are down as builders are not able to offload flats they have built as speculators are out of market. The end users who want places to live in are still buying but their numbers limited. (*Sunday Times of India*, October 12, 2008)

Year	*Cement cost per bag (in Rs.)*
2005	110
2006	150
2007	190
2008	230

The unprecedented increase in cement and steel prices has held up several infrastructure and housing projects in the twin cities. Most developers have postponed their projects with the hope that the prices would stabilise soon. Some companies are trying to pass on the extra burden to consumers. It has now become a daunting task for realty companies to provide 'affordable housing' to middle and lower middle classes. Steel and cement account for 33 per cent of construction costs and every 50 escalation in price of these materials will increase the cost of property by Rs. 75 to Rs. 100 per sq.ft. The average cost of property will end up 8-10 per cent higher than the original estimate. Member of AP Builders Forum says "the common man cannot purchase a flat in Hyderabad if the trend continues". The state government recently held a meeting and asked cement companies to cut their profit margins in order to supply cement at reasonable prices. Government's concerns run deep since the price rise can jack up the costs of its RSS to provide low-cost houses and flats to HIG and MIG. Minister for housing says "the cost of individual flat will surely go up though we promised to provide houses at rates 25 per cent less than the market prices". The cost of construction has increased in just 6 months says BRK Constructions Ltd. President and adds that realty firms were expecting prices to cool down to some extent in next 3 months. (K. Srinivasa Rao, *Deccan Chronicle*, April 25, 2008) (L.V.Reddy, *Deccan Chronicle*, June 27, 2008)

Buying a flat in Hyderabad has become costlier by upto Rs. 4 lakhs because of local cess, increasing cement prices, and hiked interest rates. (1) Builders fear that this will affect the construction industry badly, (2) Interest rates on housing loans have climbed from 8 per cent to 11.5 per cent, forcing customers to pay more money as equated monthly instalments. A bag of cement costs around Rs. 210 against Rs. 160 last year, (3) Civic authorities revised charges from Rs. 20 to Rs. 100 per sq.mt of built up area from June 16. For open plots, the charges were increased to Rs. 75 from Rs. 10 per sq.m.

A 1000 sq.ft double bedroom flat was available for Rs. 22 lakhs in areas like Dilshuknagar, Malakpet, Uppal, Kukatpally, Mehdipatnam till end of April. But now the cost of each sqft is being fixed between Rs. 2400 to Rs 2700. The AP Builders Forum has urged the govt. to reduce the burden on builders. Also said the govt should develop residential areas on the outskirts in order to reduce the land cost. (*Deccan Chronicle*, July 4, 2008)

Builders have adopted innovative methods to reduce construction costs in the wake of the sudden spurt in cement and steel prices. Several of them like Larsen and Toubro, Hiranandani Constuctions, Raheja, Unitech, DLF, Kalpataru are using fly ash based cellular light weight concrete and fabricated material to cut costs without compromising on quality. The rise in prices of steel, cement has hit the small and medium sized constructions firms the most. Steel prices surged from Rs. 30,000 per tonne in 2007 and rose to Rs. 50,000 a tonne now. Similarly, cement prices have gone up from Rs. 180 for a 50 kg bag to Rs. 230. Earlier, steel and cement used to constitute just 20 per cent of the construction cost but now it has touched 35 per cent. Nagarjuna constructions and DLF to use cellular lightweight concrete, which will reduce the weight of cement needed in beams and columns, making them more durable that would help them save Rs. 100 to 200 per sq. ft.

The use of alternative technologies such as tunnel form technology and table forms is also gaining momentum other builders using hollow concrete blocks, rubber filler blocks, stabilized mud based blocks interlocking bricks. Pre-fabricated roof and floor trusses can be assembled quickly saving time and money. Builders believe that if the government abolishes the 25 per cent import duty on steel, domestic prices will stabilize in the long term. (L.V. Reddy, *Deccan Chronicle*, May 9, 2008)

Information and Communication Technology (ICT) have often played the role of catalysts in spurring growth, bringing about awareness, reducing vulnerability and increasing resilience in communities. However, the impact is more visible in fields like environmental awareness and management and skill development, etc. In certain fields where information available is meagre or the needs of the population are not well sorted out, the role of ICT gets impeded. Housing is one such area, which nevertheless requires a lot of awareness both from the point of view of the residents as well as the administrators. Despite the spurt in information available, there is a lacuna so far as the availability of information with regard to housing along with the entire necessary adjunct information is concerned. For one, the potential house buyers have to fend for themselves in the absence of dependable information about the house and the locality most of which is gleaned from the seller's description. The perspective that one often gets on housing and land values which are a reflection of a plethora of factors. It is most often that of the sellers and hence tinted from his angle. Secondly, there is no means or measure by which the land values can be standardized and no statutory authority to control it.

As it is the dipping housing market is leading to a slump in real estate advertising in newspapers. What's worse is that a lot of that advertising may never come back to newspapers even if the real estate sector recovers because several real estate executives are making a conscious decision to move money out of newspapers and onto the

Internet as that medium grows in importance as a tool for researching home-buying decisions. (Seth Sutel, *Deccan Chronicle*, August 7, 2007)

The city of Hyderabad has witnessed a great amount of change in terms of economy thus affecting the entire lifestyle, culture and the social structure of the people residing here. The change is evident with the rise of different BPO's who cater to the needs of countries at international level. Many famous IT companies have turned towards this city which till then was not in the realm of globalization. It is now known for ITES Services, IT and Entertainment and Pharmaceuticals business. Many Business Process Outsourcing (BPO) firms, call centers, dealing with IT and other technical or technological services have come up in the city. As a result the city infrastructure has progressed at a quicker pace than any other Indian city and the city has transformed into a business centre and chosen location for information technology, software, biotechnology and business process outsourcing. Migration both from rural to urban and from urban to urban area has transformed the land use scenario and forced the city to expand in all directions. Real estate agencies see Hyderabad as a lucrative destination which ranks advantageously compared to other Indian cities. Simultaneously, some out of the international companies have established interest in real estate in Hyderabad.

Foreign companies are partnering with the local firms to undertake large scale projects ranging from gated communities, high-end villas and service apartments to commercial complexes. Foreign real estate companies anticipated Hyderabad would be one of the best international cities in the next decade. They are keen on investing in Hyderabad as the real estate prices are here low compared to other metro cities. In all 6 overseas firms have entered the city's booming realty sector recently. They include—Westport Capital of US which joined hands with Alliance Group to develop a 480 crore villa project in Hyderabad, and Malaysia's leading infrastructure company Sunway City Berhad, which partnered with city-based MAK Group for a high-rise realty project investing US$ 50 million in the city in next 3 years for other projects. PBEL a consortium of Israel-based Property and Building Corporation and Electra Real Esate Belgiums Millenium Diamond Holdings is investing $280 million to develop a huge residential and commercial project on 28 acre near ORR.

- The Alliance Group project, named 'Inner Circle' will come up in 60 acres at Shamirpet on the city outskirts. It will have 350 luxury villas each priced between Rs. 80 lakh—Rs 2 crores plot sizes ranging between 2400-6000 sqft. As there is huge demand for classy houses in Hyderabad where there is huge growth in IT and related sectors.
- MAK Group and Malaysian-based Sunway City Berhad will also jointly develop a high-end, fully integrated township near Shamshabad investing Rs. 3500 crore. 60 per cent will be Sunway City share while the remaining 40 per cent with MAK group. 360 villas will be constructed in the township in 1st phase would finish in 5years.
- Property and Building Corporation and Electra Real Esate, both based in Isreal, have announced real estate projects worth Rs. 4000 crore in Hyderabad, Chennai, Mysore. It has already purchased 125 acres for building 10 million sq. ft of world-class residential and business space in 3 cities. It has acquired 58 acres near the upcoming ORR and Shamshabad. The residential project would cater to employees of new international airport and IT companies. Hyderabad-based Incor Infrastructure will be a 10 per cent stakeholder in the project.
- Emaar MGF Land Ltd alone is going to invest Rs. 5610 crore in Hyderabad for the construction of integrated leisure and residential community project in Gachibowli.
- HUDA which is going to auction its land soon, hopes to raise Rs. 3000 crore in the current financial year as many foreign companies are keen to participate in the auctions. (L.V. Reddy, *Deccan Chronicle*, March 14, 2008) (K.Srinivaas Rao, June 27, 2008)

This ongoing process of migration has led to many issues in Hyderabad. First and foremost being the inavailability of space making the land rates soar high. Areas which were vacant till a few years ago are now in great demand resulting in a tough competition amongst the buyers. An unusual growth of the city is a result of the globalization process and is reflected in various ways. It has attracted consumer goods entrepreneurs who also are making enormous profits in the process. Super markets, music companies, electronic goods etc. find the city to be more lucrative as a result there is more stress and pressure on the limited land. Demands and needs of this population like schools, colleges, hospitals, and bus depots besides others further add to the agony. Areas like Kukatpally, Hitech City, Shamshabad, Maheshwaram which were once on the periphery of the city and hence isolated are now beyond the reach of a common man. Major convention centres, hotels, new townships, development of satellite townships, more international flights from city, exqusite shopping mall for the middle class consumers and attracting major media giants like Reuters are among the dream plans of the state. In turn it has led to steep hike in the prices of the land which is reflected in the following Tables 2.1(a) and 2.1(b).

Table 2.1(a): Steep Hike in the Land Rates of Hyderabad

(in Rs.)

Name of the Area	*Before September 2006*	*After September 2006*
Vikrampuri	5200	10400
Bowenpalli	3000	6000
Sikh Village	3000	6000
Thokatta	3000	6000
Vasavi Colony	4000	7700
Picket Main Road	8000	12000
Marredpally	10000	15000
Doodhbowli	3000	4000
Charminar	10000	12000
Patthar Gatti	8000	10000
Chandrayan Gutta	1500	2000
Barkas	1500	2000
Jubli Hills	30000	35000
Film Nagar	30000	35000
Nandgiri hills	30000	35000
Prashant nagar	30000	35000
Banjara hills	30000	35000
Srinagar Colony	30000	30000

Source: *Deccan Chronicle*, 2006.

The stamps and Registration Department had formally recommended to the State government for an increase in the market value of land in Hyderabad from 0 to 100 per cent depending on the potential of each region in the city. Yet, there is a difference of 50 per cent between Govt. rate and the seller's rate. The revision of the market value would be applicable for sale, purchase/transfers of land. At the moment, the department has decided to exempt buildings from the ambit. The revised rates are given below and the addition to the market value is very much perceptible in Table 2.1(c).

Table 2.1 (b): Hyderabad: Realty monitor: 2006

	Rental Value Independent house (4-5 bedroom) Rs/month	*Apartment (2000sqft) Rs/month*	*Capital Value Independent Plot Rs/square yard*	*Apartment Rs/square foot*
Banjara hills	35000-80000	20000-30000	25000-35000	1800-2800
Jubilee hills	35000-80000	20000-30000	25000-35000	1800-2800
Srinagar colony	25000-40000	15000-25000	18000-25000	1800-2300
Ameerpet	20000-30000	10000-20000	15000-25000	1500-1800
Somajiguda	35000-50000	15000-20000	18000-25000	1500-2000
Begumpet	30000-40000	15000-30000	18000-25000	1700-2300
Maredpally	20000-40000	15000-20000	18000-25000	1500-1900
Picket	15000-25000	8000-15000	15000-20000	1200-1500
Vikrampuri	20000-40000	15000-20000	10000-20000	1600-2000
Himayathnagar	25000-40000	12000-17000	15000-25000	1400-1700
Mehdipatnam	10000-15000	8000-12000	7000-15000	850-1400
Uppal	8000-15000	5000-9000	6000-10000	850-1200
Habsiguda	10000-18000	6000-10000	7000-12000	1000-1400
Madhapur	20000-30000	15000-25000	12000-20000	1700-2200

Source: *Times of India*, Nov. 11, 2006.

It has also been witnessed that the CBD of Hyderabad has shifted from Abids to Punjagutta—Somajiguda area, which is the new focus of transportation arteries, lies on the highways that link the rest of the city with the IT hub (HITECH City), houses the most posh shops selling designer goods and catering to an upmarket clientele, has the Governor's residence (Raj Bhavan) and also has the highest land values in Hyderabad.

Table 2.2 makes it clear that because of increasing demand for land most of the areas have become costly. Since land is considered as a lucrative investment the land rates have risen enormously. In some places the land value has hiked by even 100 per cent. Despite that there is a difference of 50 per cent between the government rate and the sellers' rate in certain areas as there is intense demand for land, as people are willing to pay more than the market value for land. Seeing this, the government introduced a fresh round of hike in the market values of lands for registrations which came in to effect on February 1 in Hyderabad (*The Hindu*, February10, 2007).

The increase in the market value does not remain uniform across the city and varies depending on the commercial potential of the area. Recently Andhra Pradesh Housing Board had to cancel an auction because it did not fetch a high bid in Kukatpally area. The officials

Table 2.1(c): Revised Market Value in Some Parts of the City (per square yard)

Secunderabad area		
	Previous	*Present*
Paradise X Roads to Garden Restaurant	Rs. 25000	Rs. 30000
YMCA Secuncerabad	Rs. 25000	Rs. 30000
Begumpet Main Road	Rs. 25000	Rs. 30000
Kavadiguda	Rs. 22000	Rs. 22000
Chilkalguda	Rs. 15000	Rs. 17000
Padmaraonagar	Rs. 18000	Rs. 22000
Monda Market	Rs. 2500	Rs. 30000
Addagutta	Rs. 5000	Rs. 8000
Parts of Cantonment Board have registered 100% increase in the market values because the revision was done after a gap of 2 years.		
Chikkadpally area		
Ashoknagar	Rs. 20000	Rs. 22000
Golconda X roads	Rs. 15000	Rs. 17000
Lower Tank Bund	Rs. 10000	Rs. 12000
Banjara Hills area		
Panjagutta to Banjara Hills Road No. 1	Rs. 50000	Rs. 50000
Market values in most of the areas at Banjara Hills have increased by 10-15%.		

Overall rate of Registration Fee:	
Prior to July 1, 2005	**After July 1, 2005**
13.5%. (*Breakup:* Stamp duty-8%, Transfer duty-5% and Registration fee-0.5%)	9.5%. (Breakup: Stamp duty-7%, Transfer Duty-2% and registration fee - 0.5%

(*The Hindu*, February 10, 2007)

expected that the bidding would be around Rs. 13 crores per acre based on its previous experience when it had sold an acre of land at Rs. 22 crores. The bidders were from Delhi who wanted to invest in Hyderabad which shows the lure of the city. (*Deccan Chronicle*, October 16, 2007).

Intellectuals think that there will be a sharp rise in land prices and that the future will be in high-rise buildings. In the peripheral areas around the city, at a radius of 20 kms, the trend will be for multi-storied complexes including far flung locations such as Shameerpet, Himayat sagar, etc. When the apartment in the core city is priced at Rs. 1 crore, an apartment at Rs. 40 lakhs in the city periphery would be seen as a good bargain and keeping in view the requirements of the city HUDA has taken up a major urban project that will have tremendous multiplier effect on the city. It will work on a 162 km 8- laned Outer Ring Road. HUDA is committed to deliver this road costing Rs. 3500 crores before the end of 2008. HUDA is also facilitating development of Radial road projects, under which 33 radial roads have been identified to connect the Outer Ring Road with the core city location, all along the Outer Ring Road. HUDA has also assessed a great potential for creation of living and work places. To ensure that the common man is not swept aside in the spiraling price rise of properties, all the townships will have provision for Low-income group and High income group housing which will be offered at fixed costs to the people. HUDA will also contribute to the improvement of traffic infrstructure. These include three flyovers being planned at Langhar Houz, Dilsukh Nagar and Uppal. Also in the offing is an elevated Expressway which connects the city to the upcoming International Airport. This is touted as the largest flyover in the country, spanning 11.4 kms *(Now completed)*. (*The Hindu*, April 14, 2006.)

There is another part of city suburb which hardly evoked any enthusiasm either among real estate brokers or prospective investors. That was till early 2005. When the property boom reached here, Chanda Nagar on the Mumbai Highway just got swamped in it. Rates kept climbing and locals recall that they fluctuated between morning and evening, and a square yard which till a couple of years ago were offered for Rs. 2000 or so zoomed high to stand between Rs. 15,000 to Rs. 20,000 per square yard. Chanda Nagar being in close proximity to Madhapur HITECH city now does not have any vacant space left. Similarly, market value of land for registration has gone up by 100 per cent in Secunderabad Cantonment area from December 2006. Market values of lands in other parts of the city have only gone up by 10 to 50 per cent. Though the stamps and registration department proposed a 200 per cent increase in some Cantonment areas, the State government decided to go for a uniform 100 per cent increase. Hyderabad District Registrar said that this was done as there was big difference between the government market value and the open market value in Cantonment. (*The Hindu*, 2007).

Vacant land has reduced in size drastically in the Secunderabad Cantonment area. There are 300 colonies under the jurisdiction of the board and as per the rules of the board; they have to set aside a certain proportion of their land for the development of parks etc. However, most of this land was either sold or trespassed during the real estate boom and now has buildings erected on it. (*Deccan Chronicle*, November 4, 2008)

Prices of land and apartments have increased by 10 per cent to 30 per cent following the government's decision to raise registration charges. This will fetch the state exchequer Rs. 230 crore. It earned Rs. 22.25 crore through registration of properties in the city and outskirts in April-May 2008. Builders complained that new rates would lead to a slowdown in the sector. Even under construction apartments have to pay the registration fee and different charges are levied for commercial and residential properties in the same locality. (L.V. Reddy, *Deccan Chronicle*, August 8, 2008)

Cumulative effect of the hike in interest rate on housing loans, service tax, VAT would drive away middle class buyers and lead to the collapse of the construction industry.

The Stamps and Registration Department proposed a unified price in place of the existing practice of charging stamp duty separately on the undivided share of land and the build up area. However, the government had decided against the proposal for registration of structures as it would have increased the burden on the property buyers. The Department charges stamp duty for the undivided share of land on the basic market value and also charges the structure per sqft. The public works wing of the department fixes the basic market value for the structure taking the Standards Schedule of Rates into consideration. 'As the procedure is confusing, the dept proposed to fix unified price rate on each sq.ft. of built up space' an official said. In Maharashtra and Karnataka too this proposal was dropped. (N.Vamsi Srinivas, *The Hindu*, Nov 11, 2008)

Real estate majors who jacked up property prices during the unprecedented boom in the property sector in the past 3 years, have suddenly realised that prices have gone beyond the reach of even the upper middle class groups. With the global economic meltdown dampening the sales prospects, several builders have decided to cut down property prices to boost sales and to avert the effects of recession. The National Real Estate Development Council, the apex realty body in the country, has decided to cut down apartment prices in the existing projects by 5 per cent. Those who plan it for future projects will be slashed by 10 per cent. City builders, however, say that the prices can be slashed further, up to 30 per cent, if only the government rolls back the multiple and double taxation policies. The government should ensure lower rates for home loans, bank credit to developers and offer a package to give a boost to the industry.

While the Can. Fin, which is an auxiliary of the Canara Bank, has been in the home loan arena from the late 1980s, other banks have made a foray into this very useful venture. The ICICI and Kotak Mahindra have entered this market by offering some very competitive interest rates which hold great attraction especially for the salaried middle class customers. (*Deccan Chronicle*, Dec. 9, 2009) Typical house prices increased 3 to 4 times during 2003-2008. This has led to a significant rise in home loans. The overall home loans excluding those to the reality sector accounted for 44 per cent during 2001-2007. This slowed down to 12 per cent in the subsequent year. This slowdown was caused by an inordinate increase in the property prices which well crossed the affordable limit. Also during the peak period in property prices, the ratio of Equated Monthly Instalment (EMI) to salary was a whopping 80 per cent. This strongly reduced the legitimate demand. The best ratio of EMI to salary ought to be 50 per cent. Hence a further correction in property prices is foreseen. (*Deccan Chronicle*, 2008)

According to Asian Development Bank estimates India's real estate sector is estimated to grow to $90 billion by 2015 from $12 billion in 2005. It will need 10 million new housing units a year by 2030. Such huge demand coupled with 100 per cent FDI in construction projects has catapulted the real estate sector to such heights that many analysts fear a property bubble is forming in India and a price correction of 10 per cent to 40 per cent is imminent. (U.Kumar Dey, July 8,)

The State government has announced a waiver of the stamp duty from 7.5 to 2.5 per cent in order to stimulate the real estate sector, which has been in a crisis for the last few months. This will enable buyers to save up to Rs. 1 lakh while registering their properties worth Rs. 20 lakh. Flats within 1200 sqft will be given reduction in stamp duty on registration. Public sector banks too announced a cut in interest rates valid for the next six months. According to Janapriya Engineers Syndicate "the government has provided a golden opportunity to the middle class by cutting stamp duty". According to Aditya Homes Pvt Ltd stamp duty exemption should be extended to

Table 2.1 (d): Charges for Commercial and Residential Properties in Hyderabad, 2008

Per sq yard	*Commercial purposes*	*Residential purposes*
Banjara hills	Rs. 53000 increased to Rs. 60000	Rs. 30000 increased to Rs. 32000
Begumpet	Rs. 38000 increased to Rs. 45000	
Narayanguda	Rs. 22000 increased to Rs. 24000	
Venkateshwara Colony/Journalists Colony	Rs. 30000 increased to Rs. 32000	
Qutbullapur	Rs. 3500 increased to Rs. 5000	
Shamshabad	Rs. 6000 increased to Rs. 7000	Rs. 1800increased to Rs. 2000
Construction charges for apts in Hyderabad for ground, 1st 2nd floors were increased from Rs. 540 per sqft to Rs. 5550. >3rd floor increased from Rs. 580 to Rs. 600. In addition to registration charge.		
Registration charges in suburbs falling in Rangareddy limits were raised by 15%		
In areas such as Kukatpally and Hitec city, govt restricted the increase to 100%		

Source: *Deccan Chronicle*, August 8, 2008.

flats for middle class buyers ranging from 1200-2000 sq. ft to stimulate this sector. SMR Holdings suggests that the cut in interest rate should be extended to all the buyers irrespective of loan amount. According to the GHBF as most buyers rely on private banks (HDFC, ICICI), they should bring down the interest rates to 9 per cent from 11 per cent. (K.Srinivasa Rao, *Deccan Chronicle*, December19, 2008)

Despite the cut in home loan interest rates announced by public sector banks buyers owning a house still is a distant dream as the majority of the ongoing residential projects in the city address only upper-middle and higher income segments. To purchase such a flat one needs to go for a loan of more than Rs. 20 lakh which is outside the package. The banks had decided to provide home loans of upto Rs. 5 lakh at 8.5 per cent interest and loans from Rs. 5 lakh to Rs. 20 lakh at an interest rate of 9.25 per cent. The concession loan package does not make much sense as properties are hardly available at this cost, even in tier-II and tier-III cities. And, moreover, the deadline for loan disbursals being June 30 it will be impossible for buyers or developers to meet this deadline.

Chairman of Bharat Infratech says that "the govt should give loans of up to Rs. 30 lakh at 6 per cent interest and loans above this amount at 8.5 per cent." Added that only such a comprehensive package would create the required growth momentum in realty, construction, cement, steel and heavy engineering sectors. (L.V. Reddy, *Deccan Chronicle*, Jan 9, 2009)

The meltdown in Indian real estate sector can be defined under 2 heads.

1. A significant drop in actual property transactions.
2. The inability of property developers to raise capital for their existing and future projects.

There are several factors causing the realty meltdown. Some are external to real estate. As the economy is de-accelerating it will leave its scars in form of Job losses, deferment of expansion plans and above all a gloom factor. People put off from taking longterm and high value decisions. Builders struggle to raise fresh capital as their overseas lenders themselves are facing problems. Real estate is a high risk and high return business and banks not in mood to take risk game for now. However, key policy steps can put realty sector on track :

(a) Providing cheap funds to realtors in meeting their commitments.
(b) Subsidising land meant for affordable or mass housing.
(c) Lowering home loan rates to 7-7.5 per cent.
(d) Raising the income tax exemption limit on home loan interest re-payments from 1.5 to 3 lakh per annum.

There was a 11.969 per cent drop in the number of property seekers and increase in number of site searchers. Property seekers from different cities have reacted differently to this slowdown. Preference to live in rented accommodation has seen a 13 per cent rise in rental seekers. The number of people looking for affordable housing (under 60 lakh) has increased by 7.79 per cent from April to June 2008 to July-Sept 2008 showing a trend of shift in demand. Seekers need to do a self-assessment before venturing into the property market. (Aditya Verma, *Deccan Chronicle*, December 12, 2008)

Apartment prices went up not only due to builders but also because of multiple taxation policies. Owners of individual houses pay tax only on the purchase of land whereas apartments are taxed 3 times higher in terms of building permission, urban development charges, power and water connection; so flat buyers end up paying up more than 30 per cent. Director, Navayuga Constructions Ltd says builders are forced to pay higher registration charges for apartments and this burden is being passed on to the customers. (L.V.Reddy, *Deccan Chronicle*, December 5, 2008)

Keeping the requirement in view the Hyderabad Urban Development Authority (HUDA) is hoping to raise more than Rs. 2000 crores by auctioning off 400 acres of land in Tellapur near HITECH City. As of now, HUDA has fixed Rs. 4 crores as the reserve price per acre of land in Tellapur. It had earlier auctioned off the lands at Kokapet at a price of Rs. 14.5 crores per acre. Tellapur falls in Medak district and is located five kilometres away from HITEC City. The plan is to set up an integrated township in the area which can also house information technology firms. The development of the township would be undertaken, in the private public partnership and the developer will get back his investments by marketing the houses and commercial complexes. (*Source*: *The Hindu*, 2007).

Kokapet is now being touted as the city's most attractive real estate location. Situated in the epicentre of prestigious IT corridor and is also strategically located between Gachibowli and the GHZone. The ORR is 1.5km from Kokapet, the metro is around 10 km away, Shamshabad airport is close enough at 17 km and the Secunderabad railway station 30 kms away. Dozens of residential and commercial projects are under various stages of construction in Kokapet. It has already been giving rich dividends to investors who came in early. Land which was valued at Rs. 10,000 per sq. yd. two years ago is now selling at Rs. 22,000. The prominent residential projects coming up near Kokapet include Lanco Hills, Aparna Sarovar, Aparna Cyber Commune, Ramky Towers, NCC Urban, Meenakshi Trident Towers, Jain Carlton Creek, Manjeera Diamond Towers, SMR Symphony and Emmar Boulders Hills. Mantra Developers and Ramky are developing commercial projects and Meenakshi Infrastructure are developing IT parks. The demand for residential property will grow further since the staff strength of companies is expected to increase further within 5 years. (L.V. Reddy, *Deccan Chronicle*, Nov. 14, 2008)

Table 2.2 represents the Municipal circles of Hyderabad of the GHMC (Greater Hyderabad Municipal Corporation) which came in to existence keeping in view the requirements of the consistently expanding city. Creation of GHMC led many developers to tap small and medium-sized companies with their projects and thus paved the way for several independent specialized infrastructure projects targeting the growing IT industry. Simultaneously, some overseas companies have evinced interest in infrastructure development in the State. A Singapore-based business group—Ascendas, has entered into an agreement with L and T Infocity Ltd, to develop a modern enclave, which will have a built-in space of about 5 lakh sq ft. To support the office infrastructure with better housing facilities, a host of initiatives are underway in and around the Madhapur region of Hyderabad, where private players have lined up a range of multi-storeyed complexes. And not to be left behind and to latch on to the emerging business opportunity, the State-owned Andhra Pradesh Housing Board, has signed up with two overseas partners—one Malaysian, and the other Singapore-based, to develop integrated townships to bridge the real estate demand-supply mismatch. Malls have become the flavour of the city and have sprouted all over. More and more retail chain stores both local and from across the country are underway. What started with mega stores such as Shoppers' Stop, Lifestyle, Pantaloon, Giant, MPM Mall, have lead to a chain reaction with more projects cropping up.

Table 2.2: Greater Hyderabad Municipal Corporation Town Planning Circles

Zone	*Circle*
Central	Circle-3 (erstwhile MCH area)
	Circle-4 (erstwhile MCH area)
	Circle-5 (erstwhile MCH area)
North	Circle-6 (erstwhile MCH area)
	Circle-7 (erstwhile MCH area)
	Malkajgiri
	Qutbulapur
	Alwal
South	Circle-1 (erstwhile MCH Area)
	Circle-2 (erstwhile MCH Area)
	Rajendranagar
East	Kapra
	Uppal Kalan
	L.B Nagar and Gaddiannaram
West	Kukkatpally
	Serillingampally (North)
	Serillingampally (South)
	Ramchandrapuram and Patancheru

Source: *Deccan Chronicle*.

Architects from the US, Britain, Singapore, Malaysia and Israel are in huge demand. In all, 6 residential projects of the city are currently being handled by foreign architects. Since, the concept of high rise building is new to local architects, the developers have opted to hire international consultants. Most developers choose foreign architects only for their large projects. It is affordable to hire an international firm to make master plans if there is a big volume of work. For smaller projects, local architects are better. (L.V. Reddy, *Deccan Chronicle*, October 31, 2008) Some projects with the intervention of international architects are listed hereunder:

1. The Maytas Hill County Project, Bachupalli, Skidmore of New York and CPG of Singapore.
2. The Sunway Open Grand, Miyapur, SAA architects of Malaysia.
3. Indu Aranya, Nagole, Surbana of Singapore.

4. Aliens Space Station and Iconia, Actins of UK.
5. PBEL City, Israel.

Apart from these RSP Architects Planners and Architects 61 of Singapore are also designing big projects in cities like Hyderabad, Mumbai and Bengaluru. In addition to these new malls—Tirumala music centre and Stanza—have come up and more are in the pipeline. In fact, a Dubai-based firm has evinced interest in developing a shopping arcade, on the lines of those developed in Dubai. Even as more such projects get lined up, the real estate biz in Hyderabad is in for exciting times.

The land market in Hyderabad has displayed a tendency to skyrocket. Though the impact of the global economic recession and a slackening of prices are felt on the peripheral parts of the city, the core city has been rather insulated from it. The prices in the Western (Jubilee Hills, Banjara Hills) and central parts of the city remain high and out of reach of the common man (Fig. 2.1). Realtors are adopting a 'realistic approach' following economic slowdown. Instead of a range of flats at Rs. 50,00,000 to Rs. 80,00,000 which are now harder to sell, they are looking for smaller functional flats for middle income groups of 800 to 900 sft @ Rs. 25,00,000. There has been a switch over from luxury flats with costly interiors to budget flats. Construction firms are accordingly altering plans in future projects (*Deccan Chronicle* Oct.11, 2008).

The Global Economic Meltdown has had a Domino Effect on the Urban Land Markets. However the Silver lining to the slowdown is that many people have a chance to call a home their own and housing is not elusive any longer. The recession did seem to have an impact on the housing market in the sense it ought to have and the sequence of steps to this build up in the pre and post recession period are highlighted in fig. 2.2.

The current stock market meltdown has hit realty stocks the hardest probably because of fears of a slowdown in the sector, with rising input costs and little chance of interest rates softening and this is an indicator that land prices are also going to change. (L.V.Reddy, *Deccan Chronicle*, June 20, 2008)

The downfall of investment banks Lehman Brothers and Merrill Lynch will also hit real estate, banking and IT sector. Both invested in 10-12 real estate companies Lehman alone invested $1billion in

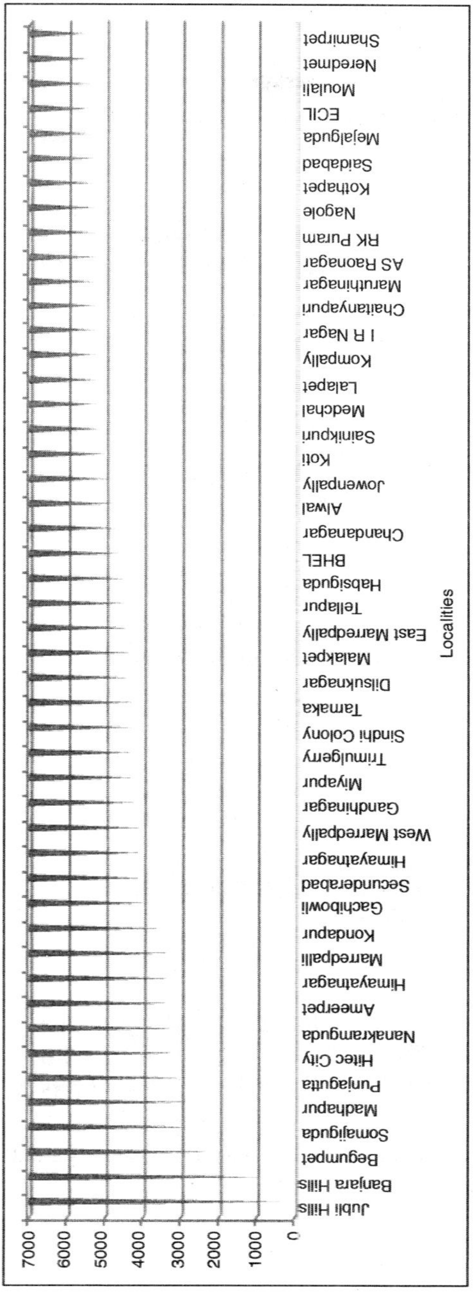

Source: Internet

Fig. 2.1: Hyderabad: Land Values, 2007

Source: Based on Prabhakar Sinha 'Housing and Dry?' *Sunday Times of India*, April 19, 2009

Fig. 2.2: Sequence of steps to build up in the pre and post recession period in Housing Market

India. ICICI, SBI, PNB, BOI, UBI HDFC which had exposure to Lehman and Merrill have suffered losses.

The Indian real estate has been through one of its worst phases with a lot of challenges to overcome. The market has slowed down, the liquidity crunch is increasing with each passing week, demand has depreciated, the stock market has crashed and the overall economic scenario is not very rosy. The finance ministry asked different sectors to cut prices to stimulate demand including the realty arena. The Government should bring down the housing loan interest to 7 to 8 per cent. However, experts feel that the realty sector can take a hit on its margins as most builders have been clocking an average net profit of over 40 per cent in the last 2 years. Also with substantial earnings in the past, real estate companies can afford to take a price cut in this grim situation. The home loan interest rate cut combined with price cuts on behalf of realtors could ignite positive sentiments and help the sector sail through choppy waters. (Rai Umraopati Ray, *Deccan Chronicle*, December 5, 2008)

The global melt down has spread gloom in the real estate sector, which had been on a roll in the last 5 years. However, maj r realtors in AP expect the industry to bounce back within six months since the traditional home market in India is very strong. The country's realty sector which is growing at 35 per cent is estimated to be worth $15 billion and would continue to grow next decade. The APBF says the real estate market will have a wonderful future in next years though the sale of Houses has been affected temporarily. Real estate companies such as Aliens, Lanco, Landmark builders feel that the situation will improve within 6 months. According to director of Aliens Group "the recession may have its impact temporarily but cannot disturb the market for a longer period" and buyers are still coming to invest in our projects including Aliens Station I and II. It indicates that the traditional home market is strong in Hyderabad. According to the Greater Hyderabad Builder's Forum the recession would not have any impact on the sale of flats meant for MIGs. "there is heavy demand for functional flats though buyers are not interested in luxury flats". (K. Srinivasa Rao, *Deccan Chronicle*, Oct 17, 2008)

Faced with rising inflation and soaring home loan interest rates, the real estate sector in the country is witnessing hard times this year pushing the cost of construction and thus hiked the overall cost of realty projects. With RBI raising its key interest rates to curb inflation there has been an across the board hike in bank lending rates.

- Major Banks like ICICI, HDFC have hiked home loan rates by a massive 0.75 per cent points.
- HDFC home loan rate priced minimum of 11.75 per cent
- ICICI from 13.5 to 14.25 per cent
- IDBI BY 0.50 per cent from 13.75 to 14.25 per cent
- Bank of Rajasthan, by 1 per cent from 15 to 16 per cent
- Punjab National Bank and AXIX Bank had also hiked their lending rates.

However, there are several PSU banks that have spared existing and future customers from latest interest hikes upto certain loan limit. Nevertheless, both the common man and the developer/builder community, who have been badly hit, are exploring newer avenues of funding to sustain their ongoing projects and plans.

As per RBI data, the growth in housing sector has come down from 25 to 13 per cent in just 1 ½ years. In 1990's home loan rates were at 17 per cent in 2003-04 increased 14.25 per cent from 7 per cent. Finally, going in for real estate investment makes sense keeping in mind the affordability, purchasing power of today. As Property appreciation counters inflation and one gets deduction of Rs. 150,000 on interest payments from annual income and finally property prices are said to be softening all over the country. (Rai Umraopati Ray, *Deccan Chronicle* August 22, 2008)

The upward revision of home loan interest rates is a major blow to the real estate market of Hyderabad, which is already grappling with the steep hike in construction cost in the last 6 months. Home loan interest rates which were hovering around 10 per cent have, rose to around 13.5 per cent now. HDFC, ICICI Banks have already announced a rise in lending rates and SBI and others would also revise their interest rates in a week. This has forced many people to shelve their plans to build their dream homes. Builders and developers say it is impossible to recover from the slump unless the govt comes forward to rescue the construction industry. Director of Landmark Builders says "builders are unable to complete the ongoing projects with the 30 per cent increase in construction cost even if finished won't be able to sell as buyers are scared with the interest rates. (K.Srinivasa Rao, *Deccan Chronicle*, July 4, 2008)

The revenue department has decided to postpone revision of land values across the state in view of the depressed land market. The department did not increase land rates in 2009 but planned to do so this year. It had just seen a huge shortfall in registration revenue and is, therefore, unwilling to risk increasing land rates. Last year the registration department fell short of its target by about Rs. 1000 crore. In a desperate bid to increase revenue, it planned to revise rates by rationalising the slabs. Many non-remunerative slabs will be withdrawn to make the registration process easy to handle. The 14 existing slabs will be trimmed to just 7. With the Central Government insisting on reducing stamp duty to 5 per cent from the existing 9 per cent, the department will lose about Rs. 1200 crore every year. It hopes to make-up the loss through revising the slabs. (*Deccan Chronicle*, May 12, 2010)

The soaring inflation on one hand and the continuous rise of interest rates on the other hand has led to a piquant situation. Private equity firms have also raised interest rates significantly because of funds shortage. Added to this, new policy by union finance on raising funds from the overseas market has also made it difficult for developers to access foreign funds. This has forced realty companies to raise funds locally either by land sales or by selling incomplete ongoing projects to big domestic realty companies. A Hyderabad-based real estate group issued advertisements seeking to generate Rs. 50 crore through bulk purchase of its housing project in the city to high net-worth investors. The real estate market has been under pressure for the past 6 months and according to market analysts, sales declined by 70 per cent and prices by 20 per cent in major cities such as Hyderabad, Chennai, Bangalore, Mumbai and Delhi.

Real estate developers pay interest rates as high as 18 per cent on funds. This would naturally make projects unviable; as a result several on-going projects are getting delayed. Though the big realty firms are more comfortable after having raised funds during the stock market boom in the last 2 years, the mid and small sized realty firms are feeling the pinch. Caught between sluggish demand and raising capital cost, construction cost, developers are deferring launch of new projects. Once the market settles down funds will automatically flow into the sector according to Hiranandani Constructions Ltd. (L.V.Reddy, *Deccan Chronicle*, July 4, 2008)

Speculation is coming to an end in the real estate sector due to the volatile/unpredictability in market. IT is estimated that a good chunk of investors, ranging between a quarter and three fourths, have been buying property more for investment than habitation. This has led to a rapid and abnormal increase in the value of residential and commercial property in major cities, which deterred genuine buyers from investing in real estate. The prices were beyond the reach of middle-class families. A large number of investors indulged in speculative buying to avoid paying taxes, and buying property is also an easy way to liquidate black money. Also much of the speculative activity in the market was driven by money being made in the stock market that witnessed a great phenomenal boom during 2006-2008.

Housing boom has it plus and minus points:

- Demand higher than supply
- Galloping prices
- Difficult for Lower and Middle Classes to move upwards
- Forced flight from the city may take place

However, in 2008 with the sensex falling below 14K the speculative markets have cooled off. The turmoil in the stock market has witnessed genuine consumers accounting for 80 per cent of buyers which is healthy and highly desirable.

Affordable Houses

While an affordable and decent house is everybody's dream, not everyone is able to realize it. The 'one size fits all' aphorism does not work in all situations. Housing has different connotations for people from different socio-economic backgrounds. In most cities, what is required is an improvement of the low income group housing; besides others, it can take the form of betterment of existing structures and provision of subsidized housing. The middle class, which is the key to the vim and vigour of the city, should be facilitated to locate and retain housing they can afford, lest the city becomes an elite commune. The city must increase aided and market price housing by collaborating with developers, builders, non-profit and financial institutions. This will have an impact on the overall social and physical fabric of the city. Otherwise, the crisis of affordability will widen gaps between groups of people.

In countries like USA an affordable dwelling is one which costs less than 30 per cent of the annual income of the people, however, in India it is defined as that which is 5.1 times of the annual income. While this definition is given by Housing Development Finance

Corporation (HDFC), which is the largest lender of housing loans in India, Ernest and Young fix 'affordable housing' at Rs. 10 lakh to Rs. 25 lakh. Property consultants Knight Frank, who surveyed the Indian Middle class with an income in the range of Rs. 3 to Rs. 10 lakhs, in the seven metropolitan cities of Mumbai, National Capital Region (NCR), Chennai, Bengaluru, Hyderabad, Kolkata and Pune. They found that people in the income bracket of Rs. 3 to 5 lakhs, are willing to compromise in terms of size of the housing unit in case they are given options of location to choose from. This aspect of location has been ignored heretofore by the builders and developers. It is, however, averred from Table 2.3 that middle class families in Kolkata, Chennai and Hyderabad can afford houses valued at Rs. 14 to 45 lakhs, whereas those in Mumbai and Bengaluru have to, with difficulty, fork out upwards of Rs. 12-38 lakhs for similar locations. On account of Mumbai's high cost of living and lifestyle, the MIG households have lower levels of affordability than cities like Kolkata, Chennai and Hyderabad. The study also reveals that while the middle class is the largest pressure group in the country, it will have an unmet demand for 2.06 million houses by 2011. (Sachdeva, A., 2009) This is amply evident from Table 2.4.

Table 2.3: Affordable House Value for the Middle Class

(*In Rs. Lakhs*)

City Income	*3-5 Lakh*	*5-8 lakh*	*6-8 lakh*	*8-10 lakh*
Mumbai	12-15	17-22	22-29	33-38
Pune	13-21	20-30	27-31	35-40
NCR	14-19	21-28	25-32	36-39
Bengaluru	13-18	19-24	24-28	33-37
Chennai	14-21	19-27	28-32	35-45
Hyderabad	15-20	22-28	31-34	35-43
Kolkata	14-20	19-27	25-32	35-40

Source: *Deccan Chronicle*, December, 3, 2009.

Thus residents of Chennai, Hyderabad and Kolkata have a greater proclivity to invest in housing as the family expenses generally are under control on account of relatively lower costs of living compared to Mumbai and Bengaluru. Affordability of housing has to be viewed in the overall ambit of the family budget as it is related to a trade off between expenses on housing and transportation. The location of one's house determines the cost incurred on transportation for various purposes like work, retail stores, recreation, social trips etc, in other words it determines one's action space. Self-sufficient localities are those which have access to roads, means of transportation, retail stores, and services of diverse types like schools, eating places, etc. and are thus efficient for residents to meet their everyday travel requirements in terms of time, money, and greenhouse gas emissions (http://htaindex.cnt.org/). Thus while housing and transportation put together account for almost 45-50 per cent of the household budget, the "Locational Efficiency" of an area depends on having self sufficient, compact and walkable lanes and localities, where access by proximity, not only makes them energy efficient, but by extension, also helps in encountering climatic change.

Table 2.4: Housing Requirement by 2011

City	*Housing Requirement (units) by 2011*	*Area Requirement (mm sq. ft) by 2011*	*Market Size (Rs. Bn)*
NCR	5,47,434	438	876
Mumbai	4,04,673	324	647
Bengaluru	3,27,694	262	524
Kolkata	2,65,242	212	424
Hyderabad	2,25,555	180	361
Chennai	1,57,471	126	252
Pune	1,34,264	107	215
Total	**2,062,333**	**1,650**	**3,300**

Source: Modified from: *Deccan Chronicle*, December 3, 2009.

Affordable housing can also be viewed from the perspective of agencies involved in the city's housing delivery system which need to focus not only on the amount of "assisted housing" produced and preserved, but the quality of the living environment that is created. The measure of quality should include high-grade construction materials, provision of open space, recreational amenities, safe access to public transportation, neighborhood schools, neighborhood retail options, and respect for neighborhood history and context (Comprehensive Housing Strategy Task Force, Washington, D.C. 2005)

Affordable housing is now attracting large-scale investments from developers. Real estate majors are undertaking low-budget housing projects, using modern technologies. Janapriya Engineers Syndicate is adopting the work and shuttering system of Germany, which will enable construction of concrete walls in place of traditional brickwork. It invested about Rs. 25 crore to adopt the technology in upcoming mega residential projects in Hyderabad and Secunderabad. It has been building houses for MIG for the last 3 decades. The innovative technologies help the builders not just to cut down costs but also to speed up work and finish their projects on time. Hundreds of 2BHK, 3BHK flats with prices ranging at Rs. 15 to Rs. 25 lakh are currently under construction in the city.

Switching to the latest machinery in construction will do wonders for the skyline of the city. Experts say all the ambitious projects in Hyderabad will be completed as per schedule only if the companies adopt advanced technology. JNTU experts say "we have been advising companies to acquire latest equipment which will give return on investments in a very short period". Some of them have started acquiring technology since they are planning to build up to 33 floors in Hyderabad. (K.Srinivas Rao, *Deccan Chronicle*, February 15, 2008)

Currently huge residential project on 12 acres in Kowkur near Alwal with 950 flats under the brand 'Arcadia' using the latest German technology are under construction. 540 of them are sold out and the entire project was expected to be finished by the end of 2009. The flats range from 925 to 1450 square feet. This project is called affordable housing since flat owners will be provided a premium clubhouse, with restaurants, gymnasium, swimmimg pool, children's park, elevators and security system.

Other realty firms like Ansals and Omaxe are also planning low-budget housing projects in smaller towns and cities. Red Fort Capital plans to invest Rs. 430 crore in the next 2 years in affordable housing projects on the outskirts of Hyderabad besides Bangalore. They will provide homes in the range of Rs. 8-20 lakh by using technology that reduces cost of construction by 15 per cent says director of RFC. The construction firms are expecting 20-25 per cent returns on affordable housing projects, which is the case in high-end investments too. (L.V.Reddy, *Deccan Chronicle*, July 25, 2008)

Six new massive residential projects were launched in the city by realty majors such as Prajay Engineers Syndicate, Golden Gate, Purvankara Projects, Modi Builders and Janapriya Engineers Syndicate. These companies have lined up Rs. 3,000 crore investments spread over 3 years. Most of it is located near Tellapur, Miyapur, Gachibowli, Madinaguda, Patancheru, HCU and Nagole. Interestingly, a majority of these segments are aimed at the middle-class and upper-class segments with apartments costing Rs. 20 lakh and villas in the range of Rs. 35 lakh. Despite the slowdown in the housing sector these are witnessing considerable demand. Realtors attribute the rise in demand in these segments to the RBI's policy to encourage banks to lend loans under Rs. 30 lakh under priority sector lending norms. They say it's the Rs. 50 lakh-plus segment that has the jitters, but the Rs. 15-20 lakh range is still selling fine. Moreover, construction costs too came down in the raw material prices. PES has launched 'Water Front' project in Turkapally spread over 72 acres developing 585 independent 'affordable villas' ranging from 1490 sq.ft. to 4500 sq.ft. with a price of Rs. 33.5 lakh. Golden Gate, launched its Commune in Hyderabad. It will build 3,500 world-class living spaces at price starting from Rs. 19.9 lakh offering 2BHK, 3BHK spread over 960-1490 sq.ft. Golden Gates Property Ltd MD says "Hyderabad has always been over the top when it came to real estate pricing, always dearer by 20-25 per cent than the prevailing rates across the country. It is hightime the realty sector steps forward to provide quality yet affordable housing solution for the common people. (L.V.Reddy, *Deccan Chronicle*, November 21, 2008)

City builders expect the coming year to inject fresh verve in the realty sector, which has been going through hard times in the last six months. People friendly measures being contemplated by the Centre in the run-up to the polls would be positive for the realty sector. "The package, which is expected from the government, is set to be a boon for the realty sector, which is facing several challenges" according to the A.P. Builders Forum. Realty majors are expecting the government to reschedule loans, cut down home loan interest rates further and bring down petroleum prices.

The builders are now concentrating on affordable housing to cater to middle-income groups. Earlier the realtors used to construct big flats ranging from 1500 to 2000 sq.ft. as IT professionals preferred spacious homes. But with the slowdown in IT and aviation sectors, they have now started constructing smaller flats. (K.Srinivasa Rao, *Deccan Chronicle*, December 5, 2008)

After reigning high for a couple of years, property prices have fallen considerably in the last 6 months bringing cheers to those planning to buy a house or plot. Realty experts say that this is the right time to buy flats and houses since the prices are 'lucrative'. To attract middle-income customers, real estate companies are offering discount schemes. Firms that developed layouts in city outskirts have reduced property prices to give tough competition to rivals. Fall of steel prices has also helped realty firms to rationalise property prices. Steel prices coming down to 32,000 per tonne has brought down the cost of construction by around Rs. 70 per sq.ft. bringing cheers to buyers and realtors. There is hope, construction cost would get reduced again with inflation coming down in a couple of months. Almost all companies have reduced prices to around Rs. 200 per sq.ft. for flats and plot rates have also been stabilised says head of Karvy Realty India Ltd. APBF (builders forum) which has studied the latest market trends felt that Hyderabad would witness a fresh boom very shortly. "It is better to book flats now; otherwise property rates may go up again once the demand increases" says President of the forum. Builders too urge the government to reduce taxes and the home loan interest rates from 12 to 8 per cent per annum to help customers. At present they are paying around Rs. 600 per sq.ft. as taxes and fee. However, financial experts say the reduction in home loan interest rates can only be undertaken after the global economy stabilises. (K. Srinivasa Rao, *Deccan Chronicle*, October 31, 2008)

The period between Diwali and the New Year is the one that witnesses a spurt in the real estate market, with several schemes being offered by the developers. While some consider it as auspicious, others think that they have an abundance of options to choose from. In 2009 too as many as 77 per cent potential buyers had soaring expectations with regard to purchase of property in the festive period. They look forward to lucrative offers. Their enthusiasm is reciprocated by that of the developers and sellers. Among the perks that are most appealing to potential buyers are cash discounts. The sellers also felt the requirement of 'affordable housing' of utmost importance and are seeking to provide in this segment. (Verma, A., 2009)

Realty firms are implementing innovative methods to attract prospective buyers so that they can complete the ongoing and proposed projects as per schedule. Several realty firms of Hyderabad are luring buyers with various offers. They are planning to make use of the down payments of the buyers to overcome the cash crunch.

Manjeera Group is planning to emulate the idea which assures the buyers that the money would be returned with interest if the market value of the property comes down in the future. Aditya Homes has announced a discount of Rs. 300 per sq.ft. in its Sunshine project at Kondapur. However, Indu Projects had sold off a majority of the flats even before the recession hence there is no scope for revision of property prices. According to Lanco hills the company's priority is to deliver the properties on schedule so completing them on war footing. (K.Srinivasa Rao, *Deccan Chronicle*, December 26, 2008)

Realty firms started off 2008 with much swagger but it did not last long. Tuning into the boom several firms such as Lanco and Aparna built 1200-1400 flats in massive apartment projects. However, recession came rolling in and they could sell only 400 flats. The situation became worse during August-September. Despite some construction firms building towering structures anticipating a boom towards the end of the year, it did not happen. Caught in the whirlpool of a slowdown, developers have now started chanting the affordable housing mantra, which is likely to be the trend in the coming year. Collapse of major Global Financial Institutions (GFI) created a major cash crunch in the market. Ironically this happened just after the city realty sector attracted large-scale FDI. Six overseas firms and, 3-4 national firms entered Hyderabad city's realty sector in 2008.

The biggest disappointments in the realty sector this year were Srisailam and Shamshabad. Land transactions worth an estimated Rs. 20,000 crore took place but much of it got stuck midway and thus created a huge liquidity crisis in the local market. Government hype on Fab City and Rajiv Technology Park bought lands near the Srisailam Highway but the projects failed to take off despite the state government laying foundation stones and signing MoUs. DLF in Kokapet too didn't take off due to collapse of GFI. Meanwhile major villa projects are being constructed in Medchal/Kompally areas by Aparna, Aditya, Ashoka, Manbhum and Ambience. New residential hubs have also taken shape in Tellapur, APPA, Bachupally, Nizampet, Maheshwaram and Shamirpet.

Lots of new local and national developers launched projects in Kukatpally, Tellapur, APPA, and Gachibowli areas. However, most developers did not look really into the affordability factor and are now struggling to sell big apartments. Local developers launched two or more projects this year and they did fairly well in early part of the year and they too faced difficulties later. International developers launched quite a few projects which include Westbridge and Alliance Joint venture in Shamirpet, Prajay with Lehman in Maheshwaram,

PBEL in APPA, TSI in Tellapur and Aparna with Morgan Stanley in Tellapur.

Liquidity was available easily in the boom months of the year but things started becoming difficult with collapse of financial institutions. The gloom must be contrasted with wild optimism in the beginning of the year when developers were vying to build the tallest and largest towers in Hyderabad. Many infrastructure companies, which showed keen interest in real estate during 2006-2007, did not venture into major projects in 2008 except Indu projects. Meanwhile land and building regularisation generated huge income for government; also positive signals from government on building regulations in the form of green channel and deferred impact fee and the actual impact of these can only be gauged in 2009. Government departments such as HUDA, Housing Board, and APSRTC had started the year 2009 with land sales, which evoked positive response but later hardly got any bids. However, the builders are optimistic about the year in the wake of cutting down of interest rates and announcement of incentives by the government (to reduce Stamp Duty and Registration Charges) to boost the housing sector. Construction firms expect the interest rates to slide down further giving a fillip to the realty sector. (L.V.Reddy, *Deccan Chronicle*, December 26, 2008)

The sate government will announce a stimulus package for the real sector, also modify the cause of mortgaging 25 per cent property to government till completion of project. The government has now decided to do away with the registration of the mortgage deed. Now only details of the property will be entered into the prohibitory register of the stamps and registration department .The HMDA and GHMC levy infrastructure impact fee (IIF) ranging from Rs. 50 to Rs. 300 per sq. yd. for buildings with more than 5 floors. The government is likely to give relief to the realtors hit by recession with IIF and has also extended the time limit for paying the same from 3 to 5 years. (N.Vamsi Srinivas, *Deccan Chronicle*, April 10, 2010)

Indian Banks Association plans to cut interest rates on home loans. This is expected to stimulate construction in the city. Home loans upto Rs. 5 lakh would be given at 8.5 per cent interest while those between Rs. 5 to Rs 20 lakh would be offered at 9.25 per cent interest. Further banks have decided not to charge any processing fee and pre-payment charges for Rs. 5 lakh loans. They will be providing free insurance cover to the properties. Though public sector banks are all set to reduce the interest rates, private banks like ICICI, HDFC reportedly not keen to bring down the interest rates to 9 per cent from the existing 11-12 per cent range. The APBF and GHBF welcomed the move of IBA and requested it also to lower interest rates for loans < Rs 20 lakh. APBF President says "this decision will help only those buying properties in outskirts where flats are less costly". (*Deccan Chronicle*, December16, 2008)

Banks, both private and public, have brought some relief to the real estate sector by cutting interest rates on home loans. The real estate sector has been facing a slump in recent times due to the high interest rates. HDFC, the largest mortgage lender, has taken the lead by cutting its Retail Prime Lending Rate by 25 basis points to 13.75 per cent. SBI, country's largest lender slashed prime lending rate by 0.25 to 12.50 per cent. Canara Bank has also reduced by 25 basis points. Corporation bank has lowered interest rates on home loans by 50 basis points. Similarly, Allahabad Bank cut down by 50-100 basis points. PNB Housing Finance too reduced by 0.5 per cent and SBH by 25 basis points. The objective behind the cut in rates is to remain competitive in the market and not to drive volume growth. However, the country's second largest bank ICICI indicated that it would review interest rates only in 2008-09. (L.V.Reddy, *Deccan Chronicle*, February 15, 2008)

Indian Banks Association plans to reduce their interest rates by around 100 basis points has cheered the realty sector, which has been reeling under the cash crunch for the last 6 months. The nationalised banks such as SBI, Bank of Baroda and UBI agreed to reduce the lending rates, which will in turn bring down the home loan interest rates to an affordable 10 per cent per annum. This will benefit both the new buyers as well as those who have already taken loans on floating interest rate.

The beleaguered real estate sector has not seen any sign of revival despite the infusion of liquidity to the tune of Rs. 2,70,000 crore in the banking system by the RBI and cut in interest rates. Private equity investments too have dried up from the last 2 months. Industry experts say that home seekers are not in a buying mood and corporates have preferred to wait and watch. The total number of deals has reduced to 20 per cent and the valuations decreased by 66 per cent. (Yogesh Mehendale, *The Hindu*, Nov 11, 2008)

While the national housing shortfall in urban areas of India is 17 million units, it is expected to soar up to 80 million units by 2012 according to the National Housing Board. More than 90 per cent of this demand is from the low income group. The proliferation of slums is a manifestation of the need for low cost housing. While the mass creation of low cost housing is the right gesture in this context, the initiative for this which can only come from the government is lacking in steam as 'it lacks the quick feel good factor' which accompanies other sops that are instant vote fetchers. (Contractor, H., 2009)

According to Cushman and Wakefield survey, real estate demand in India in all sectors would be around 1098 million sq.ft. by 2012. The residential segment will continue to drive demand in the country and will account for 63 per cent of total space in the next 4 years. While the demand for commercial office space is expected to be 243 million sq.ft., the retail and hospitality segments are expected to seek 95 million sq.ft. and 73 million sq.ft. respectively. With rupee price stabilising and almost bottoming out in some areas, and interest rates coming down, this will be the right time to buy property. (K.Srinivasa Rao, *Deccan Chronicle*, Nov 7, 2008)

Hyderabad retained its position on the preferred list of retailers with focus remaining around the commercial business districts of Begumpet, Banjara Hills Road No. 1 and 10, and stretches closer to Punjagutta circle. According to the annual report on global retail rents by Cushman and Wakefield India is placed at 24th in the world's top shopping centres. The recently released report put the monthly rental per square feet in the stretch between Somajiguda circle to Punjagutta circle/Banjara hills at Rs.110 in 2nd quarter of 2006. It retains its plum post. The annual growth was put at 69 per cent. The report also says India as the year's biggest riser in the world's most expensive shopping locations in terms of retail rents. Despite the rapid growth in mall development high-street locations will continue to be viewed favourably by retailers.

There is, however, no regulatory body to safeguard the interests of either the consumers or the agents. The utter lack of transparency makes real estate a safe haven for transactions that involve black money, which inturn result in abnormal price rises. When faced with a crisis, sellers don't want to sell and buyers don't want to buy. In such a situation the worst hit are the real estate agents. There is an urgent need to put an Independent Regulator (IR) in place to oversee the growth and developments in the realty sector and bring in greater accountability. Independent Regulator (IR) with clearly set guidelines and directives to follow will ensure fair competition and protect the interest of builders, investors and above all—consumers. (*Deccan Chronicle*, Samir, Chopra, October 21, 2009)

A Realty Index on the lines of Sensex and Nifty to track the value of a plot is planned. Despite the real estate boom of the past years, there has been no solid data on price of property in India. The state government imposes hefty stamp duties on real estate transactions, but they too have little data to indicate the change in prices. The National Housing Bank (NHB), the Housing Finance Regulator is now planning to create a real estate index for the general public. The Centre has opened up the real estate sector to FDI and billions of dollars have poured in from the US, Europe, the Middle east, South east Asia and the Far east. Investors also had been clamouring for credible data on the sector.

Though NHB had earlier launched an index for the housing segment, called NHB Residex, the data was only available to big firms tracking the residential areas prices in 5 major cities by taking into account location, construction quality, amenities and infrastructure. NHB now plans indices for 10 cities giving price appreciation figures for major cities. Finally, it would cover 63 cities and an all India index would be formulated. Plans are afoot to set up separate indices for rentals, land prices and affordability. Also plans to involve all real estate stakeholders including the government, builders, buyers and housing finance industry in formulating the index are afoot. (L.V.Reddy, *Deccan Chronicle*, May 23, 2008)

Major real estate companies are all set to build-up more pressure on the government for reduction of tax burden on the construction industry, which is reeling under economic slowdown. The Confederation of Real Estate Developers Association of India (CREDAI) with the support of state bodies such as AP Builders Forum has decided to ask the government to reduce tax burden on the real estate sector in the larger interest of the industry. It is estimated that around Rs. 700 per sqft is being collected in the form of taxes.

Taxes being imposed on realty sector:

- Value added tax
- Service tax

- Tax deducted at source
- Stamp duty on sale
- Stamp duty on land
- Income tax on profit of development, materials, services
- Municipal premiums and development charges
- Excise duty on materials
- Octroi on construction industry

According to the AP Builders Forum "the government should also take steps to bring down the home loan interest rates to 7 per cent level and also registration charges further so that more buyers come forward to take loans. It will boost the industry and stimulate economic activitiy". Some realtors felt that it was the right time to develop on Special Residential Zones (SRZ) on the lines of SEZs which would ensure affordable housing to all the sections. According to Laura Green Properties Pvt Ltd "the government should set up a Real Estate Board, which will frame guidelines and understand the needs of the construction industry". (K.Srinivasa Rao, *Deccan Chronicle*, November 21, 2008)

Low-cost housing is once again in fashion due to the escalating prices of land, cement, steel. At the prevailing rates, it is impossible for middle income families to buy land and build houses. The real estate boom and availability of easy finance has left the middle-income and economically weaker sections untouched. Builders have come up with the novel idea of setting up special residential zones on the lines of SEZ to offer low cost housing. The government will acquire land for the SRZ and provide road connectivity; builders will be responsible for construction. SRZs could be set up in areas ranging from 500 to 1500 acres and a housing unit would be constructed in a minimum of 1000 square feet area. Ideally they should be set up in the city suburbs to cut down the cost of land acquisition.

Planning Experts and Real Estate majors say state Government should encourage Special Residential Zones (SRZs) on the periphery of the city, like Special Economic Zones (SEZs). Development of Amenities and Facilities like health and educational services on the periphery of the city will help to decongest the city. The Confederation of Real Estate Developers Associations of India (CREDAI) suggested creation of SRZs as they would bring real estate within the reach of the common man. SRZs may be given Tax holidays like SEZs so that affordable housing in the private sector is made available to people. (*Deccan Chronicle*, September, 26, 2009)

"A house built in an SRZ away from the city may cost just Rs. 8 lakh compared to the cost of around Rs. 25 lakh for an average house says president of Alliance Group". He adds the low land price, tax exemption of upto 27 per cent and faster clearance through single window clearance (as SEZ) system help in cutting costs. The government is amenable to this idea but wants to impose strict norms to ensure that houses built in SRZs reach the eligible groups and are not filched away by others. (L.V.Reddy, *Deccan Chronicle*, May 16, 2008)

Choice of location for housing usually depends on connectivity to work place and infrastructure. On the other hand, the choice of a particular house or housing project depends on certain vital factors like availability of water supply, power, safety and security and certain discretionary or elective factors like the interior fixtures, availability of swimming pool, gymnasium etc. beside others.

Government involvement in the housing sector under the aegis of Basic Services to the Urban Poor (BSUP) of the Jawaharlal Nehru National Urban Renewal Mission (JNNURM) has given a ray of hope to the underprivileged. It entails construction of 20,019 houses along with infrastructure in the areas covered by Municipal Corporation of Hyderabad (MCH). The unit cost of each dwelling unit will be Rs.80,000, out of which Rs.40,000 will be the subsidy from Government of India, Rs.8,000 (10%) will be the beneficiary contribution and Rs.32,000 (40%) will be the bank loan to be arranged for the beneficiaries by the District Collector. The A.P. State Housing Corporation Limited (APSHCL) shall be the implementing agency for the BSUP of JNNURM in the areas covered by MCH. 49,000 VAMBAY houses are allotted to Hyderabad and Ranga Reddy districts under the Jawaharlal Nehru National Urban Renewal Mission (JNNURM). Each unit costs Rs. 1 lakh with Central and State Governments picking up three-fourth cost as subsidy (*The Hindu*, February 8, 2008).

Housing scheme for the poor under the Jawaharlal Nehru National Urban Renewal Mission (JNNURM) is in an indeterminate state. The GHMC has failed to construct 27,379 flats for the economically weaker sections though 3 years have passed. The GHMC was not able to provide land for the contractors. Also the unit cost of the flat which was fixed at Rs. 1 lakh in 2006 has become un-remunerative to the GHMC (*Deccan Chronicle*, August 5, 2009)

The APHB suffered a major jolt as big time realtors, buyers shied away from purchasing prime land it put up for sale in Hyderabad. Plots in prime plots in Hyderabad, however, had no takers besides a major block of land at Raidurg in Ranga Reddy district.

- A 2185 sq.yd. plot in Malkajgiri village area priced at an attractive price of Rs. 20000 per square yard, did not attract any bids. Surprise to APHB as the land is situated in the posh Mahendra Hills area where current market value is said to be around Rs. 40000 per sq.yd.
- Even plots in Gudimalkapur (1680 sq.yd.), Alwal (3993 sq.yd.) and Thokatta (1200 sq.yd.) drew a blank, according to APHB official.
- 2517 sq.yd. plot in the obscure Dommara Pochampally village found only one bidder quote of Rs. 50 per sq.yd. over the upset price of Rs. 3000.

Of the 5 plots on offer in Hyderabad, only this plot could be sold with 76.76 lakh by an individual buyer. Shocking to officials was the cold response to the Bay Ridge block of 10.33 acres at Raidurg in Ranga Reddy district, close to Outer Ring Road. APHB expected more than Rs. 200 crore but received no bids for this land, which is said to be ideal for housing ventures or star hotels. It wants to conduct the auction afresh soon. (*Deccan Chronicle*, April 17, 2008)

The year 2005 saw the real estate boom, fuelled by information technology and sustained by development of infrastructure; make rapid strides to achieve a growth rate that was inconceivable so far. Lenient lending policies, with a lending rate of 7.5 per cent as against 17 per cent in 1995-96 have further spurred real estate development and led to its consolidation, which heretofore had been unorganized and splintered (Chandrasekhar, V., 2005). Over the last few years, property prices in most Indian cities appreciated by over 250 per cent while the economy grew at 8 per cent annually. A commensurate development in the infrastructure sector would aid the development in the real estate sector more so as many expected 2010 to be the year of affordable housing. However, the reality industry is divided over a possible correction in the skyrocketing prices of residential properties in major Indian metros. (http://in.biz.yahoo.com/100628/50/bavv1j.html).

The real estate sector in India is on an upturn. In last 24 months, there has been an unprecedented growth where overall market has witnessed 35 to 40 per cent jump in capital values. It is the result of a number of positive macro and micro factors. The macro factors are driven by the spectacular economic growth resulting in growing incomes as well as low inflation and interest rates. The micro factors include growing aspiration levels, availability of better quality real estate and a far wider range of choice for the same. Research estimates have it that the real estate market is expected to grow from the current \$14 billion to a \$102 billion in the next 10 years. (*Times of India*, December 16, 2006)

Amongst the IT cities—Bengaluru, Hyderabad, Pune—the sentiment remains low with prices seeing a dip. Hyderabad has seen a correction amounting to 15 per cent while Mumbai and Kolkata remain stable with fluctuation less than 10 per cent. Chennai remains the only market bullish on realty with prices appreciating in all localities in the last quarter.

Hyderabad—the city has seen a decline in prices in the localities of Banjara Hills, Nizampet and Kukatpally in the third quarter of the year 2008 (July-September). In Banjara Hills there has been a 10 per cent correction in prices with the figure now standing at Rs. 7800 per square feet. (*Deccan Chronicle*, December19, 2008)

On a different note though related to the different manifestation of affordability, quality space on rent for commercial purposes not being an easy commodity any more has seen entrepreneurs and traders, who would otherwise have gone for 1000 square feet sprawling and swanky office/shop spaces, now proclaiming that small is beautiful as it's the only affordable way out. Space in areas like Raj Bhavan Road, Somajiguda, Banjara Hills Road No. 1 which used to the most preferred areas for setting up offices and opening shops is slowly becoming as good as forgotten, from rates of Rs. 20 to Rs. 25 per square feet for unfurnished spaces rentals, here guesstimates are now Rs. 35 to Rs. 80. For furnished space it is Rs. 100 per square feet.

A pioneer of the 'Commercial Mall cum, Multiplex' concept in the twin cities is now poised to become a 'Mega Realtor' with the construction of its ambitious project of a 60-storied commercial monument in the twin cities. The giant monumental tower, is most probably, the highest in the country. The tower will have commercial shops, multiplexes, convention centres, auditoriums, conference halls, offices, and exhibition halls. Intervening in between at the 6th floor is a helipad, the 7th to 10th floors are Consulate and Government offices, 11th to 39th floors are for multi-national companies and to make it feel like home, five star hotels in the 40th to 59th floors to take care of the catering aspect. On the 60th floor a luxurious rooftop restaurant with a 'Bird's eye view' of the city is likely to come up.

Ernst and Young highlight that the present asset class focus for developers continues to be residential followed by commercial and retail. Apart from the affordable housing segment, several 'neo-assets' like warehousing, healthcare, infrastructure and logistics will emerge as an integral part of a developer's future portfolio. The health care segment is the impetus for growth in the real estate sector in Tier II and Tier III cities. (NCR, Mumbai, Pune, Hyderabad, Chennai, Kolkata Bangalore.) (Rai Umraopati Ray, *Deccan Chronicle*, September 19, 2008) Diversification thus seems to define the shape of things to come.

The Associated Chambers of Commerce and Industry of India (ASSOCHAM) has advocated the introduction of Real Estate Investment Trusts (REITs), to bring in institutional investors and to discipline the domestic real estate market which may also help develop the Commercial Mortgage Backed Securities (CMBS) market and create a source of cheaper debt for commercial real estate. The presence of a large number of REITs could enhance liquidity for commercial real estate in the secondary market. Real estate investment trusts (REITs) are the need of the hour as they will bring more transparency into the system. REITs typically can own a variety of real estate properties, often even across geographies. They thus offer a pool of well-diversified CMBS properties resulting in a better spread of risks as compared to regional developers who offer mortgages on a few similar properties often located in the same market space. REITs play an important role in the development of CMBS. (*Deccan Chronicle*, Nov 21, 2008)

Many corporate occupiers, especially in the IT/ITES sectors, have either postponed or curtailed their expansion plans. The fund availability to developers has also been constrained due to RBI's inflation control measures. A review of the third quarter office market space in the country indicated a slack in demand. This trend started to dampen office space values across key cities, albeit in varying degrees, depending on the specific micro market and office type. In Hyderabad, the rentals have stabilised across the various micro markets and look to remain that way for a while, what with the current demand scenario and with developers postponing and further phasing out supply. Even though the real estate market scenario at present is quite subdued, there is still a cautious optimism about the future. The Indian real estate market is expected to remain an attractive, long-term proposition and once the current churn is over, the sector should embark on a high growth trajectory impelled with sound fundamentals, increased corporatisation and integration with the global economy. (*Anshuman Magazine*, *Deccan Chronicle*, December 5, 2008)

Due to the realty boom in the city and surrounding areas owners of old flats have been making good profits by selling them Realty Plus by Ernst and Young highlight that the present asset class focus for developers continues to be residential followed by commercial and retail. Apart from the affordable housing segment, several 'neo-assets' like warehousing, healthcare, infrastructure and logistics will emerge as an integral part of a developer's future portfolio. The health care segment is the impetus for growth in the real estate sector in Tier II and Tier III cities. (NCR, Mumbai, Pune, Hyderabad, Chennai, Kolkata Bangalore.) (Rai Umraopati Ray, *Deccan Chronicle*, September 19, 2008)

Due to the realty boom in the city and surrounding areas owners of old flats have been making good profits by selling them off at twice or even thrice the original price. Flats which were purchased a few years ago at around Rs. 1000 per square feet in prime localities are being sold for rates of up to Rs. 3000 per square feet now. There are increasing demands for old flats in the city since new flats have become unaffordable for middle-income people. Old flats are now being sold at rates ranging from Rs. 18 lakh to Rs. 25 lakh depending on their size and location. There is huge demand for such flats in Kukatpally, Chandanagar, AS Rao Nagar, Marredpally, Dilshukhnagar and Chaitanyapuri. Earlier banks were reluctant to provide loans to purchase old flats built 10 years ago due to depreciation of value. Now banks have relaxed rules and are providing loans even for flats built two decades ago. Earlier banks used to give 20 per cent of the cost as loan but now it is 50 per cent. The hesitation of major builders to take up new projects because of the sharp rise in prices of cement and steel have also heightened the demand for old flats. (K.Srinivasa Rao, *Deccan Chronicle*, March 21, 2008)

On a different note again, land sharks have encroached upon many small and medium graveyards in and around the city and in areas where several new colonies have come up in recent years. Of the 500-odd graveyards in the city and outskirts, 200 have been encroached upon by land sharks. The city has big graveyards only at Sanjeeva Reddy Nagar, Punjagutta, Chandrayangutta, Saidabad, Mehdipatnam, Moosrambagh and Bowenpalli. Earlier, even land grabbers used to give a wide berth to graveyards since people feared to live there. But nowadays, wily realtors make use of the graveyard development committees set up by government to encroach upon the lands.

The Katikaparula Byagari Sangham (Graveyard Keepers Association) has now asked the govt to abolish these committees to protect at least the existing graveyards. The HUDA also removed several graveyards for the construction of ORR but did not take the initiative to build alternatives in their place. Officials say though they have identified lands in several places for burial grounds but there are serious objections from locals. (*The Hindu*, November 11, 2008)

Till 2005 Chandanagar was hardly evoked either among real estate brokers or prospective investors, when the property boom came calling Chandanagar on the Mumbai highway just got swamped in it. Rates kept climbing and locals recall they fluctuated between morning and evening. A square yard which a couple of years ago was offered for Rs. 2000 or so, zoomed high to stand between Rs. 15000 to 20000 per square yard. As it is close to Madhapur and takes a 10-15 minutes drive to reach IT destinations, clean and less-crowd, big super markets, leading electronic goods sellers shops, most banks with ATM has made things easier. The rentals too have shot-up based on space; decent accommodation can be obtained for a rental of Rs. 2000 to 5000. However, the sad part: a *'space bar'* is on there. Just that not much space is available now.

The relatively quieter Chandanagar has emerged as a major residential hub of business executives, IT professionals and employees of various organizations. It has connectivity to Hitec-city, Gachhibowli, HCU, Patancheru, IDA Bollaram and Zaheerabad. The MMTS railway station has become an added advantage. With demand for flats and individual houses going up, construction activity has picked up in the area. Though the construction material cost is skyrocketing, cost per square feet is still between Rs. 2400 to Rs. 2800 here. Some builders feel that high rents in the area have also interested property buyers. The monthly rent for a 2BHK flat is between Rs. 8000 to Rs. 12000 and the demand is growing with the establishment of several companies in nearby localities. (K.Srinivasa Rao, *Deccan Chronicle*, July 25, 2008)

The first-ever experiment of fusing real estate with geriatric health care sector, one of the city-based Real Estate agents is coming up with a project that boasts of having some novel value addition features. Samvidha Senior Citizen's Treat, the 160 apartment complexes (houses) with world class facilities will tag on to the main project—Surabhi Pride Homes that are to come up at Kowkur village shortly. It will have 285 luxury houses on a plotted area of 300 square yards; the complexes for the senior citizens will have 160 suites each with a size of 600 sq.ft. Each suite in the senior citizens enclave will have a touch of luxury. Elderly citizens will get all facilities plus 24 × 7 personal care. (K. Srinivas Reddy, *The Hindu*, April 15, 2006)

The government has designed Reverse Mortgage Loan (RML) for senior citizens who are not eligible for any form of mortgage loan and is over 60 years and owning residential property. For those who want to renovate a flat, meet medical expenses or repay a loan, the bank makes periodic lump sum payments to the borrower, unlike conventional mortgage loans, hence the name Reverse Mortgage. The maximum period of the loan is for 20 years. The borrower does not have to pay instalments or interest as long as one is alive and in occupation of the property. One can apply at any scheduled bank or Housing Finance Company registered with the National Housing Board. (*Indrani Rajadurai*, July 29, 2008)

The Reverse Mortgage Scheme (RMS) for senior citizens who own property. They will be paid monthly instalments and they need not even vacate the property even after the tenure expires. Under the RMS, DHFL (Dewan Housing Finance Corporation) provides a fixed sum to the property owner based on the market value for a fixed tenure. In short, it is like the customer selling his house in instalments, even when continuing to live there. The rate of interest that DHFL has pegged on its reverse mortgage offer, christened 'Saksham' is 12 per cent. The scheme gives liberty to the customer and his/her spouse for maintaining and living in the property as long as they are alive, without the fear of having to vacate the property even after the tenure of the reverse mortgage expires. As per Saksham rates a property worth Rs. 20 lakh, for instance, will earn a customer Rs. 4,100 per month for 10 years. After adding up interest, the amount payable to DHFL would be Rs. 10 lakh at the end of the tenure. The bank will take possession of the property only after both the borrower and owner have expired. (D.M.Mathew, *The Hindu*, November 4, 2006)

In fact, Himayathnagar, Punjagutta-Nagarjuna circle stretch rates have shot above Rs. 100 to 120 per square feet. The growing demand for Hyderabad's rented commercial space has seen businesses which require lavish spaces moving beyond Raj Bhavan Road and Banjara Hills to Kukatpally and Miyapur. Naturally this had a cascading effect on the rental values there as well. (D.M.Mathew, *The Hindu*, October 21, 2006)

Miyapur is blinking on the realty radar as bright as any another premium residential and commercial spot in the city. A few km away from Kondapur and Madhapur, the area was waiting on the wings as property boom at these places escalated beyond the reach of many. With options running out at Kondapur and Madhapur, the choice for property developers was Gachibowli and Miyapur. With Gachibowli already high on price map, the focus shifted to Miyapur and in 2 years the landscape changed. There were few apartment complexes with the development of its other boundaries at Chandanagar, Nizampet, KPHB but now tall structures and duplex housing projects dot the landscape. Property prices are just shooting upwards. Double bedroom flats which were offered in the range of Rs. 6 to 8 lakhs, have become double expensive while 3 bedroom flats are sold from Rs. 16 lakhs onwards. Some duplex houses even touch a price tag of Rs. 50 lakh. The MMTS station of Hafeezpet is few kilometres away and when the proposed MRTS takes shape, another round of revision is expected to nudge the property prices further up. (T. Lalith Singh, *The Hindu*, November 4, 2006)

Apartments with world class facilities at Ameenapur near Miyapur are planned. The project spread over 35 acres of land with a total of 5 million square feet of multi-storeyed apartments will be completed in different phases. Units ranging from 1500 to 1800 sft will be offered at prices above Rs. 50 lakhs. They are targeting higher middle class and above segment. With an expected investment of Rs. 800 crores, they see a boost in employment opportunities apart from addressing upscale housing requirements with an international flair.

The Nizampet-Bachupally stretch has become a major residential hub, catering to both rich and middle class sections. The area is strategically located between the National Highway 9 and Inner Ring Road of Hyderabad. Major realtors including Maytas Properties (constructing world class integrated township in 376 acres at Bachupally offering a range of apartments, villas, bungalows, retail, hospital, entertainment, infrastructure and SEZ all incorporating the best features), Indu Projects (planning an integrated township in 100 acres at Nizampet-Bachupally), Landmark Builders (is building 90 flats under its Pristine Project), Sri Surya Builders and Developers (fixed a sq.ft. rate of Rs. 2500 which has taken up the Sri Suryavijya Icon Project in Nizampet) and Jagadamba properties (constructing 300 flats in the Divine Dwellings project) have taken up residential projects in the stretch. Flats and individual houses are being sold at rates ranging Rs. 25 to Rs. 75 lakh, based on the quality of construction, built-up area and other facilities. Nizampet will become more attractive once the ORR and metro rail projects are completed. (K.Srinivasa Rao, *Deccan Chronicle*, August 1, 2008)

With the state government clearing the ORR Growth Corridor Project recently, building activity in the city suburbs is expected to get a fillip. It will attract many urban dwellers as it is free from traffic and pollution afflictions. Builders are irked by the several conditions tagged on; including 5 per cent of total developed area to be gifted to the state government. The new norms apply to all projects in areas that fall within 1km on either side of the outer edge of ORR.

To ensure this, the government has issued regulations that the minimum plot size of apartment complexes and other non-residential buildings should be 1000 sq.m. In all 10 per cent of total area should be set aside for parks, apart from 5 per cent for EWS, housing and another 5 per cent to government. They also should set aside 2.5 per cent for social infrastructure such as schools, hospitals, specific sites for bus, auto stands and garbage collection points. Even in AP the government has insisted for allotment of 5 per cent space for EWS, LIG, MIG groups. All the properties abutting the ORR would mandatorily have a buffer of 15 mts from the outer edge.

In the special development zone, existing industries will not be allowed to expand also they would be continued only under safe conditions, certified by pollution control board and neither will permission be given for new industries. (L.V.Reddy, *Deccan Chronicle*, August 15, 2008)

The Highlights of the Growth Corridor will be:

- Minimum layout area: 10 acres.
- Minimum plot area: 1000 sq yards.
- Group commercial complexes: 4000 sq yards.
- Hyper markets: 12000 sq yards.
- Marriage Halls: 8000 sq yards.

- Theatres/Multiplexes: 8000 sq yards.
- Play Schools: 1200 sq yards.
- Schools: 4000 sq yards.
- Coaching centres/hostels: 6000 sq yards.
- Nursing Homes: 2000 sq yards.
- Hospitals: 4000 sq yards.

The commercial rental segment has at least 8 categories—malls, showrooms, offices, small shops, franchisees, dealerships, and so on. Automobile companies and their franchisees who looked for big spaces earlier are now looking only to expand beyond the city as most of them are well ensconced in the city. The demand for businesses like furniture shops, boutiques, branded garment outlets small eateries has skyrocketed.

The enormous increase in the demand for residential space has given a boost to the relatively marginal areas of residential location in most cities and Hyderabad is no exception. Places like Tukkuguda, Bachupally, Kandukur, and so on, started figuring prominently on the horizon of the real estate market. The list of projects to shape the future of the city is growing from International Airport at Shamshabad, Fab city in Maheshwaram, BITS campus at Jawaharnagar, NIMS University and IT spaces at Raidurg, Pocharam and Manikonda besides others. Infrastructure initiatives such as MRTS (Mass Rapid Transit System), elevated expressway along with a series of flyovers have further enhanced the visibility of Hyderabad on the reality map. Other factors that seem to have acted as catalysts in the real estate market have been enhanced institutional funding to developers, coming on the scene of world class developers, enlarged consumer demand due to simplified and less bureaucratic financial procedures and comprehensibility in the real estate market. Besides, public authorities like Housing Boards and Urban Development Authorities are making efforts to provide housing. While these initiatives provide a healthy competition to the private sector which is engaged in the housing market, they also provide a range of options to the consumers to choose from. The market seems poised to become the consumers' market from select perspectives.

Luxury villas are coming up in large numbers in the suburbs of the city. More than 25 such ventures are underway in various locations, from Shankerpalli to Shamshabad and from Medchal to Manikonda. The most-favoured spots for villas are Nizampet, Bachupalli,

Kompally, Shamshabad, Medchal, Uppal, Nagole, Maheshwaram, Dundigal, Shameerpet, Yapral, Ghatkesar, Srisailam Highway, Gachibowli, Tellapur, Kothur and Shadnagar. Despite being high price, there is huge demand for villas which are being built near major IT hubs and the Shamshabad airport.

Some of the tallest residential buildings in the country are coming up in Hyderabad. The Aliens group is constructing 28-storied residential towers at Tellapur near Gachibowli while Bharat Infratech has taken up the Iconia project, *(is conceptualised by Atkins of UK, which created the world famous hotel BURJ Al Arab in Dubai)* which will have 18 20-storied residential high rises offering duplex flats. Many such high-rises will dot the skyline of Hyderabad in the next 3 years as HUDA has carved out a skyscraper zone in the city. Flats in these huge residential towers will offer ultra modern facilities with swanky interiors and priced between Rs. 75 lakh and Rs. 2.5 crore. There will be around 2200 flats in the Aliens Space Station, spread over 20 acres and Iconia will have 1500 flats in 21 acres. Realty experts say that the city will witness unprecedented vertical growth in the coming yrs. (L.V.Reddy, *Deccan Chronicle*, September 12, 2008)

Amidst the recent rush for budget housing among realtors to offset current economic slowdown, Hyderabad-based Lanco Infratech is going full steam on its high-end luxury township Lanco Hills. Apart from flats, the company now plans to offer villas to tap customers from the elite category. The costliest apartment on 34th floor would cost Rs. 2.1 crore in Lanco Hills. The 110 acre Lanco hills were initially supposed to consist of high rise apartments-both commercial and residential. It had become an instant attraction. It also supposed to house one of the tallest residential towers in the world. (S.Umamaheshwar, *Deccan Chronicle*, Sept 26, 2008)

There are no building regulations to stop a skyscraper development, No height limits either in some zones. But hi-tech Hyderabad has very few high-rises. But with rapid urbanization, it's only a matter of time before the city will be dotted with skyscrapers.

High capacity growth with proper infrastructure in place is anytime better than allowing the city to keep on spreading. Land is limited, so for a given region to meet the demand for more space vertical growth is inevitable, skyscrapers offer that.

High capacity growth with proper infrastructure in place is anytime better than allowing the city to keep on spreading. Public utilities like water, sewerage and even transport will come under tremendous strain if there is too much geographical growth. Land is limited, so for a given region to meet the demand for more space vertical growth is inevitable, skyscrapers offer that. It's time a fast-growing city like Hyderabad had a skyscraper zone with no restriction on the height of the building. A skyscraper Zone would be a multiple-use zone with high-end offices, commercial, shopping and entertainment complexes. The government has demarcated a huge part of area close to the proposed Outer Ring Road (ORR), as a skyscraper zone. The Areas of Gopanpalli, Nallagadla, Tellapur besider Gachibowli has been declared by the Urban Development Agency of the city (HUDA) as High-rise Zone. This is done to enable construction of skyscrapers which will house the teaming tech population of Gachibowli. HUDA has indeed done careful planning and taken advance action. The pressure on scarce land available between Gachibowli and the Outer Ring Road would have been too heavy and the tech population in Gachibowli, would have been forced to live away, resulting in huge traffic bottlenecks and huge fuel consumption. This also translates as the need for the high rise residential structures close to these areas. Some of the highrise zones marked in the master plan would fall in Medchal, Kukatpally, Shambupur near Bolarum industrial estate, Kardanur near Patancheru, Hayathnagar, Pocharam near Ghatkesar, Rampalli Road, Shamirpet, Narsingi] Bandlaguda near Balapur, etc.

Source: Compiled by *The Cyberabad Times*, Sunday, April 22, 2007, sources include *the Hindu*, *The Times of India*.

Catering to the city's changing needs, real estate and infra companies are developing malls and multiplexes. The Lanco group is coming up with 16 theatres in its multiplex as part of the Lanco hills project at Manikonda, investing Rs. 650 crore with 2 million sft by the end of 2011. It will be the biggest multiplex in South-East Asia. GVK one, is being constructed (now constructed) with an investment of Rs. 1000 crore in Banjara hills, it will house fashion labels, hypermarkets, food courts, 5-screen multiplex. DSL Infrastructure and Space Developers Pvt Ltd, has begun the construction of a 4-screen multiplex in 5 acres in Uppal. Construction will be completed in 18 months and it says 'Multiplexes will rule the entertainment industry as spending power has increased'. Manjeera projects has acquired 6½ acre for the construction of a 5-screen multiplex along with a shopping mall and residential project. These firms are also giving top priority to parking as it has become a major problem in existing malls and multiplexes. (K.Srinivasa Rao, *Deccan Chronicle*, October 3, 2008)

Luxury villas at the 531 acre 'Boulder Hills Golf' and 'Country Club' complexes built by Emaar MFG Land Ltd are being sold at prices ranging from Rs. 8 to Rs. 20 crore. These are the costliest villas to be built in the city. There are about 100 villas in the Rs. 5610 crore project, all of which have been booked by prospective buyers. Emaar MFG, a joint venture between Dubai-based Emaar group and Delhi-based MFG Ltd, claims that the USP of the complex is the 192 acre 18-hole golf course built according to international standards. Other developers are building villas priced between Rs. 2 crore and Rs. 5 crore plots ranging from 180 to 320 sq.yds. The built-up area extends from 1100 to 4500 sq.ft. Interestingly the Asian Township Shankerpalli is offering low cost villas priced at Rs. 24 lakh to Rs. 38 lakh. These are 167 villas in 18 acres plots ranging from 167 to 267 sq.yds.

'People are moving towards suburbs due to congestion in cities' according to Vasudeva Realtors which is developing 150 villas in 20 acres in Tellapur cost varies from Rs. 2.5 to Rs. 4 crore. Other big projects underway are Bloomfield Ecstasy in Tellapur with 150 villas in 20 acres, Palm Meadows in Kompally with 337 villas in 59 acres. Gorlas Paradise in Medchal with 433 villas in 104 acres, Hill county in Bachupalli with 43 villas in 68 acres and Galaxy Vistas in Shamshabad with 500 villas in 100 acres. Most of these projects wil be ready by the end of 2009. Most villas offer superior design, structure and elevation and have luxury amenities. Further most villas have incinerators, garbage and sewage treatment plants and provision for rain water-harvesting and centralised security. (L.V.Reddy, *Deccan Chronicle*, August 1, 2008)

Hyderabadis can look forward to a thriving real estate industry in 2008. Some of the just completed, ongoing, upcoming projects conceived by 20 prominent builders in the city are:

- Lahari estates which offers 180 independent houses in its gated community, Lahari Green Park. Lahari Jade Residence has 160 apartments, it is also coming up with independent

Source: Skyscraper Blog Skyscraper City Forums

Fig. 2.3: Skyscrapers in Hyderabad: An Assorted View, gives an insight into the skyscraper culture that is developing in Hyderabad.

bungalows worth Rs. 1 crore. All these ongoing projects are located at Bhanur. The 60-room Lahari resorts at Bhanur is another running project.

- Aditya constructions is coming up with nearly 10 million square feet of residential and commercial spaces in Hyderabad with gated communities at upcoming high-end areas like Empress Park at Shiekpet Jubilee Hills, EDEN WOODS at Tellapur, Villa Grande and Beverly Park at Kompally, High Rise apartments at Tellapur and Nallagandla and high rise towers at Kukatpally in the year 2008. Another ongoing project is Windsor in HITEC city and Green Field at Kondapur.
- Indu Projects just launched Indu Aranya based on the theme of 'Life is Green' at LB Nagar. The 35-acre project with greenery and forestry consists of 250 villas ranging between Rs. 60-80 lakh. They were to be handed over to buyers in 2008.
- IVRCL just completed their Hill Ridge villas Gachibowliand are also coming-up with top class housing and commercial ventures at Madhapur. There will be another apartment complex at Kukatpally and their Ella Compass hotel is nearing completion.
- Obili's current project includes Obili My Green City at Kandawara. This 200 acre project will be completed in 3 phases. It has open plots, independent houses starting from Rs. 25 lakh and duplex houses with a starting price of Rs. 39 lakh. Another 100 acre residential project within My Green City is Obili Elite. It will have independent luxury villas priced at Rs. 1 crore each.
- Prajay has about 15-20 projects in their pipeline. Prajay Homes on 42 acres has 300 independent houses priced at around Rs. 20 lakh each in Masjidpur. The 13 acre Celebrity Villas at Shamirpet has 84 luxury villas. The end 600 independent clubhouses on 71 acres—'Prajay Waterfront City' is another project. Windsor Park will house <than 2000 flats ahead of Uppal. Residential projects in Gachibowli are also on the anvil.
- NCC Urban Infrastructure Ltd has completed Nagarjuna Residency at Gachibowli. It has 460 flats on 9.64 acre priced at Rs. 1crore each. Another upcoming villa project is at

Kompally of 34 acres. It will have 200 villas costing around Rs. 1crore each.

- Dasha's NRI Platinum City, close to Shamshabad on Nagaram main road is a 10 acre project. Dasha Residency offers 300 villas on 12 acres priced within 20 lakh close to Maheshwaram. They also have plans for another project in 2008. The 15 acre housing project will have independent and duplex houses in Sankerpally area which cost less than Rs. 25 lakh.
- MAK projects Banyan Tree Retreat is an ongoing project on Srisailam highway. The 100 acre project houses 350 high end villas with all modern facilities priced at Rs.1crore. Its integrated project at Miyapur is M3 Towers. The 1 million square feet area houses a business class hotel with 250 rooms, commercial retail and 200 apartments. It is also coming up with 200 countryside farmhouses near BHEL at Sankarpally on 125 acres.
- Saket Engineering just completed their luxury, gated community Saket Mithila consisting of 101 villas at Kapra. Another ongoing residential project with 25 floor luxury apartments called Saket Sriyam is priced at Rs. 35 lakh. They have just started another township, Saket Pranam for the senior citizens. Besides luxury apartments, it will house a restaurant and a 15-bed hospital. Saket also has 50 acre project near Medchal and at Kollur village coming up in 2008 for luxury villas.
- Anuradha's new 80 acre project is Aura County before Shamirpet on the Karimnagar highway. This has 200 open plots with size ranging from 200 to 1400 square yards. Another running venture of 150 acres is Galaxy Vistas on the Bangalore Highway near Shamshabad. There are > than 300 plots priced about Rs. 3,500 per square yard. Its 10 acre ongoing project Orient Vistas is at Kompally on Medchal Highway is priced at Rs. 7500 per square yard.
- Aliens Elite is the freshly completed venture from Aliens. It is a residential five floor apartment at Miyapur. The 20 acres Aliens Space Station1 was to be ready by January 2008. Each flat of this 30 floor is priced at Rs. 40 lakh. Work on 100 acre project of 30 floors apt at Shamshabad Space Station 2 will commence from 2008. Aliens hub at Srisailem road is a

1000 acre project that will feature golf course, malls, resorts and work will start in 2008.

- The 108 acre project Lanco Hills at Manikonda was Lancho group's biggest venture in 2007. More residential apts are in the offing from Lanco Hills also come up. Besides Lancho Hills, there's a 22 acre land bank project at Kokapet for a residential complex which is under discussion.
- Manjeera's latest ongoing project is Manjeera Diamond Towers near Gopanpally. It has 88 apts on 11 acres each of the 3 bedroom flats are priced at Rs. 62 lakh. Manjeera Heights with 126, 2 and 3 bedroom flats at Saroornagar was completed this yr. Its phase II with 152 flats will be completed by the end of 2008.
- Sree Vensai's ongoing project Bramhani Avenue is an elite gated community spread over 130 acres near the International Airport at Shamshabad.
- Vintage Avenue has come up with projects like Vintage Classica, Vintage Olympia and Vintage Celeste. Former has 10 independent houses while the later on Srisailem road is another housing project on 150 acres. Its latest offering is the 50 acre Vintage Flora at Nandigama situated on Bangalore National Highway and located close to Vintage Classica and Olympia. Residential complexes will be constructed with customers' choice. It will have both picturesque villages along with all modern city amenities.
- Green Home is coming up with a 30 acre gated community Knights Park at Shamshabad. It will house 150 duplex villas, a shopping complex, and clubhouse. The price will range from Rs. 1 crore to 2 crore. Besides, the 150 acre Metro city and 200 acre gated community Princeton on the Bangalore Highway have just been completed. Another ongoing 100 acre project of open plots on Srisailem road is El Dorado. Work on apts at Shamshabad will also begin shortly.
- Ashoka's Buiders and Developers ongoing residential project is Ashoka A-la-maison. This is a 60 acre gated community with 300 villas at Dullapally near Kompally. The price of the villas range from Rs. 1.5–2.5 crore. Ashoka Metropolitan Mall on road No. 1 was just completed. Other upcoming projects include Ashoka Golden Mall at Kukutpally, Ashoka Park on 1 lakh sq.ft, which will be a corporate office building

at Banjara hills. Work on Ashok'a Info Park at Madhapur on 25 lakh sqft will start in 2008.

- Modi Builders have got 6-7 projects, among these are Nilgiri Homes with 95 row houses and bungalows, at Rampally on 6.5 acres. It's a gated community with all modern facilities; 40 acre Silver Oak (phase III) consists of 400 elegant duplex bungalows at Cherlaplly and Silver Oak apt on 1acre has 120 flats; Greenwood Residency with 345 flats on 6 acre near Bollaram; Mayflower and Paramount Residency at Nagaram.
- Splendid Aparna Habitat's latest joint venture is Palm Meadows. It's a 95 acre residential villa project of the Aparna Group and Splendid Group of companies. Located near the ORR at Kompally amidst greenery, it houses 330 villas with plots sizes ranging from 533 square yards to 840 square yards completed by the end of 2008.
- Sri Sairam Projects Ltd—Sri Sairam Towers is a completed project on 7.5 acre having 26 per cent built up area and 74 per cent open space with 8 blocks of Excellently Designed Apts. Three-level parking, with14 floors it has 578 residential apts ranging between 1500 to 5400 sq.ft, 3-bedrom, 4/5 bedroom duplex with triplex terrace.

(*Deccan Chronicle,* December 29, 2007)

Hyderabad-Bangalore National Highway 7 is now witnessing a real estate boom with the proposal of HUDA. HMDA is going to oversee planned growth in outskirts; it will replace the existing HUDA. It will cover 6856 sq.km covering 5 districts—Hyderabad, Rangareddy, Mahabubnagar, Medak, Nalgonda on the lines of NCRD (national capital region of Delhi). Realtors are expecting huge construction activity in and around Kottur, Shadnagar of Mahabubnagar in the next two years as the state government is keen on developing this area to decongest the core city. It's the right place for investment with the proposal of Textile Park, Apparel Park, aero hub, star hotels, IT parks and industrial estates. Connectivity to ORR project is an added advantage. Suchir-India, Vintage Avenue Private Ltd, JSR real estates, Jaimata Di Villas Private Ltd, Hema estates, DLF, and several other real estate companies have already taken up various projects anticipating future growth in the route. (K.Srinivasa Rao, *Deccan Chronicle*, August 8, 2008)

Maheshwaram is developing a whole horde of world-class infrastructure projects and reflects the perfect urge to be at the right place at right time. In the vicinity of FAB city, Hardware Park, International Park, International airport and several IT and ITES companies, the location is ideal and keeps free from the city's hustle and bustle. It offers matchless resources to translate the idea of perfect living into reality. Gold Coast located close to the prestigious Hyderabad-Vijaywada National highway—NH 9 and the world class Mount Opera multi theme park offers perfect option for investment. (*The Times of India*, December 31, 2006)

Brief realty radar, citing highlights with plus factors in few areas which incidentally are on the city outskirts is given below in Table 2.5.

One of the oldest areas of Hyderabad, Mehdipatnam, has always been buzzing with commercial activity. The area has gradually changed from a lower middle class locality to one that has become the latest destination for NRI investors. However, it still balances modernism and traditionalism, with some parts still retaining the old world charm of Hyderabad. The real estate boom struck Mehdipatnam a couple of years ago. The International airport at Shamshabad and new ventures in Gachibowli began to take concrete shape, property rates here were directly affected owing to its proximity to the proposed hot property zones. In 2005, residential ventures charged Rs. 5,500 per square yard, but in 2006 it was above Rs. 15,000 per square yard. Even the official values have doubled so the market rates were bound to go up even more (it may be mentioned here that the real market rates are always greater than official values of property). Similarly, rentals have also shot up owing to the increasing purchasing power of IT employees who look to Mehdipatnam as an alternative to the affluent Banjara and Jubilee Hills areas. The rent for apartments is around 5-6 per cent of the capital value and the rates are a function of proximity to main road.

The building and construction activity in the area is also on the rise. Though there is hardly any land available, there are cases of independent houses being given to developers to convert them into apartments and even commercial complexes. Construction activity is gradually veering more towards the residential areas in the interiors of Mehdipatnam. High-end construction is also scheduled to take place with the proposal of building a flyover from Mehdipatnam towards RGI Airport. "High quality construction of residential layouts is pushing the real estate prices and the fact that it is centrally located

Table 2.5: Gist of Reality Scenario in Hyderabad, 2006

Medchal • Peaceful and pollution free • Preferred for residential colonies • Prices register a steady rise • Good road connectivity with city • Positioned as a long-term yet safe investment option	Jawaharnagar • BITS city campus • Shameerpet a property hot spot • Prices are on the rise • Realtors active along Rajiv Rahadari
Madhapur • Teeming with activity • More IT facilities here • Apartment culture fast catching up • Land in scarcity, prices quite high • Preferred for residence and investment as well • High prices at Kondapur and Miyapur	Kukatpally • Fast appreciating • Residential growth continues • Malls and multiplex add new vitality • Spinal road pushes prices further • Frenzied land sale along highway • Malaysian Township ready
Gachibowli • Hot spot of city's realty growth • Demand spreading all along • Favoured IT destination • Stadia and green environs • Manikonda and Raidurg are hot properties	Jubilee Hills • Prices are going up, up and up • Record auction bid of Rs. 1.42 lakh per square metre • Limited land availability • Fast gaining a commercial hue
Shamshabad • International Airport completed • Hardware park in the vicinity • Abnormal rise in land prices • An acre costs, more than Rs. 1 crore • High demand likely for ancillary setup • Exercise caution before buying land • Check zoning regulations • Verify property rights	Pocharam • Singapore Township • Raheja IT Park on 106 acre site • Property abutting Ghatkesar road in demand • Rates still affordable for many • NIMS University proposed • Annojiguda and Medipally popular spots
Outer Ring Road • Favoured destination for all • High appreciation expected • Townships to dot the ORR • High standard facilities assured • Multi-modal connectivity planned	Ramoji Film City • City continues to expand here • RFC major attraction • Stretch popular for resorts/ recreational facilities • Prices have almost stabilised here • Favoured as a safe investment bet
Fab City • 1200 acres of land in Tukkuguda • Rs. 13500 acre computer microchip industry • Around 10000 jobs • Property prices have already hit the roof • Demand likely for both residential & commercial space	

(Compiled from: *The Hindu*, April 15, 2006)

is also working to its advantage. However, the rise of property rates here will be steady and will be governed more by demand and supply rather than speculation". (Anushya Rajagopalan, *The Times of India*, September 16, 2006)

Rental values	*Capital values*
Apartments: Rs. 7000 to Rs. 10000 (for 1100 square feet)	Apartments: Rs. 900 to Rs. 2200 per square feet
Independent houses: Rs. 15000 + (for 1000 square feet)	Land: Rs. 25000+ per square yard
—	Independent houses: Rs. 20,000 per square yard
—	Retail space: Rs. 2,700 to Rs. 5,500 per square feet

Property prices in twin cities have more than doubled in the last three years. Builders and government are blaming each other, but both have no solutions to offer. A 1000 sq.ft. luxury flat was available for Rs. 15 lakh in 2005, now it costs Rs. 30 lakh in the city outskirts. Similarly, in residential areas like Jubilee hills and Banjara hills the square feet rate was Rs. 2500 in 3 years ago but has now gone up sharply. In Kukatpally, Dilshuknagar and Marredpally too, rates have gone up from Rs. 1000 per square feet to more than Rs. 2500 now. Rise in steel prices, cement, sand and other building material has played a role in this, moreover builders too are artificially jacking up prices in certain areas to get huge returns within a short span of time.

Steel used for construction was available for Rs. 25,000 per tonne in 3 years ago but now costs around Rs. 45,000. A bag of 50 kg cement was available for Rs. 140 in 2005 now it costs around Rs. 230 per bag. Likewise a truckload of sand that cost around Rs. 2500 in Hyderabad 3 yreas ago is available now for Rs. 10,000. The surging land prices have played a role in increasing the flats rates in twin cities. The actual construction would stabilise the flats' prices while frequent plots transactions would lead to escalation in prices. Each builder has to invest at least Rs. 1 crore for the purchase of 1000 square yard, which is mandatory by GHMC for building an apartment complex. (K.Srinivas Rao, *Deccan Chronicle*, May 23, 2008)

In view of silver jubilee progress of Malkajgiri municipality its officials proposed to take up works under the World Bank-funded

AP Urban Reforms and Municipal services project for Rs. 157.97 crore that include road widening—Rs 22.4 crore, central lighting Rs. 2.04 crore, solid waste management Rs. 1.77 crore, storm water drain Rs. 30.66 crore, underground drainage Rs. 90.42 crore, water supply Rs. 10.8 crore and parks Rs. 35 lakh. (*The New Indian Express*, December 26, 2006)

The main highlights of this project are:

- AP Urban Services for Poor is innovative partnership project between the State Govt and UK-based Dept for International Development (DFID) which include Comprehensive Municipal Action Plan for Poverty Reduction (CMAPP), third quality assurance, professionals introduction like community organisers and livelihood promotion associates.
- School health programme under APSUB is implemented as a pilot project in the municipality where in October 2005 a programme was conducted for primary and upper primary schools supplying first aid kits, weighing scales.
- Women and Child Welfare Department sanctioned 18 childhood development centres for eradicating illiteracy among children in many slums
- To collect garbage from commercial establishments exnora tricycles and twin dustbins were allotted to colonies of Malkajgiri Municipalty.
- Safilguda tank was beautified by removing all encroachments.
- Citizens' charters were introduced.
- Established grievance redressal cell for public.

Quthbullapur Municipality was formed on February 24, 1987 by merging 5 gram panchayats—Quthbullapur, Jeedimetla, Pet Basheerabad, Suraram and Gajularamaram. To meet the growing demand the municipal authorities took up several developmental activities at a cost of Rs. 29.02 crore.

The main highlights of these activities are: Amount spent on development of roads was Rs. 2.25 crore, that on public toilets Rs. 10 lakh, sewerage drains Rs. 8.27 crore, water supply Rs. 6.67 crore, parks and playgrounds Rs. 2.79 crore and street lights Rs. 3.15 crore. Besides various welfare programmes are being taken up with funds under various schemes—National Slum Development Programme (Rs. 2.24 crore), AP Urban Services for Poor (Rs 8.15

crore), Integrated Low Cost Sanitation (Rs 1.07 crore) underground drainage (Rs 3.65 crore), Eleventh Finance Commission Funds (Rs 74.17 lakh), AP Urban Reforms and Municipal Services Project (Rs 1.98 crore), old age pension is being given to 1224 beneficiaries under the INDIRAMMA scheme. 8045 houses are being constructed under Rajiv Gruha Kalpa as also 3,258 more dwellings under the pucca urban housing scheme. These houses are being constructed at Suraram, and another 2 projects will be taken up at Gajularamaram, Jagadgirigutta.

The property tax collection has increased substantially from Rs. 80.70 lakh last year to Rs. 1.38 crore this year. This is due to the use of GIS where unassessed properties were assessed. Garbage collection system from door to door has been introduced. (*The New Indian Express*, December 26, 2006)

An unprecedented Information Technology boom coupled with rapid development of infrastructure in the city has sent land rates and rentals skyrocketing in Kukatpally. Once a dusty, residential -industrial belt with pollution hazards in tow, it has now turned into a seller's paradise. Proximity to the cyber hub of Madhapur has made Kukatpally area a functional dream home destination. (M. Srinivas, *The Hindu*, September 30, 2006)

Kukatpally municipalty has been termed as one of the best local bodies in the state. Infact, KPHB colony is the biggest such colony in Asia and the APUSP has declared it as the top Municipality in empowerment of the poor. Several prestigious government institutions like JNTU, NRSA, CITD, HAL, SISI, BHEL, IDPL, fall under the KKPM. Under the Rajiv Gruhakalpa Scheme 4356, UPHS 1858, INDIRAMMA 258 and VAMBAY 899 beneficiaries have been selected. Work connected with housing is going at a brisk and is expected to be completed by March 2007.

The sudden rise in rental prices is due to:

- The new Spinal Road that connects HITEC city main road with JNTU, it hardly takes 10 minutes to reach HITEC city with new access.
- Several new ventures grounded by leading real estate companies have supplemented the boom here.
- Announcement of a multiplex theatre, a star hotel and shopping mall is a major facelift to the entire area. This is to

come up in 9 acre site located on Mumbai National Highway NH-9 right in front of JNTU.

- Well connected by train services from HITEC city and bus facility from Kukatpally main road.

Now software engineers are shelling six month's rent as advance payment. Earlier rents which ranged between Rs. 2500 to Rs. 3000 have now increased to Rs. 8000. Duplex flats cost Rs. 1.5 crore, double bedroom kitchen costs Rs. 25 lakh and 200 square yard of plot commands a price of 50 lakhs now. So purchasing a flat or land in Kukatpally is fast turning out to be a formidable task.

Ten plots at Kukatpally Housing Board (KPHB) were put for auction with a HIG plot in 5th phase fetching the APHB a price of Rs. 40,200 per square yard. Six of the 10 plots spread out in phase 5, 6, 7 and 9 put for auction were taken, APHB stands to earn around Rs. 5.41 crores. A 116.66 square yard plot in phase 7 went for Rs. 35,600 per square yard while another plot measuring 445.52 square yard had a biding of Rs. 22,600 per square yard. (*The Hindu*, November 4, 2006)

Luxury is fast getting redefined these days in crores. It means acres, 6 to 7 bedrooms, 4 to 5 rooms for servants and maid, swimming pool, Jacuzzi and Spanish architecture. Of course the price runs into crores. Forty-four such signature Spanish Casas, Villas, Palacios, Quintas, 'Casa E tebana' are to come up around 12.5 km from Paradise Junction and close to Satyam Technology Centre at Medchal.

The mega-sized residencies are planned over 50 acres and individual plots measuring between ½ an acre to 1.25 acre. Getting to individual units each is to come with Spanish style patios, breakfast rooms, a home office, learning room, table tennis room, sound proofed room, a party lawn, 2-level landscaped gardens, covered garages for 3-5 cars, and more with area ranging from a minimum of 7,650 square feet to a maximum of 16,500 square feet. The project costs around Rs. 220 crore. Based on size the units are expected to cost between Rs. 4 to 12 crores. The developers hope to bring Spanish royalty to the city of Nizams. (T. Lalith Singh, *The Hindu*, October 14, 2006)

The concept of service apartments is fast catching up in the city and promising to usher in a new dawn in this sector is the project taken up at Hill Ridge Springs, Gachibowli. It's an exhilarating blend where one can reside for a day, a month, a year for that matter and in complete luxury with ready to use facilities and one feels at home with a home like ambience. Given the large number of IT workforce with disposable incomes, dynamic and ever increasing job market in the BPO sector and a huge tourism potential, the concept becomes common place. Service Apartments (SA) or luxury suites will be highly cost effective compared to 5-star hotels. Worldwide these SA are 15-30 per cent cheaper than star hotels offering same quality of living. (M. Sai Gopal, *The Hindu*, October 21, 2006)

Pictures of luxury service apartments at Hyderabad

Fig. 2.4: Myriad Views of Service Apartments

Service Apartments are preferred by executives who stay for long, foreigners, Non-Resident Indians visiting Hyderabad with their families (NRIs) and other frequent travelers. They offer the services of a hotel with the seclusion of home and a budget suitable for all pockets. In addition to the rooms they have fully furnished kitchens as well.

The new concept of service apartments is becoming a major trend in Hyderabad's hospitality sector to cater to high profile visitors. They offer the facilities of a star-hotel along with a homely ambience. A shortage of star hotels in the city has given way to luxurious service apartments that promise to offer the best of both worlds. Major hotels rent out rooms for rates ranging from Rs. 3000 to Rs. 15000 per day. But the tariff for a double bedroom in a service apartment is between Rs. 1500 to Rs. 4000 per day. Every service apartment has a living cum dining room. The concept of service apartment is gaining ground because of the scarcity of rooms. Several big firms are planning to set up service apartments in Hyderabad in a big way. Over 50 of them are located in areas such as Madhapur, Jubilee Hills, Banjara Hills, Basheerbagh and Lakdikapool. (K.Srinivasa Rao, *Deccan Chronicle*, February 29, 2008)

Unlike luxury projects, boutique homes are extremely unique residential propositions. The latest development on Indian residential properties is rather noteworthy—luxury housing (in the Rs. 80 lakh to Rs. 1 crore+) which had taken a back seat during the meltdown, is also making a convincing comeback. Interestingly, while many large developers are concentrating on getting volumes in this there is a category of builders who are cashing on—the boutique homes category. Luxury boutique homes are selling better today than volume luxury properties, since there is a scarcity. The demand for such properties had risen by 30-40 per cent over the last year. It is possible to construct them within 6-8 months, volume projects take longer to complete.

Boutique Homes focus exclusively on end users. They are defined by quality rather than volume, there will be no more than 5-10 units to a project, luxuriously outfitted. They depend on the availability of redevelopment opportunities in high profile areas. Developers of Boutique Homes throw in all high-end amenities into such properties and cater to customised specifications, as well. These are best suited for developers who address the market as micro-segments. (Raminder Grover, *Deccan Chronicle*, November 20, 2009; Samir, Chopra, *Deccan Chronicle*, October 21, 2009))

A gated housing project located near the Bangalore-Hyderabad highway, close to two upcoming Special Economic Zones (SEZ) and the Infosys campus 'designer' was launched. These are designer villas spread over 25 acres with 123 villas of European style i.e. Italian and Spanish, which will be built in 320 square yard each, with built up space in the form of 3600 square feet of duplex complexes. It would be among the first Gated Community in the city to have complete underground cabling and broadband connectivity. Water purifier plant and WIFI enablement are also on the anvil. (D.M.Mathew, *The Hindu*, October 28, 2006) Gated Communities are residential complexes that have just one entrance, maximising the security factor. Also these communities come with amenities like good roads, club houses, restaurants, shopping malls, common facilities like schools, polyclinics, lifestyle luxuries and so on. Gated Communities were earlier for the richer class only—several customers who look at this as a second investment.

On the Hyderabad-Vijayawada highway and just a 30 minute drive away from the city, customers can purchase plots ranging from 200, 400, 600, 800 and 1000 square yards. There is also an artistically designed guest house to cater to the visitors and residents requirement alike. The area boasts of cottages that are of 400-450 square feet in area with a sloping roof, hall, bedroom and sit out and equipped with modern amenities. Another venture located on a sprawling 70 acres in the heart of Genome Valley near Shameerpet has elegant, sophisticated, stylish and well integrated township with world class facilities. (*The Times of India*, December 31, 2006)

The State Government has allotted large pieces of land in the suburb to multinationals, as it did in Gachibowli a couple of years ago. This has made Shameerpet not only the fastest growing suburb of Hyderabad but also a major bio-tech hub. Realtors are making a beeline for Shameerpet, located in Rangareddy district center 30 km North of Hyderabad, 22 km from Secunderabad and about 50 km from the Shamshabad airport and property prices naturally, shot past the reach of the Middle Income Group. A square yard in the suburb now costs between Rs. 5,000 to Rs 10,000 while not many years back the price was just Rs. 600. It is a knowledge hub with good educational institutions such as IVY League Academy, Nalsar Law University, BITS campus and XLRI setting up campuses here. Now, the government is also planning to set up a Giga city, an IT and knowledge destination in 2000 acres, which will be four times the size of Cyberabad. It will have commercial complexes, shopping malls and multiplex theatres. Anticipating a surge of highly-paid professionals, several world class residential townships are coming up in the area, the major one being the Inner Circle villa project built by a Bangalore-based real estate company which states that once the access to ORR is completed, property prices would go further up. The urban landscape of this area is in for a major transformation from residential areas nestled in rurban environs to a near supra-urban setting with modern infrastructure. (L.V.Reddy, *Deccan Chronicle*, March 28, 2008)

One of the leading property developers of Bengaluru-Plans 21 projects on the outskirts of Hyderabad; it will have 5,000 homes in Moinabad, Medchal, Timmapur, Maheshwaram, Mamidipalli and Shamshabad. It has come up with concept of resortomes combining the lavishness of a resort and practicality of an efficient home. Located at Moinabad 'resortomes' have 200 villas ranging from Rs. 55-60 lakhs. (*The Hindu*, November 25, 2006) It also caters to 9000 houses within Gated Community spanning across Bangalore, Pune, Hyderabad and Chennai. Each villa is priced at Rs. 40 lakh and above making it affordable for the mid income segment. These prices are much lower than what villas in Gated Community are available at. (Nirmala Govindarajan, *Times of India*, December 16, 2006)

Jain Housing Constructions Ltd involved in residential developments in cities like Chennai, Bengaluru, Cochin, Coimbatore, Mysore, Pune and now in Hyderabad is launching its mega residential project Carlton Creek at Khajaguda near Gachibowli, a 13 acre monumental project located at a mere 15-minute drive from Jubilee hills. Tucked away amidst ornate gardens, this landmark houses a captivating selection of 1120 spacious and well-ventilated 2 and 3 BKH apartments. It blends an impressive selection of high-end lifestyle amenities and alluring recreational facilities in a comfortable resort-like ambience. Another venture named Jains Salzburg—a 5 acre opulence located near to the APPA, ORR junction at Bandlaguda centrally between the Shamshabad airport and the Gachibowli Bank. Each venture is home to several amenities making truly urban and contemporary lifestyle complete with every conceivable comfort. Quality interiors match the exquisitely-done exteriors with landscaped gardens, lawn, pool, club-house and gym that add halo to life in the Pearl City. (*Deccan Chronicle*, August, 22, 2008; April, 25, 2008)

Vintage Valley is located on the Hyderabad-Vijayawada highway and is a 30 minute drive away from the city. Customers can purchase plots ranging from 200, 400, 600, 800 and 1000 square yards. There is also an artistically designed guest house to cater to the visitors' and residents' requirement alike. Bloomz boasts of cottages that are of 400-450 square feet in area with a sloping roof, hall, bedroom and sit out and equipped with modern amenities. Romana County is located on a sprawling 70 acres in the heart of Genome Valley near Shameerpet. Elegant, sophisticated, stylish in nature it is a well integrated township with world class facilities. (*The Times of India*, December 31, 2006)

In the peripheral areas around the city at a radius of 20 km, the trend will be for multi-storeyed complexes including locations such as Shamirpet that was in a dormant stage till recently. When the apartments in core city are sold at Rs. 1crore, an apartment at Rs. 40 lakhs in city periphery would be seen as a good bargain. However, with vertical growth made easy with the doing away of Floor Space Index (FSI) and density concepts, the city will be in deep trouble and demand for housing without commensurate infrastructure, road network, traffic planning and efficient public transport, may dip. (M.L.M.Maitreyi, *The Hindu*, March 17, 2007)

Another view expressed across the cross section of society is that the middle class in twin cities are 'right in the middle of nowhere' today. They cannot afford housing even on the outskirts. Property prices burn fingers and vaporize hopes. Chances of owning an independent house or an affordable apartment in twin cities is fast dwindling for urban middle class. A brief lull in construction activity under new regulations in the past six months has further narrowed down the alternatives for middle class families. Stiff penalties under the rules are impractical so builders stopped taking new projects fuelling sudden rise in prices even for ongoing projects. Now only suburban areas like Ghatkesar and areas beyond Ramoji Film City are the options left. (M.Sai Gopal, *The Hindu*, October 28, 2006)

The construction activity was hit badly for months after builders refused to take up new projects citing restrictions imposed under G.O.Ms.86 as unviable. Shortage of cement and skyrocketing prices of construction material and land compounded the problems. All of a sudden, construction came to a grinding halt all around, forcing those with moderate pockets to wait. With no new ventures, flats that were available went for a premium. The government finally made a few relaxations, following a sustained campaign by a section of builders and rising concerns over the real estate fate. This would help reduce apartment costs as well. However, builders vigorously opposed the mortgage issue, which wanted a builder to hand over a certain floor. An amendment has relaxed this to 10 per cent of the built-up area or a floor, whichever is less, for mortgage.

Builders were lobbying for it to be set at 5 per cent, but are now content with 10 per cent. The argument was that the condition affected those taking up projects on development basis. With landowner and developer sharing 50 per cent each being a common practice, the latter would be forced to pledge 10 per cent from his share and put for sale the remaining 40 per cent. The construction industry is not yet certain on the procedures of handing back mortgaged property. Builders want their representative to be on the committee that will release the mortgaged floors. President of Greater Hyderabad Builder's Forum (GHBF) says that "from compound wall to pillars, no deviations are allowed but there is some freedom for internal changes, though with a penalty".

The amendments put in place include encouragement of semi-detached residential buildings in group housing schemes and exemption of mortgage for individual buildings up-to 300 square metres. Builders had to restrict building around 22 sq.ft. from 28-30 square feet per yard. These changes, developers feel, would see a rush for building approvals as most plans were put on the backburner since the G.O was announced. The industry also feels that if construction work picks up in a right measure, prices of apartments could come down. At the same time, they feel that the unrealistic rise in land cost could hinder the prices sliding down to the pre G.O.86 phase. (T. Lalith Singh, *The Hindu*, December 9, 2006)

Amendments to GO 86 make the builders happy. But the public remain confused. Building plans are being drawn and redrawn. The latest changes have brought forth the charge that the government was reintroducing floor space index through 'backdoor' even while professing maximum use of space, besides giving an escape route to structures built without the sanctioned plan.

Under the NHP (National Housing Policy) and the JNNURM the centre has asked all the states to ensure shelter for the poor. In Hyderabad they also have to earmark 5 per cent land free to HUDA, apart from another 20 per cent for road network, parks, playgrounds, open spaces and social infrastructure. But Andhra Pradesh Builder's Forum says the orders would cause chaos and would create ill-will between the rich and the poor as both have to live in the same premises. It suggested that the government should implement exclusive housing schemes for poor without creating a scenario of social conflict. Developers fear there will be in trouble if MIG and LIG don't come forward to purchase land in posh localities. Therefore:

- The land, which is allocated for them, should not be used for other purposes.
- Maximum plot size should be upto 100 sq.mts
- Builders should allot 5 per cent to economically weaker sections, 10 per cent to LIG and 10 per cent to MIG's. (K. Srinivasa Rao, *Deccan Chronicle*, June 13, 2008)

"Cellar and stilt floor parking was allowed for constructions of plot size 500 square metres to 750 sq.mts and height up to 12 metres but inexplicably cellar permission was removed." There is also this strange stipulation that balcony projections are not to be allowed for non-multi-storied buildings—those of less than 18 metre height. Permission for extra floor for the owner under transferable development rights too is baffling. Questions arise as to why parking space for built-up area outside MCH is reduced when that in surrounding municipalities is growing spectacularly in recent times and also why the rules do not mention residential, commercial zones. (V. Geetanath, *The Hindu*, December 16, 2006)

The 'tatkal' service of giving permits in 48 hours for layouts approved by HUDA/MCH was launched on July 7, 2007 after a successful pilot programme in the L.B. Nagar circle. Kukatpally and Serilingampally circles too have begun the service and gradually it will be extended to 18 circles for permission for Ground and an upper floor. The site should not extend for >300 square metres or 360 square yards. The applicant has to pay Rs.500 per floor to avail the scheme. Not only is the GHMC promising a hassle free service but it is also offering to pay Rs. 50 per day for any unexplained delay on its part. It's also planning to have online clearance of building plans. However, houses planned for more floors will take more time since the mortgage clause comes into the picture and 10 per cent of the total built-up area has to be mortgaged as a guarantee against any illegal deviation from the sanctioned plan. They should not have dues of taxes to GHMC.

While no permission is required for houses to be constructed in less than 100 square yards in an approved layout, plan details have to be filed. Usually NOC from Mandal Revenue Officer (MRO) concerned, Urban Land Ceiling Act (ULC Act) affidavit for construction in more than 1000 square metres, ownership documents, duly attested by a gazetted officer are required. For multi-storied buildings of above 10 metres height documents like NOCs from the Joint Collector, land use certificate from HUDA, feasibility certificate from HMWSSB, structural stability, soil testing report are required. (V. Geetanath, *The Hindu*, July 7, 2007)

The Urban Land Ceiling Act of 1976 was repealed in March 2009. This entails unlimited ownership in notified urban areas, where ownership heretofore was restricted to 1000 square metres. This may be a boon to the housing sector which has been facing a slump. The prices of prime lands are likely to come down, facilitating construction activity. (*Deccan Chronicle*, March 27, 2009)

Builders are now required to register themselves with the GHMC. Maintaining a register of builders and giving them licences is a noble idea writes V.Geetanath. With the mortgage clause and now with the threat of licenses being revoked in case of constructions deviating from the sanctioned plan, building activity can be regulated to a large extent. Issuing of license to builders will herald a new phase in the reality sector and they are more organized now. (V. Geetanath, *The Hindu*, July14, 2007)

The state government was positively considering the Municipal Corporration's suggestion to exempt the mortgage clause for plots up to 300 square metres and relax setback rules for plots between 500 and 1000 square metres besides giving flexibility in setback area depending upon the number of floors. Corporation would also deploy security guards at dumper bins whose duty will be to ensure that garbage is disposed in the bins and not thrown around it. (*Deccan Chronicle*, November 5, 2006)

The Real Estate Management (Regulation and Control) Bill set a stir among developers and builders in the city. Though the proposal is still in a nascent stage and no concrete laws have been set for the State, the proposed Bill has evoked negative responses from the industry. Some complain that the regulations are very bureaucratic in nature; others fear it would deter the growth of industry in the city. (Anuhya Rajagopalan, *The Times of India*, November 11, 2006). The salient features of the bill are:

- Ban developers from issuing advertisements till the project is cleared by a proposed regulator.
- Regulator will give the nod only after checking that the title deeds are appropriate and transaction records for the land to be developed have been examined for the last 30 years.
- Pre-launch bookings a big no no. Builders are barred from accepting advances or deposits from buyers unless a sale agreement has been executed.

- Advance payments for particular projects should be deposited in a separate bank account, earmarked especially for the venture.
- Mortgage of land is prohibited.
- Developers should deposit 25 per cent of the development cost in the form of a bank guarantee.
- Sale cannot be cancelled unilaterally. Promoters should issue notices and give buyers enough time to respond before cancellation. Money collected and the interest thereof must be returned.
- Late clearances of dues will be penalized to the tunes of 1 per cent of the cost of the house.

Earlier 'Golconda X Roads' was a typical middle class locality but now a 3-Bedroom Kitchen Hall apartment with 1600 square feet is about Rs. 40 lakh which is simply not affordable to even those earning Rs. 16,000 to 20,000 per month. Even for used 2 Bedroom Kitchen Hall apartments of 100 square feet in Ameerpet the rates are about Rs. 28 lakhs. In Tarnaka, Habsiguda, A.S. Raonagar used 3 Bedroom Kitchen Hall would not be less than Rs. 15 to 18 lakh. The rental scenario is also not that rosy. In Alwal, Uppal, Kapra rents are little reasonable. Prices in Miyapur industrial belt and far off places like Hafeezpet too are skyrocketing with Rs. 2000 to Rs. 2800 a square feet. Now Uppal on the eastern extremity of GHMC too is on upswing, as the rates may touch Rs. 3000 per square feet. On the whole apartments are virtually out of the common man's reach now.

Uppal, which is just 7 km from Secunderabad railway station, has become a middle class paradise and a real estate hotspot. Foreseeing the growth in the area, many MNCs such as Genpact and Dell have already opened their offices. Microsoft and other firms are also setting up their offices here. Though the growth is slow when compared to other areas of the city, the land prices have shot up from Rs. 140 per square yard in 1990s to Rs. 15,000 per square yard at present. Land prices are set to go up even further with the coming of the international airport in Shamshabad since Uppal is adjacent to the ring road connected to the Shamshabad National Highway.

Uppal is all set to become the next information technology hub after Madhapur. Major infrastructure companies are showing interest in developing IT parks and in uppal where land is available at an affordable price compared to Gachibowli and Madhapur. These moves will boost economic and real estate activity in area and its surroundings in the next 2 years. Major firms like DSL Infrastructure and Space Developers Pvt Ltd, Bhagyanagar Infrastructure and Iconic Company have decided to develop IT parks in Uppal, which is 10 km away from Secunderabad. Meanwhile, Top Notch has proposed an exclusive SEZ for software companies in the area. Each firm is likely to invest around Rs. 300 crore for the development of IT parks while the SEZ would need around Rs. 1000 crore. The government is also encouraging infrastructure majors to set up IT parks and SEZs in Uppal by providing facilities under Software Technology Parks of India scheme, which gives various benefits including a tax holiday. Chairman of DSLI says "Uppal is considered a strategic location to provide connectivity to all parts of the city including Secunderabad and Shamshabad". (K.Srinivasa Rao, *Deccan Chronicle*, May 9, 2008)

Areas surrounding Uppal, including Habsiguda, Tarnaka, Medipally, Ramanthapur have also witnessed increase in land prices after the opening of the International Cricket Stadium and the outlet of IT major GE on the Tarnaka-Uppal Main Road. Though it has become a township of sorts, it still retains its village greenery. (L.V.Reddy, *Deccan Chronicle*, February 15, 2008)

Several residential and commercial projects are coming up in areas around the Warangal Highway where land rates are quite affordable ranging from Rs. 4000 to Rs. 5000 per sq yd. These areas are close to core localities 10 km from Uppal, 17 km from Dilsukhnagar, 18 km from Secunderabad and 19 km from Koti. Moreover, several professional colleges located here with Good transportation facilities. With the launch of Raheja Group's Mindspace IT Park and Software giant Infosys second campus in these areas has lifted the spirits of builders. There will be much demand for apts, independent houses among IT employees of these parks. Major residential projects under various stages of construction in Annojiguda and Pocharam include Emarald Heights and Emarald Park by Modi Builders. All these factors will make this locality the next IT destination says Keshav Naidu of GSK Constructions.

In all 829 flats in the range of 1360-1895 sq.ft. are being built in Emarald Heights and 192 independent villas of 252 sq.yd, are coming up in Emarald Park. The Government is planning to set-up a Giga City in 2000 acres in Jawaharnagar, close to Warangal Highway. Inorbit Malls, subsidiary of the Raheja Group, is building a large shopping mall spread over 106 acres called Retail Value Village in Pocharam. While an independent house spread over 133 sq.yd costs

Rs. 15 lakh, for 150 sq.yd. it is Rs. 20 lakh and Rs. 23 lakh for 200 sq.yd. house. A 1100 sq.ft. flat can be bought for < than Rs. 20 lakh. (L.V.Reddy, *Deccan Chronicle*, December 19, 2008)

The realty sector is banking on the IT/ITES/BPO sectors for its next boom in the city. After Madhapur IT corridor it's now Tellapur Techno-city in the Gachibowli IT corridor to give a boost to the realty market, in the western part of the city. A consortium led by US Constructions Tishman Speyer and ICICI venture is developing India's largest integrated township on 400 acres in Tellapur in partnership with Nagarjuna Construction Company. The project includes 30 million square feet of stylish residential and office buildings apart from retail, civic, and cultural amenities and is expected to cost Rs. 200 crore. This would house 30,000 people and provide office space that will generate 35,000 jobs. It is the first township to be developed in public-private partnership.

These are already has IT companies like Microsoft, UBS, Franklin Templeton, Wipro, Polaris, Computer Associates, Infotech, ICICI, SBI, Infosys and several IT companies have come forward to set up shop in Gachibowli IT corridor and consequently demand for residential and commercial property is expected to rise. Developers are taking-up extensive construction of residential and commercial buildings to cater to this demand. Most buyers are IT professionals as several global and national firms set up operations in Gachibowli IT corridor apart from this, the government has set-up a Skyscraper zone in Tellapur where buildings should have at least 30 floors. At least 30 construction companies, including builders from other states are keen on taking-up projects in this area.

- The first to get approval for construction of high-rise buildings is Aliens Space Station coming in 20 acres out of which 4 acres are earmarked for commercial buildings and for residential purposes. The project is estimated to cost Rs. 1200 crore and has 13 stations with 28 floors will have nearly 2000 flats.
- DLF is also constructing a huge commercial complex.
- Other major projects on stream are NCC Urban and Ramky Tower. (L.V.Reddy, *Deccan Chronicle*, July 18, 2008)

More and more people from other states are investing in real estate in Hyderabad, as property prices have skyrocketed in other states. Despite the realty boom, prices of flats and houses in Hyderabad are lower than in other metropolitan cities. A survey done by Many people from North India were acquiring properties in Hyderabad as they find the cost per square feet cheaper here between Rs. 2,500 to Rs. 4,000 per square feet. They also prefer to invest in APHB flats to have clear title deeds and to avoid problems in the future. More than 400 out of 2080 flats in the Singapore Township developed by APHB at Pocharam were sold to North Indians. (K.Srinivasa Rao, *Deccan Chronicle*, March 14, 2008)

HUDA is selling away 75 acres of prime land in Kokapet to New Delhi based real estate developer Omaxe Ltd at one-third the market price. Omaxe paid Rs. 12 crore per acre for 25 acres at an auction also came with a joint development proposal. However, several developers are opposing over increasing preferential treatment to select companies and to the proposal. (N.Vamsi Srinivas, Jan 27)

Gulf property majors are shunning India's economic indicators and are betting high on the Indian realty scenario. The investment arm of Ras al-Khaimah plans a US$5 billion business centre in Hyderabad. Ras al-Khaimah Investment Authority (RAKIA), which manages the funds of the Emirate, part of the United Arab Emirates, said that it had recently signed an initial agreement with the Andhra Pradesh Industrial Infrastructure Corp to set up Hyderabad Economic City, which would offer financial and healthcare services. The demand for affordable housing is immense and the returns will be good for long-term investors. (*Deccan Chronicle*, November 21, 2008)

For the middle class own house in Hyderabad just become dearer due to huge demand, new building rules and soaring prices of cement and steel. It has become possible for a middle class man to construct an independent, single bedroom house in a minimum area of 650 square feet at a cost of Rs. 6.5 lakh, provided they have plot. Similarly, for double bedroom independent house in a minimum area of 1000 square feet can be built at cost of Rs. 9 lakh.

To build a single bedroom house the minimum land required is 85 to 100 square yards, for a double bedroom house it is 100-125 square yards. According to one estimate which undertakes low-cost construction in the city, the prevailing market rate for each square feet construction is Rs. 900 to Rs 1000 including total construction, electrical wiring, drainage etc. remaining expenditures like flooring and others will vary depending on the labour charges. If the owner supplies all the material to the builder the cost will come down to

Rs. 750 per square feet. (L.V. Reddy, *Deccan Chronicle*, January 25, 2008)

Buying a flat in Hyderabad has become costlier by upto Rs. 4 lakhs because of local cess, increasing cement prices, and hiked interest rates. (1) Builders fear that this will affect the construction industry badly. (2) Interest rates on housing loans have climbed from 8 to 11.5 per cent, forcing customers to pay more money as equated monthly instalments. A bag of cement costs around Rs. 210 against Rs. 160 last year. (3) Civic authorities revised charges from Rs. 20 to Rs. 100 per sq.m. of built up area from June16. For open plots, the charges were increased to Rs. 75 from Rs. 10 per sq.m.

Increasing Cement Prices from 2005 to 2008

Period	*Average Price (Rs. per bag)*	*Increase since December 2005 (in Rs.)*
Dec 2005	158	
Jan 2006	163	5
Feb	175	17
Mar	189	31
Apr	199	41
May	200	42
Jun	201	43
July	201	43
Aug	201	43
Sep	202	44
Oct	205	47
Nov	208	50
Dec	209	51
Jan 2007	209	51
Feb	212	54
Mar	225	67
Apr	226	68
May	226	68
Jun	227	69
July	229	71
Aug	231	73
Sep	231	73
Oct	231	73
Nov	231	73
Dec	230	72
Jan 2008	231	73

The unexpected fall in consumption had brought down cement prices from Rs. 230 per 50 kg bag to Rs. 200. The Federation of

Andhra Pradesh Chambers of Commerce and Industry is hoping that cement prices would come down to Rs. 150 per bag so that construction cost would also come down drastically. Steel prices had already come down from Rs. 50000 to Rs. 30000 per tonne. RBI had lowered the repo rate by 100 base points, following this ICICI Bank had announced reduction in home loan rate from 13 per cent to 11.5 per cent for loans up to Rs. 20 lakh. Others too are likely to reduce. Much delighted are city realtors with a fresh boom in the construction sector. (K.Srinivasa Rao, *Deccan Chronicle*, December 12, 2008)

In fact a fall in cement prices as a consequence of fall in the price of its raw material—limestone—has brought down property prices in Hyderabad and other parts of Andhra Pradesh. The excess of supply over demand has made for a fall in cement prices by 30 to 40 per cent. Steel prices have also come down and the real estate companies have brought down prices by at least 25 per cent. Some builders are also offering gifts like cars, diamond necklaces, air conditioners and laptops to lure customers, so that the construction activity is sustained. (*Deccan Chronicle*, November 21, 2009)

A 1000 sq.ft. double bedroom flat was available for Rs. 22 lakhs in areas like Dilshuknagar, Malakpet, Uppal, Kukatpally, Mehdipatnam till end of April. But now the cost of each sq.ft. is being fixed between Rs. 2400 to Rs 2700. The AP Builders Forum has urged the government to reduce the burden on builders. They also said the government should develop residential areas on the outskirts in order to reduce the land cost. (*Deccan Chronicle*, July 4, 2008)

However, after square feet and square yards, it was 3-Bed Room flats and triplex and now acreages that have caught the fancy of property investors and real estate dealers. As options dry out fast in the city and its vicinity and prices soar beyond reach, both green field and parched lands on the city outskirts have started drawing investors in big numbers. The trend has caught up in a radius of 80 km to 150 km from the city encompassing places as far off as Siddipet, Chevella, Ghatkesar, Shankarpally, Zaheerabad, Sadashivpet, Mansanpally, Ramayampet, Sangareddy and so on. Realtors now look to develop on the city outskirts snug cottages with a patch of greenery.

However, agricultural field on the city outskirts are slowly giving way to multi-storeyed apartments in Madhapur-Kondapur stretch. Desolate suburbs and beyond turn into beehives of activity and forsaken pastures come to bustle with row after row of dwellings. Property aspirations were confined to areas such as Marredpally,

Banjara Hills, Masab Tank, Jubilee Hills with Madhapur and Kondapur a couple of years ago. Next were colonies in Tarnaka, Bowenpally, Nallakunta and so on. Now distances do not matter much. Most are willing to commute and this is resulting in the radius for suburbs getting stretched further.

Real estate activity has gathered momentum in the city suburbs due to the future connectivity that the metro rail project promises in these areas. There is much activity now in areas located towards the south of Hyderabad stretching between Nagole Nadargul, Kothapet, Karmanghat, Snehapuri, Hastinapuram, Turkayamjal, Batasingaram, Dilshuknagar and Hayathnagar. Property rates range from Rs. 2,000 to Rs. 3,000 per sq.yd., though located just 12 km away from the city. Flats are available in these areas ranging from Rs. 13 lakh to Rs. 15 lakh.

It planned to take the Metro rail beyond Shilparamam to Sankarpalle on the line 3 and to Patancheru beyond Miyapur on line 1. In both the places, it is intended to build mega residential and commercial ventures, including Hill County spread over hundreds of acres. Nine lakh passengers are already travel everyday on the LB Nagar-Kukatpally stretch, and 26 lakh passengers are likely to travel by 2026. (N.Vamsi Srinivas, August 8)

A dozen apartment projects and 5 independent house projects are currently under construction in Mansurabad, Vanasthalipuram, R.K. Puram, Saroornagar, Nagole, Manneguda, Tatti Annaram, Almasguda. SSVS builders is constructing 15 flats in its Jockey Classic each spread over 1425 sq.ft. to 1575 sq.ft. SV Constructions is developing 30 flats in 'SV Arcade' in Saroornagar. Sai construction is building 25 flats under Sai Balaji project in Saroornagar and MRP Housing is constructing 90 flats in MRP Towers at Mansurabad. Malhar Constructions is developing 80 independent houses in GVR Colony at costs ranging from Rs. 20 lakh to Rs. 25 lakh. Jaideep Constructions, Sri Sri Estates are all developing independent housing ventures. Construction activity is also on in Chaitanyapuri, Ramachandrapuram, Snehapuri. Interestingly these areas are also famous for 'readymade houses' built by small-time contractors and sold at competitive process. (L.V. Reddy, *Deccan Chronicle*, December 12, 2008)

Acquiring agricultural lands in the city outskirts and developing them into IT and bio-tech parks, luxurious villas and gated communities have become the latest fad in the State Capital. In the quest for a dream house the urban middle class, unable to afford a house or an apartment within 15 to 20 km radius of the city, is also heading towards the outskirts. Developers with deep pockets and resources seldom have trouble in cross-checking the background of the tenant farmer or landlord whose land they are about to purchase. As agricultural lands are abundant in the city outskirts one must make sure to verify the revenue records like Khasra Pahani and Protected Tenancy Register with the Mandal Revenue Official and check whether land is transferable or not. Finding out the nature of the land up for sale is also very important. The agricultural land in question could be an 'Assigned' or Inam land which was abolished in 1997 and so this fact needs to be checked by the buyer. Assigned lands are generally lands given to ex-servicemen or to members of SC and ST communities. Hence, the buyer has to verify whether the seller does have an Occupancy Right Certificate, which is as good as a title deed. (M.Sai Gopal, *The Hindu*, December 2, 2006)

The massive repository of land registration records, a few of which even date back to late 1800s, are arguably among the country's largest collection of records of land sales, lands given in the form of gifts, mortgages and a variety of transactions. However now Registration and Stamps office is keen to make the records fully digital. Prior to 1999 all the records were in paper format. Over 30 lakh pages in the 6,000 volumes of transactions, including sale, purchase, will deeds, mortgages and others including city maps, old plans and registrations are being carefully scanned, digitised and stored in CDs for posterity. (M.Sai Gopal, *The Hindu*, January 27, 2007)

Rights given to farmers during the Nizam period are affecting the HUDA drive to remove unauthorized structures and encroachments in and around the lakes in the city as these cause inundation of low-lying areas during rains. The Nizam order, HUDA fears, would make it difficult to implement the Chief Minister's recent order to restore city water bodies. HUDA officials say the Nizam government had issued Sikham Pattas (SP)—issued in Telangana particularly Hyderabad—to locals enabling them to grow crops on the lake beds when the water level decreased. Now 1000s of acres are with SP holders; some of them sold their land to realtors who built houses on the lakebeds and shores of more than 400 lakes. According to officials 3,000 houses were indentified in Ranga Reddy (RR) district alone and 400 acres of land was in illegal occupation. Some SP holders were carrying on cultivation near Pedda Cheruvu and Fox Sagar and other tank areas. However, local politicians were objecting to the removal of encroachments, arguing that the government could not take back lands from the patta holders. (*Deccan Chronicle*, Nov 23, 2006)

Plots in 'unauthorized layouts' come cheap. Predictably, demand is huge. But, there is no provision for amenities like drainage or drinking water. Transaction in such plots should be made punishable as in some other Indian cities. Unauthorized layouts will result in unplanned development. These unauthorized layouts are of different categories:

- Plots sold for residential purposes in zones earmarked for green belts, recreation areas, open spaces, tank beds and their catchments.
- Plots sold in zones where layouts are permitted but roads, open spaces and amenities are inadequate in terms of width and sizes and with no internal development like drainage, electricity and drinking water.
- Plots sold in zones where layouts are permitted, space standards are met but no development is carried out.

Experts say buying plots except in approved layout should be made financially punitive rather than rewarding. To steeply escalate the property value of those who benefited by major projects may contribute to the funds for the major projects. (*The Hindu*, November 4, 2006).

City 'boundaries became elastic', but construction activities stayed put to a much-berated GO. Some of the snapshots of real estate in Hyderabad in 2006 (T. Lalit Singh) revisits the year's roller coaster reality ride.

- Real estate cavalcade rolls on to unexpected parts of the city outskirts and expands the property map to unheard of sizes.
- Remote corners that never figured on local maps shot into prominence as real estate agents scouted for vacant lands to cater to the rising demand.
- Unlike the initial phase of realty boom when demand for property was restricted only to peripheries of IT zones such as Madhapur, Kondapur and Gachibowli, these days one witnesses rapid strides in areas where even common amenities are not available.

- Though there are several projects that promised to transform the 400 year old city to a real modern one, not much progress has been achieved. Some plans such as ORR, FAB City that propelled realty boom to new highs, ran into controversies and got delayed.
- Places like Medchal, Uppal, A.S. Rao Nagar and Dundigul that remained in the flanks waiting for IT driven locations to exhaust themselves, finally managed to get into the spotlight resulted in a changing landscape here.
- Shamshabad continued to remain hot and many ventures along the road heading for Srisailam sprang up.
- Names like Timmapur, Pulimamidi, Mansanpally, Gudur, Kandukur, Chinna Mangalaram jostled their way to the realtors' vocabulary.
- The period from March till late November saw builders putting a halt to their projects objecting to certain provisions promulgated under the GO 86. It created unease in the industry and impacted the overall real estate situation to some extent as apartment construction was brought to a grinding halt.
- The said orders were revised few times and construction industry which in particular was peeved at the mortgage clause and deviations, did express satisfaction with the modifications done recently.
- The mid-year is also witness to a scare caused by severe shortage of construction material. Cement in particular turned dear and available stocks were sold for as high as Rs. 195 per bag. Sand and supply of stone too was hit for brief spells but industry absorbs the shocks.
- The auctioneering by the HUDA and APHB set new land price records whether it was at Kokapet or Kukatpally. The trend seemed to have slowed down a bit as the year came to a draw.
- There has been a subtle shift in the house design pattern too. Designs of duplex, triplex, row houses and villas have gained wider acceptance.
- The projects that made really big news is Casa Estebana that came up over 1.25 acres priced at Rs. 12 crore. However, one project that generated lot of noise but failed to get

acceptance was HUDA's MIG housing at Jawaharnagar. (T.Lalith Singh, *The Hindu*, December 30, 2006)

Townships are sprouting from Thumukunta on Karimnagar road to Manasanpally Kandukur on Srisailam Highway to Annojiguda near Ghatkesar and deals are sealed instantly. Initially seen suited for the affluent classes with only villas, costly duplex, triplex houses but as demand grew, row houses, apartment blocks, and independent housing too are fast picking up in these places with developers announcing ventures. With the sky rocketing of property prices—an open plot was auctioned for Rs. 58,500 per square yard recently—plots are turning sparse in the city. Choking of the city has contributed to the situation. (T. Lalith Singh, *The Hindu*, November 11, 2006)

A flat in the city on an average costs Rs. 35 lakh to 50 lakhs, while the same on the outskirts comes for a little over Rs. 20 lakhs. In the last one year, prices of land in parts of surrounding districts, that have direct access from the city, have gone up. The present prices range from Rs. 75,000 to Rs. 1,50,000 per acre, based on distance from the city, connectivity from main highway, internal access and nearness to a major project or development centre, those closer to city come in a price range of Rs. 3 lakh to Rs. 10 lakh. (T. Lalith Singh, *The Hindu*, February 24, 2007)

The real estate activity spread itself widely and brought into its fold what were then treated as 'suburbs' and redefined the contours of city sprawl and growth, new dimensions are being added to the boom with projects which were once unheard of here. By 2012, Hyderabadis, can boast of having the tallest residential complex in the world—100 storied-Signature Towers with state-of-the-art facilities. Not only the residential complex, IT parks and bustling commercial establishments and 16 multiplexes for entertainment, all at one place are being developed on a sprawling 100 acres land at Manikonda. The works on the Rs. 5,500 crore project commenced in 2007. The IT parks alongside the Signature Towers, when ready will accommodate 75,000 software professionals in modern working environment. A multi-level parking area is developed to park more than 12,000 cars on the complex premises. Apart from the walk to work concept, this will also offer the employees the luxury of shopping, dining out and entertainment within the campus. Manikonda is near to both the Shamshabad airport and the IT zone at Gachibowli and Madhapur. In the commercial zone, the project also has 5 star premium hotels of 400 rooms and a deluxe business hotel offering 350 rooms alongside a lake developed on 25 acres. A mega convention-cum-exhibition centre will also be part of the development activities planned. (M.Srinivas, *The Hindu*, July 7, 2007)

With the big infrastructure projects taken up in Manikonda, properties are now worth lakhs of rupees. In 2000, Infosys was allotted 50 acres here, then came the Urdu University, ISB, Emmar Hills Township, Wipro campus, Microsoft campus and Lanco Hills. This changed the face of the entire area. Residents are delighted as the value of their property has escalated. In 1990 the Secretariat staff, employees of Raj Bhavan and Assembly purchased plots. They bought all the 72 acres for about Rs. 80,000 and divided it into 600 plots of 200 square yards and 300 square yards. (*Deccan Chronicle*, February 1, 2008)

The much-touted Integrated Township project of HUDA along the ORR is set to become a reality with the Tellapur Integrated Township, first of such projects awarded to a consortium recently. The objective is to ease traffic congestion in the twin cities and to meet the growing need for residential, commercial and office spaces. The cost of 400 acres of land itself would come to Rs. 1686 crores that would be paid to HUDA over 3 years. It is estimated to cost about Rs. 3500 crores. But with such amount the affordability remains a question.

The GHMC is also planning to provide increased space in the city by encouraging cluster housing. This will be a boon for the congested areas of Abids, Sultan Bazaar and the old city. Incentives will include relaxation from the required road width—which can be of 30 feet and setbacks—which will not be insisted upon. Plot owners shall combine their plots and the minimum site area ought to be 1000 square metres. The scheme will encourage redevelopment of congested areas, where roads can never be widened and provision of infrastructure is becoming a nightmare due to the overcrowding. (*Deccan Chronicle*, 2008)

HUDA is coming up with some projects that will take real estate market to new heights:

- *The integrated township in Tellapur* which comes up in 400 acres is in advanced stage with big names competing to grab it. About 30 companies were short listed based on quoting the price for the entire township. Besides independent residential houses (minimum 300 to maximum 2000 sq.yds) there would be also apartment complexes, IT offices and recreational facilities. Although the developer is free to fix price for all properties, HUDA will decide the price for houses to be built for the economically weaker sections—LIG—within the township.

- *Exclusive NRI villas and golf course at Budvel* in about 400 acres with locational advantage of being close to ORR and International Airport. The will be built soon each on 1acre land with tennis courts, swimming pool and 200 acre golf course. Buildings will be of plot owner's choice from the options of Italian, Spanish, English and Indian style. The built up area will not be high—about 10 per cent of plot area in view of restrictions around twin water bodies of Himayathsagar and Osmansagar. HUDA will sell plots and select buyers through a draw; it is expected to run into crores of Rupees.
- *Hotel cluster near International airport in Shamshabad* of about 160 acres with 10 hotels—5-star, 3-star and budget hotels. Land will be auctioned to the highest bidders. The detailed project report is in process. The former 5-star, 3-star hotels are exclusively for long established business houses and the budget hotels are open for new entrants.

To fulfil the need of funds for ORR and Elevated Expessway, HUDA will use these upcoming projects that would be grounded soon to raise resources. It also plans to develop integrated townships in Srinagar and Uppal Bhagat. Kokapet auction alone fetched Rs. 750 crores to the organization. (N.Vamsi Srinivas, *Deccan Chronicle*, November 11, 2006)

The GMR group which leads a consortium that is taking up the Rs. 2,283 crore Greenfield Airport at Shamshabad is planning to build an 'Aerotropolis' in 1000 acres around the airport. 'It makes sense to do business in its vicinity', thus took shape the concept of Aerotropolis—a planned city hinged to airport. It would have multi-modal logistics support, connecting the arteries of the city proper. It would have space for offices, residential areas, exposition facilities and entertainment areas. It would have direct impact on a radius of

25 km and indirect impact up to 90km. (K.V. Kurmnath, *The Hindu*, February 24, 2007)

Construction of flats is going on in full swing around the RGI Airport in Shamshabad. Presently, major construction work is going on in villages surrounding the international airport such as Bandlaguda, Gandhamguda, Peeram Cheruvu, Hydarsha Kota and Kismathpura. The govt's launching the ORR project has further fuelled real estate activity in these villages. Realty rates have nearly doubled in the last 2 years in these areas and more than 10 big residential projects involving nearly 2000 flats are currently underway in Bandlaguda and Hydersha kota. Developers are taking up residential projects that suit all kinds of people in the villages between the Airport and Gachibowli IT corridor. Overall flats ranges from 800 sq.ft. to 1250 sq.ft. Giridhari Constructions named 'Executive Park' underwhich it is developing 518 flats ranging 1250 to 1800 sq.ft. The Fortview Project undertaken by Theme Ambience has 285 flats ranging from 1170-1800 sq.ft. Star Construction and Symantic constructions among others. (L.V. Reddy, *Deccan Chronicle*, July 11, 2008)

Hyderabad is set to witness an abundance of major infrastructure projects. HUDA is actively associated in the planning and implementation of these initiatives. A major urban project that will have tremendous multiplier effect on the city taken up by HUDA is the 162 km, 8-laned Outer Ring Road (ORR). Hyderabad Urban Development Authority (HUDA) now rechristened as Hyderabad Metropolitan Development Authority (HMDA) is committed to deliver this road costing Rs. 3,500 crores before the end of 2008, however, Phase II of this ORR will be ready by December 2012 according to the State Chief Minister (http://www.business-standard.com/india/news/outer-ring-road-phase-ii-to-be-ready-by-2012/387113/). It is also facilitating development of Radial roads project, under which 33 radial roads have been identified to connect ORR with the core city locations. All along the ORR, HUDA has also assessed a great potential for creation of living and work spaces. HUDA is going to capture this potential in the form of its flagship Integrated Townships Project. An internal survey has revealed the demand for about 20 townships altogether, of which HUDA is rolling out three to begin with and the rest in a phased manner. All the townships will have provision for Lower Income Group (LIG) and Middle Income Group (MIG) housing which will be offered at fixed costs to the people. It will also contribute in the improvement of traffic infrastructure. These include 3 flyovers being planned at Langar Houz, Dilshuknagar and Uppal. Also in the offing is an elevated express way which connects the city to the upcoming International airport, the longest flyover in the country, spanning 11.4 km *(note: now completed)*. (Jayesh Ranjan, *The Hindu*, April 15, 2006)

A special compensation package for those displaced by ORR was also announced by the State Govt. Described as the most generous package ever announced for the displaced in the country, it would cost the exchequer Rs. 1,250 crores. The affected would get a cash compensation of Rs. 8 lakh to Rs. 25 lakhs an acre besides plots in developed layouts and for land for those losing more than 80 per cent of agricultural lands. (*The Hindu*, December 9, 2006)

The general view is that if the focus is on decongesting the city, then townships should be affordable for a large chunk of population than the going rate of apartments and houses in the city. As the name suggests, integration is not for exclusivity but for inclusiveness. HUDA needs to ensure that Integrated Township does not become the 'exclusive domain' of some adding a snob value to the residential address.

RBI's decision not to cut interest rates may further add to the housing industry slowdown caused by the high cost of mortgage financing. As the rate remains stagnant, high levels in interest rates will continue and the impact will be felt mostly in the residential sector. This may also force developers in some areas to sell their products at lower rates according to the SBH. (*Deccan Chronicle*, February 1, 2008)

Tata housing was formed by the legendry J.R.D.Tata when real estate was not a transparent business. He wanted to set a trend and the company became the 1st corporate to get into the real estate business in 1984. Brotin Banerjee MD and CEO Tata Housing, says that "the slackness in demand will continue until the economy starts to improve. People have been told to wait and watch. The government needs to put money into the economy to stimulate demand, interest rates must come down to 9 per cent, loans must be disbursed faster and developers have to bring down prices." Developers have claimed to have brought down prices by 10-20 per cent. But if prices had gone up 150 per cent in the last 5 years, bringing it down by 10-20 per cent will hardly make difference. If prices fall below 40 per cent then developers will not be able to repay the banks. Prices of inputs from cement to steel had increased. Steel, for instance, went up from Rs. 20000 per tonne to Rs. 50000. Real estate hike 60-70 per cent was driven by investors and not users. He also says that the present crisis in the real estate industry will actually turn out positive as developers will focus on customers and quality. Of course, the pain in this sector will continue to stay for 8-9 months. (*Deccan Chronicle*, January 5, 2009)

Sentiment, supply and affordability are the main forces that impact the rental pack of the real estate market. While non-affordability and oversupply-led correction will drive the commercial market in India to support tenants in the short term, in the long term it will transform into a land—lord driven market yet again. The suburban micro markets have come up in response to encouragements from the government, at times by way of value addition through additional infrastructure. Huge projects were planned on relatively cheap land on the periphery of the city consequent to the real estate boom and the escalation of the land values in the established CBD. (*Deccan Chronicle*, April 10, 2009)

Andhra Pradesh government had however, launched certain flagship programmes like the Indira Awas Yojana for the underprivileged, however, it has been sullied by corruption in the AP State Housing Corporation. More than 5 lakh ineligible people benefitted from this scheme and the government had to axe several functionaries in the Corporation. "Involvement of politicians and middlemen, lack of proper supervision and greed among the beneficiaries are other ills plaguing the scheme". Fund for this scheme had been slashed in the year 2009-2010 as according to the state government the Union Government is also spending heavily on Indira Awas Yojana and Rajiv Awas Yojana in the rural areas which will provide shelter to every family in the state. (*Decean Chronicle*, August 9, 2009). However, at a later review of this scheme, the Andhra Pradesh Government is planning to scrap the Indira Awas Yojana (*Deccan Chronicle*, February 2, 2010) and invoke the Revenue Recovery Act against ineligible persons.

The state government, which reaped a rich harvest by selling land in and around Hyderabad and helped create a real estate boom, has now been hit by the ebb in the market affecting investment in land in the city. It unabashedly pursued its real estate interests through agencies like HUDA, APHB, APIIC contributing to the abnormal spurt in land values in the last four years. They are now feeling the impact of the crash in demand as they are finding it difficult to sell even prime land. HUDA's Empire project at Kokapet lowered the upset price by Rs. 2 crore per acre but still found no takers. APHB could not find takers for its Bay Ridge block.

Reasons for this slowdown not only in Hyderabad but other parts of the country as well include: the economic slowdown, the fallout of the dollar, volatility in the stock market and a liquidity crunch and companies tied up with project development. However, government agencies are not willing to give up on the market. (D. Surya, *Deccan Chronicle*, April 18, 2008)

Six new massive residential projects were launched in the city during the last four weeks by realty majors such as Prajay Engineers Syndicate, Golden Gate, Purvankara Projects, Modi Builders and Janapriya Engineers Syndicate. These companies have lined up Rs. 3000 crore investments spread over 3 years. Most of it located near Tellapur, Miyapur, Gachibowli, Madinaguda, Patancheru, HCU and Nagole. Interestingly, majority of these segments aimed at the middle-class and upper-class segments with apartments costing Rs. 20 lakh and villas in the range of Rs. 35 lakh. Despite the slowdown in the housing sector these are witnessing considerable demand. Realtors attribute the rise in demand in these segments to the RBI's policy to encourage banks to lend loans under Rs. 30 lakh under priority sector lending norms. They say it's the Rs. 50 lakh-plus segment that has the jitters, but the Rs. 15-20 lakh range is still selling fine. Moreover construction costs too came down in the raw material prices.

PES has launched 'Water Front' project in Turkapally spread over 72 acres developing 585 independent 'affordable villas' ranging from 1490 sq.ft. to 4500 sq.ft. with a price of Rs. 33.5 lakh. Golden Gate, launched its Commune in Hyderabad. It will build 3,500 world-class living spaces at price starting from Rs. 19.9 lakh offering 2 BHK, 3BHK spread over 960-1490 sq.ft. Hyderabad has always been over the top when it came to real estate pricing, always dearer by 20-25 per cent than the prevailing rates across the country. It is hightime the realty sector steps forward to provide quality yet affordable housing solution for the common people. (L.V.Reddy, *Deccan Chronicle*, November 21, 2008)

Gated Communities: A Measure of Exclusivity!

Gated Communities have been a new age phenomena in the urban areas of all parts of the world, spanning all continents. These are exclusive residential enclaves of the upper echelons of the society who go in for clearly defined and distinct residential localities where the perimeter is demarcated by a wall and entry is controlled through a gate. They are more a characteristic feature of areas which have a large proportion of nouveau-riche population, who prefer not to mingle with many people in the neighbourhood and seek certain isolation from the rest of the locality. The need for placid surroundings by these people, with least amount of social friction and also a non involvement in the mundane day to day affairs of the neighbourhood, besides a certain snob appeal that these neighbourhoods cater to, are among the flip points addressed by these localities. While the Gated Communities have distinct social and psychological overtones on one hand, they also mirror the economic profile of their inhabitants on the other, apart from showcasing the interplay of demand and supply factors in the real estate market.

Rich and upper middle class people nowadays prefer to buy villas in Gated Communities as pollution; heavy traffic and commercial activity have crept into most residential colonies but are kept at bay in Gated Communities. Professionals who get good salaries are keen on buying villas since they get higher income tax relief if they do so. There is also the fact that they face exasperating maintenance problems in apartments. Villas in Gated Communities are available at prices ranging from Rs. 80 lakh to Rs. 1.5 crore depending on the size, amenities and locality. Most of them provide 50 per cent open space, compound wall with solar energy fencing, BT roads with avenue plantation, landscape and a rain water harvesting system. They also offer health club, swimming pool, children's play area and amphitheatre. They are coming up in areas where reputed schools, colleges, hospitals, super markets and banks are located. Banks are ready to provide loans for purchasing villas as most of them are built with prior approvals from the HUDA. Also in case of violations builders generally hesitate to violate rules since they are investing huge amounts. (L.V.Reddy, *Deccan Chronicle*, April 4, 2008)

Hyderabad, which is a top notch city in the IT bracket of India is not oblivious to this rage of the Gated Communities, which are proliferating at a terrific pace especially on the outskirts in the western and north eastern parts of the city, where the better off localities in general are located.

The concept of gated community too caught up quickly. A majority of the builders have their projects drawn up on these lines.

A horde of projects are in various stages of completion along Maheswaram, Medchal, Timmapur, Mamidipally, Shamshabad and Kondapur. According to developers, though the concept initially caught the fancy of IT employed young investors, it picked up with almost all the classes. To cater to different wallets, the builders have projects with units that come in a wide range starting from Rs. 20 lakhs to a crore and more making the land almost occupied everywhere.

Layouts are also being processed at Chinna Mangalaram. The leading projects include City Square's plans to develop 5000 units spread over Moinabad, Medchal, Timmapur, Maheshwaram, Mammidipalli and Shamshabad and Koncept Ambience's plans of 'The Neighbourhood' at Gundla Pochampally and 'Casa Estabana' near Satyam Tech centre at Medchal. All this ranges from Rs. 20 lakh to a crore and more. No pollution to worry, no traffic congestions, lots of free and open space, green environs, good infrastructural amenities, malls, recreational facilities etc. have given a boost to it. (T. Lalith Singh, *The Hindu*, November 11, 2006). A gated community, in a massive expanse of sylvan marvel near the International Airport with a DTCP mega layout surrounding stunning environs is being built on 30 acres. Several industrial houses of international repute and many developers are planning to set their base at Shamshabad. (*Deccan Chronicle*, November 11, 2006)

Twenty-one gated communities with 5,000 homes spread over Moinabad, Medchal, Timmapur, Maheshwaram, Mamidipalli and Shamshabad are launched. Plots/homes are available in a price range from Rs. 29 to Rs. 51 lakh in the investment properties segment, while in the lifestyle segment, villas are available for Rs. 1 crore and above. Each Gated Community is a world unto itself with demarcated retail, educational entertainment and medical zones. (*Deccan Chronicle*, November 11, 2006)

A pioneer of 'gated community' concept in the city—Anwar Aziz says "a gated community, be it independent houses or apartments complexes, gives a tremendous sense of identity with its own spin-off benefits. Houses designed as Spanish or Italian Villas is more of a selling gimmick, a house should reflect local climate, culture, and socio-economic life and a design should give residential satisfaction". He has several Gated Community projects comprising individual and row houses in varying plot size to his credit. In the peripheral areas around the city at a radius of 20 km, the trend will be for multi-storeyed complexes including locations such as Shamirpet that was in sleep mode till recently. When the apartments in core city are sold at Rs. 1crore, an apartment at Rs. 40 lakhs in city periphery would be seen as a good bargain. But he cautions that with vertical growth made easy by doing away with Floor Space Index (FSI) and density concepts in the real estate, the city will be in deep trouble and demand for housing without commensurate infrastructure, road network, traffic planning and efficient public transport, may dip. He says with sharp rise in prices, the future is in high-rise buildings as in Mumbai. (M.L.M.Maitreyi, *The Hindu*, March 17, 2007)

Hyderabad has seen a slow transformation from being a culture of people living in independent houses to people living in apartments since the 90s. But recent phenomenon has been the sudden growth of 'gated communities' shaping up. Though they have existed in the city, its only now with the emerging young and upwardly mobile segment, there is a need for exclusive living spaces, where established, there is a need for exclusive living spaces, where established people in their respective fields sharing a common view and likeminded ideas want to live together. This has popularized the concept of GC in the city. Today they offer the best of amenities and services. Some of the newer projects are proposing to offer exceptional amenities include Hi-tec security systems, state-of the-art automation, golf courses, artificial lakes, helipads, emergency services and so on.

In the pursuit of offering quality and value added solutions for the customer, developers have been trying to blend and accommodate people of different socio-religious backgrounds and demographics into a 'one co-existing and prosperous community says I. Shyam Prasad Reddy, CEO Indu projects (*Deccan Chronicle*, February 1, 2008)

Here an effort is made to look into the social, psychological and economic profile of the residents of one such Gated Community in Hyderabad—Ayyappa Society located in the western part of the city, close to the IT hub of Hyderabad. The perception of the residents on various counts sheds light on the reasons for migrating to these Gated Communities and also the comparison that they draw with the localities of their old residence on various counts.

Most of the residents of the Gated Community under consideration are high on the scale of income and education and represent a cosmopolitan blend of language and caste types. They also seem to have a very wide field if one considers the catchment area of the Gated Community. Their previous residence could have been a locality nearby or a city in another country. They seem to have chosen this locality for reasons of nearness to their workplace, a greater security as also for the peace and quiet that prevails there. They are quite proud of the amenities and facilities which exist within the fortified space and these are very many. The physical fortressing of localities has visible psychological ramifications as well.

This study is based on a survey of the households in the Ayyappa Society Gated community in the western part of the suburbs of Hyderabad, which by itself is a high profile area. The survey was conducted through a structured questionnaire, administered on a random basis and the results are presented in this paper.

A study of Table 2.6 leads one to infer that while gated communities are thought of as the exclusive enclave of the upper echelons of the society which in India translates as a high on caste besides income and education, this is not always so with regard to all the factors.

Table 2.6: Ayyappa Society—Social Composition of Residents, 2006

S. No.	*Castes*	*Number*
1	Sikh	4
2	Christian	3
3	Muslim	1
4	Priestly Caste ***	8
5	Landed castes*	7
6	Business castes**	4
7	OBC	31
8	SC	5
9	ST	4
10	OC	20
11	No response	9
12	Others	5

Note: * Velma, Reddy, Kamma
** Aggarwal, Gupta, Marwadi
*** Brahmins

Source: Field Survey

While the castes which are considered at the top of the Hindu pantheon—like the priestly caste—Brahmins, the various business and landed castes like Aggarwal, Gupta, Marwadi, Velma, Reddy and Kamma, put together occupy only about 19 per cent of the houses in the gated community, the OBC and SC and ST communities who are placed lower down the socio-economic ladder occupy a whopping 40 per cent. Diversity or inclusiveness of communities is also seen by way of the presence of the Sikh, Christian and Muslim religion groups in the gated communities. The obliteration of caste and religious barriers in acquiring prime property is very much evident in this region.

The measure of symbiosis comes along with occupation, income and qualifications of the inhabitants. It is found that a stupendously large majority of persons staying in the gated community (Table 2.7) are software engineers (28%), followed by those working in private organizations (19%), professionals (18%) and those engaged in business (15%). A small proportion (10%) are government officials, bank employees (3%). Thus most of the inhabitants seem to be in well paid jobs.

Table 2.7: Ayyappa Society—Occupational Structure of Residents, 2006

S. No	*Occupation*	*Numbers*
1	Government officials	10
2	Private organizations	19
3	Software engineers	28
4	Bank employees	4
5	Business	15
6	Professionals	18
7	Defence Services	3
8	Others	4

Source: Field Survey

However, Table 2.8 pertaining to income patterns does not reinforce this in ample measure as most incomes seem to be understated. Table 2.9 on the other hand, gives an insight into the asset ownership pattern of the residents of gated communities. About 58 per cent own land elsewhere and 66 per cent own other buildings and all of them have vehicles of their own—a large number of them being 4 wheelers. Multiple vehicles ownership by a household is also not uncommon.

Following on from this, a look at Table 2.10 suggests that most of the people (47%) say that they travel by four wheeler vehicles, ostensibly cars and 5 per cent alternate between a car and a bike. Most of them also travel a very short distance to their workplace – 54 per cent of them travel a distance of less than 4 kms and almost 80 per cent of them do not go beyond 7 kms for work purpose (Table 2.11).

Table 2.8: Ayyappa Society—Income Pattern of Residents, 2006

S. No	Income classes	Sum
1	<100000	5
2	100000-200000	20
3	200000-300000	31
4	300000-400000	20
5	400000-500000	14
6	>500000	10
7	no response	1
	Total	**101**

Source: Field Survey

Table 2.9(a): Ayyappa Society—Assets Owned by Residents, 2006

S.No	Opinion	Land	Buildings
1	Owned	58	66
2	Not Owned	5	5
3	No response	38	30
	Total	**101**	**101**

Source: Field Survey.

Table 2.9(b): Ayyappa Society—Types of Assets Owned by Residents, 2006

S.No	Vehicles	Number
1	2 wheeler-1	8
2	4 wheeler-1	8
3	2 wheeler+4 wheeler (single units)	8
4	2 wheeler+4 wheeler (multiple units)	5
5	Vehicle type not specified	67
6	No response	3

Source: Field Survey

Sixty-four per cent of the residences are occupied by the owners themselves and 36 per cent are occupied by tenants (Table 2.12). This emphasizes the fact that most often these residences are not purchased as just another investment option, but that they are lucrative places to stay in and the owners prefer to enjoy the benefits of stay.

Table 2.13 drives home what has been said earlier with the help of Table 2.7. 52 per cent of the people are in possession of a post-graduate degree which includes 12 per cent with a professional post

Table 2.10: Ayyappa Society—Mode of Travel of Residents, 2006

S.No	*Mode of travel*	*Sum*
1	4 wheeler	47
2	2 wheeler	27
3	Vehicle	4
4	Company car	9
5	Both car, bike	5
6	No response	4
7	Others-bus, by walk, cycle/scooter	5

Source: Field Survey.

Table 2.11: Ayyappa Society—Distance to Work Place of Residents, 2006

S. No	*Distance—work place*	*Sum*
1	Nearly	2
2	Upto 2 kms	25
3	2 to 4 kms	27
4	5 to 7 kms	25
5	8 to 10 kms	8
6	>10 kms	9
7	No response	5

Source: Field Survey

Table 2.12: Ayyappa Society—Residence Type, 2006

S.No	*Residence type*	*Number*
1	Owned	64
2	Rented	36
3	No response	1

Source: Field Survey.

Table 2.13: Ayyappa Society—Qualification of Residents, 2006

S.No	*Qualification*	*Number*
1	Degree	17
2	Professional Degree	23
3	Post Graduate	40
4	Professional Post Graduate	12
5	Study abroad	4
6	Doctorate	2
7	Others	2
8	No response	1
	Total	**101**

Source: Field Survey

graduate degree another 23 per cent possess professional degree which may not be a post graduation. Thus 75 per cent of the residents of this gated community have either a professional degree (UG or PG) or any other PG degree, which is a very high level of education attainment in any cultural context. This has acted as a prop and facilitated their ascendancy on the spatio-economic ladder.

Most of the residents of gated community 63 per cent have occupied it as a result of relocation from another locality in the city (Fig.2.5 and Table 2.14), 24 per cent have come from outside the city but within the state of Andhra Pradesh, while about 13 per cent are from other states of India and one from abroad. Of the total about 10 to 15 per cent come from other upper or upper middle class localities as in evident from a thorough perusal of Fig 2.5.The rest have made it from the middle class localities.

Table 2.14: Ayyappa Society—Place of Stay Before Coming to Gated Community, 2006

Location	*No*
Hyderabad	64
AP	24
India	13
Abroad	1
Others	3

Source: Field Survey.

Most of them are relatively new to the locality – 80 per cent of them having come in within the past five years (Table 2.15) and 42 per cent within the past two years. This speaks about the recency of occupance of these properties and in all probability an upward mobility of most of the residents of this area.

Table 2.15: Ayyappa Society—Duration of Stay of Residents, 2006

S.No	*Period*	*Sum*
1	0-1	14
2	1 to 2 years	28
3	2 to 5 years	38
4	5 to 10 years	16
5	> 10 years	3
6	no response	2

Source: Field Survey.

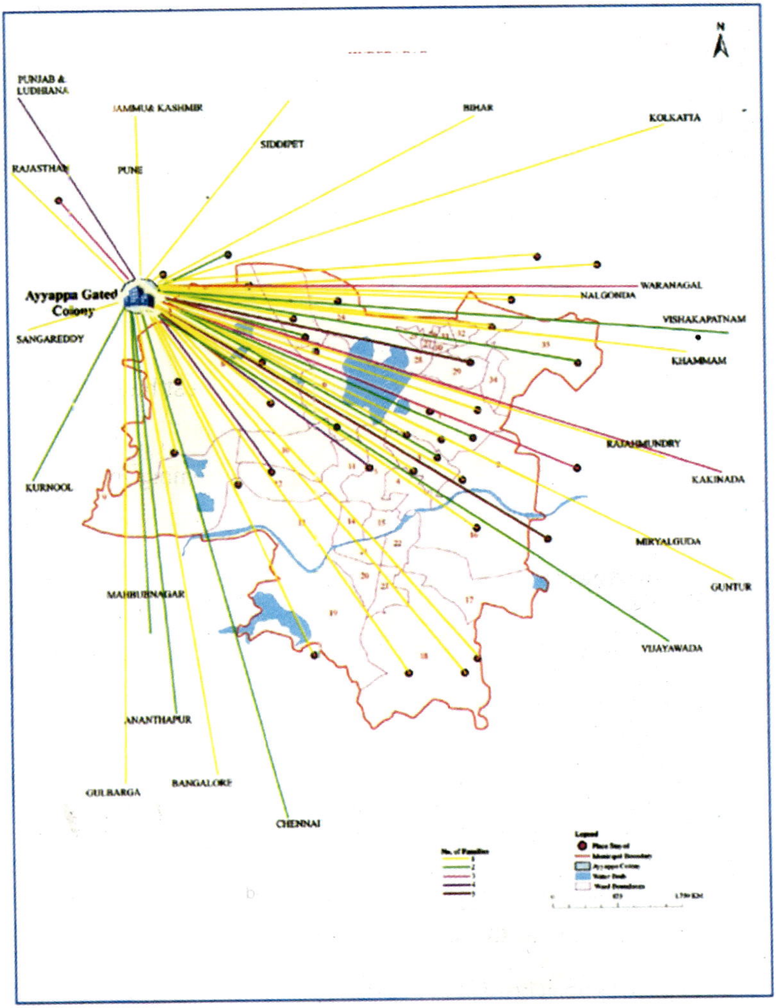

Fig. 2.5: Previous Residence of Gated Community Residents—Ayyappa Colony 2006, Hyderabad

About 75 per cent of them have their kith and kin present within the city (Table 2.15 and Fig. 2.6) and most of them are parts of north Hyderabad and Secunderabad. Very few are from other urban agglomerations units of Hyderabad and also from parts of south Hyderabad—showing thereby the social relations of this group, which

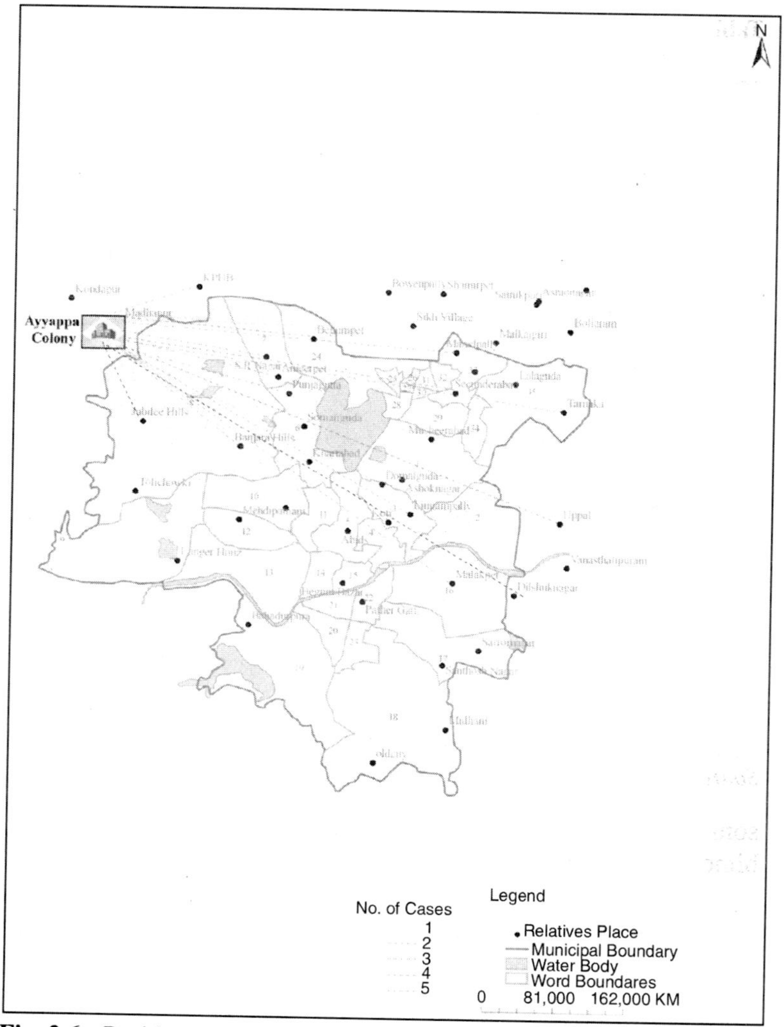

Fig. 2.6: Residence of Relatives of Gated Community Residents—Ayyappa Colony 2006, Hyderabad

bind them to other similarly placed persons in other parts of the city—the relatively better off localities in north Hyderabad and Secunderabad.

Not only do these residents have a good base of kinsfolk in the city (Table 2.16), but they also have a sustained pattern of interaction with them (Table 2.17).They visit their relatives quite frequently—

Table 2.16: Ayyappa Society—Relatives of Residents in Hyderabad, 2006

S. No	Relatives in Hyderabad	Sum
1	Yes	72
2	No	23
3	No response	6
Summary		
Urban agglomeration		**11**
Secunderabad		**27**
North Hyderabad		**30**
South Hyderabad		**7**

Table 2.17: Ayyappa Society—Visit to Relatives Places by Residents, 2006

S.No	Visits	Sum
1	Weekly	14
2	By- weekly	3
3	By-monthly, fortnightly	7
4	Monthly once	18
5	Yearly	4
6	Festivals, functions, holidays	6
7	Leisure time	2
8	Quite often, regularly	5
9	Rarely	8
10	No response	34

Source: Field Survey

some (14%) of them weekly, some (18%) monthly and others (7%) bimonthly and bi-weekly (3%).

The houses in the gated community under consideration are quite spacious (Table 2.18) are going by numbers, it is quite evident that most houses have a large number – 63 per cent having three to five rooms and 27 per cent six to eight. Smaller houses with one or two rooms constitute just about 9 per cent of the total.

Table 2.18: Ayyappa Society—Rooms Per House, 2006

S. No	Rooms	Number
1	1 to 2	9
2	3 to 5	63
3	6 to 8	27
4	no response	2

Source: Field Survey.

Most of the residents occupy this location for economic or work related reasons (Table 2.19) – 49 per cent citing official purpose and 8 per cent as business purpose—in other words proximity to the work place. 26 per cent of the people say that they occupy this location on account of a good physical environment, the measure of which are a peaceful environment or development or security.

Table 2.19: Ayyappa Society—Reason for Residence, 2006

S. No.	Reason for residence	Sum
1	Economic factors	57
2	Physical environment factors	26
3	Infrastructural factors	12
4	No response	6

Source: Field Survey

People were asked to evaluate their old and new that is the present residence, in terms of various social, physical and infrastructural characteristics. It is found that (Table 2.20) while most people said that most of the items were equally good in both the places, the outstanding thing is that the residences in the gated community were found to have better physical surrounding, better social set-up, infrastructure facilities like Gym and private parks, where as the earlier residences of the people were found to have better common halls, swimming pool facilities and religious places by a large majority of the people. The element of subjectively however, cannot be ruled out from the replies that have been given by most of the people and while they have given equally high points to both the old and new residence, it appears that while on the one hand they cannot break off from their allegiance to and liking for the old residence, the novelty of the new residence is equally fascinating.

A glance at Table 2.21 reveals that most of the residents of the gated community under consideration (58%) prefer to go on holiday tours during vacation, most of them outside Andhra Pradesh. Another 19 per cent prefer to go to their native place during the vacation period. Thus distance is not a constraint for these people, when it comes to choosing a locale for the vacation.

Conditions in the Gated Community

Residents were quizzed with regard to the conditions prevailing in

Table 2.20: Ayyappa Society—Comparison of Old and New Residence, 2006

S.No	*Categories*	*Old residence*	*New residence*	*Both*	*No response*
1	Security	10	35	37	19
2	Friendliness of people	34	14	50	3
3	Helpful nature of neighbours	41	13	44	3
4	Social relations and interaction among neighbours	36	18	42	5
5	Better physical surroundings	18	45	34	4
6	Social setup	22	29	28	22
7	Amenities				
(a)	Drinking water	11	28	59	3
(b)	Sewarage	12	29	54	6
(c)	Garbage disposal	11	26	55	9
8	Infrastructure				
(a)	Common halls	30	27	13	31
(b)	Gym	22	25	5	49
(c)	Swimming pool	12	10	6	73
(d)	Roads	18	23	52	8
(e)	Religious places	44	9	32	16
9	Linkage to the rest of the city	16	22	45	18
10	Leisure facilities & amenities such as:				
(a)	Private parks	22	32	21	26

Source: Field Survey

Table 2.21: Ayyappa Society—Choice of Place for Vacation by Residents, 2006

S. No	*Categories*	*Number*
1	Religious	5
2	Native place	19
3	Holiday tours	
	(a) Within AP	19
	(b) Outside AP	28
	(c) All over India	8
	(d) Abroad	3
4	Others	6
5	No response	13

Source: Field Survey

the gated community like the social atmosphere in the gated community upkeep, internal governance, public property and infrastructure within the precincts enclosed by the gates.

A glance at Table 2.22 leads one to infer that according to most of the residents of the gated community, there is a tradition of attending each other's function celebrating festivals together, holding meetings and discussing general and neighbourhood issues. In other words, there is a social cohesiveness in the community which is manifest functionally too.

Most of the residents (73%) are happy with the general upkeep of the premises (Table 2.23) and while 24 per cent of them pay Rs. 1000 to 1500 towards the general upkeep of the area, 19 per cent pay Rs. 500 to Rs. 1000 (Table 2.25).

A large proportion of people (44%) observe that the area outside the gates has a high rate of crime (Table 2.25) compared to those who say that it does not have a high rate of crime (24%) thus highlighting the perception of a high level of security within the gated community compared to areas outside.

The perception of the people as portrayed in this table also leads one to believe that 25 per cent of the people feel that land value is high even outside the gated community, whereas 16 per cent feel that it is not so and other feel that land values are moderate (11%) or low (5%).

Table 2.22: Ayyappa Society—Customs in Gated Community, 2006

S. No	*Categories*	*Yes*	*No*	*No response*
1	Attending each other's functions	65	7	29
2	Celebrating Festival together	60	5	36
3	Discussing neighbourhood issues	36	11	54
4	Discussing general issues	42	6	53
5	Holding any other General Meetings	43	12	46

Source: Field Survey

Table 2.23: Ayyappa Society—Perception on Upkeep of Premises, 2006

S.no	*Perception*	*Number*
1	Good	73
2	Bad	2
3	No response	19
4	Others	7
	Total	101

Source: Field Survey

Table 2.24: Ayyappa Society—Contribution per Family towards Upkeep of Premises: 2006

S. No	*Amount*	*No*
1	>500	11
2	500-1000	19
3	1000-1500	24
4	>2000	7
5	no response	30
6	no idea	10
	Total	**101**

Source: Field Survey

Table 2.25: Ayyappa Society—Perception with Regard to Crime outside Gated Community, 2006

Perception of Incidence	*No.*
Yes	44
No	24
No response	33
Total	**101**

Source: Field Survey.

Most of them (41%) also say that they have paid a premium price for obtaining residences in this prime zone (Table 2.26).

They have further reiterated (Table 2.27) that there is a protection for their families in the secluded environment of the gated community as also a certain camaraderie, bonhomie and community lifestyle (Table 2.28).

The internal governance and control in the gated community (Table 2.29) pertain to routine maintenance, security and maintenance of rules and regulations.

In summarizing this study on one of the gated communities of Hyderabad, that is, Ayyappa Society located on the western part of the city outskirts; it is found that security and the lure of a better physical environment have attracted people to this locality. They find the physical surroundings and the social setup of this locality quite conducive for stay. The better security set- up in these communities enhances their rating in the minds of the people.

Table 2.26: Ayyappa Society: Premium Price Paid for Acquiring Residence in Gated Community, 2006

Response	*No.*
Yes	41
No	21
No response	39
Total	**101**

Source: Field Survey

Table 2.27: Ayyappa Society—Perception with Regard to Protection of Families, 2006

Perception of Protection	*No*
Yes	71
No	8
No response	22
Total	**101**

Source: Field Survey.

Table 2.28: Ayyappa Society—Community Life Style, 2006

Perception on Existence of Community Life	*No*
Yes	54
No	25
No response	22

Source: Field Survey.

Table 2.29: Ayyappa Society—Existence of Internal Governance in Gated Community: 2006

S. No.	Type	Yes	No	No response
1	Routine/Regular Maintenance	74	2	25
2	Rules and Regulations	64	5	32
3	Security	65	3	33

Source: Field Survey.

The gated communities are a good representation of plural society having a fair mix of caste and religious groups. The community is thus inclusive in terms of caste and religious groups. The element of exclusivity of these communities comes when the income, educational attainment and occupation of the people is taken into consideration, where people from the upper echelons get sucked into the vortex of these communities which have become a rage in the present day urban scenario.

It may be said by way of summing up this chapter that the economic cycles have been related to the housing market. The commercial property has been compared to the residential and the ups and downs have been registered. It is noted that the owning a house is still a far-away dream as the majority of the ongoing residential projects in the city deal with only upper-middle and higher income segments. The frenzy for Gated Communities is also witnessed in certain pockets of the city especially in the western and northern part of the city. Concepts in living like 'Service apartments' 'Boutique homes' 'Designer Villas' and 'Luxury apartments' are also now common-place.

The high inflation on one hand and the continuous rise of interest rates on the other hand has led to a strange situation. Also the increase in tax rates etc. are relegating the middle class to the background in the housing market. Moreover, it is also found that people from other states of India are buying property in a big way as property in Hyderabad comes at a more competitive rate when compared to the other metros. Hyderabad also has a large number of International players in the real estate market. However, the global economic meltdown has to some extent facilitated in placing housing within the reach of the common man. Real estate majors are taking up low-budget housing projects, using modern technologies and affordable housing seems to be the catchword. There is also an increasing demand for old flats in the city. The indecisive nature of builders owing to rising costs of building material has also led to a demand for old flats. Most of the localities on the periphery of the core city have witnessed an increasing spurt of building activity. A flight of the city population to the suburbs which are low on the pollution and traffic radar is also expected and hence they need proper planning so as not to repeat the blunders of the core city. Skyscrapers are also seen as a solution to the space constraint in the city and these are coming up in plenty on the city outskirts, of course at a fabulous price, keeping the employees in the IT sector in perspective. The core city is also witnessing re-energization in some places. All this has led to an escalation of property prices.

3

Neighbourhood Characteristics

Hyderabad has witnessed an immeasurable change in its economy and attendant lifestyle as well as culture and the social structure of the people. The change is co-terminus with and is evident from the shift in emphasis from the secondary and tertiary sectors of the economy to the quarternary and quinnary sectors. Globalization and liberalization have brought in their wake an emphasis on IT, ITES and BPOs, which translate as augmented disposable income. Migration, which followed in response to employment opportunities, has colossally altered the dimensions of the city which has expanded in all directions. The upshot of this has economic, demographic and structural connotations, manifest in greater diversity and demand. The demand encompasses all types of consumer goods and services, which include besides others housing in a big way. In this study, the growth of Hyderabad is examined *vis-à-vis* the aspirations and perceptions of the residents with regard to the housing scenario as well as the outlook of the stakeholders involved in the housing market (Fig. 3.1).

Fig. 3.2 pertaining to own versus rental housing in Hyderabad drives home one fact very clearly and unequivocally. The citizens of Hyderabad have a penchant for 'own houses' if and when they can afford. This conveys among other things a sense of security and economic and emotional stability to them reflecting their traditional mindset. A glance at the attribute table for this figure reveals that 94 per cent of the localities report a preponderance of 'own houses'. This is especially so for the Municipal Corporation of Hyderabad (MCH) as well as the surrounding municipalities which form part of the Hyderabad Urban Agglomeration (HUA). However, Fig. 3.2

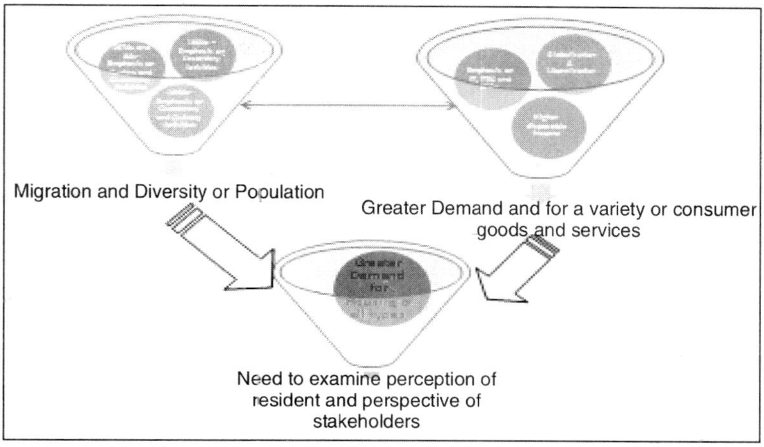

Fig. 3.1: Economic Change and Housing Demand in Hyderabad

conveys that the incidence of rental housing though low in comparison with that for owned houses is relatively more in central parts of both Hyderabad and Secunderabad. This speaks of the relatively higher proportion of mobile population, whether it is inter-regional or intra city migrants. Besides a higher proportion of rental housing *vis-à-vis* own houses is also related to higher interest rates and lower disposable incomes.

A glance at Fig. 3.3 reveals that people in central city locations are generally less satisfied with rents compared to those in the periphery; this is quite understandable in view of the high rents in central city locations owing to the presence of better accessibility and infrastructure in those areas. People in the eastern parts of Secunderabad display a relative satisfaction so far as the rent of house is concerned, so is also the case with regard to the Banjara Hills and Jubilee Hills areas and some pockets in the Central part of the MCH area like Ashok Nagar, Chikkadpally and Khairatabad. While people in the Banjara Hills and Jubilee Hills are relatively well off and rent constitutes a small proportion of their income, those in the other central city locations including Secunderabad, either occupy low value smaller houses owing to their proximity to all facilities and amenities in the city or do not mind trading off a larger chunk of their income in order to benefit from easy accessibility to most locations, amenities and facilities. Instances of the latter are also witnessed in an ample

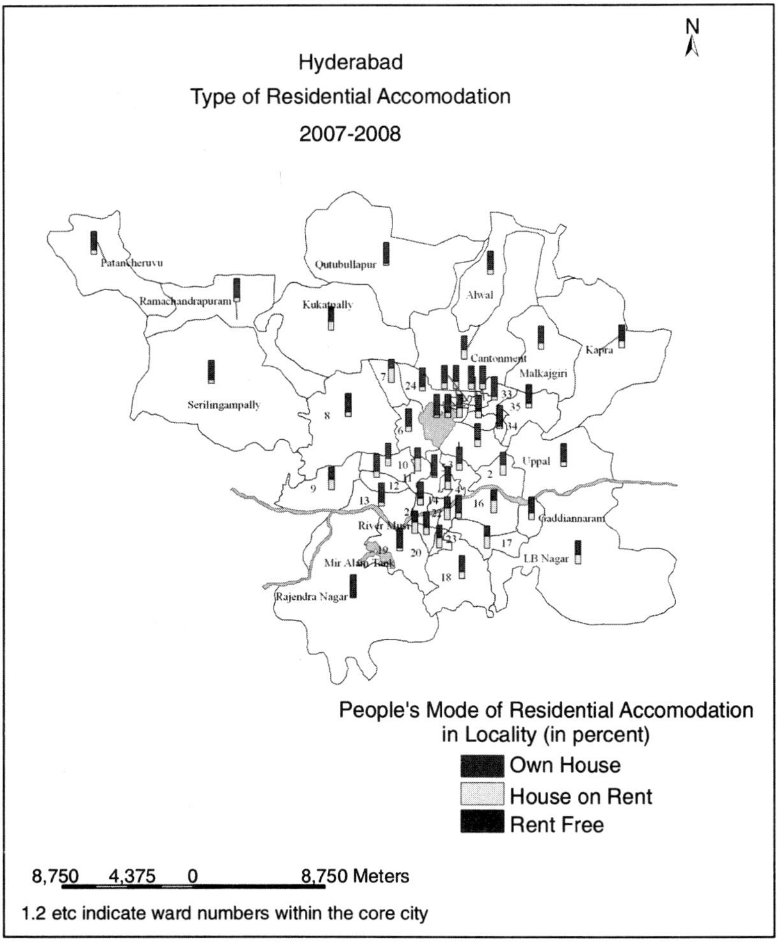

Source: Field Survey

Fig. 3.2: Type of Residential Accommodation, Hyderabad, 2007-08

measure. More than 50 per cent of the people in these areas are satisfied with the rent. However, in other areas within the MCH limits only less than 50 per cent of the people are satisfied. A glance at the picture prevailing in the peripheral municipalities reveals that most of them in the western part are satisfied with rent. The rental vales in the peripheral parts are not as high and hence within the reach of the residents, which makes for relatively higher levels of satisfaction on this count.

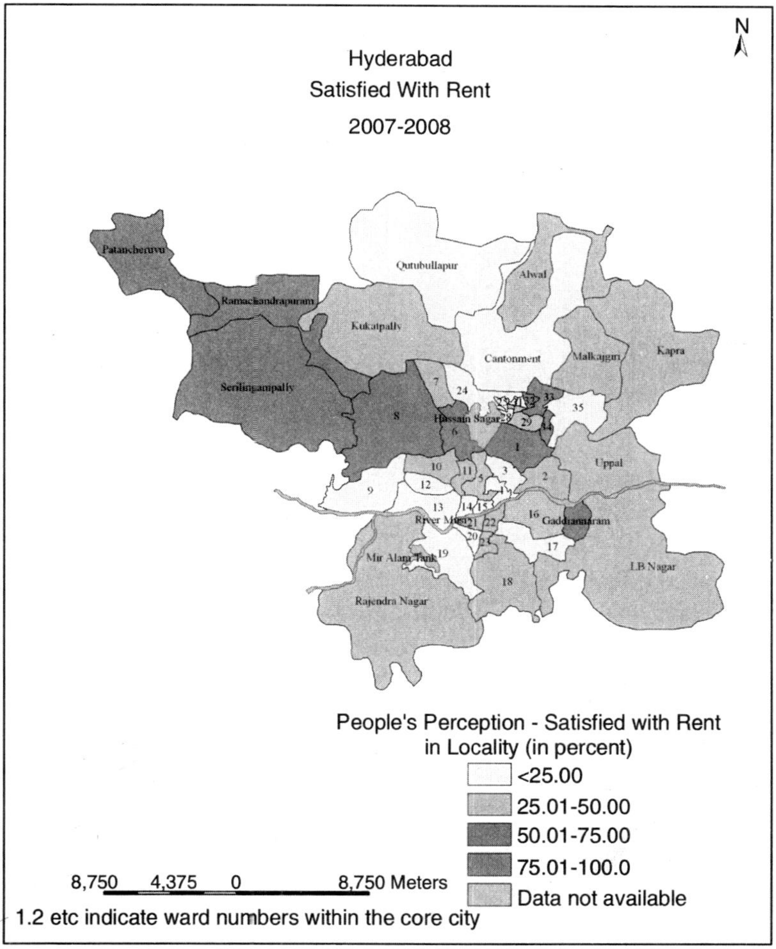

Source: Field Survey

Fig. 3.3: Satisfied with Rent, Hyderabad, 2007-08

Fig. 3.4 also conveys that most often people in the city do not have the advantage of being in ancestral houses. Those bestowed with this advantage are far and in between and relatively sizeable proportions are confined to small pockets in the central parts of the twin cities apart from Kapra Municipality.

Fig. 3.5 pertaining to the year of construction of house indicates a mixed basket, meaning that houses were constructed during all time periods in most parts of the city. While residents in many localities

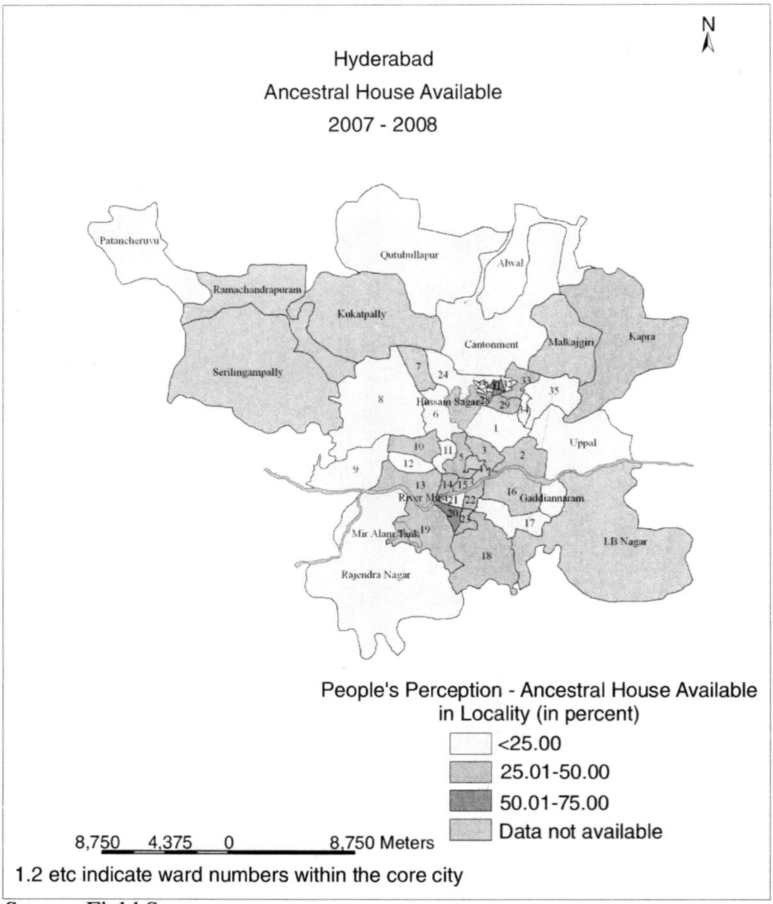

Source: Field Survey

Fig. 3.4: Ancestral House Available, Hyderabad, 2007-08

do not give the year of construction of the house or as in rental accommodations are not aware of it, certain definitive tendencies are visible. Whereas, recent constructions i.e. in the years 2003-2007 mark almost all parts of the city, those in the eastern parts and more so the peripheral municipalites display this characteristic more indicating in all likelihood that these are the areas of recent settlement to a large extent. It is also found that a large proportion of houses in the central parts of Hyderabad and Secunderabad have been constructed before 1967 vouching for the fact that these are the old

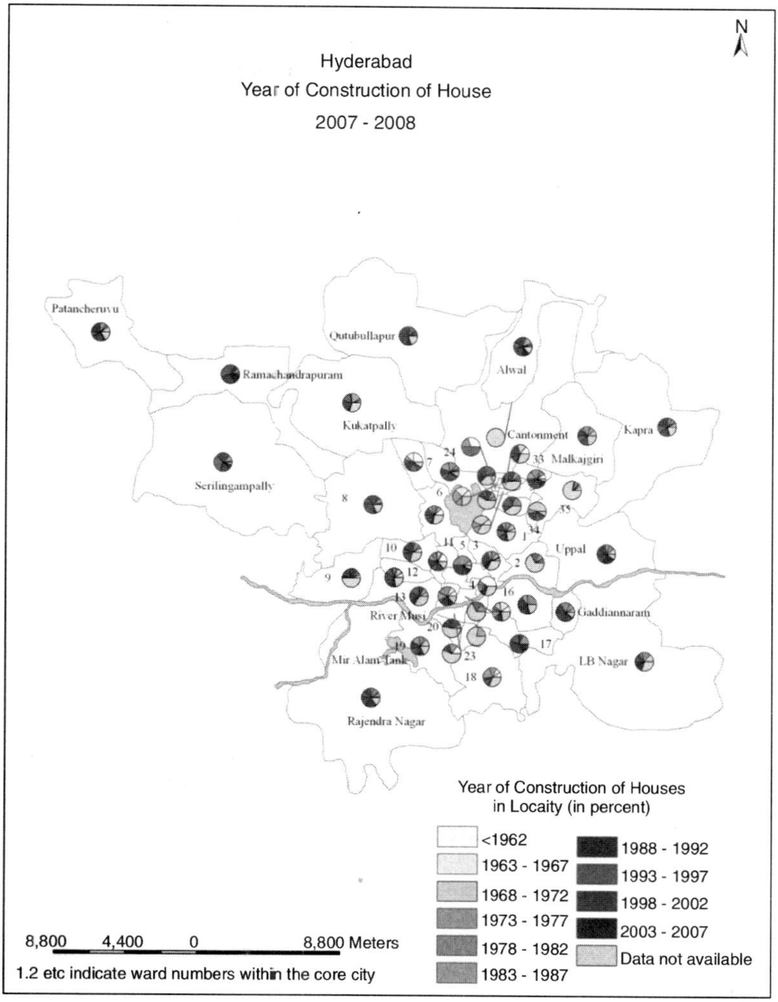

Source: Field Survey

Fig. 3.5: Year of Construction of House, Hyderabad, 2007-08

settled parts of the city. The peripheral municipalities display a larger proportion of constructions in the period after the 1980s. This tendency seems to be magnified in municipalities like Serilingampally which houses Madhapur (the IT hub of Hyderabad—which developed only in the post Globalization era in a major way).

A look at Fig. 3.6 reveals that of the houses with 1 to 3 rooms,

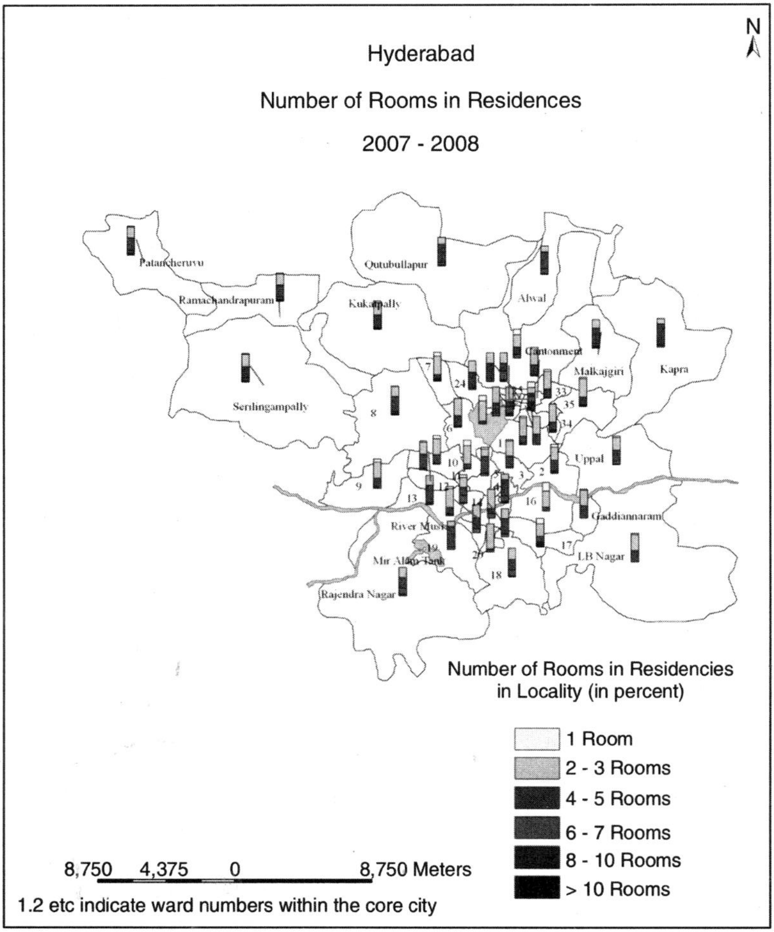

Source: Field Survey

Fig. 3.6: Number of Rooms in Residences, Hyderabad, 2007-08

most are located in the MCH area, apart from some in the Cantonment, Gaddi Annaram, L.B. Nagar and Uppal, the latter three colonies being of a middle level socio economic grade. It is pertinent to mention here that the largest majority of the houses (45.85) in the city have two to three rooms (Table 3.1) followed by those with four to five rooms (38.9). A glance at the attribute table reveals that 4-5 rooms in a house is the modal class in 27 per cent of the city units surveyed. These include Banjara- Jubilee Hills, Begumpet, Abids, Sultan Bazar,

Table 3.1: Hyderabad: Number of Rooms in Residences, 2007-2008

Number of Rooms in House	*Percent of Houses*
1	4.68
2-3	45.85
4-5	38.9
6-7	7.27
8-10	2.66
>10	0.63

Source: Field Survey.

Devibagh, Doodbowli and Gowliguda in the MCH limits and Rajendranagar, Malkajgiri, Kapra, Ramachandrapuram, Patancheru, Qutbullapur and Alwal in the peripheral municipalities. In fact a glance at the attribute table also conveys that ward 8, which houses the Banjara and Jubilee Hills area, displays a tendency where about 94 per cent of the houses have more than 3 rooms. This speaks about the relative exclusivity of this ward and the localities therein, so far as the spaciousness of accommodation is concerned. It is also evident from Fig. 3.5 that larger houses with more than six rooms are located in the peripheral municipalities.

Figs. 3.7, 3.8 and Fig. 3.9 depict the spatial pattern of sources of funding for building houses in the city. It is evident from Fig. 3.7 that people in many localities have made use of their savings for building houses. This is more so in the CBDs of Hyderabad and Secunderabad, which house the traditional population, who pool in their own resources to build houses and may be disinclined to avail loans even if they are available. This may also be extensively the case with Uppal on the eastern periphery of the city and Alwal on the northern periphery. The western part of the city also has a preponderance of such groups in traditional areas like Devi Bagh, Doodh Bowli, Mehdipatnam and Rajendranagar. Besides, some of the affluent citizens in Banjara Hills, Jubilee Hills and Khairatabad, prefer to invest their own resources in the real estate sector. Relatively less number of people in L.B. Nagar and Kapra depend on savings for house construction. Those in L.B. Nagar supplement their fund with loans from formal lending agencies, like government, banks, housing finance sources, etc; while those in Kapra supplement it with loans from local credit sources that are available (Fig. 3.8 and 3.9). The preponderance of employees in the former case makes for their dependence on formal sources of funding to some extent. It is also found (Fig. 3.9) that a relatively large, though not sizeable proportion

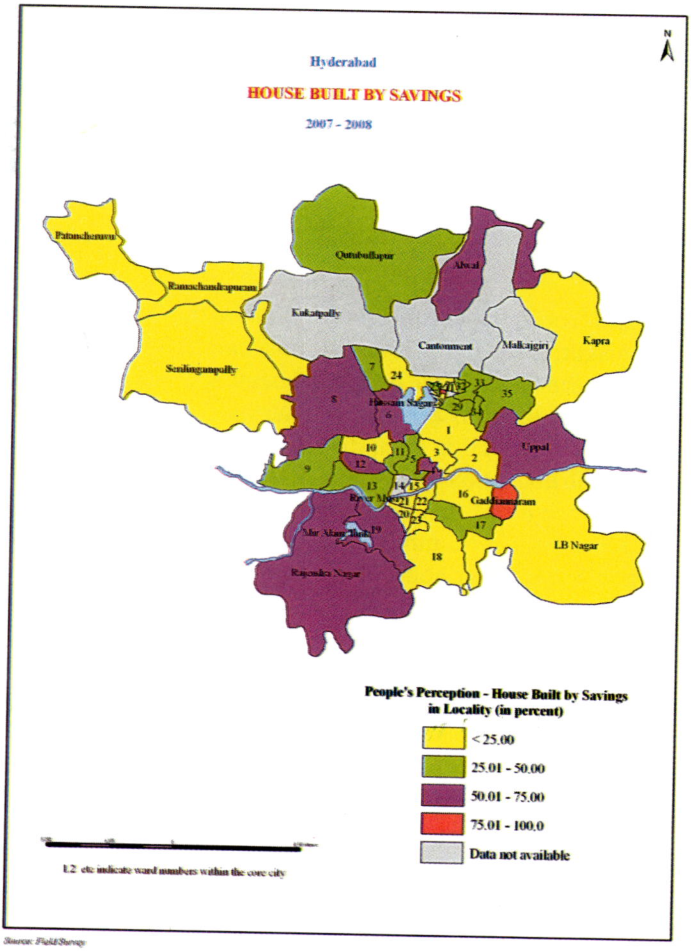

Source: Field Survey

Fig. 3.7: House Built by Savings, Hyderabad, 2007-08

of people in the central parts of Hyderabad and Secunderabad constituting 14 and 24 per cent of the cases respectively, rely on local credit sources. The traditional nature of work of these people makes for their dependence on informal sources of funding. This however is notwithstanding the fact that people in these parts also rely on funds from formal sources of funding (Fig. 3.8). A summary picture of the scenario present in Figs. 3.7, 3.8 and Fig. 3.9 is presented in

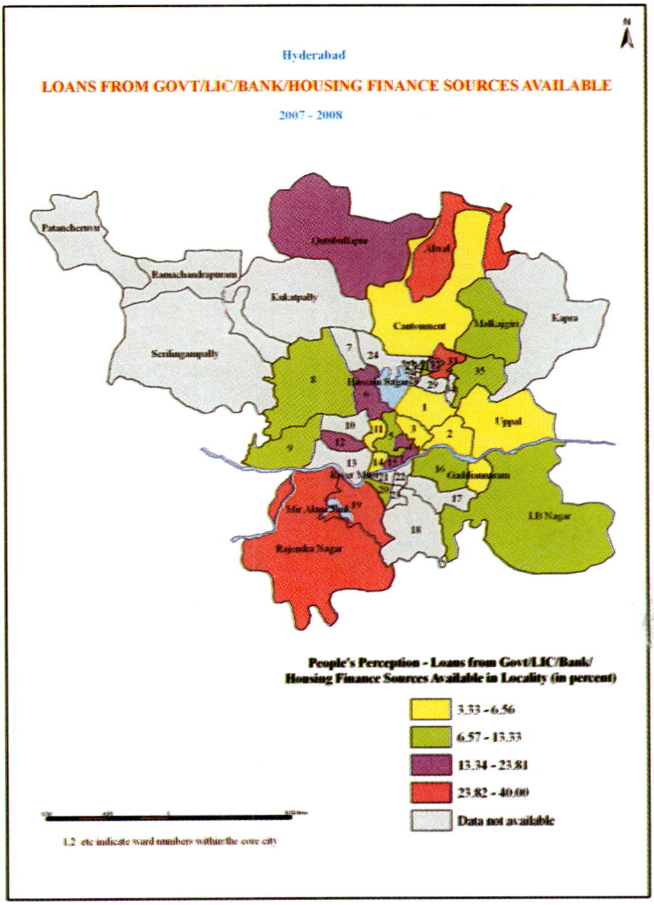

Source: Field Survey

Fig. 3.8: Loans From Govt/LIC/Bank/Housing Finance Sources Available for house construction, Hyderabad, 2007-08

Fig. 3.10 and it gives a synoptic view of the housing finance situation. It is found that people in general rely on savings for house construction, though those localities which have employees in a large measure rely on formal sources of finance and those which are traditional or house the relatively new migrants into the city as also those who are not placed very high on the socio economic scale rely on local credit sources.

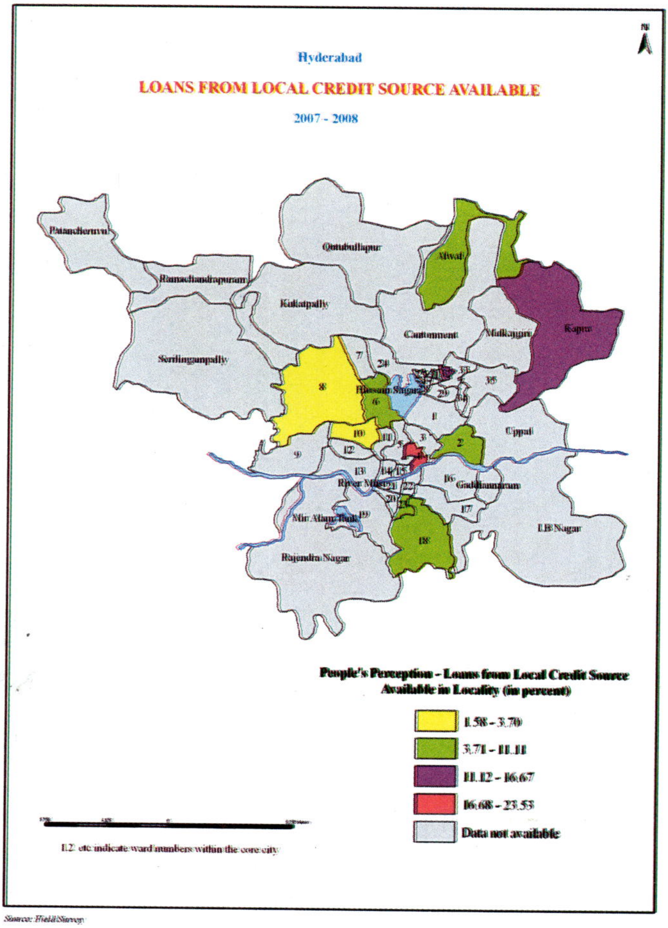

Source: Field Survey

Fig. 3.9: Loans from Local Credit Source Available for house construction, Hyderabad, 2007-08

A glance at Figs. 3.11 and 3.12 indicates that most people depend on friends and relatives for search of rental housing indicating that traditional structures are in place in most localities. The south eastern part of the city manifests this tendency to a large extent and the rest of the city presents an assorted picture with some areas having a greater dependence on relatives and friends and some less so. In some instances self-search complements and supplements the mode of

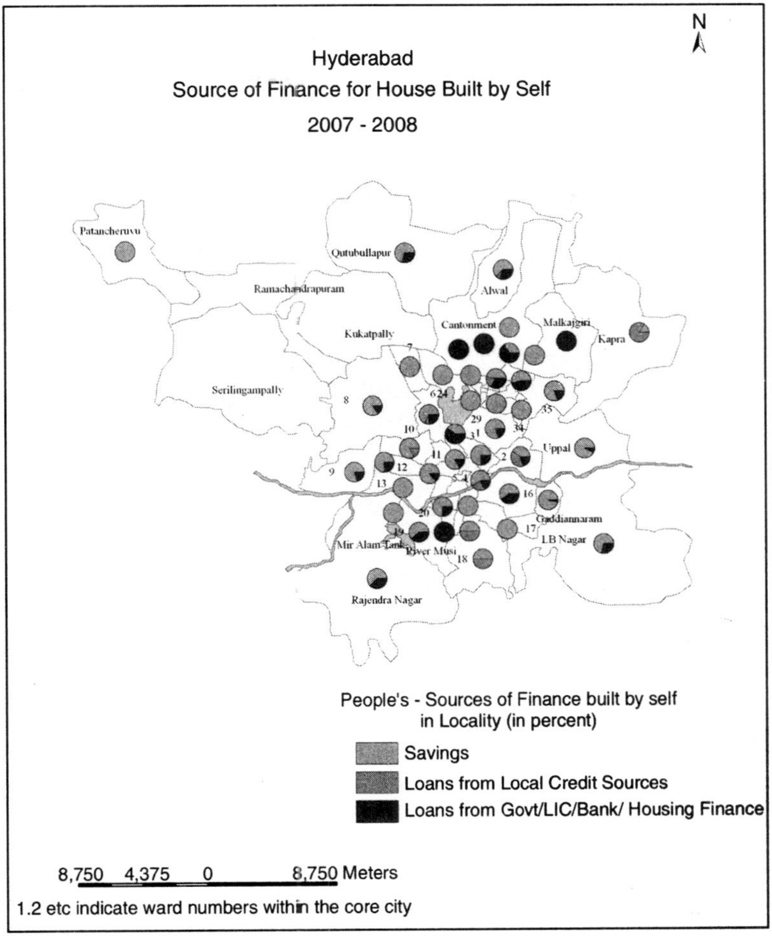

Source: Field Survey

Fig. 3.10: Source of Finance for House Built by Self, Hyderabad, 2007-08

search for rental accommodation. Such localities incidentally are more in the core city (where people have stayed over a longer period of time) rather than the peripheral municipalities. A glance at the attribute table for 'search for rental accomodation' indicates that very few if any people depend on press advertisements and real estate agents to avail rental accommodation.

An analysis of the reason for change in residence in the past five years brings out certain dominant factors. It is found that larger

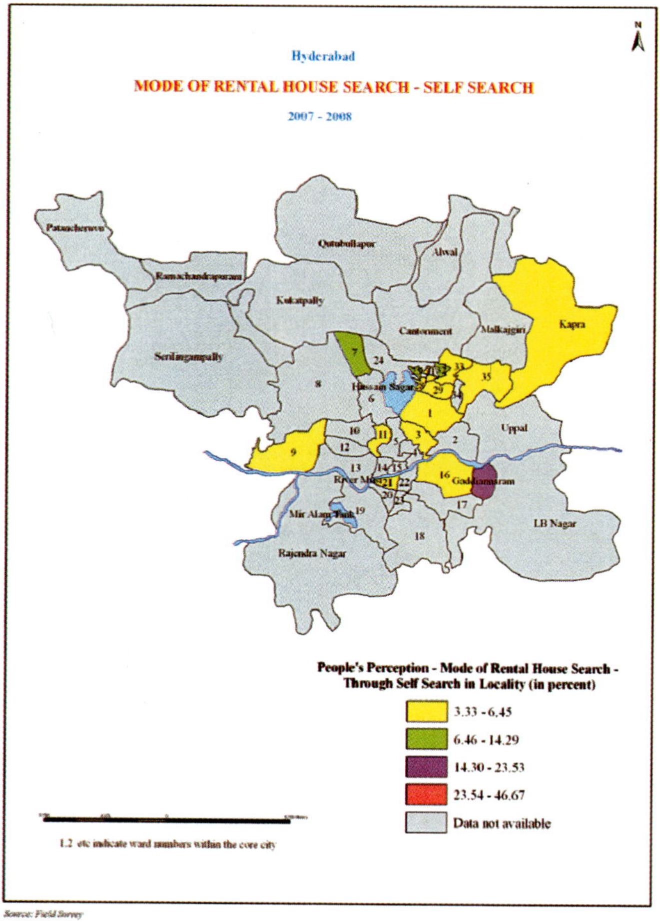

Source: Field Survey

Fig. 3.11: Mode of Rental House Search-Self Search, Hyderabad, 2007-08

accommodation, better locality and occupational mobility are the chief reasons for the shift of residence, the reasons, however, are not cited mutually exclusively by the respondents i.e. sometimes a combination of reasons are cited for the move (Fig. 3.13, 3.14 and Fig. 3.15). It is found that larger accommodation is more the drawing factor in the peripheral localities, where people seem to have migrated to the peripheral localities because of spacious accommodation available there. This is the case in the eastern as well as the western peripheries

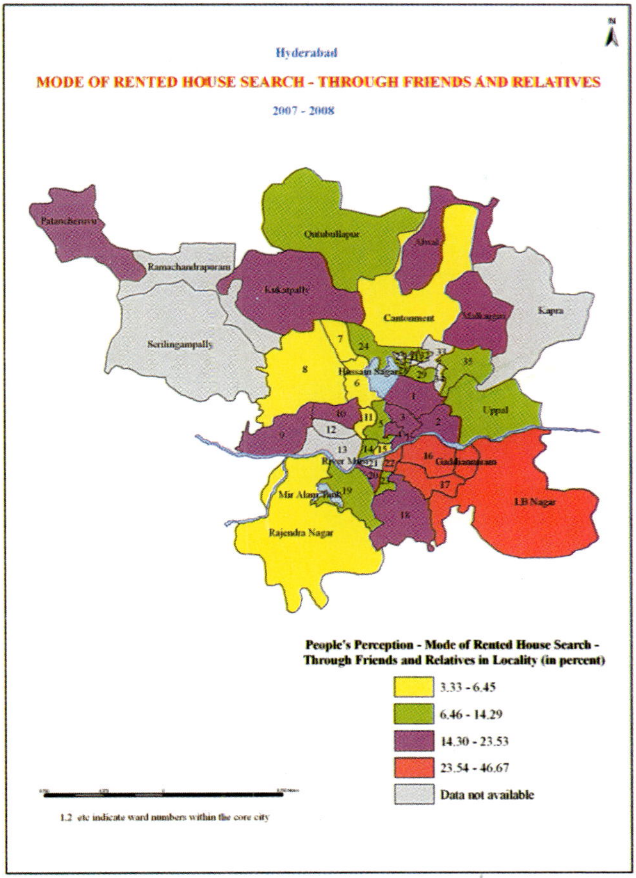

Source: Field Survey

Fig. 3.12: Mode of Rental House Search—Through Friends and Relatives, Hyderabad, 2007-08

of the city (Fig. 3.13). People have most likely escaped crammed locations to occupy houses in these localities, many of which were upcoming localities five years back from the time of survey. A miniscule proportion of the population seems to have migrated to places in the core city for similar reasons. Citizens have also rated these localities as better than others and have cited this as one of the reasons for opting to stay there. Apart from them even places like Banjara, Jubilee Hills, Ashok Nagar, Chikkadpally and Rajendranagar

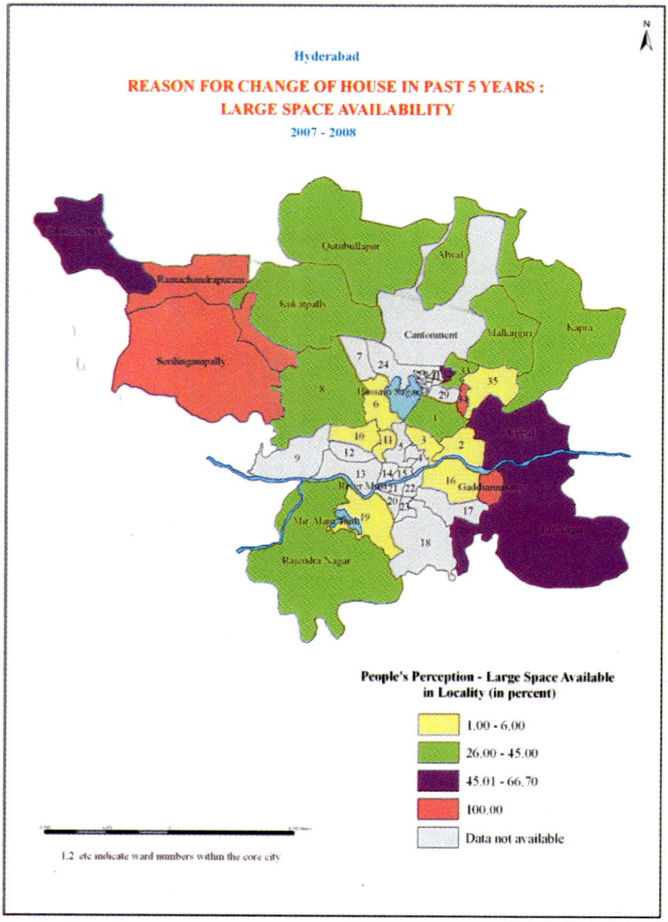

Source: Field Survey

Fig. 3.13: Reason for Change of House in Past 5 years: Large Space Availability, Hyderabad, 2007-08

are cited as 'Better Localities' and reasons for shifting residence to them in the last five years (Fig. 3.14). Generally, speaking a lesser proportion of people cite places in the core city as being better localities. On a different measure many of these localities seem to wanting from the point of view of the physical, social or built environment and hence the relatively lower rating with regard to residential preference.

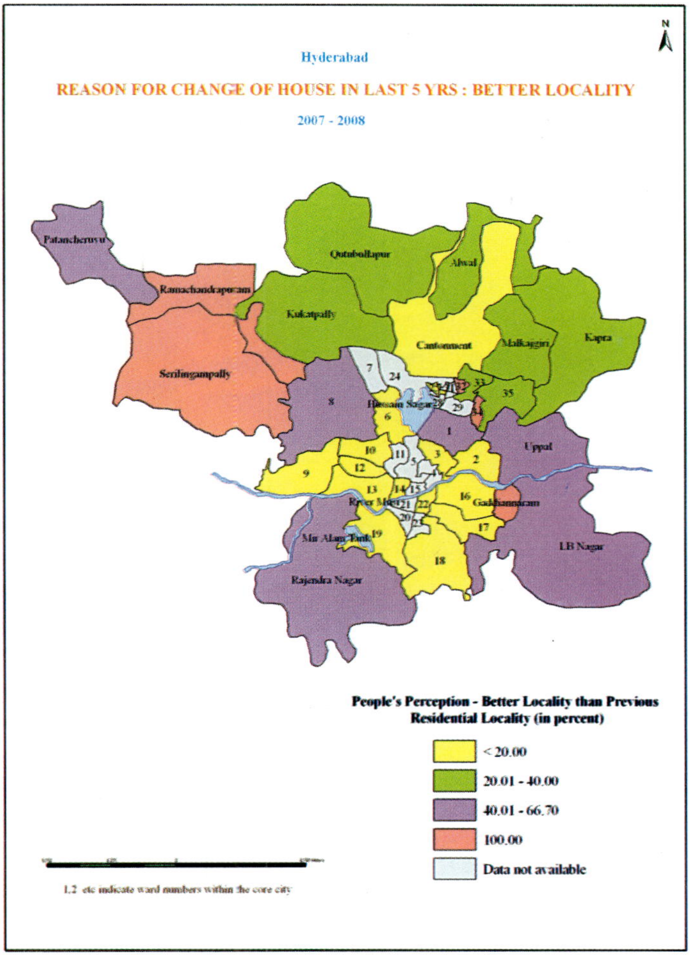

Source: Field Survey

Fig. 3.14: Reason for Change of House in Past 5 years: Better Locality, Hyderabad, 2007-08

Occupational mobility (Fig. 3.15) is by and large the reason for change in residence in the past five years in the peripheral localities than in the core city. It is also noted that the in- migrant population is staying in the peripheral parts of the city, more so close to the industrial areas and the IT centres which are the main providers of employment to them.

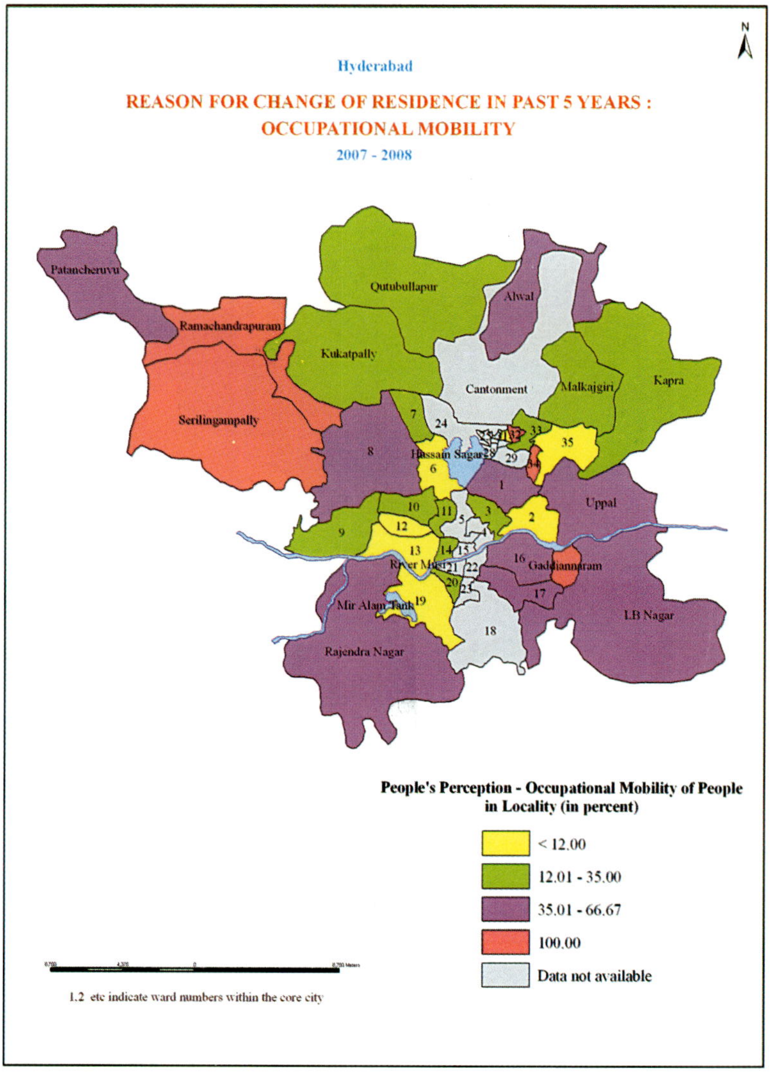

Source: Field Survey

Fig. 3.15: Reason for Change of Residence in Past 5 years: Occupational Mobility, Hyderabad, 2007-08

Fig. 3.16 pertaining to the plan of the residents to stay in their residential locality conveys an overall sentiment where most people want to stay lifelong in their locality. However, there are shades of

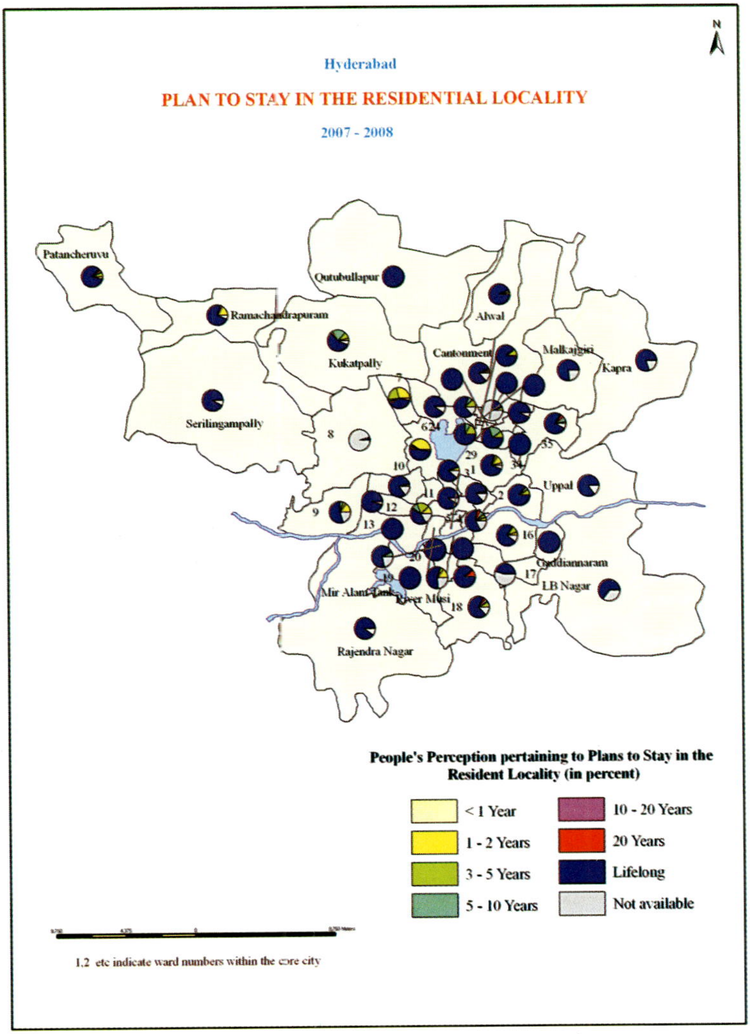

Source: Field Survey

Fig. 3.16: Plan to Stay in the Residential Locality, Hyderabad, 2007-08

variation when it comes to the minutiae. A large majority of the people in south Hyderabad prefer to stay lifelong in their locality. People in central and to some extent in the western part of the city exercise a medley of options so far as choice with regard to duration of stay in the city is concerned. The nature of the jobs of some of them may

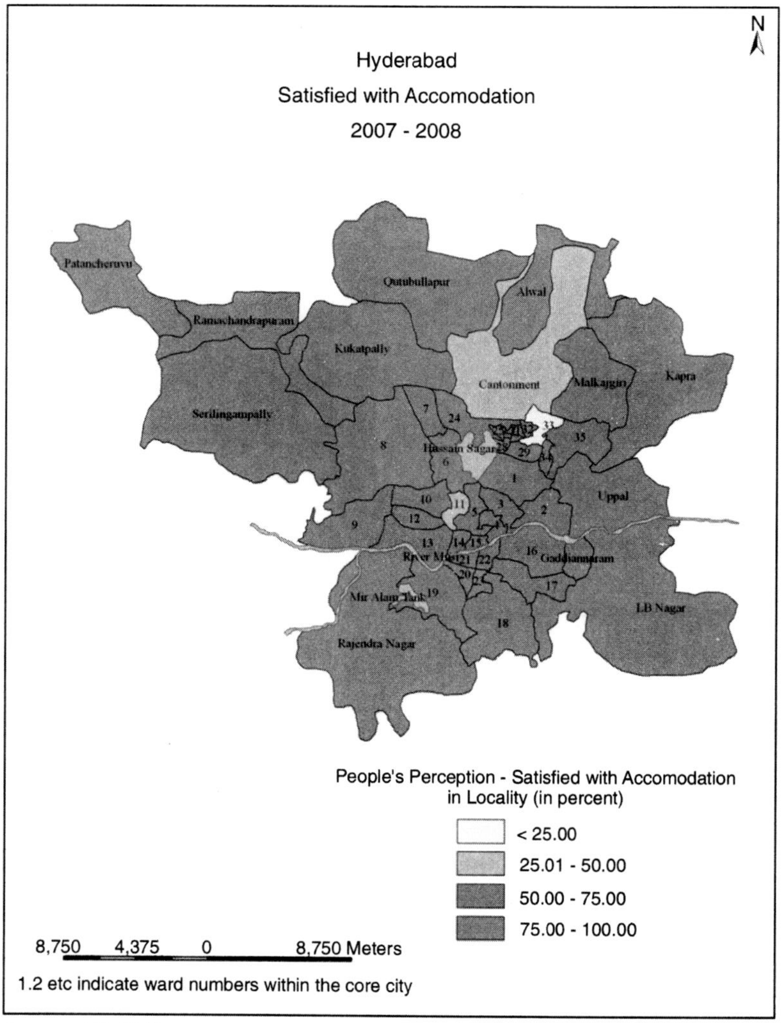

Source: Field Survey

Fig. 3.17: Satisfied with Accommodation, Hyderabad, 2007-08

warrant this kind of an option—where quite a few of them are in transferable government jobs or keep their options open with regard to occupational mobility. Many of them cite 1 to 2 years of expectancy of stay or that of 5 to 10 years in keeping with their tenure till the next transfer or their need to continue in the present job.

A glance at Fig 3. 17 drives home the fact that people are by and

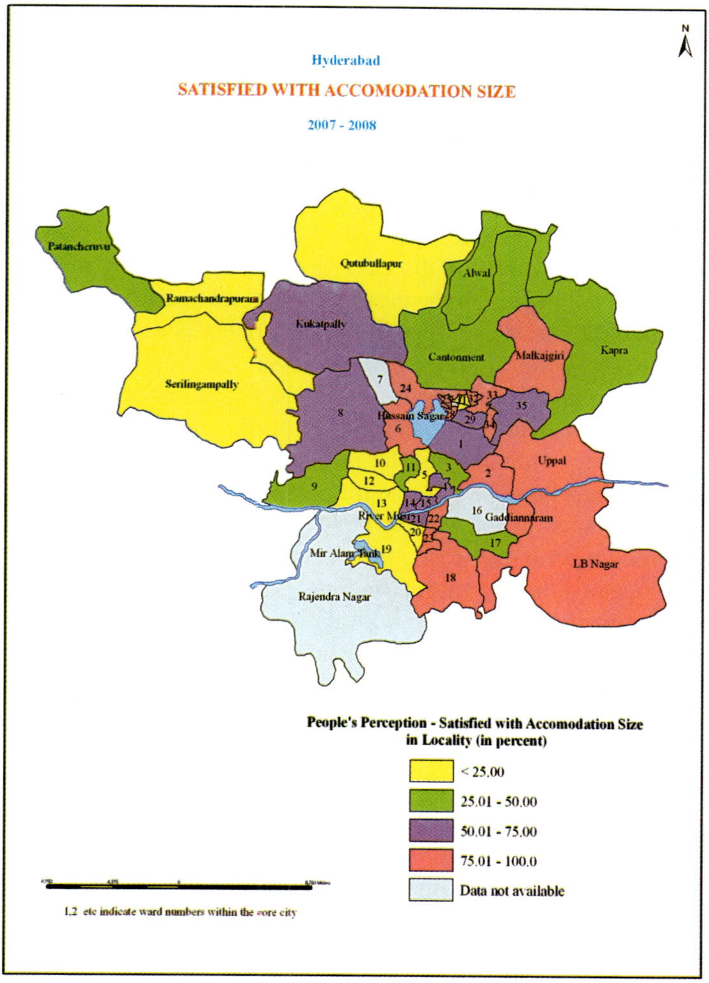

Source: Field Survey

Fig. 3.18: Satisfied with Accommodation Size, Hyderabad, 2007-08

large immensely satisfied with their accommodation in most parts of the city constituting almost 92 per cent of the units surveyed. It is only in West Marredpally along with Erukula Basti in the Secunderabad part of the twin cities that people seem to be visibly dissatisfied with accommodation. The existence of the slum with its attendant problems could be an explanatory factor in this case; otherwise people in the

Cantonment and Red Hills display a slight measure of dismay on this count, which could be explained in terms of their higher expectations. The two sets of cases explained above fall in two disparate groups at two ends of the social spectrum and yet express a similar displeasure at the accommodation that they are saddled with.

Fig. 3.18 pertaining specifically to satisfaction with regard to accommodation size conveys that while people in the municipalities on the western peripheral areas are not much satisfied with the size of accommodation, those on the eastern periphery are very much so. A majority of the houses in the eastern peripheral municipalities belong to the middle class, while those in the western peripheral municipalities belong to the lower middle class. However, so far as localities within the MCH area are concerned, it is found that there is an element of discontent in a section spanning a large portion of the central part and extending into some parts of the core area of Secunderabad too. This belt also spans large parts of south Hyderabad or the old city as it is called. A glance at the master table reveals that the actual size of accommodation is not essentially related with satisfaction on that count, meaning thereby that at times people living in small, even single room tenements are satisfied with the size of accommodation and at times even those residing in larger houses of six rooms or more also are not satisfied with the size of accommodation. It has been observed that most of these people who seem satisfied are at a lower level on the socio economic ladder, working as tailors, carpenters, auto drivers or labourers. They have an educational level which is equal to or less than Intermediate and a monthly income in the vicinity of Rs. 2000 to Rs. 5000. Also quite interestingly 74 per cent of them live in rented houses. On the contrary, many of those staying in larger houses of even up to 8 rooms and engaged in business or in well paid government jobs or working as doctors etc. and staying in posh locations are not satisfied with the size of their accommodation. This has a lot to do with the relative sensitivity of people who are well placed in society and are not willing to handle even the slightest displeasure or irritants. Conversely those lower down the socio-economic ladder are more resilient and adaptable and do not have many complaints, among other things, with regard to their living conditions, environment and accommodation.

Though the people are generally satisfied with the accommodation that they have, they do not display a similar level of satisfaction when it comes to the locations (Fig. 3.19) they live

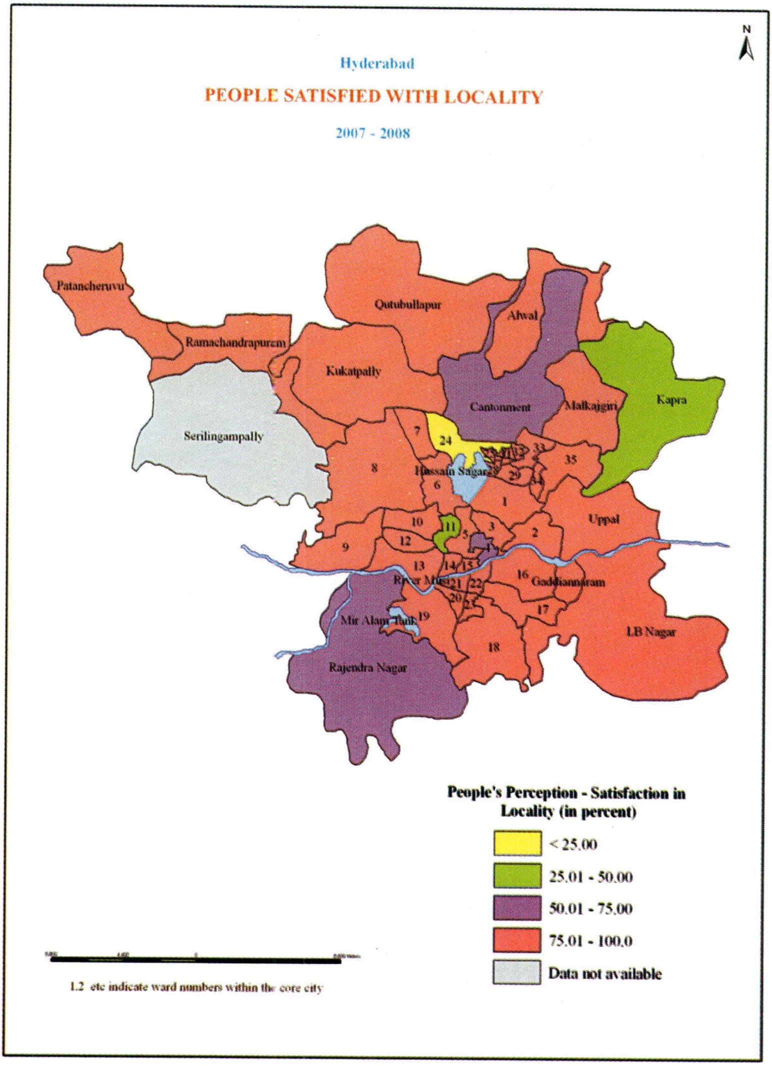

Source: Field Survey

Fig. 3.19: People Satisfied with Locality, Hyderabad, 2007-08

in. While people in central city locations and those on the eastern and northern periphery of the city are generally satisfied when it comes to their perception with regard to location, this is not so with

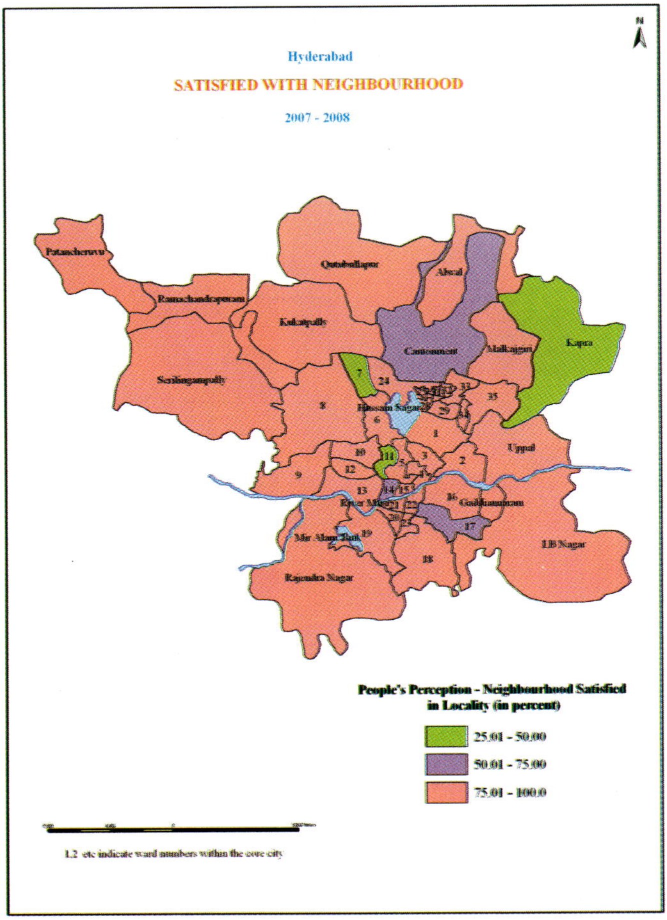

Source: Field Survey

Fig. 3.20: Satisfied with Neighbourhood, Hyderabad, 2007-08

those on the southern periphery of the city, especially Rajendranagar and Kapra Municipality in the north east. Those in Begumpet, in close vicinity to Hussain Sagar lake, in the heart of the city, also display dismally low levels of satisfaction with their location. It is evident from the attribute table of this figure (Fig. 3.19) that not even 10 per cent of the respondents are satisfied with the locality and they aver that the facilities in the locality are inadequate. Besides, the stench from the lake is also obnoxious at times

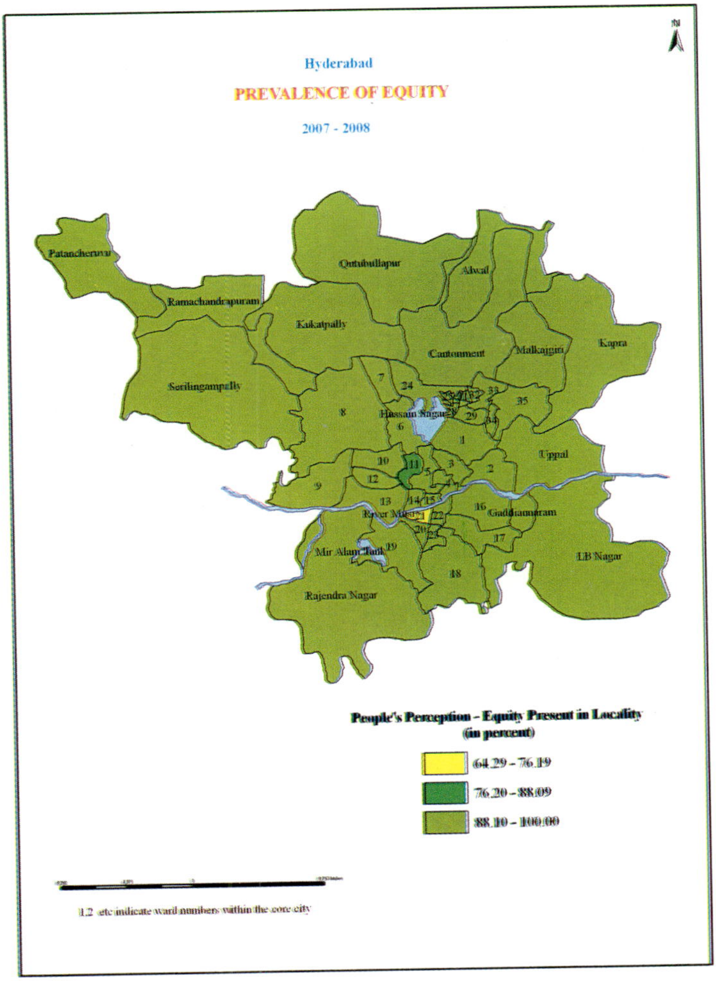

Source: Field Survey

Fig. 3.21: Prevalence of Equity, Hyderabad, 2007-08

especially during the summer season. Problems with regard to drainage and water supply have also tinted the response of the respondents in Kapra, as is again imminent from the attribute table of this figure (Fig. 3.19). This area also has an unbearable smell at times which is related to the industries located in this area.

Fig. 3.20 pertaining to the satisfaction of the respondents with

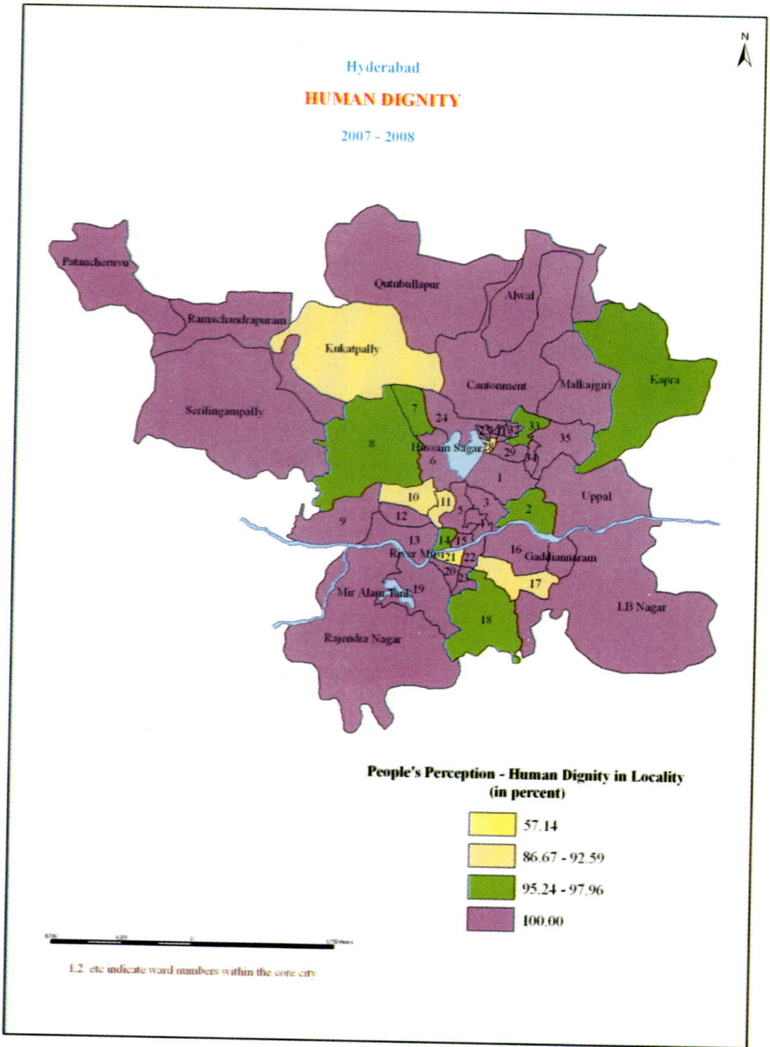

Source: Field Survey

Fig. 3.22: Human Dignity, Hyderabad, 2007-08

regard to neighbourhood, also points out a relatively high dissatisfaction of the people of Kapra. Low level of satisfaction is relatively more in the eastern part of the city and some locations in the central parts like the industrial and institutional segments in Sanatnagar and Red Hills. Quite interestingly, people in central belts spanning large extents in

Secunderabad, North Hyderabad and South Hyderabad express a high level of satisfaction with regard to their neighbourhoods.

Fig. 3.21 pertaining to satisfaction of the residents with regard to equity reveals that a surprisingly large majority of the people (in 96% of the study units) are extensively satisfied on this count and feel that there is even-handedness in the social and economic environment as also the housing scenario about which they were specifically quizzed. However, those in Red Hills and Gulzar House, in the central part of Hyderabad, display relatively low values yet they are high when the absolute measure of the variable is taken into consideration. Thus, fairness in dispensation is unmistakeably portrayed.

Fig. 3.22 pertaining to Human Dignity illustrates that 100 per cent of the people in 73 per cent of the localities find that human dignity is maintained in the locality of their residence. In fact the rating on this variable is high in most of the localities and the lowest of the low values is 57.14 in Gulzar House, which is relatively low down on the economic scale. 86.67 to 92.59 of the people in Vijaynagar Colony, Red Hills, Saroornagar, Ranigunj and Kukatpally are satisfied with regard to the maintenance of Human Dignity and 95.24 to 97.96 per cent of the people in Banjara, Jubilee Hills, Ameerpet, Amberpet, Goshamahal Barkas and Kapra articulate this sentiment. Thus, barring stray cases a sizeable majority of the people report that human dignity is upheld in their localities.

The picture presented above is by and large mirrored in Fig. 3.23 which shows the prevalence of Social Justice, in the locality with regard to housing, as it is perceived by the people. The gradation of the localities by and large remains the same, though the intensity of variation so far as the affirmation on this count is concerned is marginally scaled down in this figure. In most cases it is found that it is either the very affluent or those at the other extreme of the economic scale, who are not as well satisfied with the dispensation of Social Justice or the prevalence of Human Dignity. Thus, it is either those Below Poverty Line (BPL) who do not have much of an expectation or those who have higher levels of education and income and hence display higher levels of anticipation with regard to fair play in dispensation at various levels including housing.

Fig. 3.24 depicts a sense of solidarity among the residents in the locality. The picture presented by this variable is also not much different from that presented in the earlier figures. It appears that in 75 per cent of the units under study 96.78 to 100 per cent of the

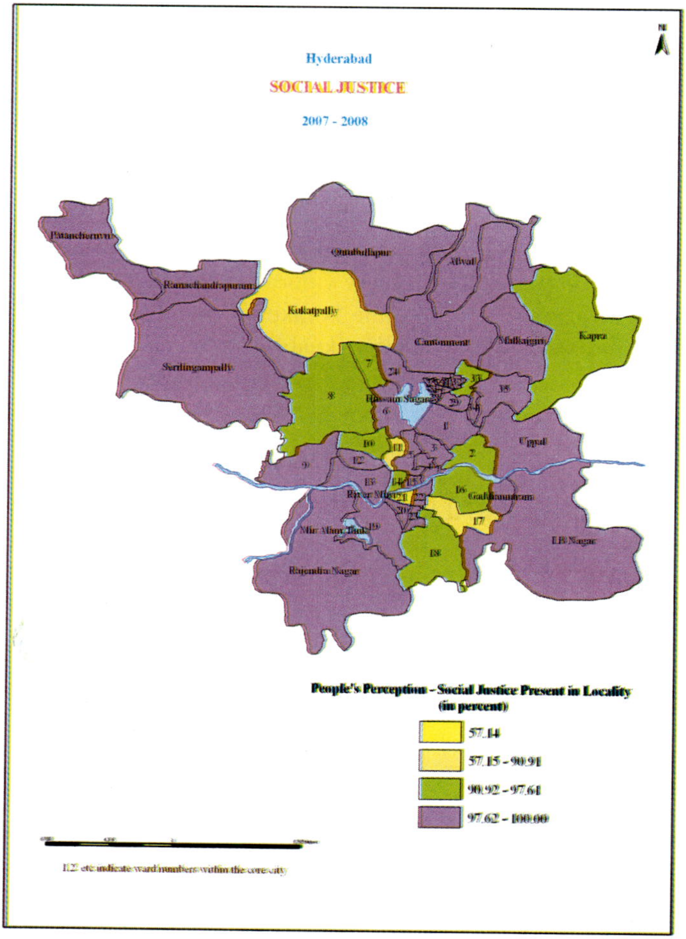

Source: Field Survey

Fig. 3.23: Social Justice, Hyderabad, 2007-08

people feel that there is a sense of solidarity among the housing units in the locality.

Fig. 3.25 illustrates the freedom of choice in residential location. About 71 per cent of the localities report a 100 per cent free choice so far as housing is concerned. The rating of localities is quite high so far as this variable is concerned. The least is 50 per cent in Gulzar House, followed by Vijay Nagar Colony, Red Hills, Gowliguda, Saroornagar, Ranigunj and West Marredpally along with Erukala Basti

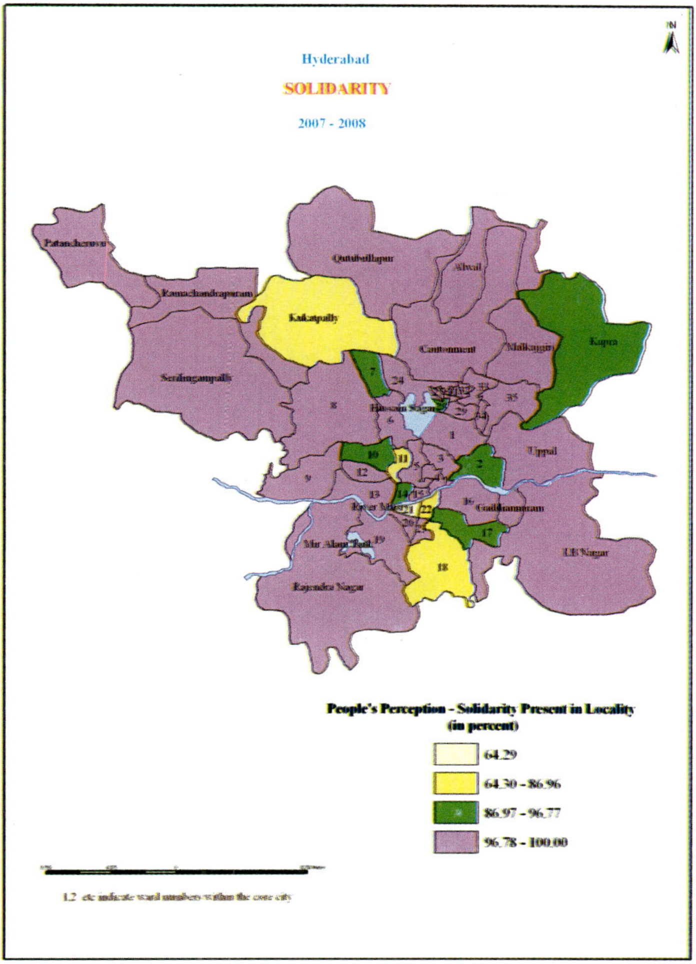

Source: Field Survey

Fig. 3.24: Solidarity, Hyderabad, 2007-08

with a range of values of 83.33 to 92.59 per cent on the score with regard to free choice of residences. Values in the range of 95.24 to 98.11 occur in Kukatpally, Kapra, Ameerpet, Jubilee-Banjara Hills, Ashok Nagar, Chikkadpally, Amberpet and Goshmahal.

Similarly 71 per cent of the localities report a free movement (Fig. 3.26) to the extent of 100 per cent. Most of those localities which report a relative low on this count (93%) are in the central part of

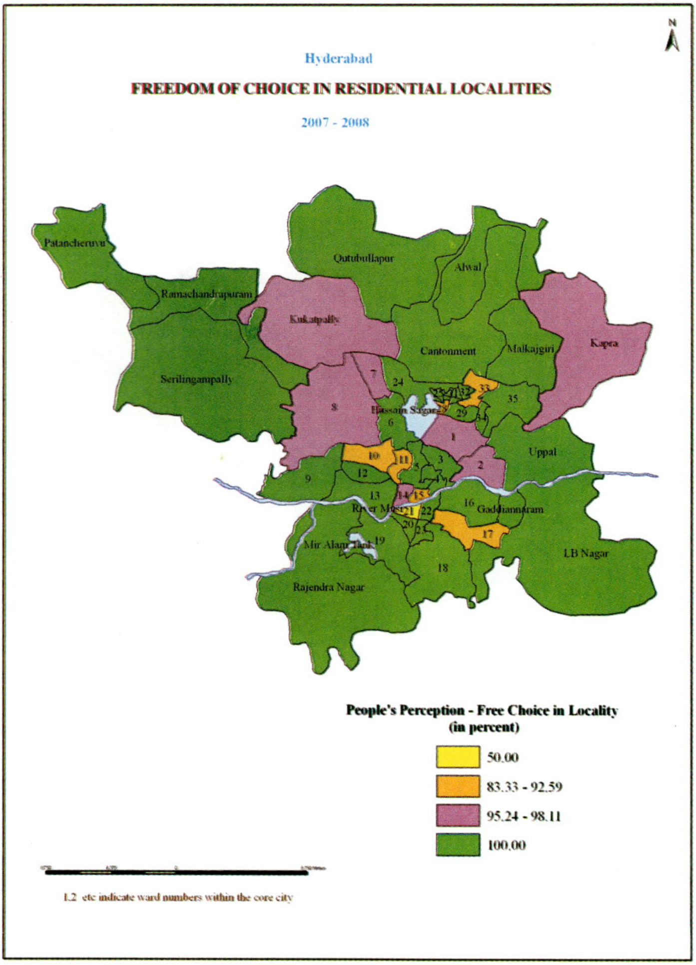

Source: Field Survey

Fig. 3.25: Freedom of Choice in Residential Location, Hyderabad, 2007-08

Hyderabad. Even in these localities the confirmatory values are in the range of 64 to 98 per cent which are high values in their own right.

Fig. 3.27 shows the civic participation by the residents. It is evident from this figure that civic participation is more in the northern, western, central and southern parts of the city compared to the eastern part in general. The preponderance of middle classes in the eastern part makes for them to invest their time in economically remunerative

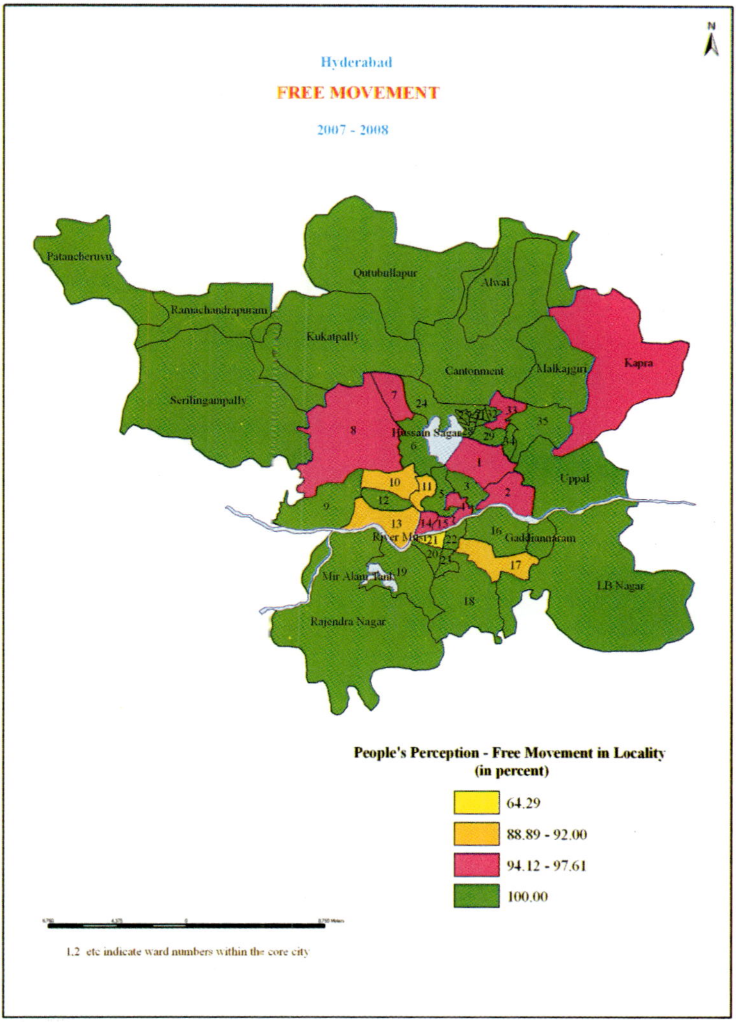

Source: Field Survey

Fig. 3.26: Free Movement, Hyderabad, 2007-08

activities. So is also the case with people in Golconda, Langar House, Mehdipatnam and Amberpet in a big way.

It may be said by way of summarizing this chapter that the residents of Hyderabad exhibit an tendency for own houses rather than rented houses, yet the predominance of rented houses in the city

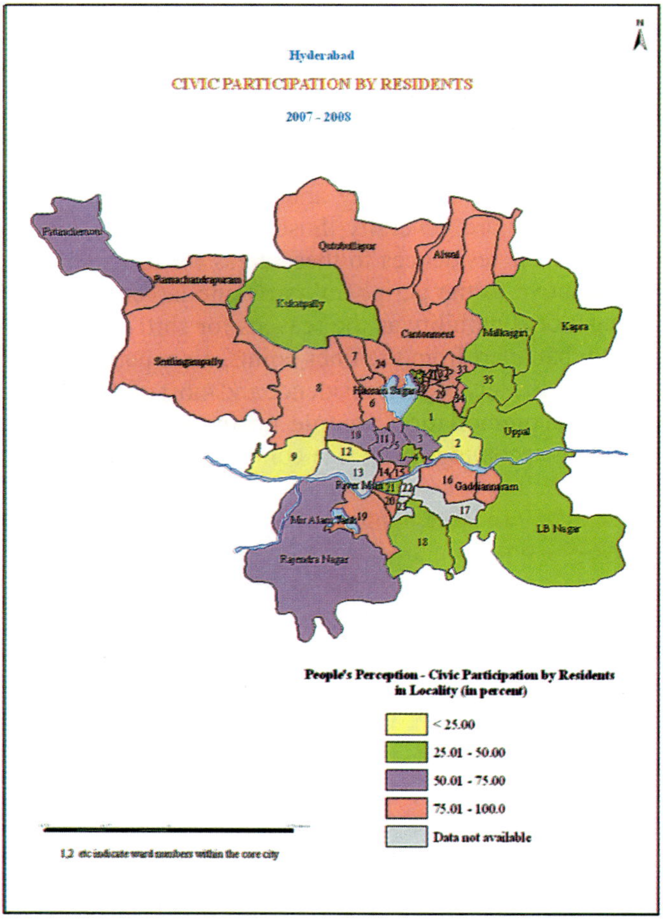

Source: Field Survey

Fig. 3.27: Civic Participation by Residents, Hyderabad, 2007-08

core speaks of a relatively mobile population in that part. These areas also have high rents and people seem generally less satisfied with them. It is also found that most of the people living in inherited houses are confined to central city locations. Most of the constructions in the central part of the city date back to the years prior to 1967, while the peripheral municipalities have seen building activity in a major way only in the 1980s and after. Most of the people seem to have made use of their savings for building the house. Localities which have more of government employees depend on formal sources of funding like bank loans, etc. Some in the CBDs of Hyderabad and Secunderabad depend on informal sources of credit. Most of rental house search is done with the help of friends and relatives—a rather traditional mode. Most of the houses are changed for reasons of larger accommodation; better locality and occupational mobility. While 'better localities' are generally those in the centre of the city and people shift their residences to these areas for this specific reason, those who move to the peripheral parts cite larger accommodation and occupational mobility as the reasons for shift of residence. It is also found that apart from the finer points, most people want to stay lifelong in the locality of their residence and most of them are satisfied with their accommodation. People on the eastern part are quite satisfied with accommodation size compared to those in the eastern part of the city. The relative sensitivity of the better off making for a lack of satiation and adaptability of the not so well off; making for better levels of satiation are the explanatory factors. Most people in the city are generally happy with their neighbourhoods. Most people also seem satisfied with the dispensation of social justice, human dignity and prevalence of equity, solidarity and free choice in residential location apart from free movement. Civic participation seems to be more in the northern, western, central and southern parts of the city compared to the eastern part in general. The preponderantly middle class population in the eastern part engages in more economically paying propositions.

References

Anushya Rajagopalan, *The Times of India*, September 16, 2006.

Chandrasekhar, V., Indicators of Real Estate cycles: Implications for India:http://in.search.yahoo.com/search?p=Indicators+of+Real+Estate+Market&fr=greentree_ff1&ei=utf-8

Comprehensive Housing Strategy Task Force, Washington, D.C. 2005.

Deccan Chronicle, April, 10, 2009.

Deccan Chronicle, Feb1, 2008.

Deccan Chronicle, February, 2, 2010.

Deccan Chronicle, Jan 5, 2009.

http://in.biz.yahoo.com/100628/50/bavv1j.html

Lalith Singh T., *The Hindu*, October 14, 2006.

Lalith, Singh T., *The Hindu*, February 24, 2007.

Maitreyi, M.L.M., *The Hindu*, February 10, 2007.
Maitreyi, M.L.M., *The Hindu*, March 17, 2007.
Mathew, D.M., *The Hindu*, October 28, 2006.
Nirmala Govindarajan, *Times of India*, December 16, 2006.
Reddy, L.V., *Deccan Chronicle*, Feb 15, 2008.
Reddy, L.V., *Deccan Chronicle*, January 25, 2008.
Sai Gopal, M., *The Hindu*, October 21, 2006.
Sai Gopal, M., *The Hindu*, October 28, 2006.
Sinha, Prabhakar 'Housing and Dry?', *Sunday Times of India*, April 19,2009.
Srinivas, M., *The Hindu*, July 7, 2007.
Srinivas, M., *The Hindu*, September 30, 2006.
Sunday Chronicle, August 9, 2009.
The Hindu, April 15, 2006.
The Hindu, November 25, 2006.

4

Perception of Amenities

The developing countries are witnessing a change in their national landscape with regard to the rural-urban scenario. Their large cities are marching towards a Mega-city status, towns are being transformed into cities and villages are turning into towns. All this is unmistakably accompanied by rural to urban migration. The processes set in motion by rural-urban migratory trends have an impact not only on the urban areas under consideration, but also on the national economies of the countries concerned. The destination cities in most of the Third World countries do not have the capacity to absorb the in migrant streams of population. Moreover, the migrants are mostly unskilled and hence not suitable for the job requirements of these cities (McKee, 1994). In such cases employment in menial jobs on one hand and circular migration tendencies on the other cannot be ruled out (Prothero and Chapman, 1999).

Most of the cities in Asia and Latin America are impacted by globalization, where rapid flow of information and capital is blurring urban-rural administrative boundaries. Urban scholars refer to this process as "mega-urbanization." Prosperous, interconnected cities that are emerging in East and Southeast Asia increasingly resemble cities in North America's northeastern corridor (McGee and Robinson, 1995).

The problems of urban areas manifest themselves in different forms in varying parts of the world. In the developing world, they appear in the form of growing number of slums and street children; in the industrialized world, they are seen in the form of social exclusion, urban ghettos and homelessness. Whatever the propensity of the problem, one thing is clear that the problems that urban areas confront manifest themselves in the form of poverty, social segregation and marginalization, whether it is in the slums of the developing countries or the urban ghettos of USA.

Though globalization today favours democratization, decentralization, worldwide communication and information exchanges, yet there are macro-economic disparities that create an even more polarized world (Rabinovich, J., 1998). Rural poverty is being exchanged for urban marginalization. Paradoxically enough, urban poverty is not only a problem, but also part of a solution for rural poverty.

In the developed countries, the shifting distribution of population within urban agglomerations, rather than between urban and rural areas, is the most significant source of urban population change. Decentralization followed by counter-urbanization, re-concentration and flight to the exurbs have been the successive tendencies in the last more than five decades. (Champion, 1989; Summers *et al*, 1999). These shifts have further compounded the problems that the squalor infested urban areas face.

A wide variety of problems ranging from housing subsidies which exacerbate concentration of people in low income housing along with its myriad manifestations to the booming informal economic sector with its insufficiencies multiplied with every in-migrant wave that inflates its size, glare one in the face rather defiantly in the urban centres of the developing countries.

A look at the Figures (Figs. 4.1, 4.2 and 4.3) unfolding the rating of their residential locality on a seven-point scale of preference by the people in the different wards and municipalities of Hyderabad acquaints one with the priorities of the people. The average scores of each locality have been plotted in the figures and reveal that the rating of localities cascades on the scale from the Physical surroundings, followed by Amenities and Infrastructure, Social Environment and Security in that order (Fig. 4.1).

A deeper look at the picture presented (Fig.4.2 and 4.3) reveals that while none of the localities have been ranked at 7 on any count on the scale on an average (though certain individuals have done so); most of the cases fall in the range of 4 to 6 on all four counts enumerated. Speaking in relative terms, it is found that while the rating on the physical surroundings scale is by and large high in central city locations, it is low in the peripheral municipalities. Incidentally, Begumpet, Barkas, Aliabad and Secunderabad Cantonment are rated below 4 on the physical surroundings scale and each of them has its own reason. While the first three are in the crowded central parts of the city, Secunderabad Cantonment by and large houses the upper middle class, which has people who are over-sensitive to the environment and any aberrations from the norm are not viewed favourably. However, 52.08 per cent of the unit areas (Wards and Municipalities) under consideration report a ranking of between 5 and 6 on the Physical Surroundings score. This compares with 39.58 per cent for Social Environment, 37.5 per cent for Amenities and Infrastructure and 33.33 per cent for Security, meaning that the people are more satisfied with the conglomerate of variables which constitute Physical surroundings rather than Social Environment, Amenities and Infrastructure and Security.

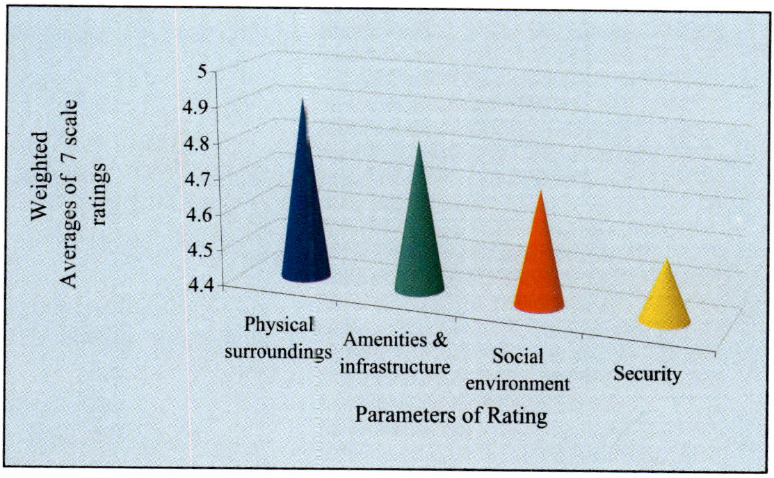

Fig. 4.1: Rating of Locality on a Seven Point Scale of Preference, Hyderabad, 2007-08 (Column Graph)

So far as the Social Environment is concerned, it is found that people in places like Saidabad Colony, Lalapet, Warasiguda, Begumpet and Marredpally along with Yerukala Basti seem to be mighty satisfied and rank their localities highest on this count. While Lalapet has a number railway employees and Saidabad Colony has employees from the research labs, a sense of camaraderie amongst them may be the reason for this; Yerukala basti is a slum and people in slums are known for their social cohesion, bonding and fellow feeling. So is also the

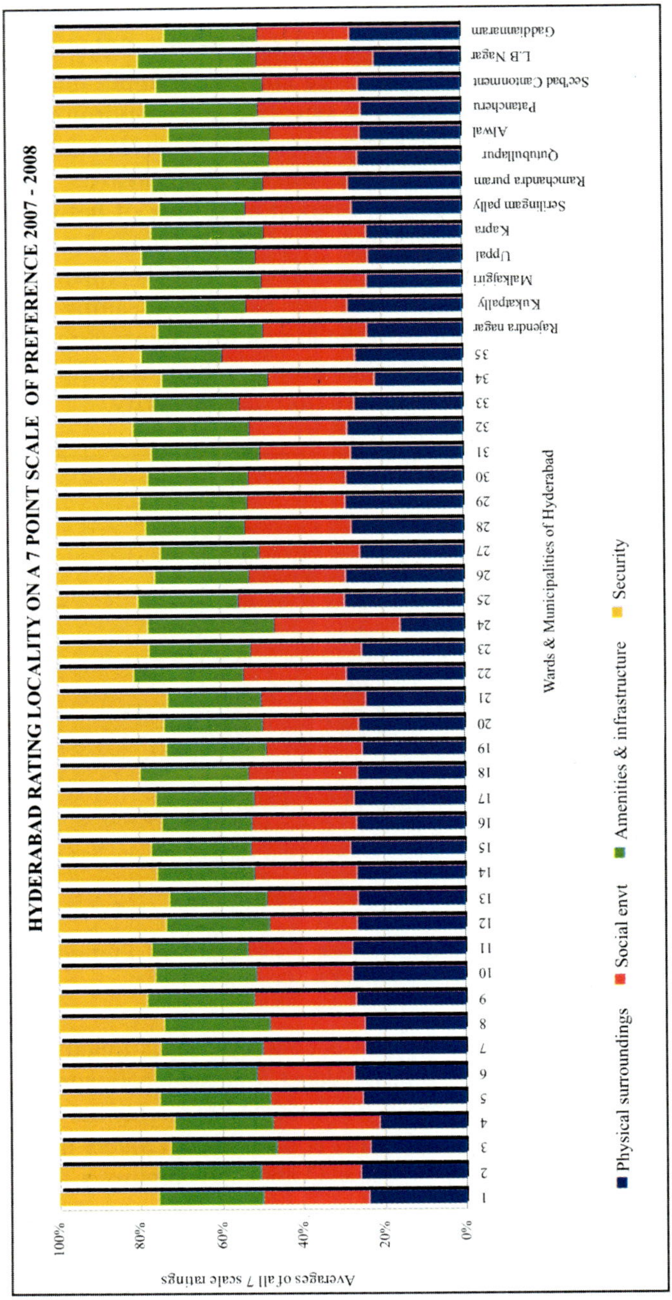

Fig. 4.2: Rating of Locality on a Seven Point Scale of Preference, Hyderabad, 2007-08 (Bar Graph)

case with other middle class habitats like Warasi Guda and Uppal, L.B. Nagar and so on. A sense of disappointment on the social environment facet is witnessed in Ramachandrapuran, Aliabad, Barkas, Secunderabad Cantonment, Mehdipatnam, Pathergatti, Monda Market and Serilingampally. Ramachandrapuram is an Industrial area and social bonds between the residents may not be as strong. Though Aliabad and Barkas have a large Muslim population it is fractured along Shia-Sunni lines and also on the socio- economic scale. While on the one hand, it has people who are not educated at all and engage in petty business, on the other hand it has some highly qualified people like doctors. Serilingampally and Mehdipatnam have people in a wide variety of occupations ranging from labourers to lecturers and there may be hardly any social bonding among such disparate groups. These factors describe the poor rating of certain localities on the scale of 'Social Environment'.

With regard to rating of localities on the 'Amenities and Infrastructure scale', it is found that while people in Regimental Bazaar, Begumpet, Warasiguda, L.B. Nagar, Kapra, Malkajgiri and Uppal give a very high rating to their localities on this scale, those in Lalapet, Aliabad, Barkas and Serilingampally rate their localities as low on this count. Notwithstanding the socio-economic variations within and among respondents in these localities, the ratings are commensurate with the ground reality. Accessibility as one among the various indices by which this dimension is measured, is high in places like Uppal and L.B. Nagar because of their proximity to the Outer Ring Road. Begumpet also occupies a central location in Secunderabad and has a very high degree of connectivity. Their higher scores on some of indices outweigh inadequacies if any on certain other counts. However, lower ranking of Lalapet, Aliabad, Barkas and Serilingampally means that the planning authorities need to take cognizance of these areas so far as planning for amenities and infrastructure is concerned.

Many of the localities seem to be wanting, so far as security is concerned. Inadequacy on this count seems to overshadow that on all other counts in most localities in the city, more so those in the eastern and northern part of the city. At times the old localities of the city do not seem to have adequate security, among them Mogulpura, Pathergatti, Aliabad and Barkhas may be cited. The core area of Secunderabad comprising Ramgopalpet and Monda Market may also be cited here. Besides these, pockets like Ramachandrapuram and

Patancheru, which have industries located in a large measure report inadequate security. So is also the case with Lalapet, the area which has the railway quarters.

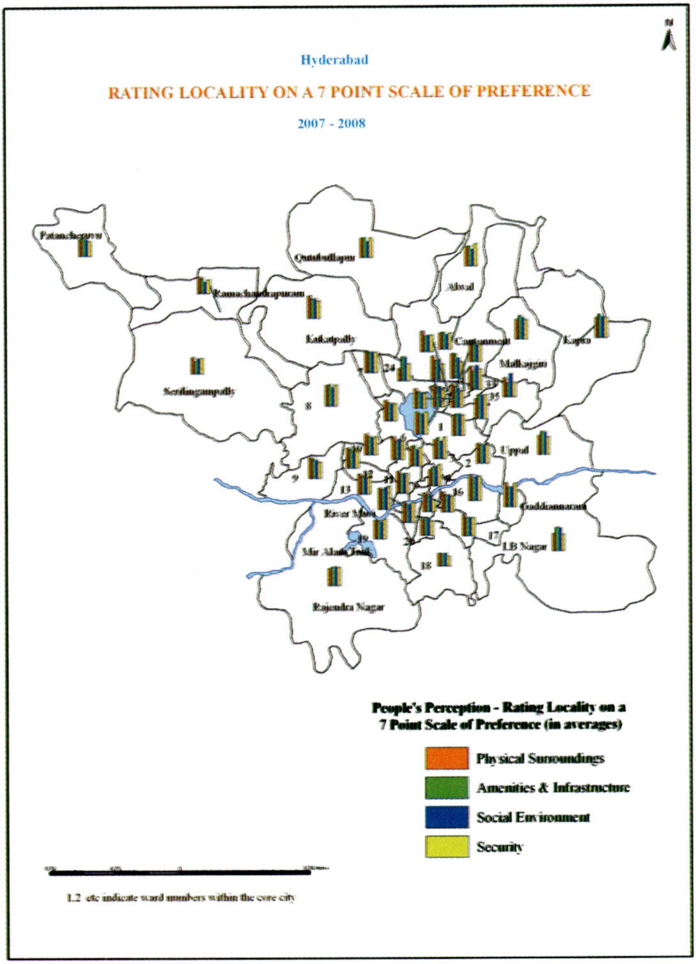

Source: Field Survey.

Fig. 4.3: Rating of Locality on a Seven Point Scale of Preference, Hyderabad, 2007-08 (Map)

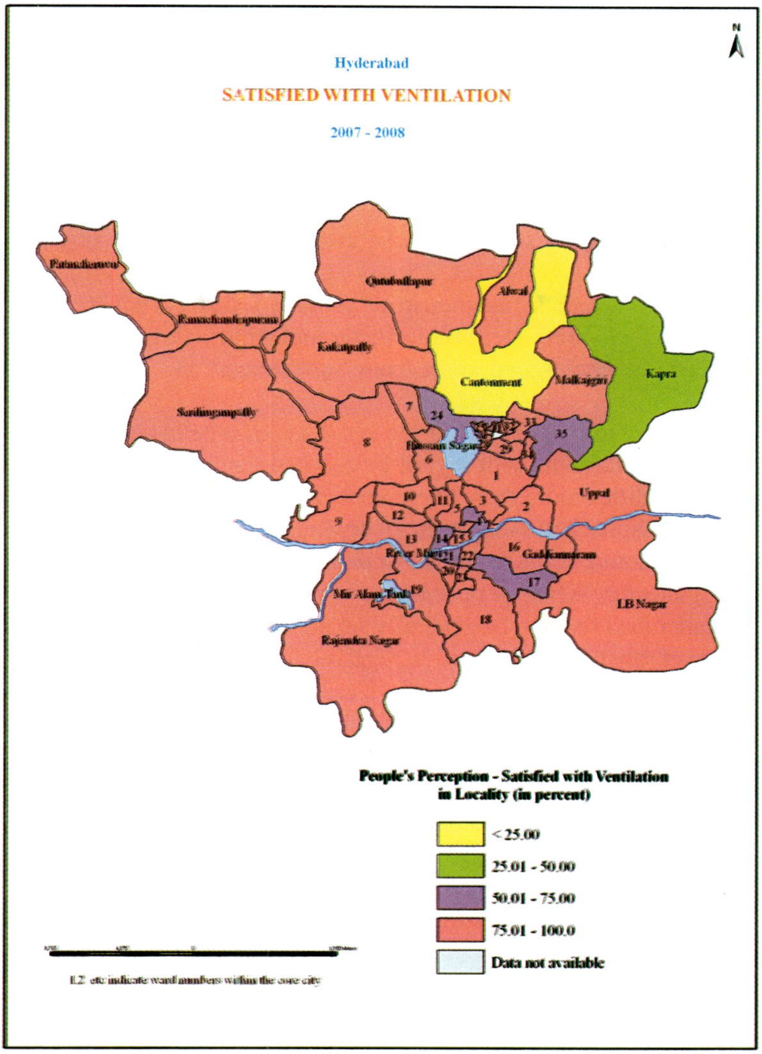

Source: Field Survey.

Fig. 4.4: Satisfied with Ventilation, Hyderabad, 2007-08

An enquiry is also made into the perception of specific amenities and facilities in the house as well as the locality by the residents. Fig. 4.4 pertaining to perception with regard to ventilation present in the house conveys that while most people in the city seem reasonably satisfied, it is just those in Kapra and the Secunderabad Cantonment who seem less satisfied. The relatively higher degree of dissatisfaction in these two localities could be linked with a more educated and hence a more sensitive population. While it is the migrants to a substantial extent in the former case, it is the government employees in the latter case who have a higher level of expectation and are not easily satisfied with their environmental conditions.

Residents in these localities are also not very much satisfied with regard to garbage disposal. This is apart from other localities like Kukatpally, which is an industrial suburb, Lalapet—which houses the Railway Colony etc, Sultan Bazar and Abids—which constitute the CBD of Hyderabad apart from Saroornagar and Mehdipatnam (Fig. 4.5).

More than 50 per cent of the residents in other parts of the city express satisfaction with regard to garbage disposal. In 58 per cent of the localities more than 75 per cent of the people are satisfied with garbage disposal and that is the overwhelming feature of this figure.

The picture with regard to drainage facility (Fig. 4.6) is not so very pleasing. While people in the central parts of Hyderabad and Secunderabad seem to be generally satisfied with drainage facility, the degree of satisfaction seems to be relatively less in Hyderabad compared to Secunderabad. It is again observed that some of the peripheral localities in the northern part of the city present a dismal picture on this count. These extend latitudinally from Ramachandrapuram in the north-west to Kapra in the north- east and encompass Kukatpally and Secunderabad Cantonment on the way. Saroornagar in the south eastern part also presents a bleak picture on this count. An extension of relatively lower levels of satisfaction with regard to drainage is also found as an extension of this area towards the south western part of the city. Thus, while people in the northern and southern peripheral parts of the city exhibit a lower level of satisfaction with regard to the drainage facility, those in the central part seem to be quite satisfied and this satisfaction extends out towards the eastern and western peripheral parts of the city.

In further corroboration of what has been said above, it is observed that the general profile on the sanitary front (Fig. 4.7) is gloomy in the south western part of the city, which houses the lower middle class localities, as well as in the Ramachandrapuram area which is an industrial enclave as also Saroornagar, which has been rated low on the count of both garbage disposal and drainage facilities. The central

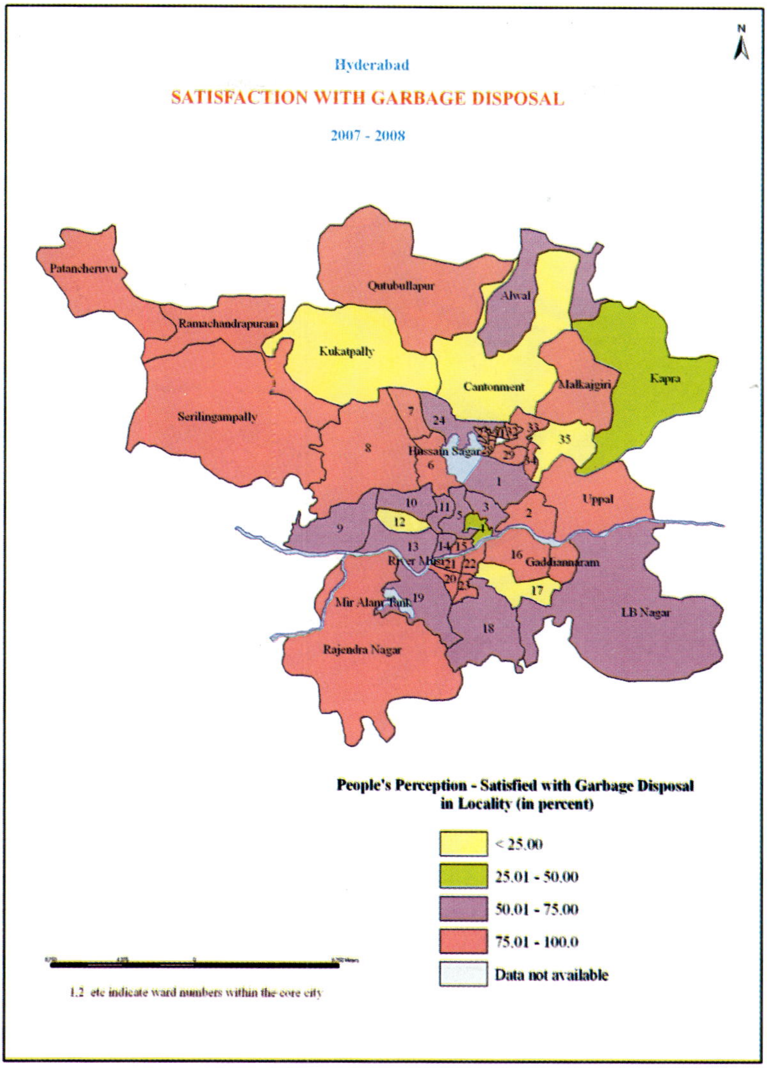

Source: Field Survey.

Fig. 4.5: Satisfied with Garbage Disposal, Hyderabad, 2007-08

part of Secunderabad and to some extent Hyderabad and their extensions into the western and eastern periphery of the city exhibit a relatively higher level of satisfaction on the count of sanitary

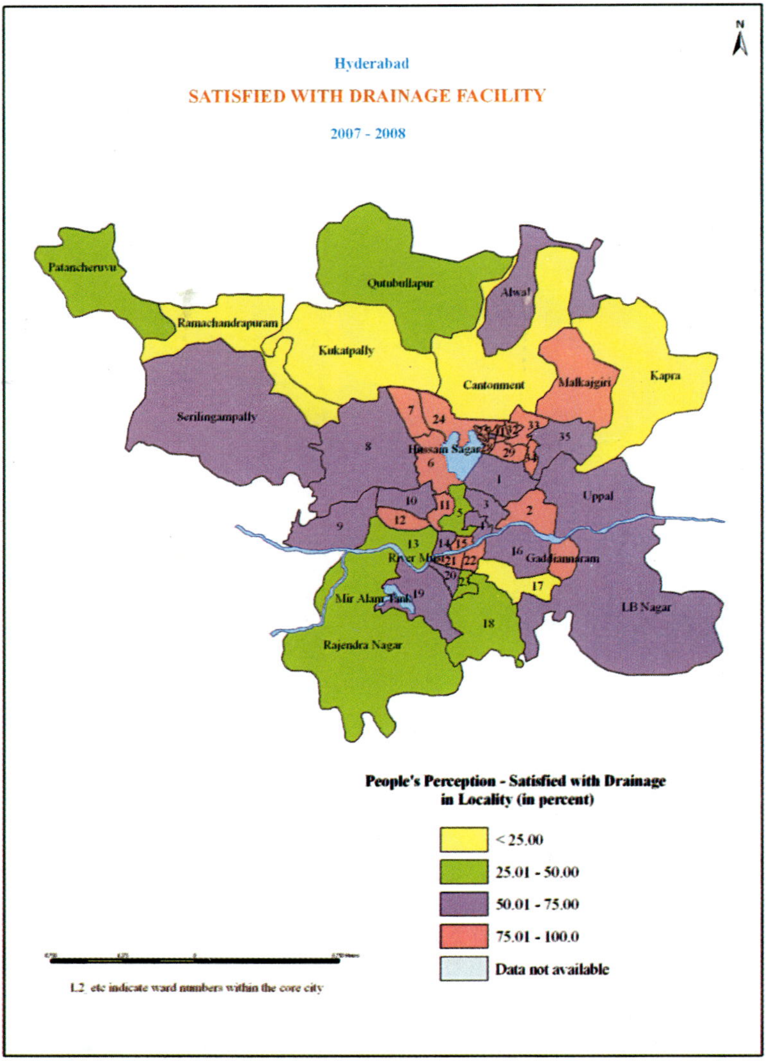

Source: Field Survey.

Fig. 4.6: Satisfied with Drainage Facility, Hyderabad, 2007-08

facilities. Thus while central city locations seem to be generally satisfactory on this count; those on the periphery are not as fortunate.

The core-periphery dichotomy with regard to satisfaction and

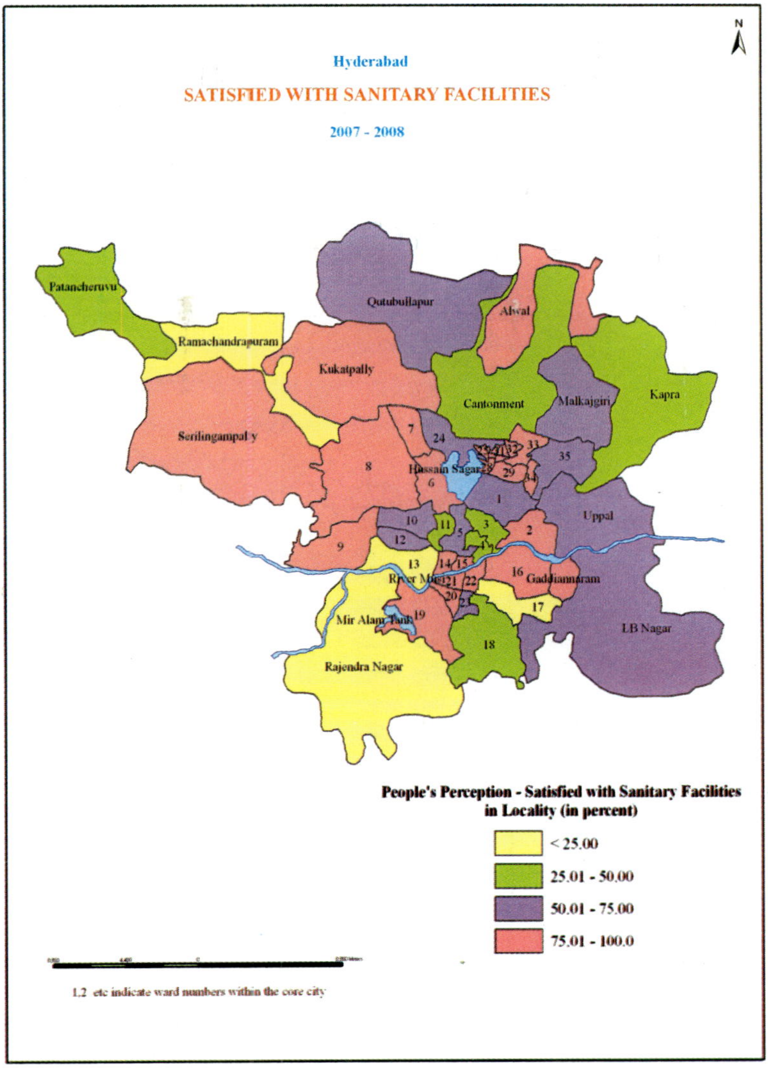

Source: Field Survey.

Fig. 4.7: Satisfied with Sanitary Facilities, Hyderabad, 2007-08

dissatisfaction as perceived by the residents is also maintained so far as the water supply situation is concerned (Fig. 4.8). While most components of the core city display a relative contentment with regard

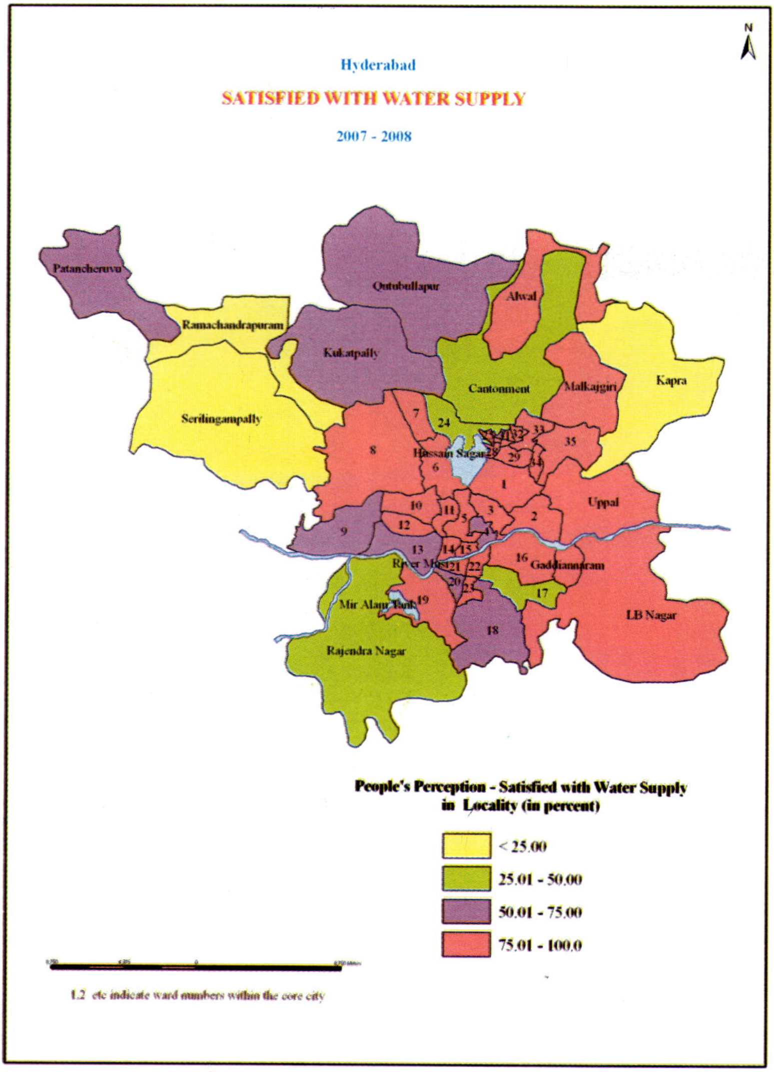

Source: Field Survey.

Fig. 4.8: Satisfied with Water Supply, Hyderabad, 2007-08

to the water supply situation, some of the peripheral areas in the south west, north-west and north-east display a relative discontent with regard to the availability of water. However, so is not the case with the eastern periphery of the city. The eastward trending slope of the city, facilitating digging of borewells with adequate supply of water may be one of the factors facilitating this kind of an outlook.

Street lighting is an equally important facility in the urban areas, more so as they are prone to crime vis-à-vis the rural areas. Proper street lighting provides a relatively safe environment to the denizens, so far as their movement is concerned. It is found that people are relatively satisfied with street lighting in the central parts of Hyderabad and Secunderabad and such areas fan out into the eastern, western, north western and south eastern part of the city (Fig. 4.9). The south western part and the north eastern part are wanting on this front. The fact that it includes better localities like West Marredpally, Begumpet and Ameerpet, besides Secunderabad Cantonment reflects on the needs and aspirations of these people, some of whom are educationally and economically better off and hence have higher levels of expectation and lower adjustability to annoying environmental conditions. The government needs to be cognizant of the needs or even the perceived needs of these areas while making further developmental plans.

A glance at Fig. 4.10 reveals that people in most localities point out and rightly so that Main Roads are present in their localities. The high density of roads in Hyderabad is the reason for this. However, some in the western part of the city allude to this statement in a lesser measure. The sparse nature of roads in some of these areas and greater interstitial distances between them are the reason for this and this fact can be considered while planning for the city, where there may be an apparent perceived apoplexy at one end and anemia at the other. Fig. 4.11 reveals that all those localities which report adequate existence of Main roads also report quite understandably their use in an equal measure. Figures 4.12 and 4.13 convey the presence and utilization of Arterial roads. It is evident from these figures that most localities in the centre of the city, for the most part report a rich presence and commensurate use of arterial roads. The arterial roads seem to be relatively scarce and so is also their usage in the peripheral localities. The derivations from the above four figures finds manifestation in Fig. 4.14 where most people in the central part of the city seem to be satisfied with accessibility, but this may not be strictly so with the peripheral localities, which seem to be underprovided on this count. The needs of such localities—especially Kapra and Rajendranagar can be taken into consideration in formulating future plans. It is also

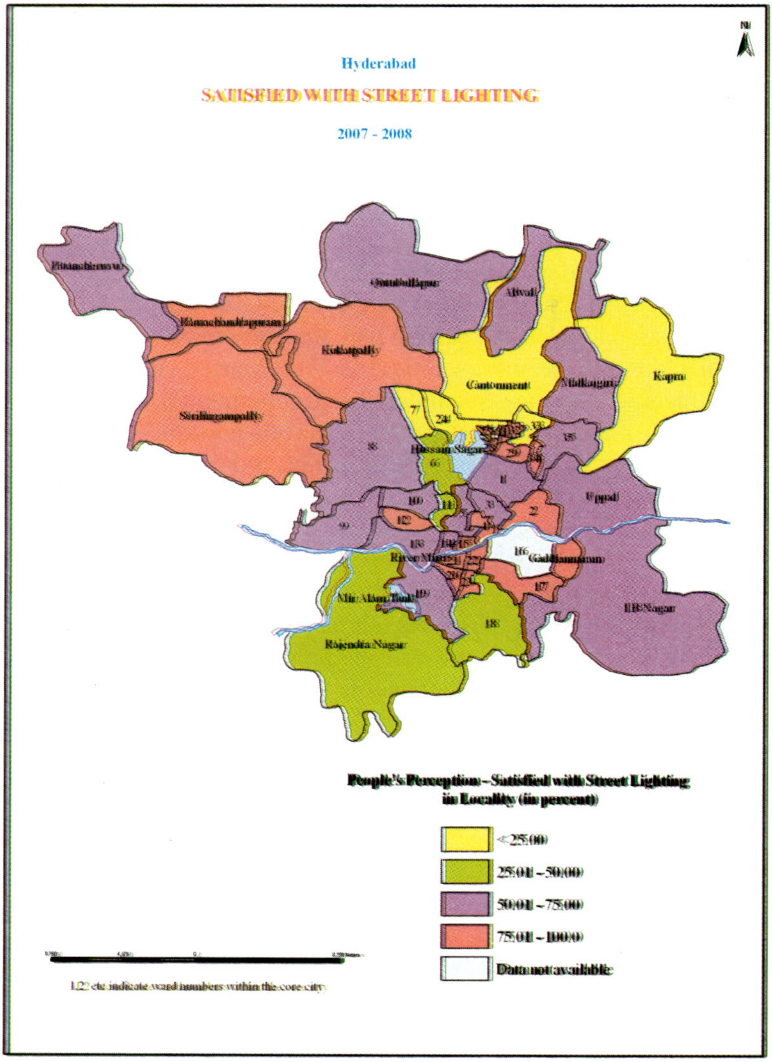

Source: Field Survey.

Fig. 4.9: Satisfied with Street Lighting, Hyderabad, 2007-08

pertinent to note here that some of the central city localities like Red Hills and Hussaini Alam seem to be wanting on this count. So is also the case with Lalapet and Goshamahal to some extent.

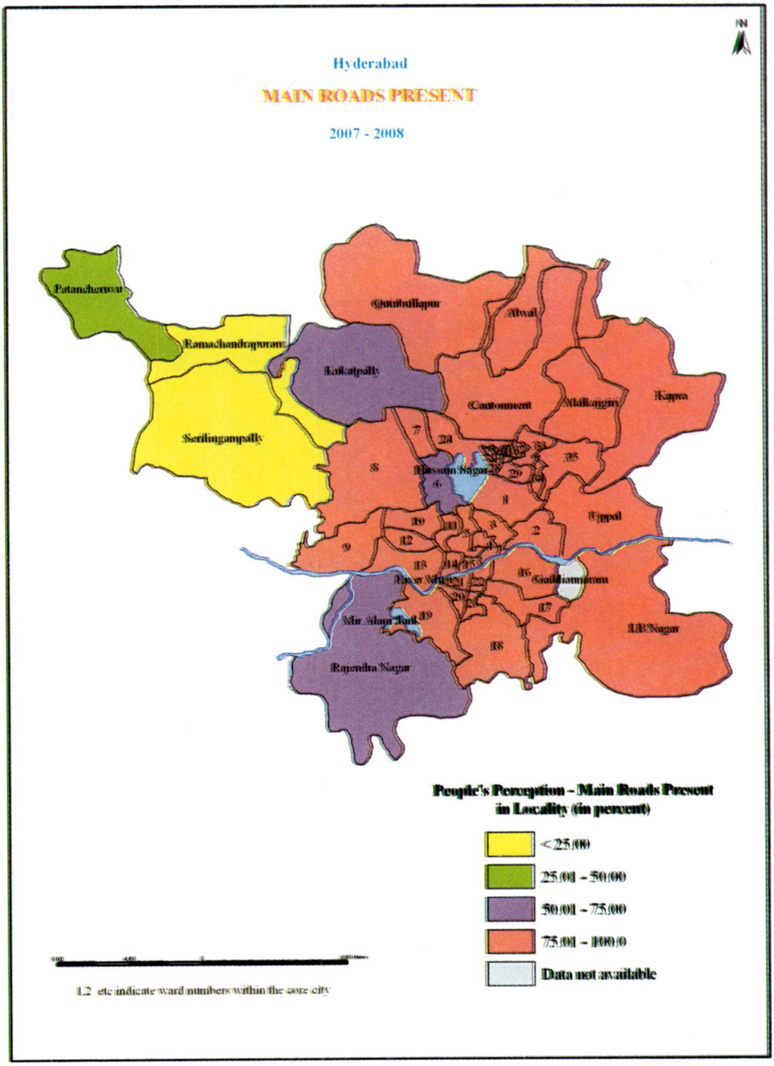

Source: Field Survey.

Fig. 4.10: Main Roads Present, Hyderabad, 2007-08

Fig.4.15 pertaining to the satisfaction of people with regard to Traffic Movement in the city shows that people in 46 per cent of the peripheral municipalities are satisfied only to the extent of 25 per

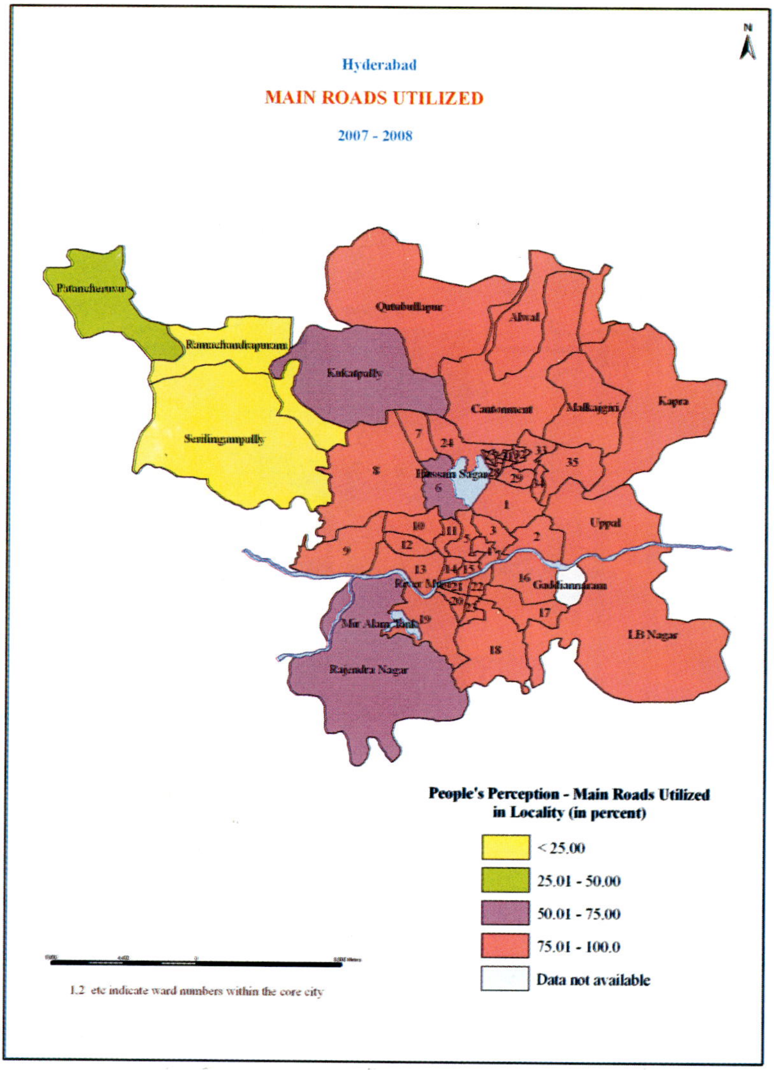

Source: Field Survey.

Fig. 4.11: Main Roads Utilized, Hyderabad, 2007-08

cent with Traffic Movement, whereas in the core city this is so with only 14 per cent of the residents. Hence, core city residents are generally more satisfied with traffic movement compared to those in the peripheral municipalities. This again reflects on general issues

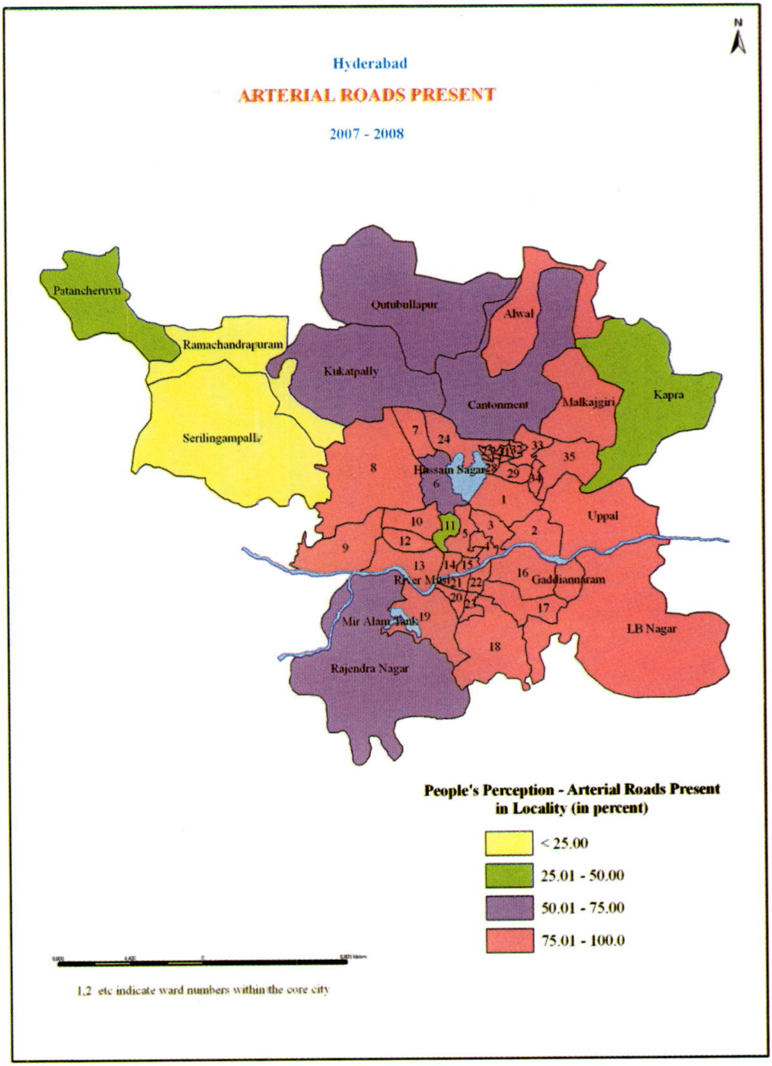

Source: Field Survey.

Fig. 4.12: Arterial Roads Present, Hyderabad, 2007-08

with regard to road networks and accessibility in a core- periphery context. Fig. 4.16 and Fig. 4.17 reflect on the near ubiquitous presence of bus stops in most localities and by implication their universal utilization.

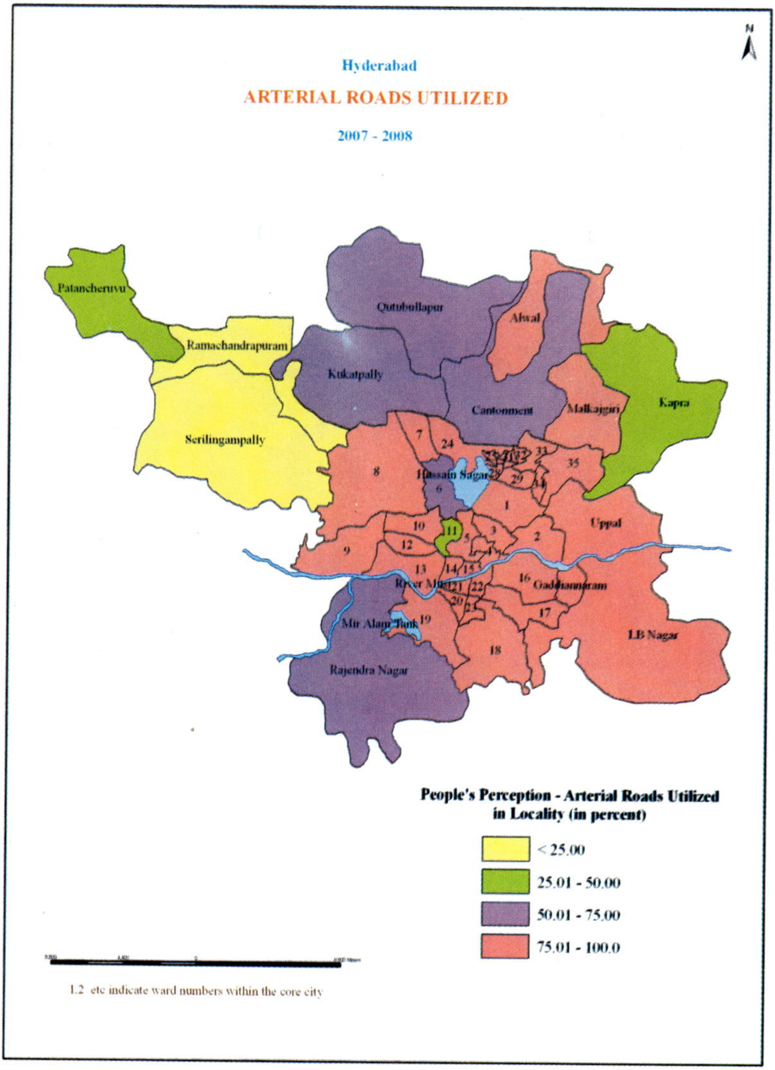

Source: Field Survey.

Fig. 4.13: Arterial Roads Utilized, Hyderabad, 2007-08

With regard to the presence of Primary Schools, it is evident that people in most parts of the city cite the presence of this amenity, only Ramachandrapuram and Kapra on the city outskirts and Goshmahal

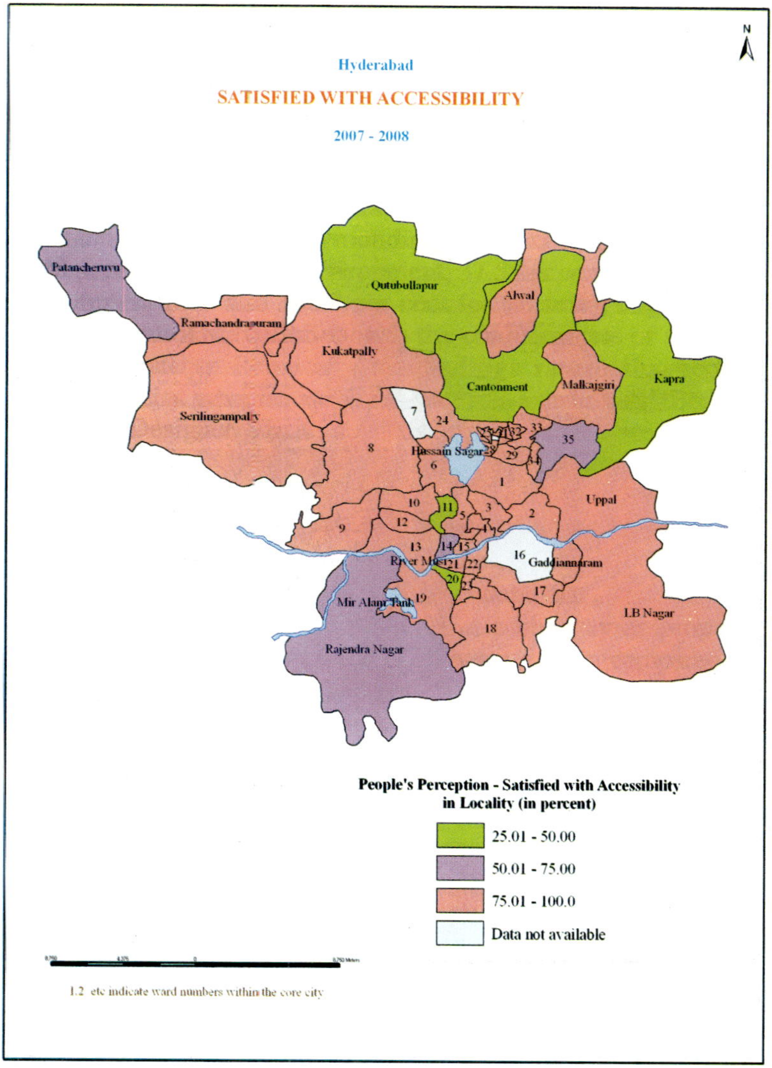

Source: Field Survey.

Fig. 4.14: Satisfied with Accessibility, Hyderabad, 2007-08

in the city centre seem to be wanting on this count to some extent (Fig. 4.18). Surprisingly enough, this facility does not seem to be utilized by the denizens in the measure in which it is reported to be present. The vocations of the people coupled with the absence of

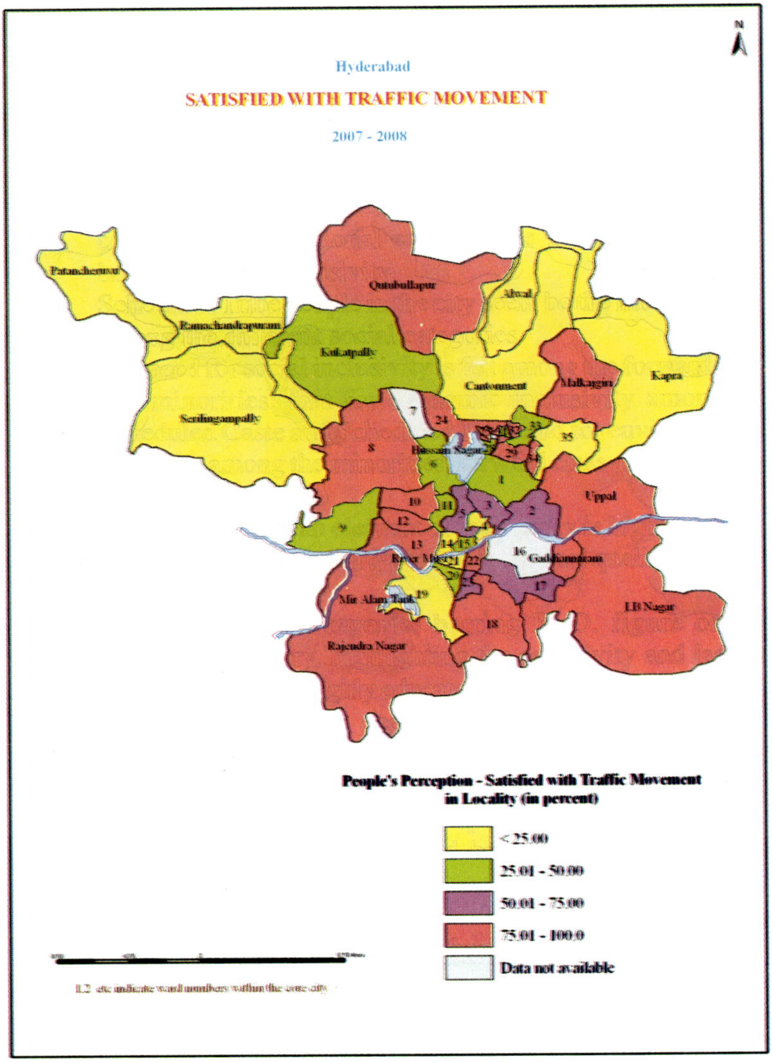

Source: Field Survey.

Fig. 4.15: Satisfied with Traffic Movement, Hyderabad, 2007-08

children in the primary school- going age group are the explanatory factors for this phenomenon. Gowliguda, Doodhbowli and Ramachandrapuram report the lowest level of utilization of this service

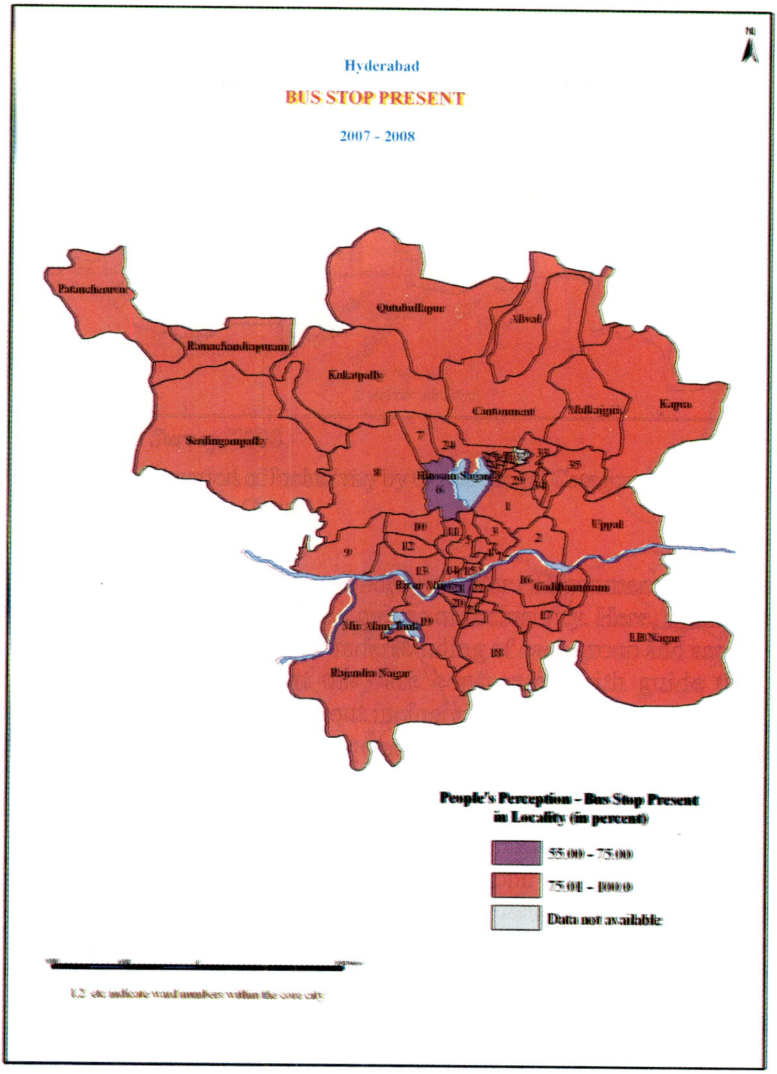

Source: Field Survey.

Fig. 4.16: Bus Stop Present, Hyderabad, 2007-08

for the above mentioned reasons. Other parts which report a relative low on this count are located in the not so well off central-western and southern part of the city as also Kukatpally and Alwal in the

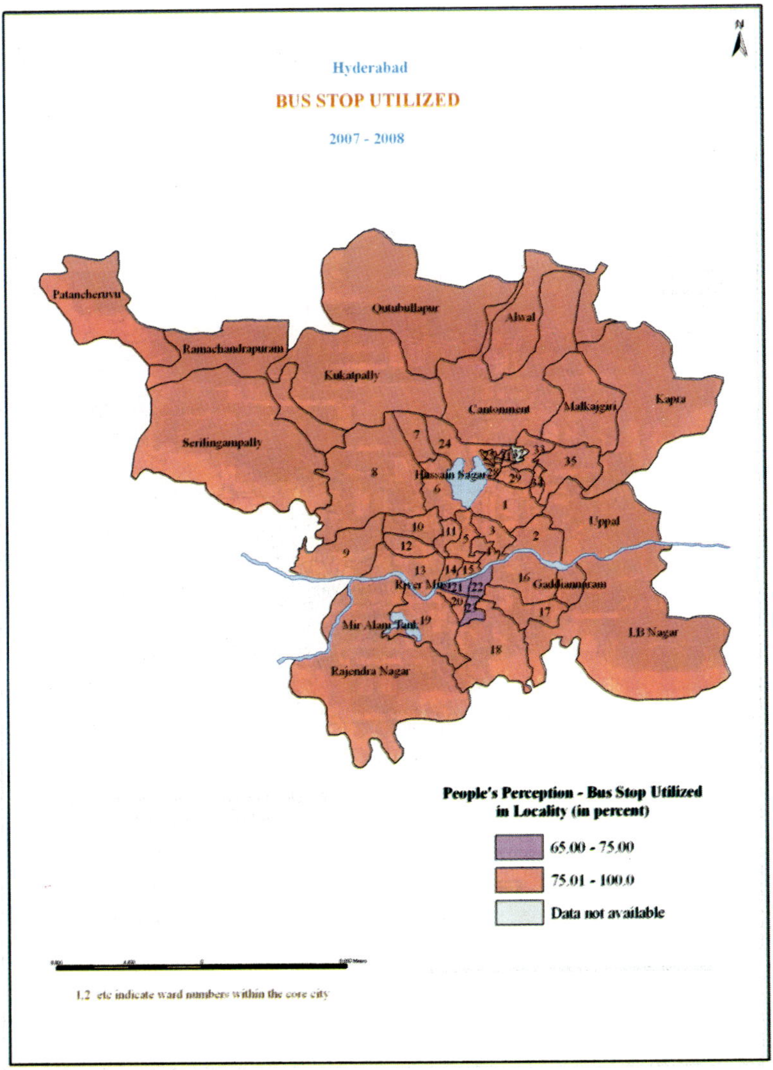

Source: Field Survey.

Fig. 4.17: Bus Stop Utilized, Hyderabad, 2007-08

northern part and certain areas in the vicinity of Ranigunj in Secunderabad.

The picture with regard to the presence of High School is also not much different from that presented by the Primary school with

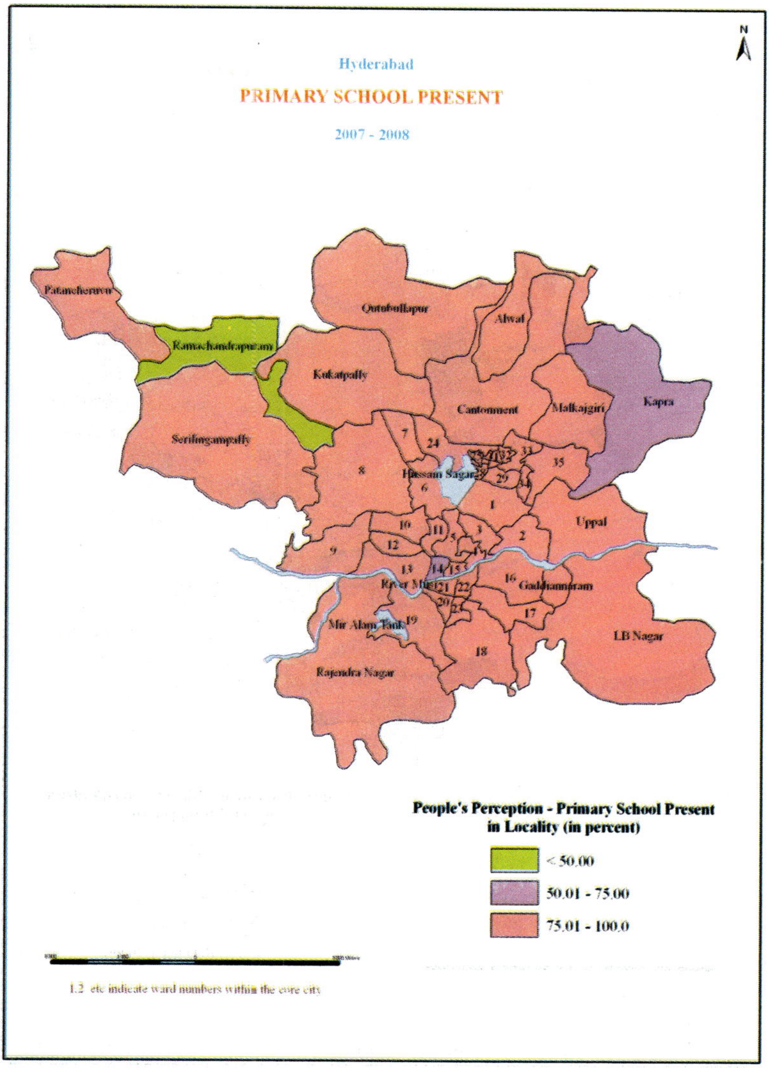

Source: Field Survey.

Fig. 4.18: Primary School Present, Hyderabad, 2007-08

regard to the generalities, though the specificities may vary (Fig. 4.20 and 4.21). Most parts of the city are perceived to have High Schools in an ample measure though the perception with regard to

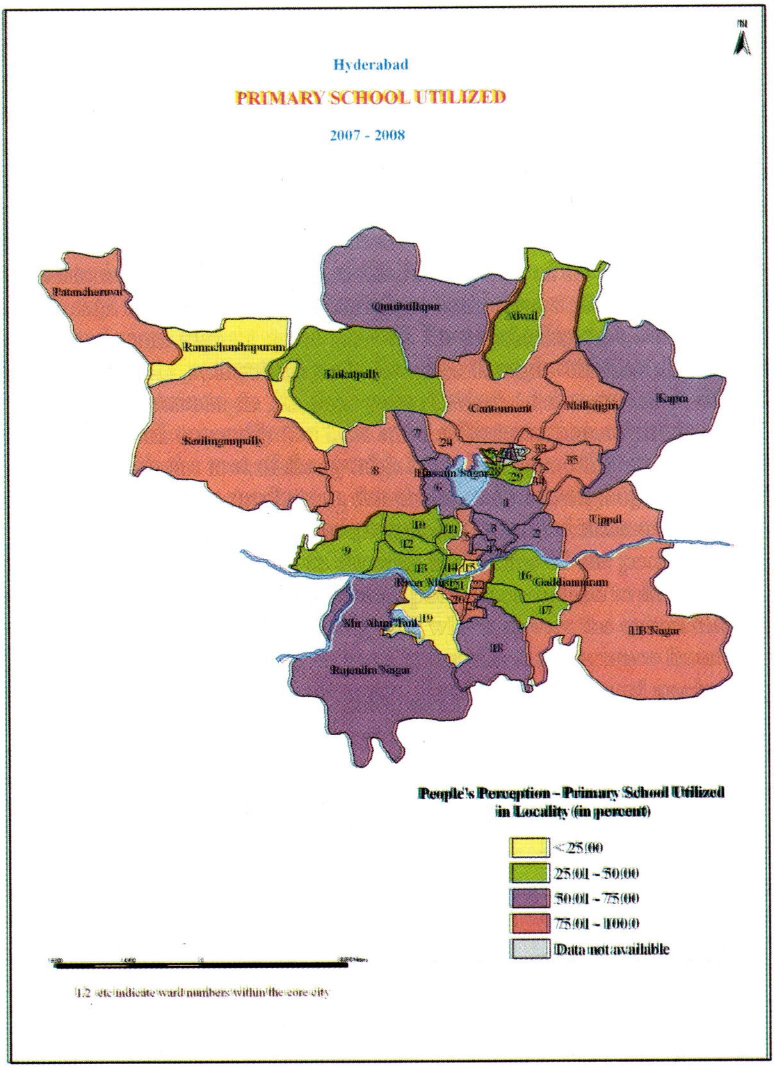

Source: Field Survey.

Fig. 4.19: Primary School Utilized, Hyderabad, 2007-08

Ramachandrapuram is on a slightly low count. Utilization of this facility generally shows a low in the central and southern parts of the city. The western, northern and eastern areas show a high level of utilization of this service, in keeping with the ethos and outlook of

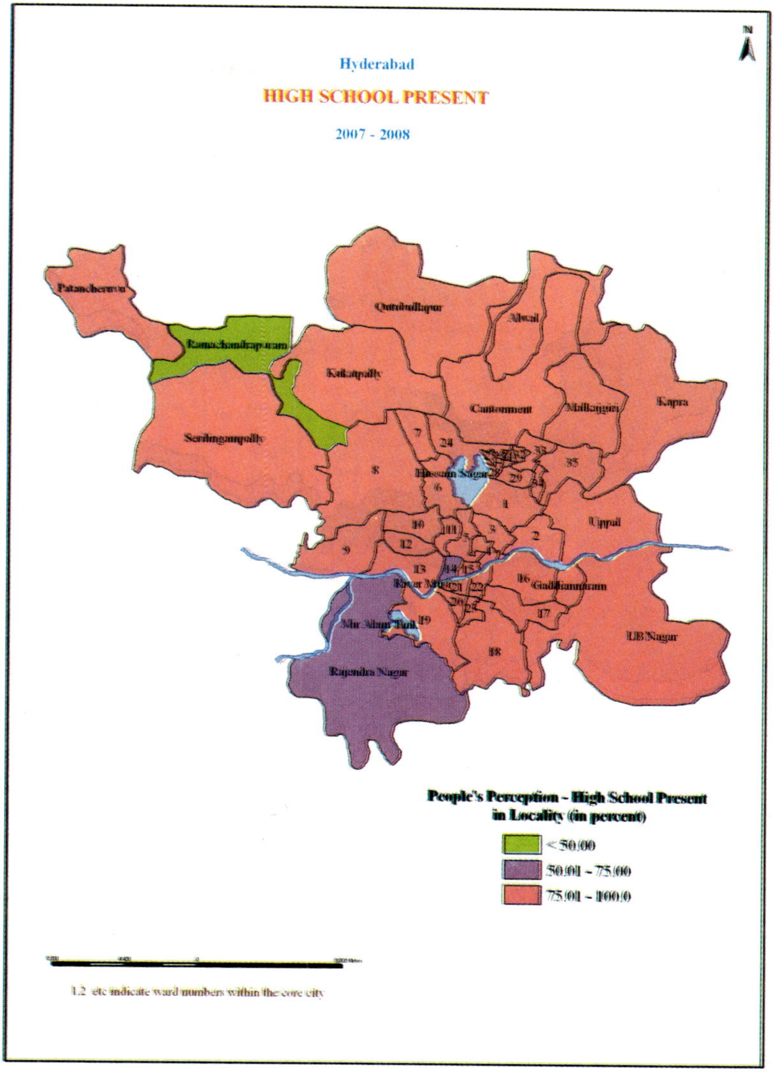

Source: Field Survey.

Fig. 4.20: High School Present, Hyderabad, 2007-08

the people in these areas, who view education as a step towards the attainment of success and prosperity in life.

Looking at higher levels of educational services, like college

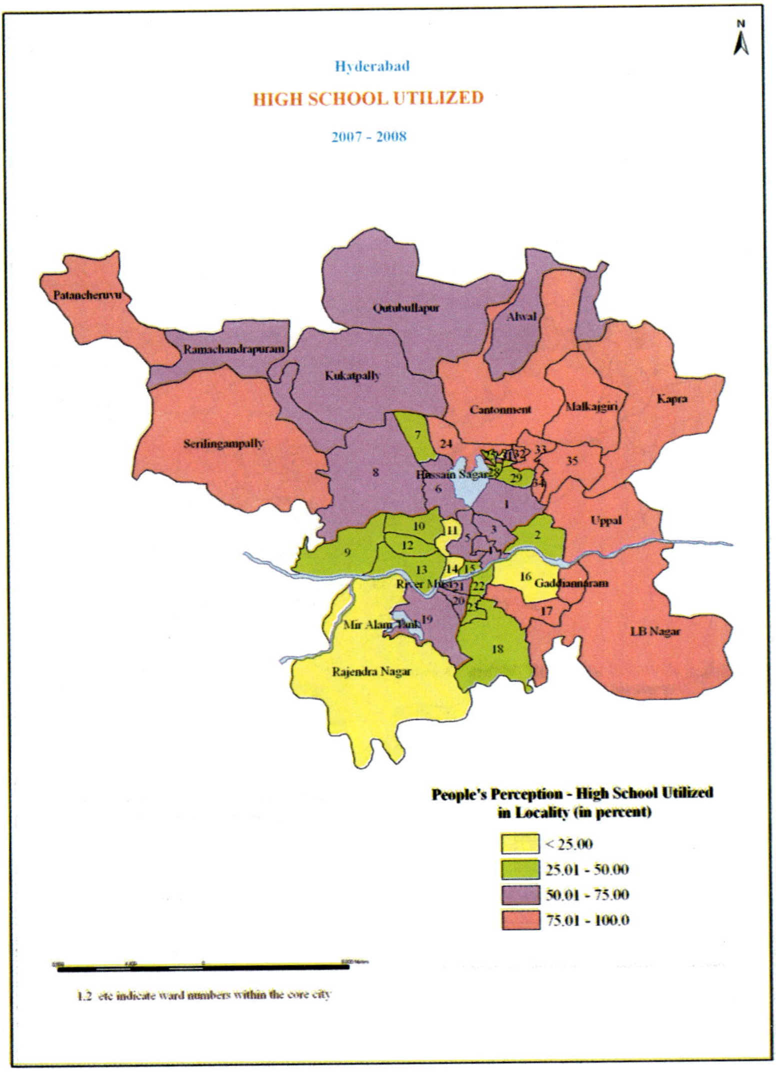

Source: Field Survey.

Fig. 4.21: High School Utilized, Hyderabad, 2007-08

service, one finds that most parts of the core city, barring Gosha Mahal to some extent, have it in an ample measure (Fig. 4.23) and quite understandably so, considering the importance of Hyderabad on the educational map of Andhra Pradesh. The utilization pattern of this

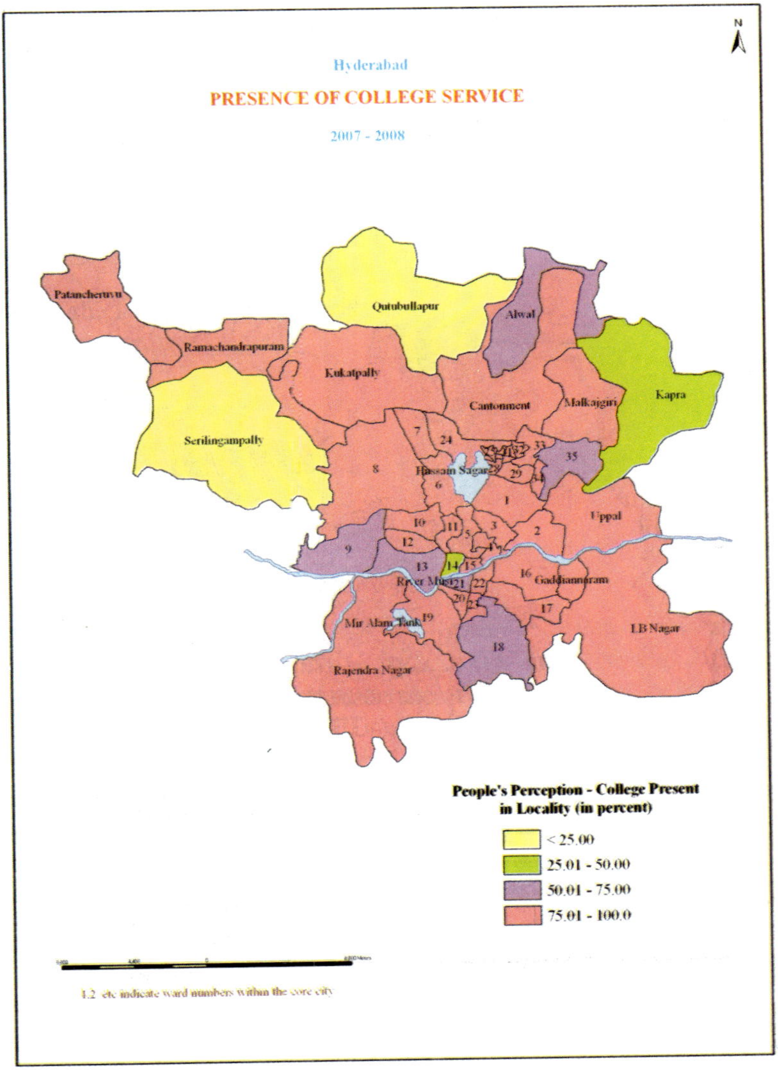

Source: Field Survey.

Fig. 4.22: Presence of College Service, Hyderabad, 2007-08

service is not commensurate with its presence in the various localities (Fig. 4.23). While the municipalities to the north eastern part of the city and contiguous areas in Secunderabad like Begumpet and Regimental Bazar utilize this facility in an ample measure; those in

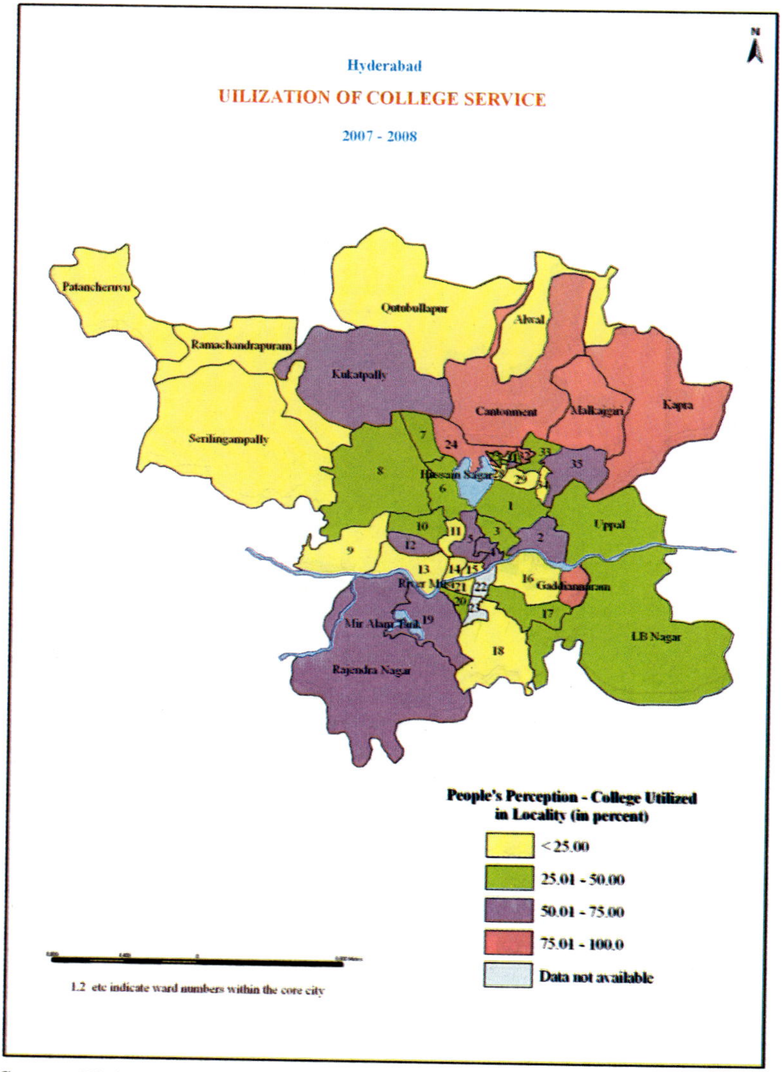

Source: Field Survey.

Fig. 4.23: Utilization of College Service, Hyderabad, 2007-08

the southern, central eastern and also the north-western and northern part do not utilize this facility in an ample measure.

However, barring few exceptions, most people in the city are

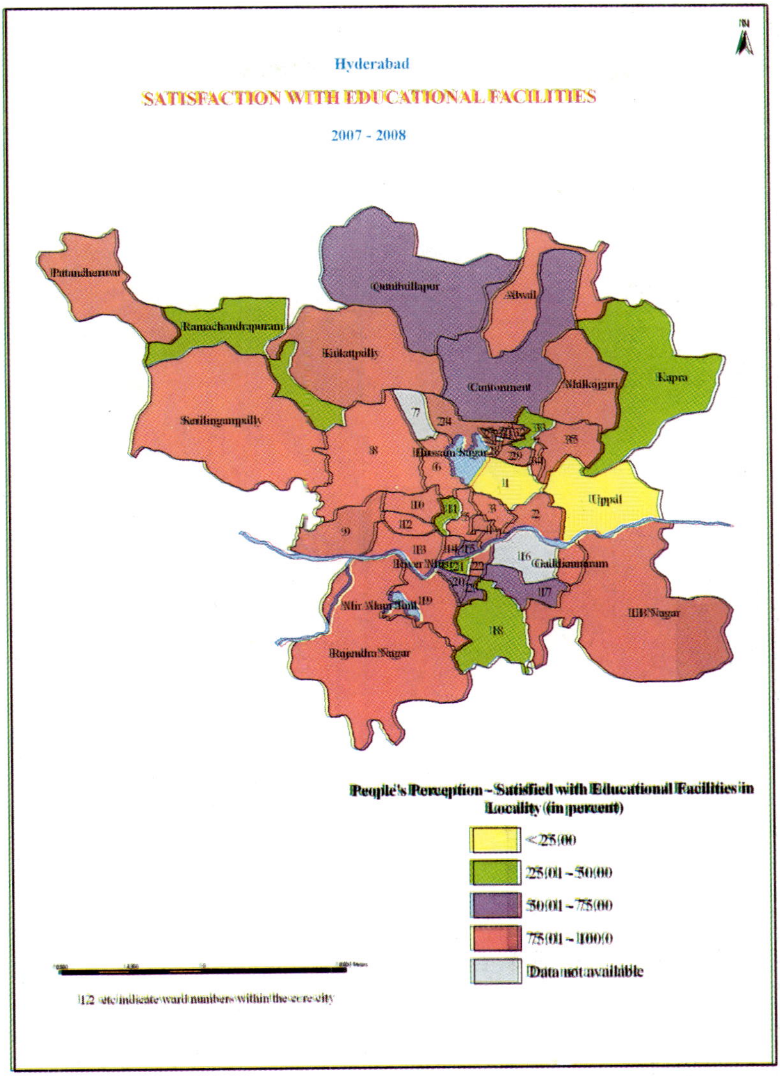

Source: Field Survey.

Fig. 4.24: Satisfaction with Educational Facilities, Hyderabad, 2007-08

satisfied with educational facilities as is evident from Fig. 4.24. Those who are satisfied in a big way far outnumber those who are less satisfied. In the part of the city north of the Musi such people account

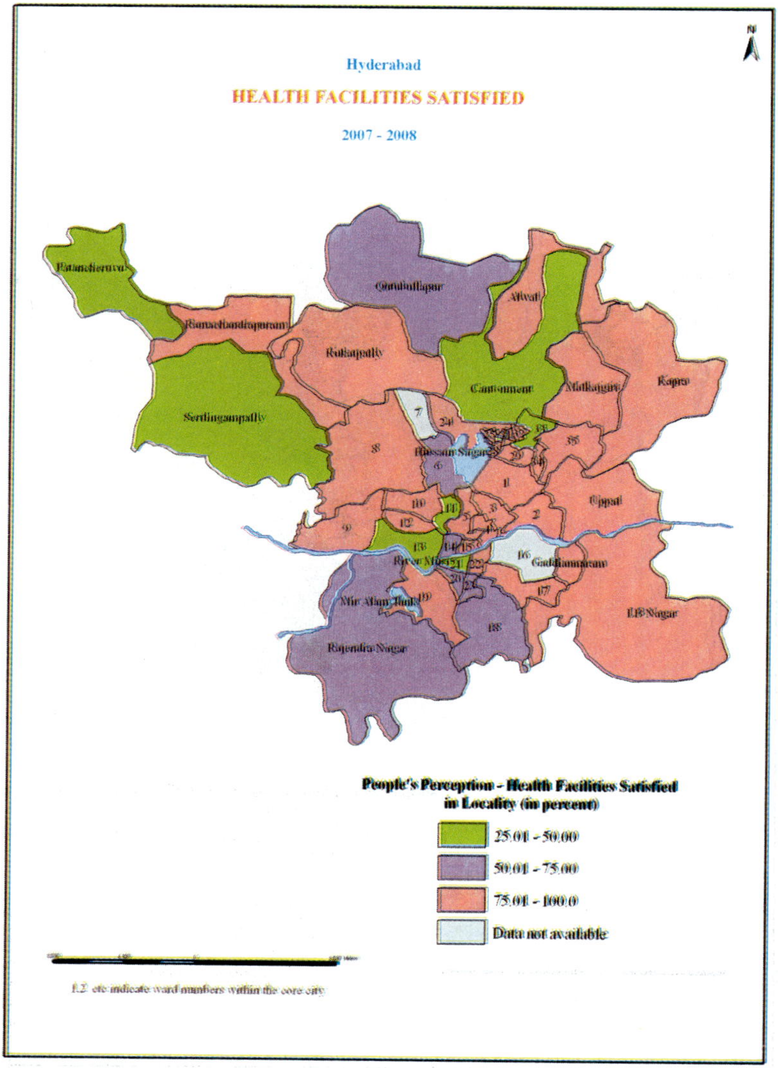

Source: Field Survey.

Fig. 4.25: Health Facilities Satisfaction. Hyderabad, 2007-08

for 72 per cent of the total and to the south of the Musi for 40 per cent.

Fig. 4.25 pertaining to the satisfaction of people with health facilities conveys that most of them in the eastern, central and to a large extent the western part of the city are satisfied with it. It is those in the peripheral municipalities on the western part like Patancheruvu and Serilingampally as well as the Secunderabad Cantonment who exhibit an element of dismay on this count. So is also the case with regard to relatively central city localities like Erukula Basti, Red Hills, Karwan and Gulzar House. While the case of a sense of deprival in the peripheral Municipalities/Localities can be explained by the relative absence of better health facilities in them, the case of certain central city localities which display disappointment on this count can be explained by the lack of where-withal with the residents which denies them access to the health facilities. This is notwithstanding the fact that barring a minuscule proportion, all localities in the city, report the presence of Government hospital (Fig. 4.26). An upgradation of facilities in Government hospitals and making the others within the reach of the common person may be read as the clarion call here. Though Government hospitals seem to be present in almost all localities in the city, they seem to be underutilized in the eastern part as also the central part of the city and the core of Secunderabad (Fig. 4.27). The presence of corporate hospitals and the access provided to them by the employers in many instances are the explanatory factors in these cases.

Fig. 4.28 and 4.29 show the presence of private doctors and the utilization of their services in the different localities of the city respectively. It is found that they are present in a fair measure in most parts of the city, though some localities report them in a low number only in relative terms and these are to a large extent in the southern part of the city and to some extent the western part. Barring Pathergatti and Mogulpura in the old city, the other localities seem to utilize the services of the private doctor in an adequate measure. At times even if they have less of this facility in their own locality, they seem to access it from others.

Most parts of the city report the presence of cinema houses (Fig. 4.30), which are still a source of entertainment, despite the electronic revolution and the presence of means of entertainment within the houses of many people. The parts which report a relative lack of them are Warasiguda, Saroornagar, Gowliguda Chaman, Gosha Mahal and Rajendranagar. A comparison of Fig. 4.30 and 4.31 leads one to infer that in most of the localities this facility is underutilized. The spread of other means of entertainment could be an explanatory factor in a general sense where they seem to be making inroads into the

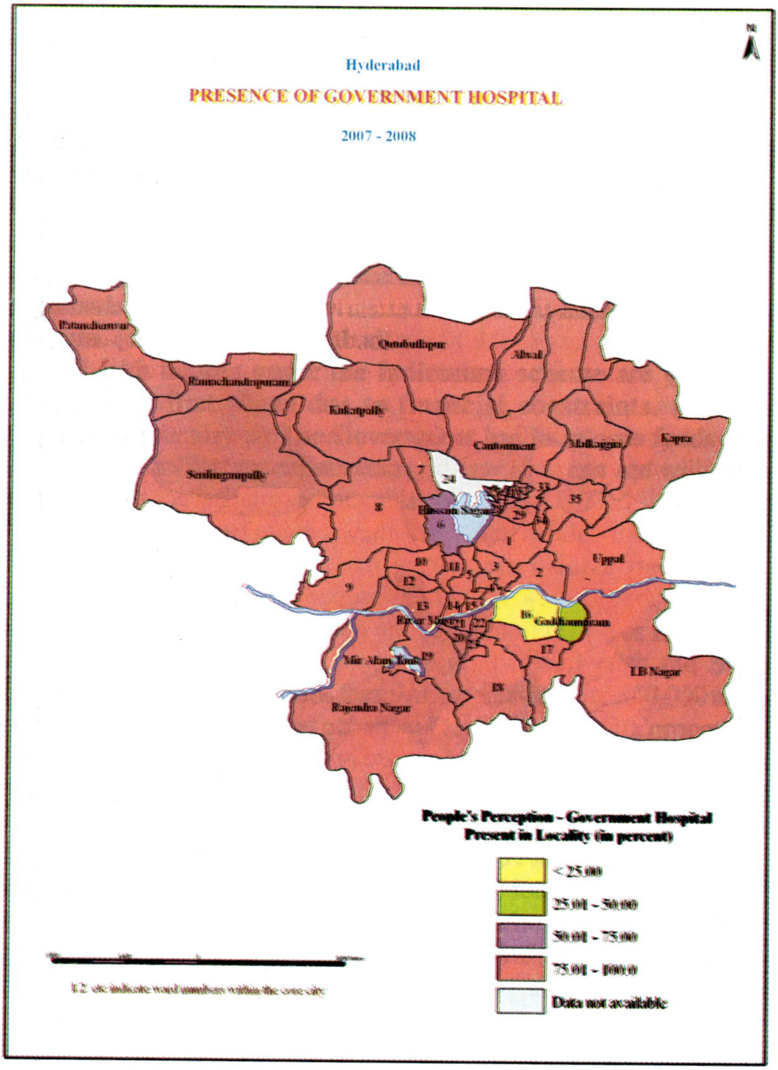

Source: Field Survey.

Fig. 4.26: Presence of Government Hospital, Hyderabad, 2007-08

market captured by cinema. The case with regard to the eating places also seems to be more or less similar. While they are present in an ample measure in most localities of the city (Fig. 4.32), they are not utilized in a commensurate proportion in a good number of parts

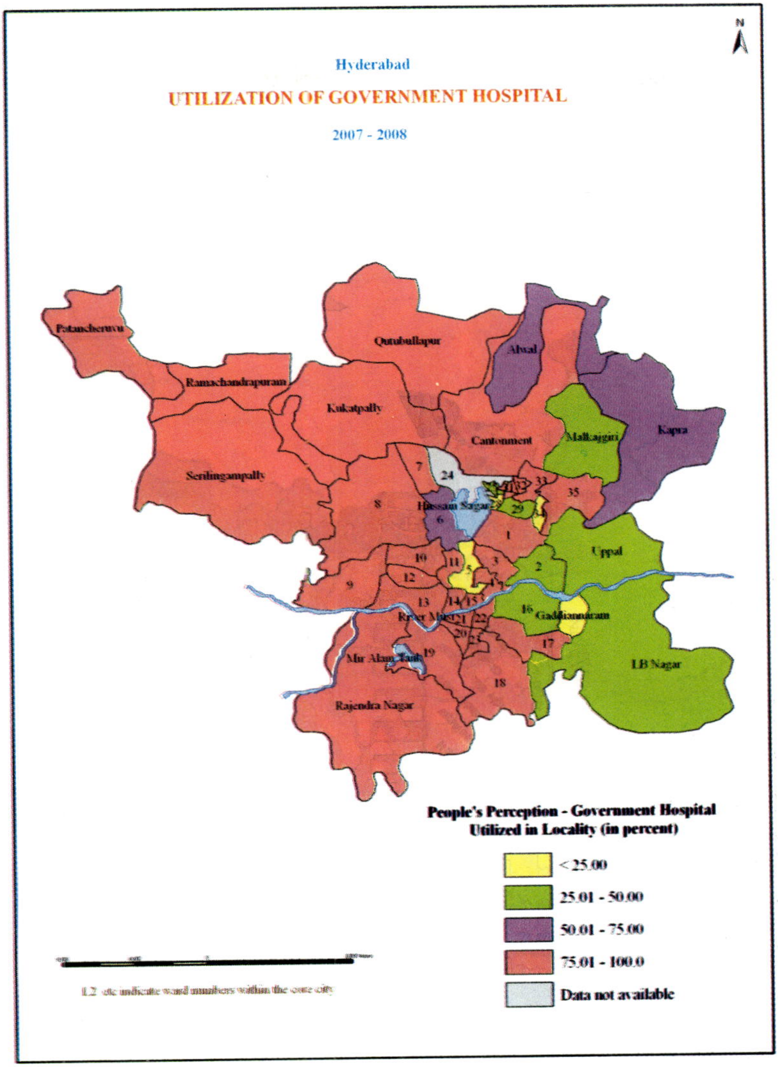

Source: Field Survey.

Fig. 4.27: Utilization of Government Hospital, Hyderabad, 2007-08

(Fig. 4.33). Aliabad, Gulzar House, Kapra and Alwal seem to figure prominently among such localities. The general ambience of these localities coupled with the standards of living in most of them and their neighbouring areas may be the factors accountable on this front.

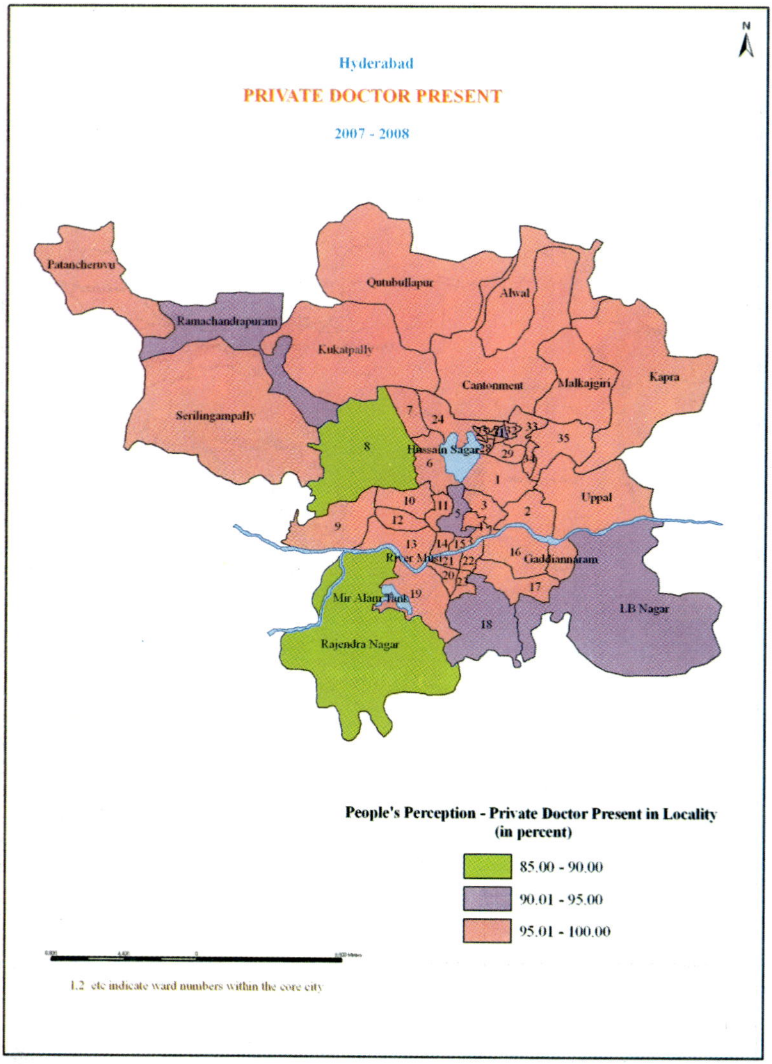

Source: Field Survey.

Fig. 4.28: Private Doctor Present, Hyderabad, 2007-08

Fig. 4.34 and 4.35 pertain to the presence and utilization pattern of parks in Hyderabad. Parks are reported in a very less number of localities and even when they are reported, a dismally low proportion of people seem to utilize them. Development of parks and gardens

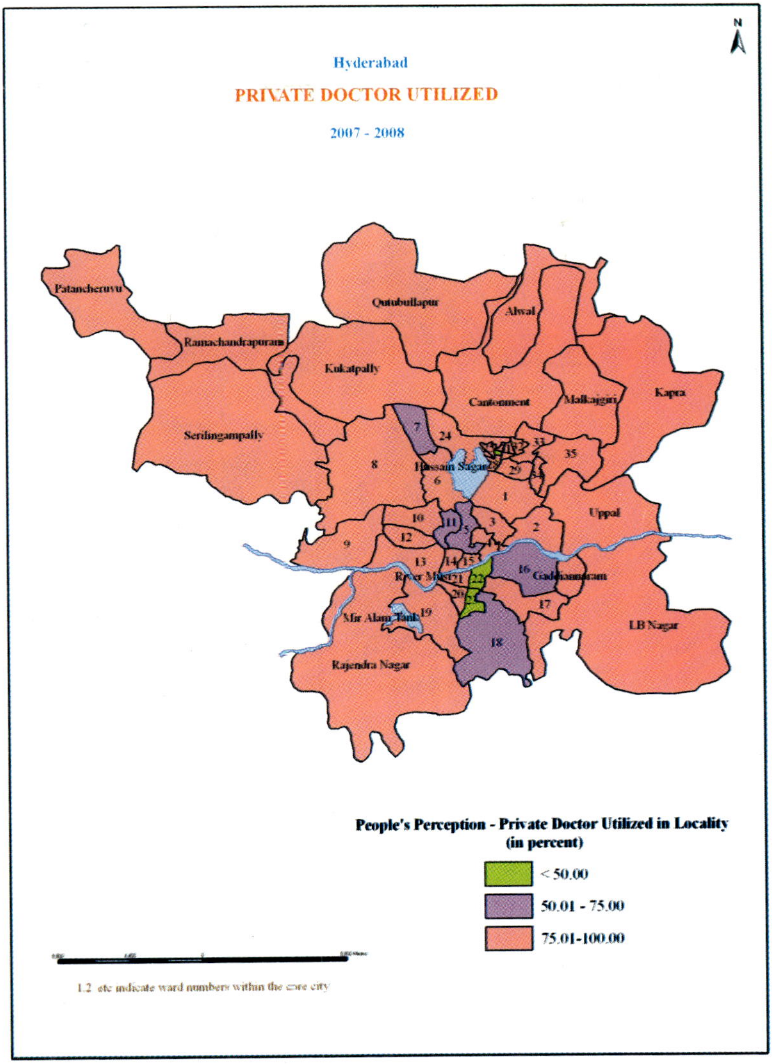

Source: Field Survey.

Fig. 4.29: Services of Private Doctor Utilized, Hyderabad, 2007-08

and sensitization of the people towards them may be the crucial factors that the government can look after, more so as they serve as lung spaces in an otherwise congested city. The apathy on the part of people

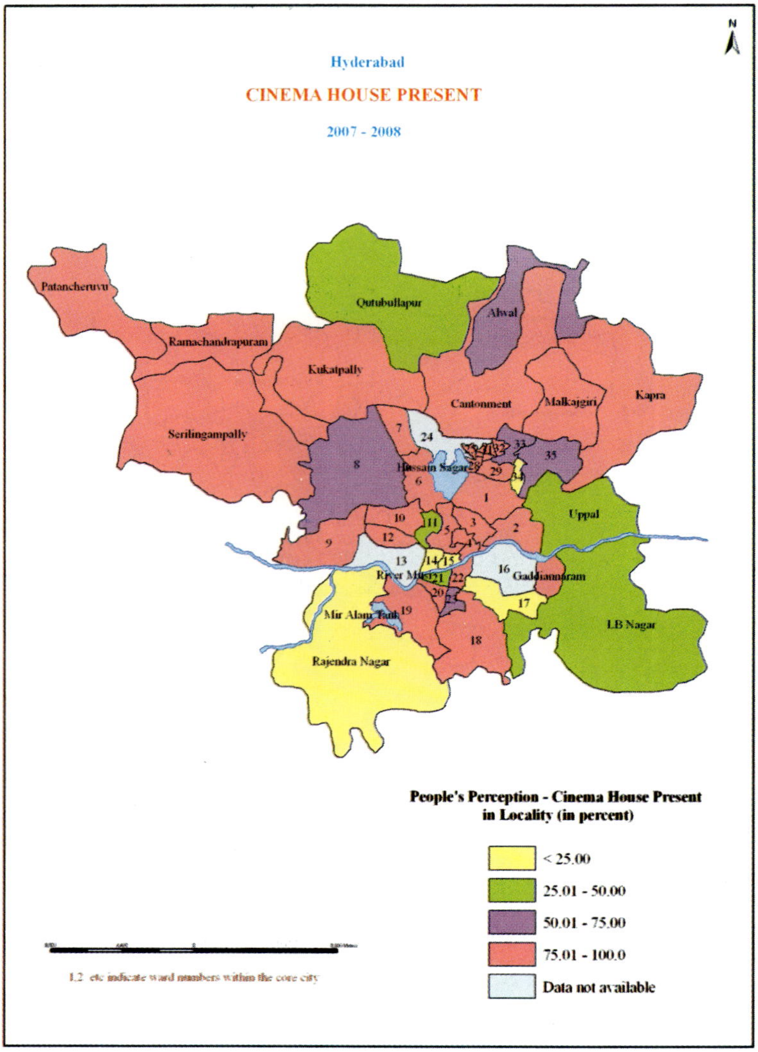

Source: Field Survey.

Fig. 4.30: Cinema House Present, Hyderabad, 2007-08

parks in the peripheral localities is more conspicuous. The picture with regard to the presence and utilization pattern of play grounds (Fig. 4.36 and 4.37) is also not much different. They seem to be present

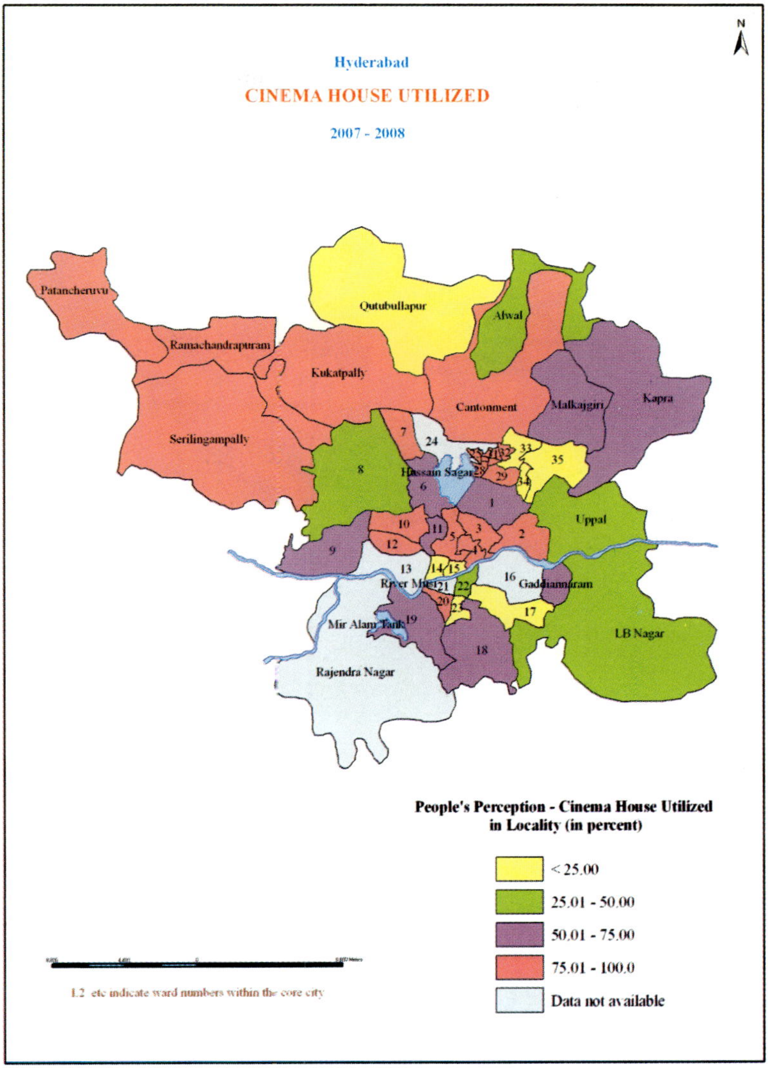

Source: Field Survey.

Fig. 4.31: Cinema House Utilized, Hyderabad, 2007-08

in select locations, more in the central city locations when compared to the peripheral areas. But their utilization as reported by the residents is miserably low. Open Spaces are also present in select locations and quite understandably, more on the periphery of the city (Fig. 4.38).

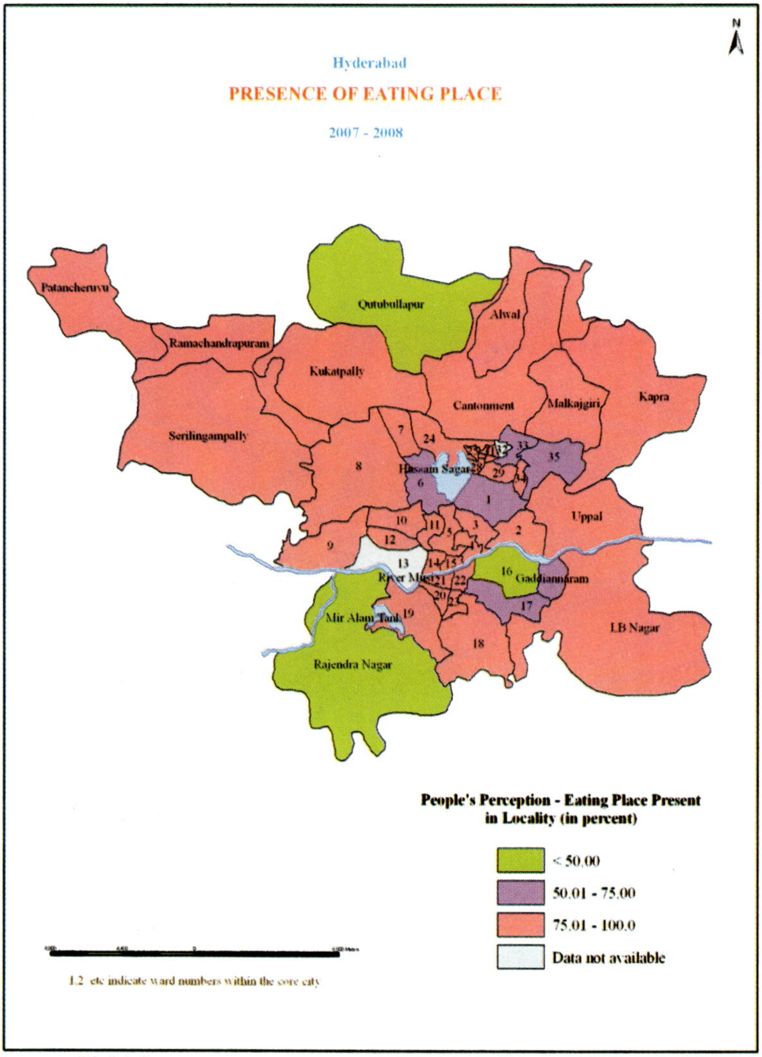

Source: Field Survey.

Fig. 4.32: Presence of Eating Place, Hyderabad, 2007-08

The land use pattern (Fig. 4.39) is most often in keeping with the availability of this endowment. Most localities in the city (69%) exhibit a satisfaction quotient of more than 50 per cent so far as recreational facilities in the city are concerned. Hussaini Alam, Lalapet

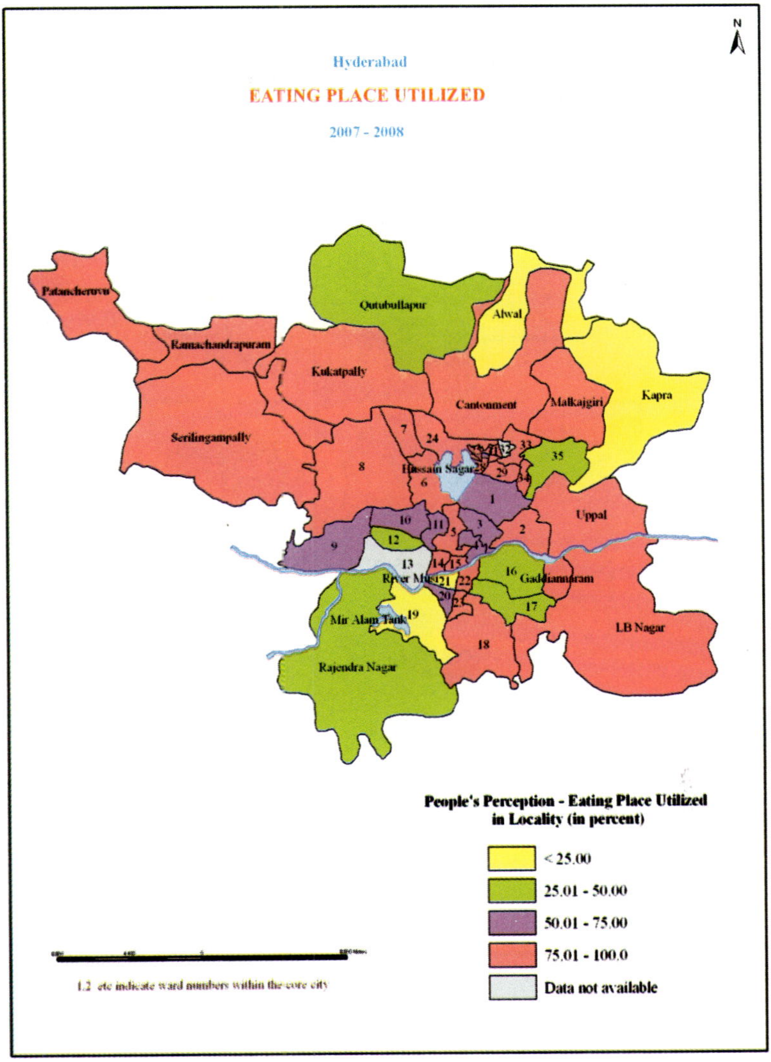

Source: Field Survey.

Fig. 4.33: Eating Place Utilized, Hyderabad, 2007-08

and Malkajgiri seem to be wanting on this front to a large extent. Planning authorities can take cognizance of this in their endeavours towards planning for recreational facilities.

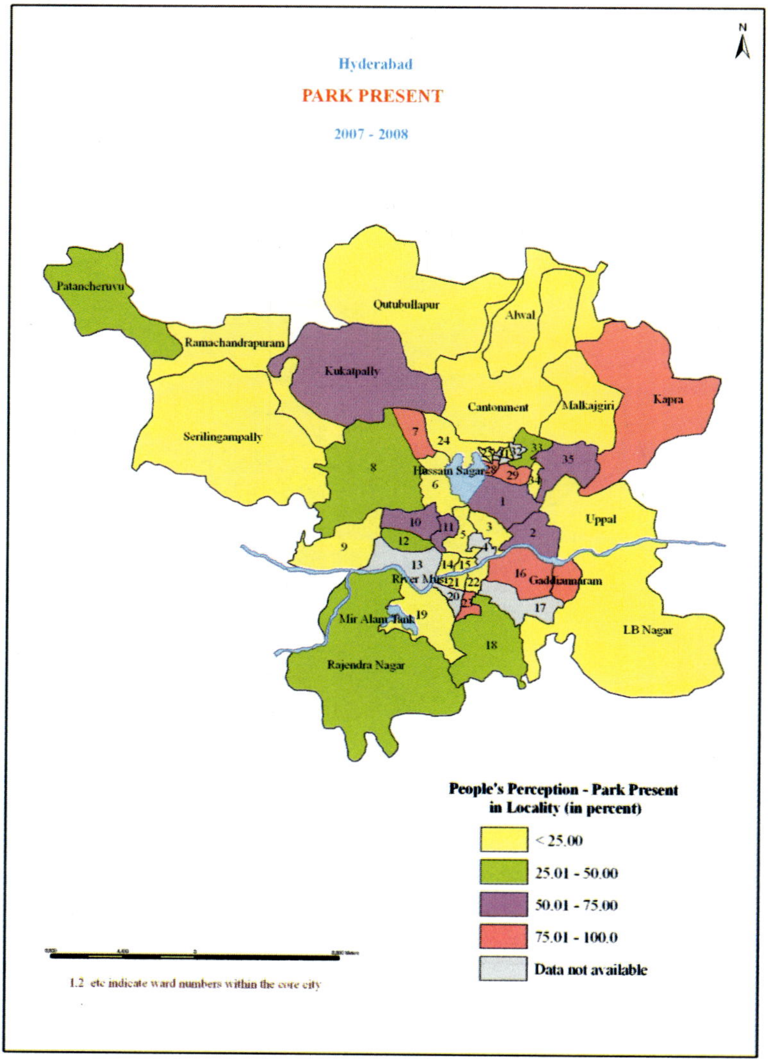

Source: Field Survey.

Fig. 4.34: Park Present, Hyderabad, 2007-08

Financial institutions like banks, which are a near basic requirement in this era of globalization, are ubiquitously present in all the localities of the city (Fig. 4.41), their utilization pattern is

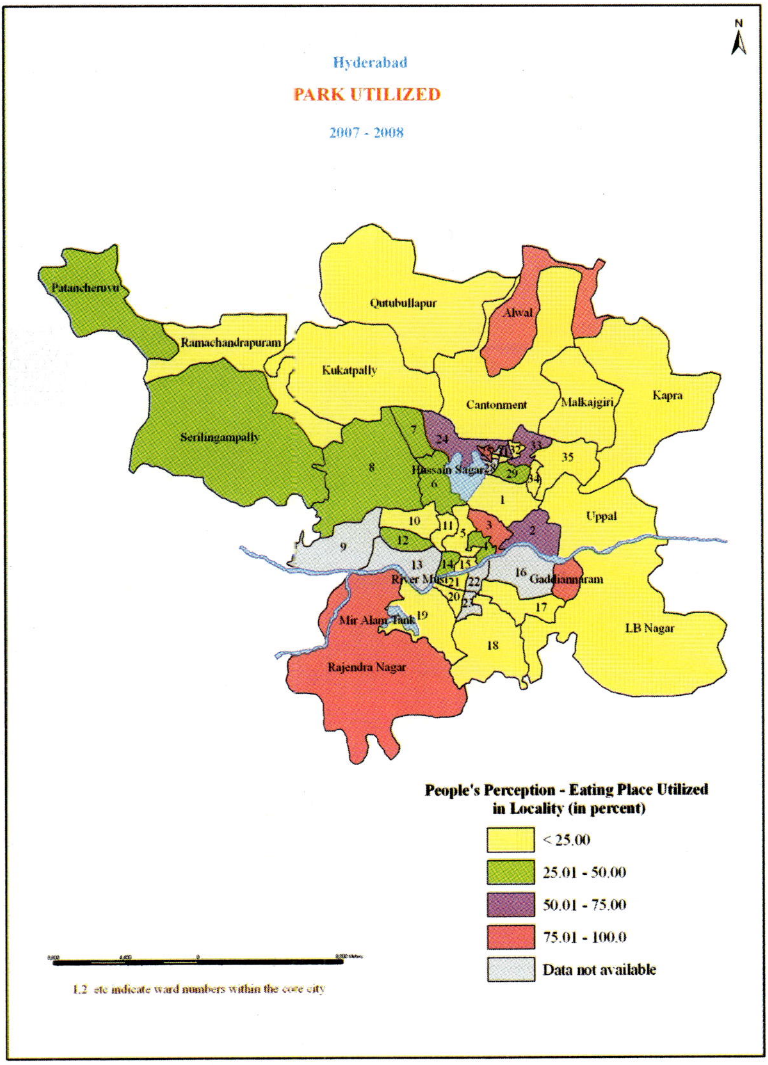

Source: Field Survey.

Fig. 4.35: Park Utilized, Hyderabad, 2007-08

slightly at variance with their presence. For one, the service seems to be slightly underutilized in the old city, which is to the south of River Musi. The traditions and mores of the resident Muslim community

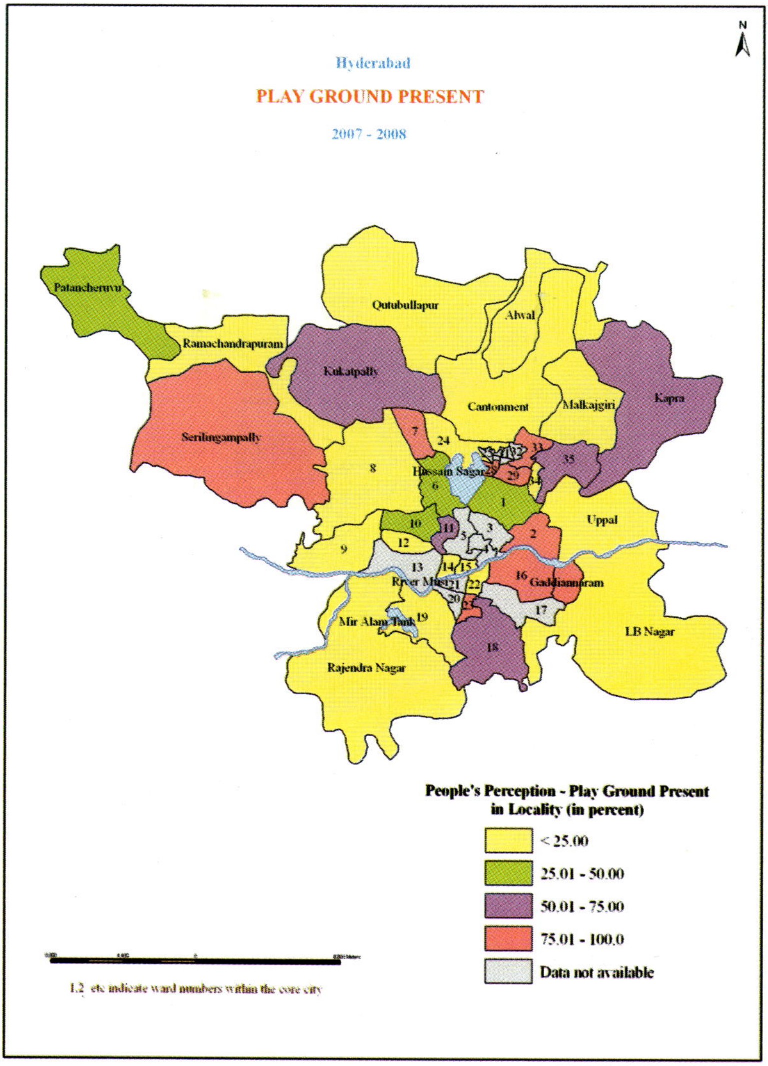

Source: Field Survey.

Fig. 4.36: Play Ground Present, Hyderabad, 2007-08

which do not favour earning interest on money, are in a large measure responsible for this phenomenon. Apart from that the not so well off Erukala Basti and Kapra have less than 50 per cent of the people making use of the bank facility.

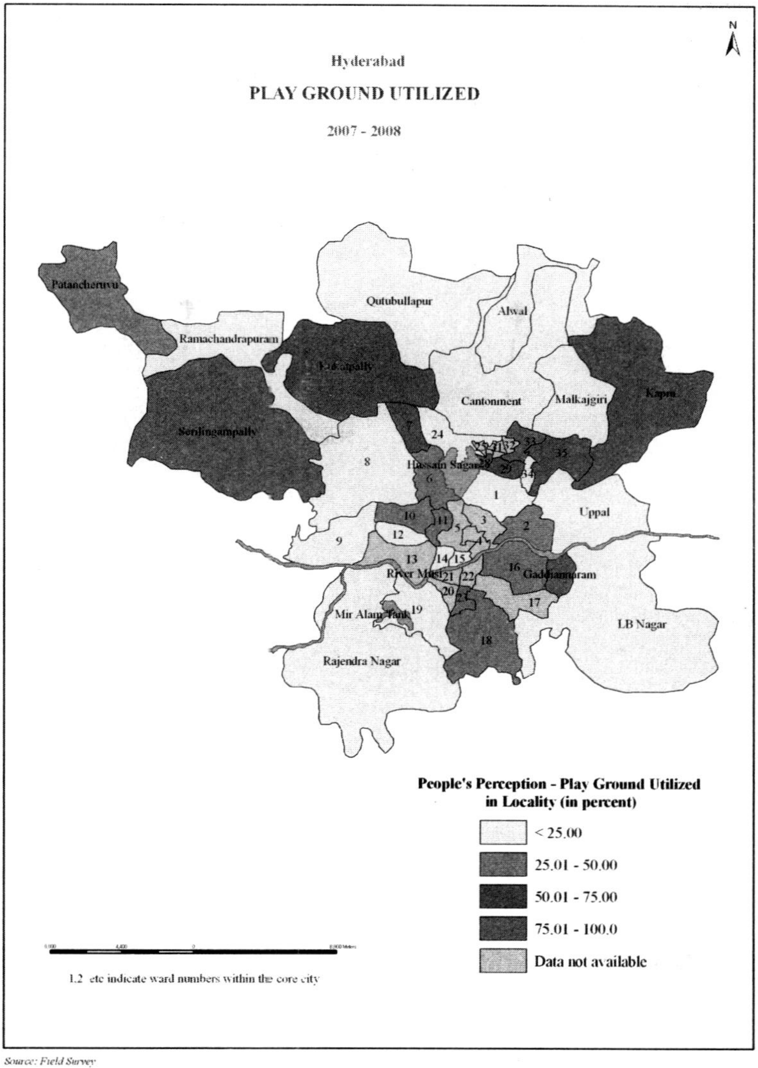

Source: Field Survey.

Fig. 4.37: Play Ground Utilized, Hyderabad, 2007-08

ATM facility is present again in most of the localities in a fair measure (Fig. 4.43) though less than 50 per cent of the people report its presence in the Sabzimandi- Karwan area. The facility again seems

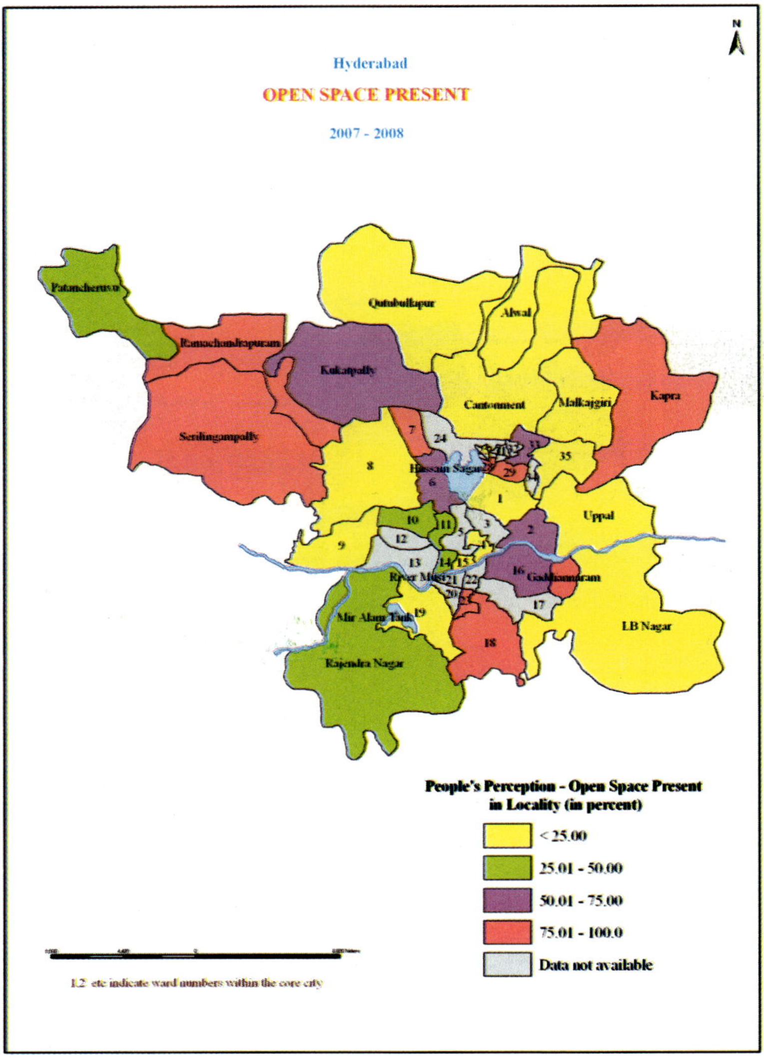

Source: Field Survey.

Fig. 4.38: Open Space Present, Hyderabad, 2007-08

to be underutilized in most of the localities (Fig. 4.44). While people are aware of its existence they are not utilizing it to the optimum level. This is again so more in the Sabzimandi- Karwan area, Erukala Basti and Saidabad Colony. Greater utilization seems to have a radial pattern

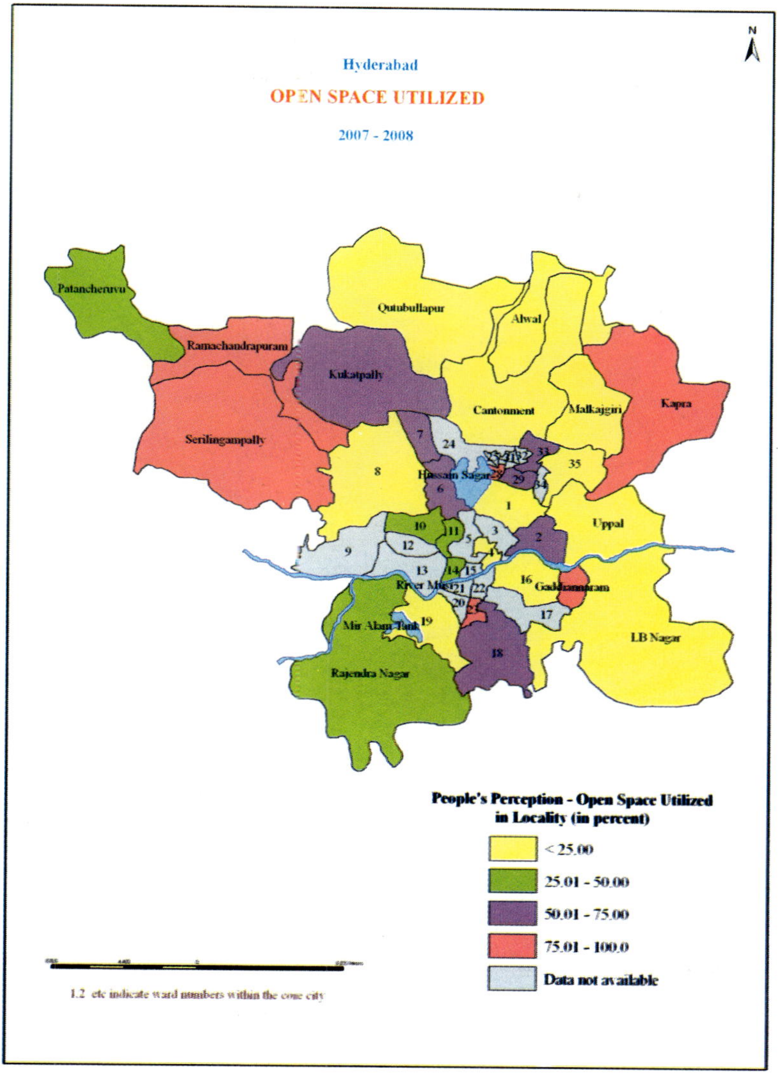

Source: Field Survey.

Fig. 4.39: Open Space Utilized, Hyderabad, 2007-08

from the centre of the city towards the north- west and north- east. In that sense, it seems to be more astride the main transportation arteries.

Most people have reported adequate presence of Post and Telegraph facilities in their localities (Fig. 4.45). Their utilization

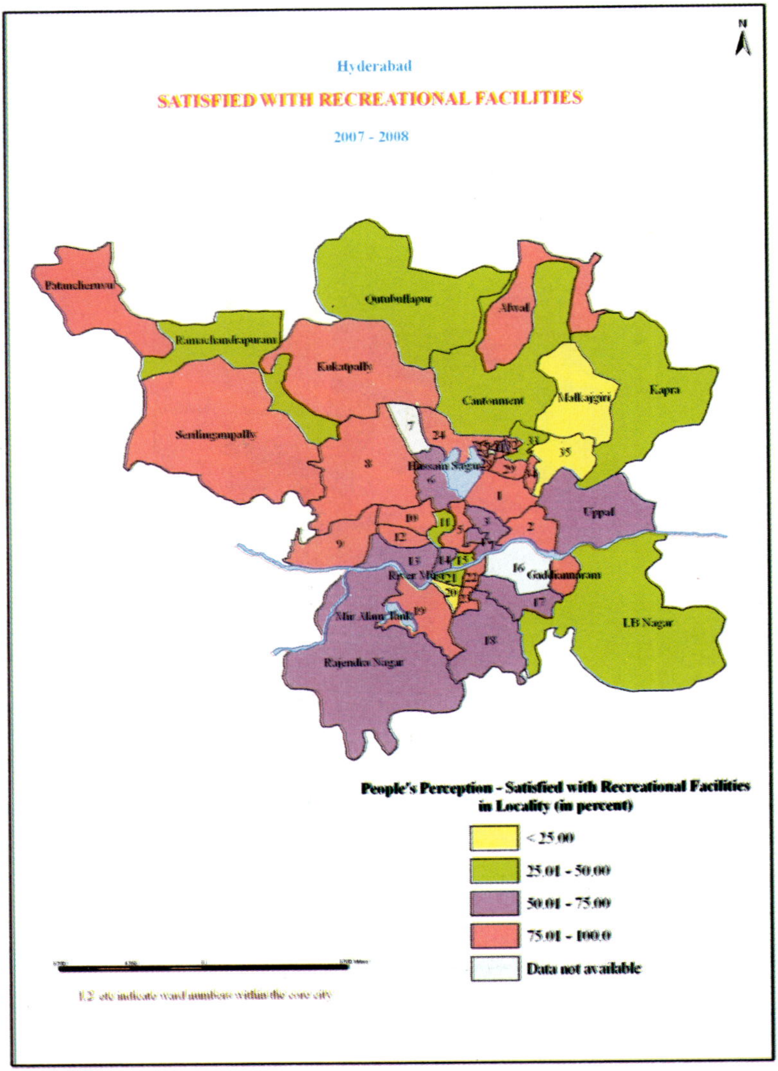

Source: Field Survey.

Fig. 4.40: Satisfied with Recreational Facilities, Hyderabad, 2007-08

pattern, however, is at vaiance with the presence of this facility (Fig. 4.46). The facility seems to be less utilized as the digital revolution and the coming on the scene of faster modes of communication have out-spaced the traditional modes of communication. Another basis

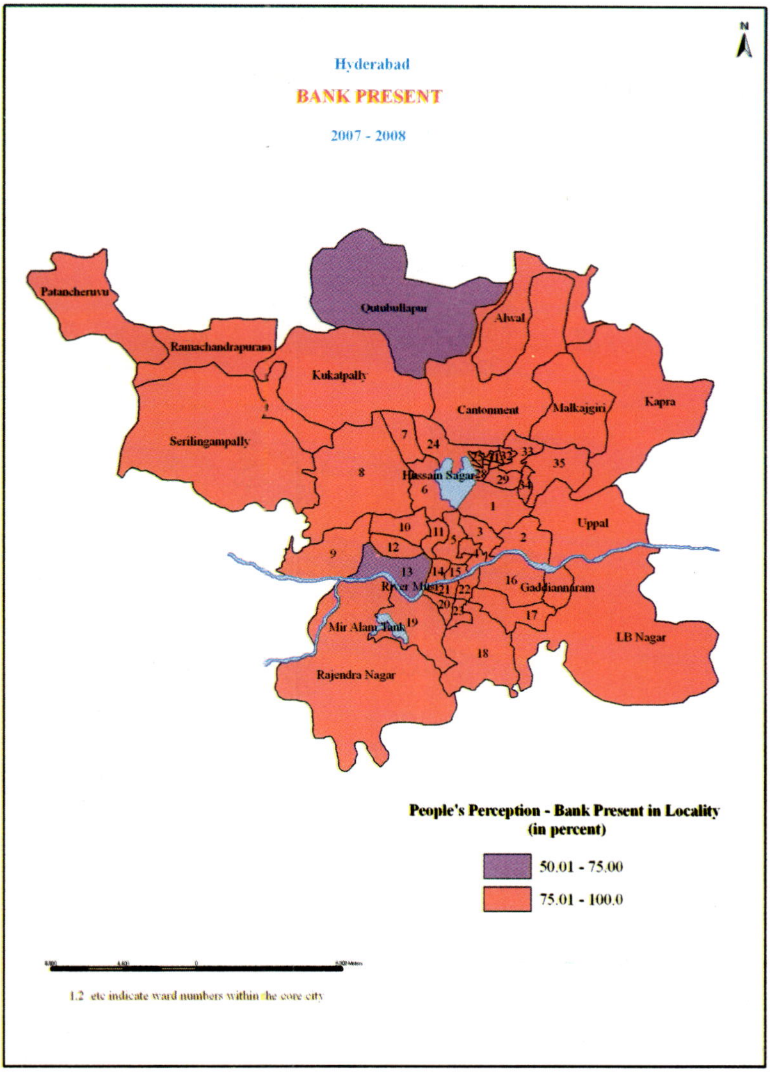

Source: Field Survey.

Fig. 4.41: Bank Present, Hyderabad, 2007-08

for this could be the relatively low level of interaction of certain pockets of the city like Karwan, Moghalpura, Gaddiannaram, Rajendranagar and so on. with the outside world.

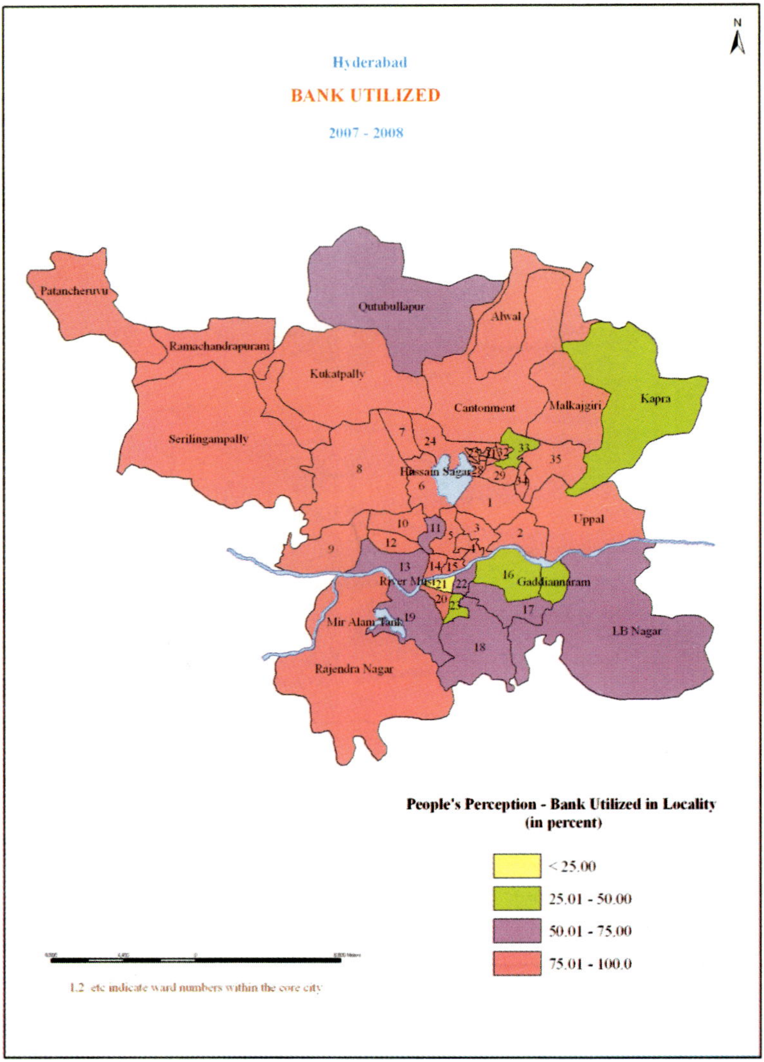

Source: Field Survey.

Fig. 4.42: Bank Utilized, Hyderabad, 2007-08

Fig. 4.47 and 4.48 relate to the presence and utilization of the services of the motor mechanic. It is found that while this service is present in an abundant measure in all parts of the core city and even beyond, it is not used in a matching proportion in many parts, especially those to the

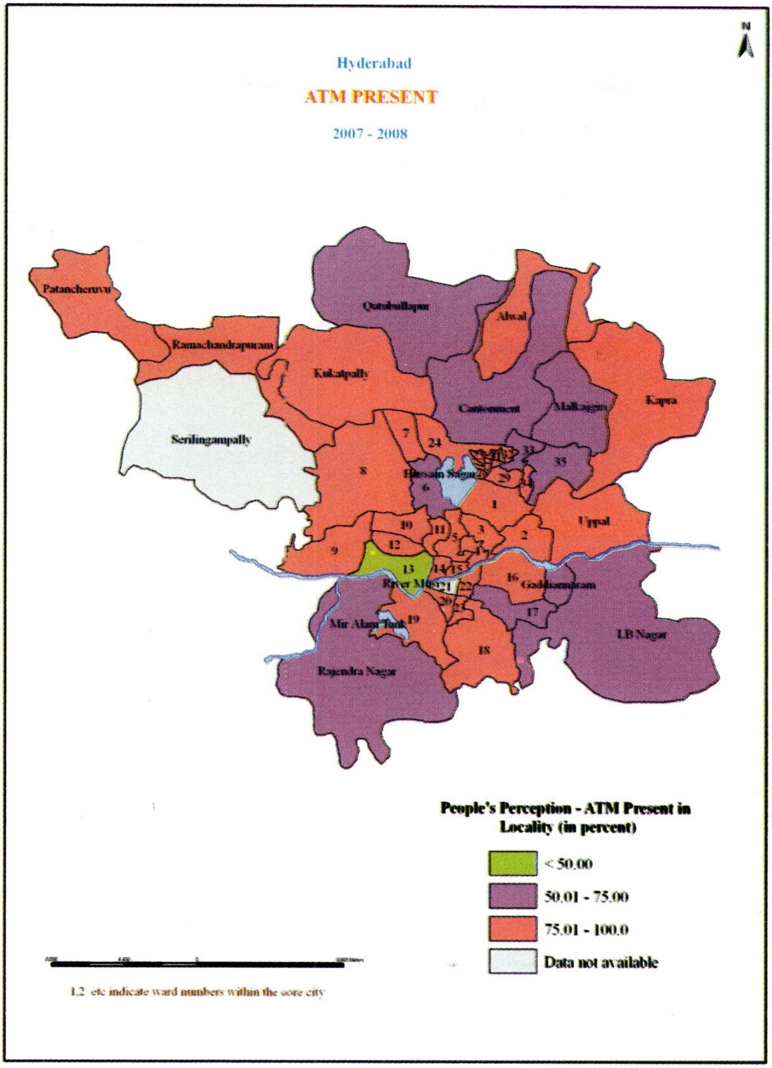

Source: Field Survey.

Fig. 4.43: ATM Present, Hyderabad, 2007-08

south of the river Musi. Lack of personal vehicles may be one of the reasons for this. This is apart from the fact that this service can also be used in localities other than the resident locality of the respondents.

The case with regard to the super markets (Fig. 4.49 and 4.50) is

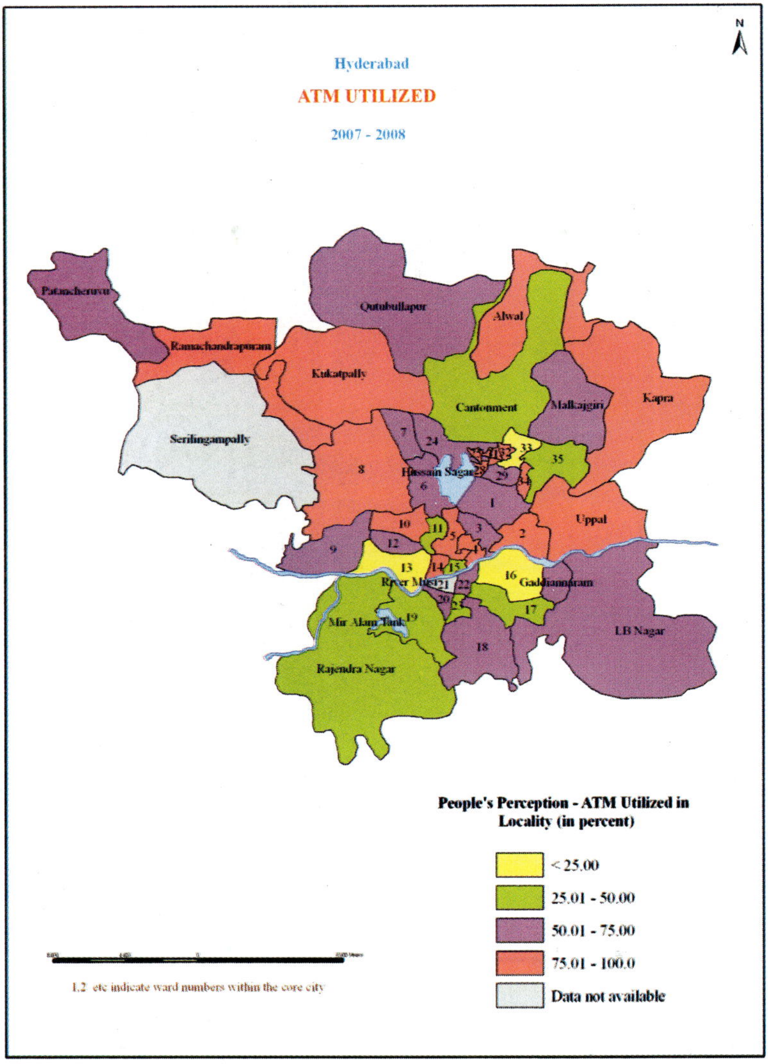

Source: Field Survey.

Fig. 4.44: ATM Utilized, Hyderabad, 2007-08

also the same, where the facility seems to be underutilized in most of the localities. The utilization pattern is not commensurate with the presence of the facility. Yet people seem to be more or less satisfied with shopping facilities in most of the localities (Fig. 4.51). This is a

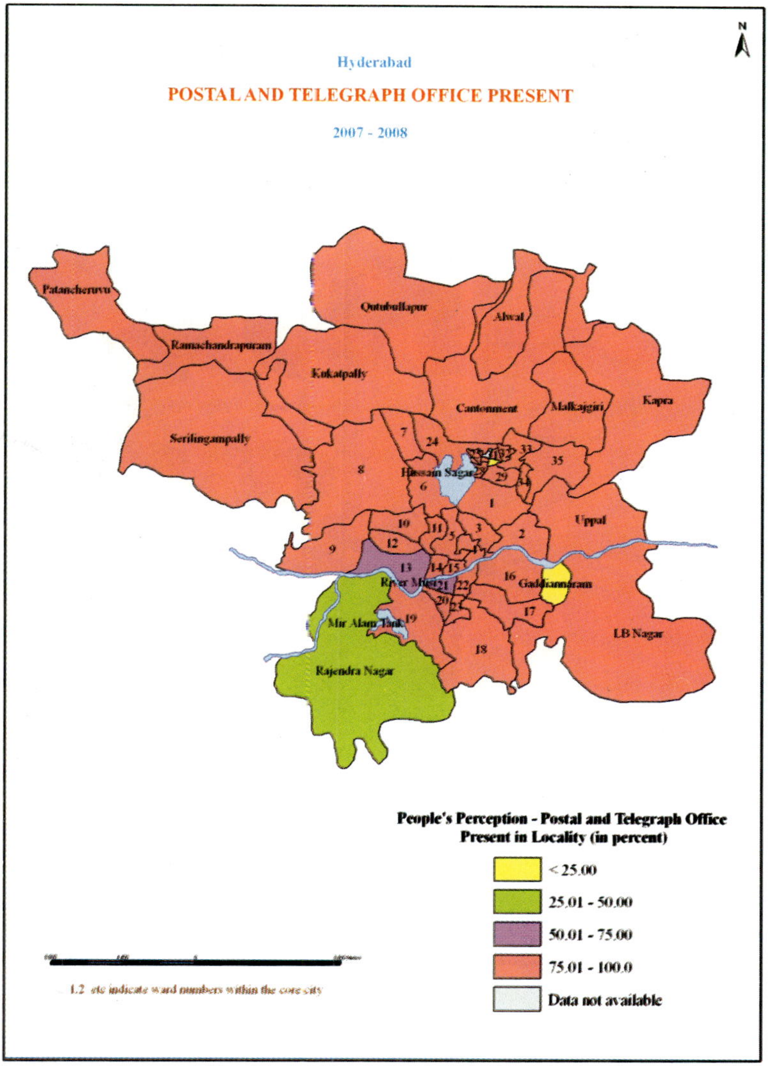

Source: Field Survey.

Fig. 4.45: Postal and Telegraph Office Present, Hyderabad, 2007-08

reflection of the fact that despite underutilization of a higher end service with regard to shopping like super market, people are well able to meet their requirements on this front.

It may be said in recapitulation of what has been said in this chapter

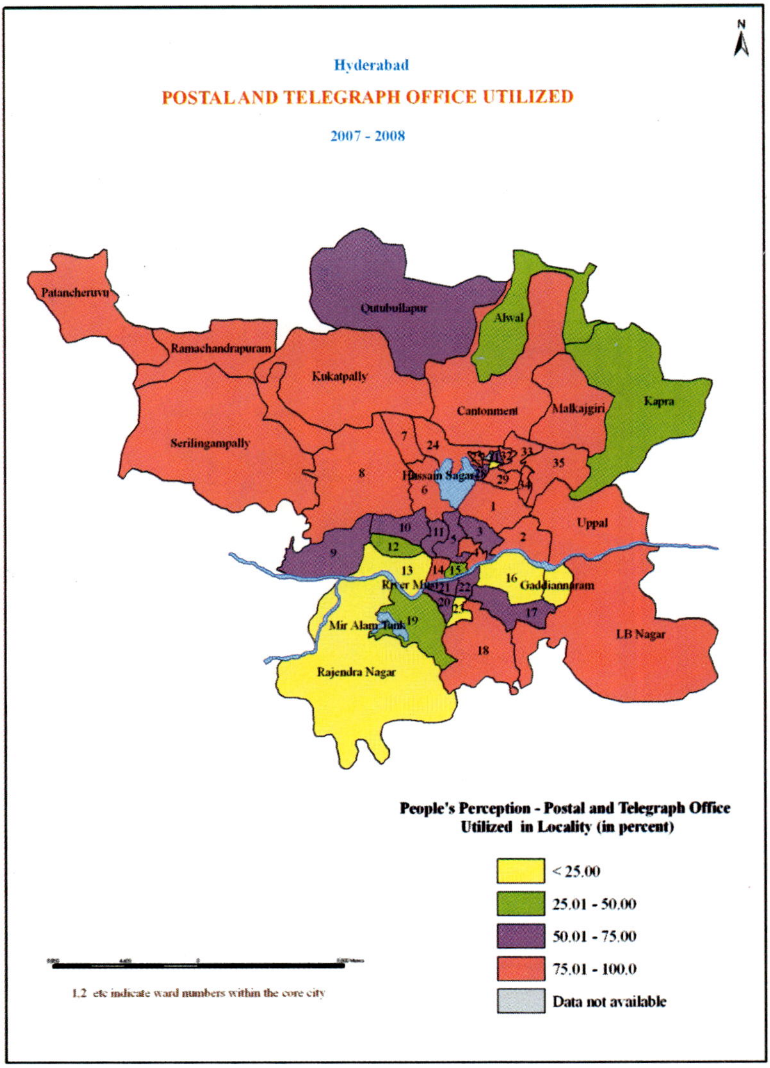

Source: Field Survey.

Fig. 4.46: Postal and Telegraph Office Utilized, Hyderabad, 2007-08

that most people in the city place their locality high on the physical surroundings scale; this tendency is more manifest in central city locations than peripheral locations. This variable is followed by ranking on the scale of Amenities and Infrastructure, Social Environment and

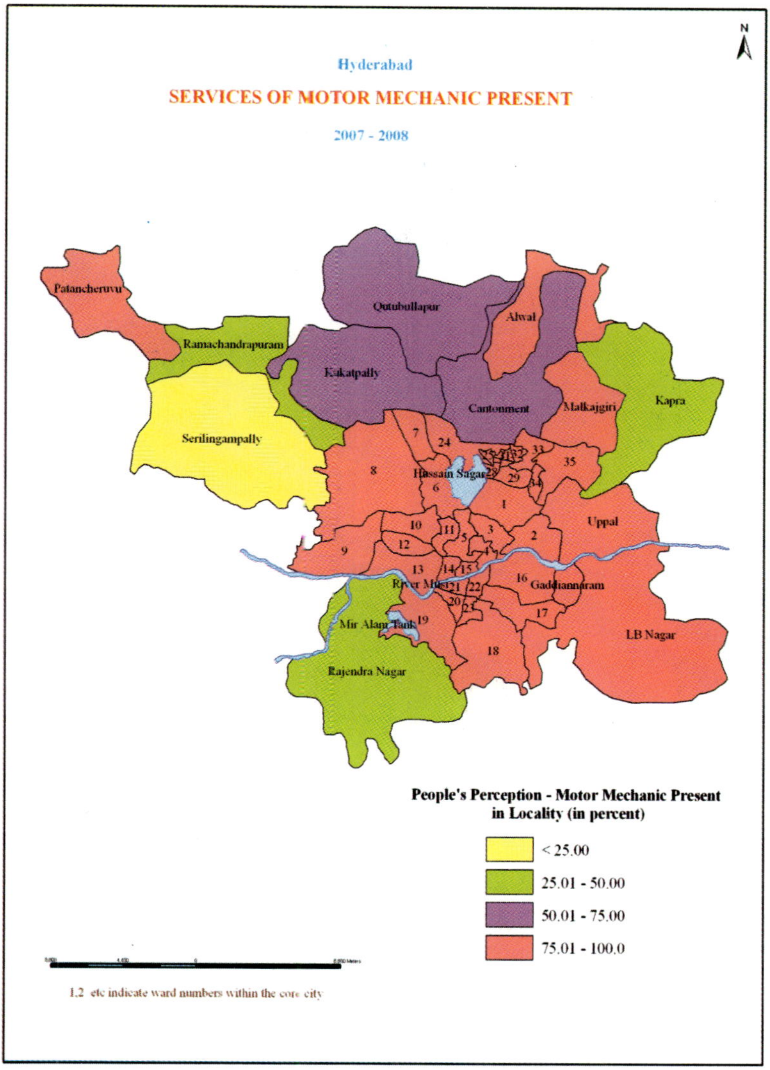

Source: Field Survey.

Fig. 4.47: Services of Motor Mechanic Present, Hyderabad, 2007-08

Security. So far as specific amenities and facilities in the house and locality are concerned, most people in the city seem to be satisfied with ventilation in the house. Also more than 50 per cent of the people seem to be satisfied with garbage disposal. However, so far as drainage

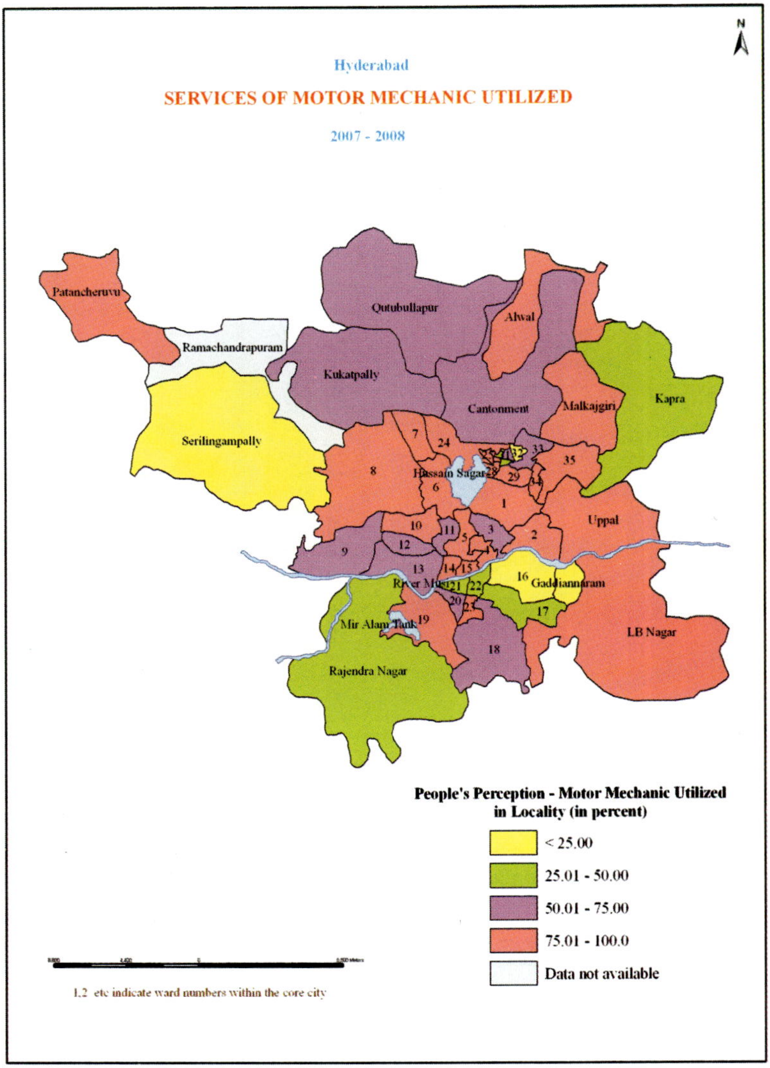

Source: Field Survey.

Fig. 4.48: Services of Motor Mechanic Utilized, Hyderabad, 2007-08

facility is concerned most people in the Hyderabad part of the twin cities and the peripheral localities are not satisfied with this facility. A core-periphery scenario seems to be noticeable so far as sanitation

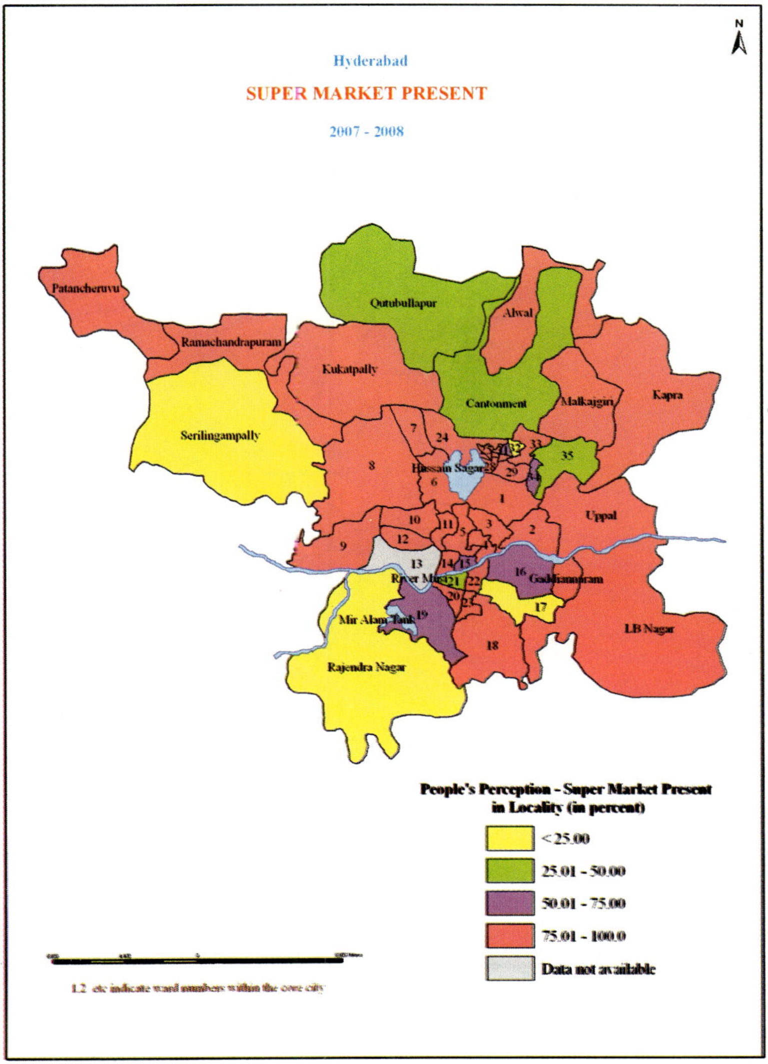

Source: Field Survey.

Fig. 4.49: Super Market Present, Hyderabad, 2007-08

and even other variables like water supply situation, street lighting, roads, traffic movement, accessibility, satisfaction with regard to health facilities, etc. are concerned. While the core areas exhibit a relative

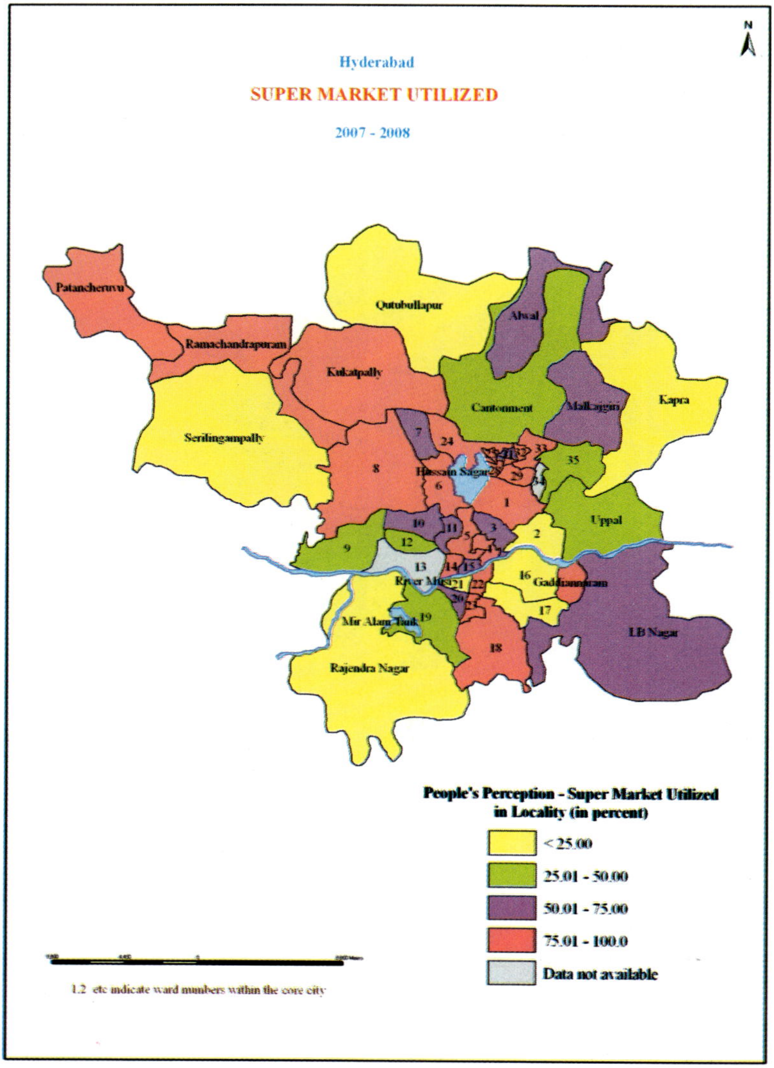

Source: Field Survey.

Fig. 4.50: Super Market Utilized, Hyderabad, 2007-08

contentment, the peripheral areas are not so content. Primary and High Schools seem to be present in most of the localities of the city. Colleges are also present in an ample measure in most parts of the city. However,

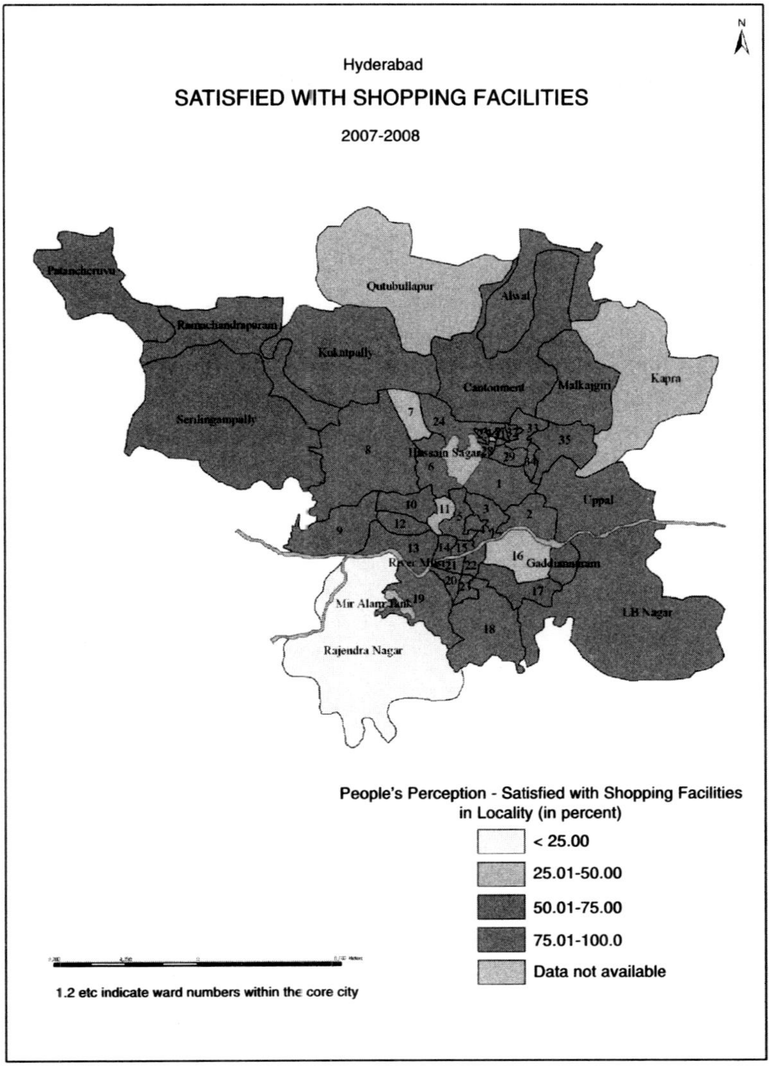

Source: Field Survey.

Fig. 4.51: Satisfied with Shopping Facilities, Hyderabad, 2007-08

the utilization pattern of these facilities shows that they are underutilized in the central and southern part of the city, speaking for the need to increase the awareness among the parents for education.

Private doctors are also present in almost all localities and at times their services are accessed from other localities also. Cinema theatres and eating places are present in an adequate measure in most parts of the city, though there is an element of underutilization so far as their use is concerned. Parks seem to be present in select central city localities, but their use is dismally low. Open spaces are more on the periphery of the city and by implication also utilized in those areas in a greater measure. Banks are present in all parts of the city though their use is slightly restricted in the Muslim dominated southern part of the city. Though ATM facility is present in most parts of the city it is utilized more along the main roads. Post and telegraph facilities are also adequately present all over the city, though their use pattern is less in comparison to its presence, owing to for one the digital revolution and secondly the low level of interaction of some of the localities with the rest of the world. It is also found that while not all people utilize super markets in the measure in which they are quoted to exist, yet all sections of the people are satisfied with commercial facilities present in their localities.

References

Anita, A. Summers, Paul C. Cheshire, and Lanfranco Senn, (eds.), *Urban Change in the United States and Western Europe: Comparative Analysis and Policy*, Urban Institute Press, Washington, DC, 1999.

Anthony, G. Champion, ed., *Counter urbanization: The Changing Pace and the Nature of Population Deconcentration*, Edward Arnold, London, 1989).

D'souza, Alfred and Singh "*The Indian City*" Manoher Publishers, New Delhi 1978.

David, L. McKee, *Urban Environments in Emerging Economies*, Praeger Publishers, Westport, CT 1994.

Deccan Chronicle October11, 2008.

Deccan Chronicle September 29, 2008.

Denton, Nancy A. and Douglas S. Massey. *American Apartheid: Segregation and the Making of the Underclass*, Harvard University Press, Cambridge, 1993.

Jonas, Rabinovich, First Forum of the World Alliance of Cities Against Poverty, *Proceedings*: 12-14 October 1998, Lyon, France.

Mansell Prothero, R. and Murray Chapman, *Circulation in Third World Countries*, Routledge & Kegan Paul, London, 1985.

Markandey, Kalpana, 'Inclusive Cities in an Era of Globalization: A Case for a Shelter Programme for Hyderabad' Unpublished UGC Project Report, 2008.

Market Beat, *Hyderabad Residential Report*, A Cushman and Wakefield Research Publication, 3Q, 2009.

Mazumdar, Sharbnani, *Social Development of Slums*, Hindustan Publishing Corporation, New Delhi, 1990.

Mehta, Dinesh, *Rural India to Modern Era*, New Delhi Publications, New Delhi, 1991.

Michael, Harrington, *The Other America: Poverty in the United States*, Macmillan Publishing Company, New York, 1962.

Patel, Sheela Director, Society for the Promotion of Area Resource Centres (SPARC), quoted in the *TV-Evideo series, Life II, "City Life,"* Programme 1, 2001.

Paul, A. Jargowsky, *Poverty and Place: Ghettos, Barrios, and the American City*, Russell Sage Foundation, New York:, 1997.

Rao, K.R. and Rao M.S.A. *Cities and Slums—A Study of a Squatters' Settlement in the City of Vijayawada*, Concept Publishing Company, New Delhi, 1984.

Rao, Ratna, *Social Organization in an Indian Slum*, Mittal Publications, New Delhi, 1990.

Richard, Stren, "Thinking About Urban Inclusiveness," paper prepared for the 18th Session of the Commission on Human Settlements, entitled, "Bridging the Divided City: A Dialogue on Social Inclusion in Cities," 14 February 2001. See http://www.unchs.org/govern/

Saskia, Sassen, Professor of Sociology, University of Chicago, quoted in the *TV-E video series, Life II, "City Life,"* Programme 1, 2001.

Source The Hindu, Feb.8 2008.

Sunday Times of India, October 12 2008.

Terrence, G. McGee and Ira M. Robinson, *The Mega Urban Regions of Southeast Asia University of British Columbia Press*, Vancouver, Canada, 1995.

The Hindu, Feb.8 2008

UNCHS, Global Report on Human Settlements 2001, Earthscan Press, London, 2001, p. xxviii and pp. 15-23.

UNCHS, *State of the World's Cities 2001*, Nairobi, 2001, p. 109.

UNDP, Human Development Report 2000, Oxford University Press, New York, 2000, pp. 31-41.

UNDP, *Human Development Report 2000*, Oxford University Press, New York, 2000, pp. 31-41.

United Nations Development Programme, "Human Development Report," Oxford University Press, New York, 1999, p. 2.

5

Housing Finance

The State Government has given 1,022.95 acres of 'surplus land' in Hyderabad city and Ranga Reddy district to the HUDA, APIIC and APHB for 'optimum utilisation in public interest.' Under the order, HUDA got 384.62 acres, APIIC 482.15 acres and APHB 156.8 acres. The government had earlier taken over these lands under the Urban Land Ceilings and Regulation Act, 1976 and officials said that the lands would cost over Rs. 1500 crore. (*Deccan Chronicle*, August 3, 2008)

A medley of schemes have been put in place by various governmental agencies for providing houses to the marginalized and less advantaged sections of society. Among these the better known ones and those which have a wider ambit are the VAMBAY Scheme, Indira Awas Yojana and Rajiv Gruhakalpa to name.

10000 houses which came up on a 100 acre government land at Jawarharnagar near Shamirpet will be regularized by revenue authorities. These include houses and structures in Nanamurinagar, Giriprasad Nagar, Devendranagar, New Devendranagar, Gabbilalapet and other colonies. (*Times News Network*, March 4, 2008)

Government Initiatives in Housing for the Poor

The Andhra Pradesh Housing Corporation Limited, Hyderabad is responsible for taking up housing schemes particularly for the weaker sections. During the period from 1997 to 2002, the Andhra Pradesh Housing Corporation constructed houses in Hyderabad and adjoining Ranga Reddy districts; these included almost 45,000 houses for the poor (Table 5.1).

Table 5.1: House Construction by A.P. Housing Corporation

Year	*Hyderabad District*	*Ranga Reddy District Urban*	*Ranga Reddy District Rural*
1997-1998	1542	837	5064
1998-1999	3034	1007	6309
1999-2000	4854	1046	4117
2000-2001	1045	1005	4507
2001-2002	536	240	4151
2002-2003	495	389	5018
Total	**11506**	**4524**	**29166**

Source: HUDA, 2003.

It may be noted that most of the urban components of Ranga Reddy District and sizable parts of Rural Ranga Reddy District fall in HUDA jurisdiction.

Thus the above figures of around 8000 houses per year for weaker sections can be considered the figures for HUDA area. This is to be viewed against the annual demand of total houses of around 80,000 all together. The demand for the lower income groups would be at least 80 per cent of the total demand. Thus there is a big gap in the demand and supply for this group, part of which is met by the gray market, the unauthorized sector.

The Andhra Pradesh Housing Corporation has the following types of Urban Housing Schemes:

Table 5.2: Housing by Andhra Pradesh Housing Corporation

Scheme	*Unit cost*	*State subsidy*	*Central subsidy*	*Total*	*Loan*	*Benefi-ciary contribu-tion*
EWS Urban	25000	3000	0	3000	20000	2000
EWS Special	30000	3000	0	3000	25000	2000

Source: HUDA, 2003.

The target groups have reservations for Scheduled Caste and Scheduled Tribes, Minorities and EBCs. The Special Housing covers groups like Beedi Workers, Fishermen and Weavers.

The Urban Housing taken up by the Andhra Pradesh Housing Corporation ranges in plinth area from 20 to 24 square metres. Type designs are provided for some of the schemes. The schemes emphasise

Self-Help and Mutual help of beneficiaries. The target groups for Urban Housing are families whose annual income is Rs. 126,000 and Rs. 18,000 for EWS and Special EWS respectively.

Housing for the Lower Income Groups

While the private developers and builders have built most houses in HUDA area, the supply is mostly by way of large plots of land and apartments for the upper middle and higher groups.

No urban development or Municipal legislation in Andhra Pradesh has any specific concessions for the urban poor. Supply of serviced land for housing in urban areas is largely left to the private real estate trade.

Vambay Scheme

About 49,000 houses are allotted to Hyderabad and adjoining Ranga Reddy district under the Jawaharlal Nehru National Urban Renewal Scheme (JNNURM). The 195 SFT single room tenements (Fig. 5.1) with an attached bath and toilet are being constructed on a vast 86 acre site, few kilometres across from the highway. The GHMC is handling the housing portfolio project now. Although work had started 15 months ago, it has picked up in the last few months and houses are to be handed over to the identified beneficiaries by March end (*Source*: *The Hindu*, February 8, 2008). Each housing unit costs of Rs. 1 lakh, with Central and State Governments picking up three-fourth cost as subsidy, another grant of Rs. 3,750 is for for toilet and the beneficiary contribution is Rs. 6,250. They are "liveable" with all basic amenities. Some of the houses will also be made disabled friendly in consultation with beneficiaries and experts in the field. Disabled and old persons will be given preference for ground floor. It is planned to build 50,000 houses by October end with at least 20,000 to be ready in a month (from February, 2008).

The Vambay Housing Scheme (Valmiki Ambedkar Awas Yojana) is one of the schemes being offered by the Government for housing the urban poor and the disadvantaged. Most of the developmental efforts under this scheme are aimed at relocation and some at regularization. Data for this scheme has been analysed from 2001-2001 to 2003-2004 for Hyderabad.

Fig. 5.1: VAMBAY Housing

While some of the schemes aim at relocation of houses of the benificieries, others aim at regularization. During 2001-02, 35 slums in Hyderabad benifitted from the relocation scheme, in 2002-03, 10 benifitted from relocation and 44 benifitted from regularization and in 2003-04, 13 benifitted from regularization (Fig. 5.2 to 5.4).

A glance at Figures 5.5 to 5.7 reveals that the Scheduled Caste population and rightly so is the largest beneficiary of this scheme, other benificieries include Scheduled Tribes and Backward Castes among others. This is corroborated in detail by the picture presented by Fig. 5.8, 5.9 and Fig. 5.10 for individual slums, where it is found that Scheduled Caste and/or Scheduled Tribe population are invariably the benificiaries—sometimes the sole and sometimes substantial in most of the slums (85% in 2001-02 and 2002-03 and 77 per cent in 2003-04).

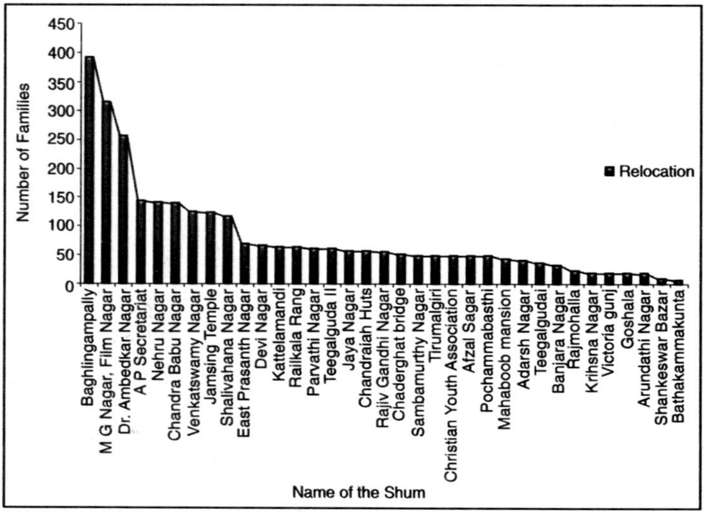

Fig. 5.2: Mode of Development Under VAMBAY Housing Scheme, Hyderabad, 2001-02.

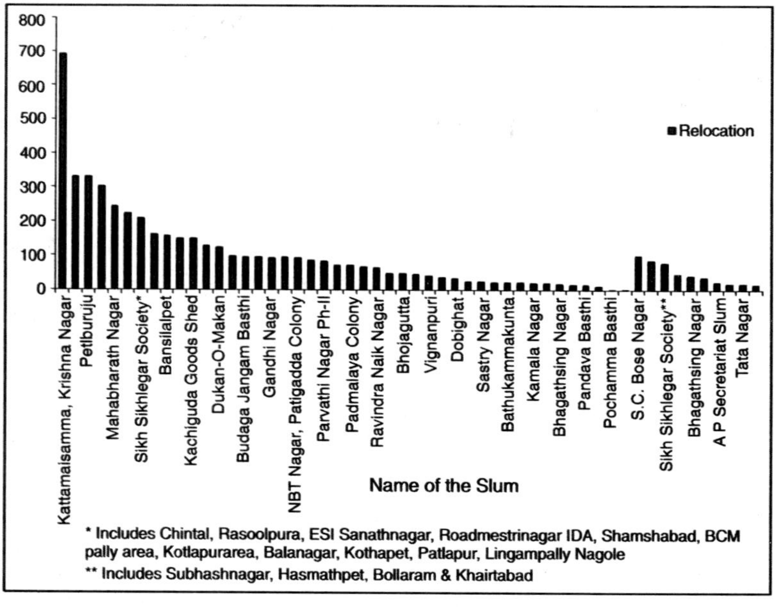

Fig. 5.3: Mode of Development Under VAMBAY Housing Scheme, Hyderabad, 2002-03

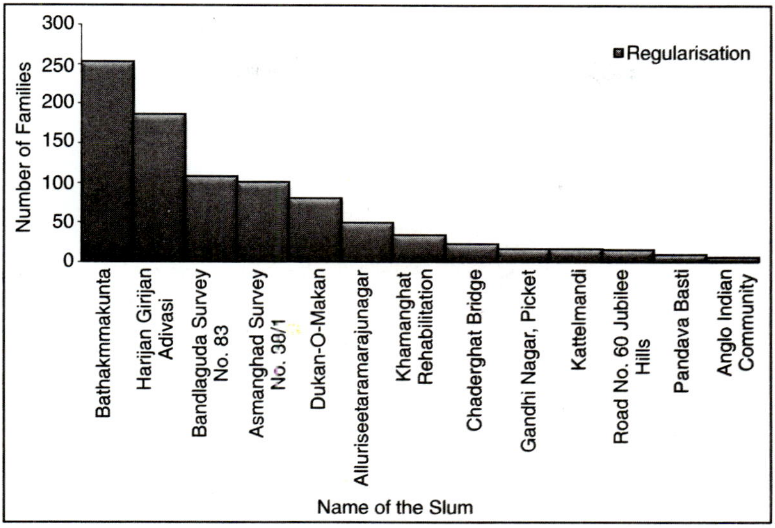

Fig. 5.4: Mode of Development Under VAMBAY Housing Scheme, Hyderabad, 2003-04

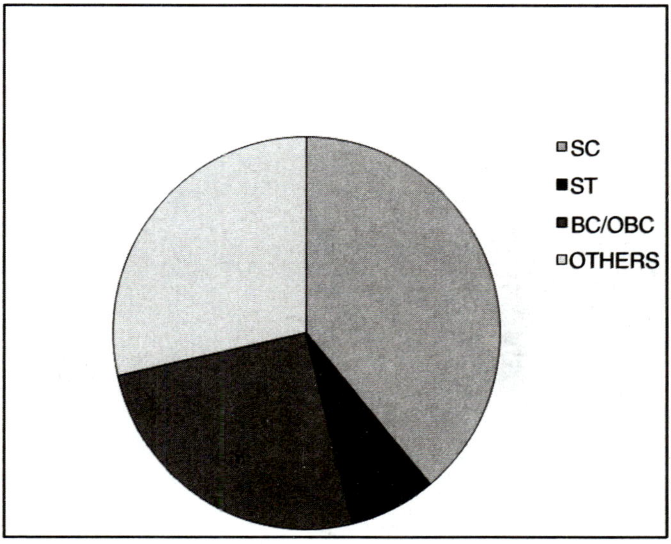

Fig. 5.5: **Caste-wise Breakup of Proposed Houses Under VAMBAY Housing Scheme, Hyderabad, 2001-02 (Pie Graph)**

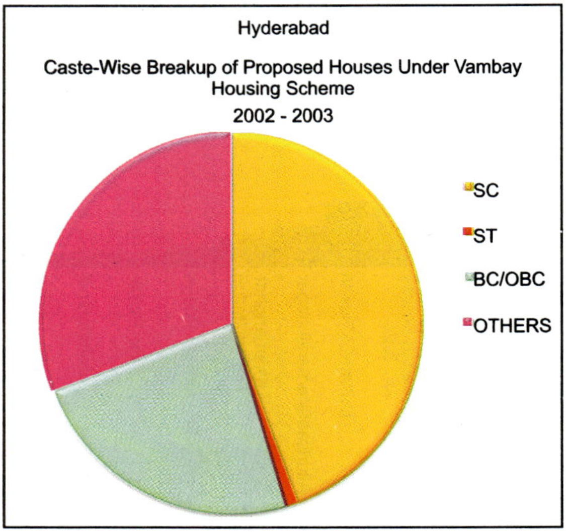

Fig. 5.6: Caste-wise Breakup of Proposed Houses Under VAMBAY Housing Scheme, Hyderabad, 2002-03 (Pie Graph)

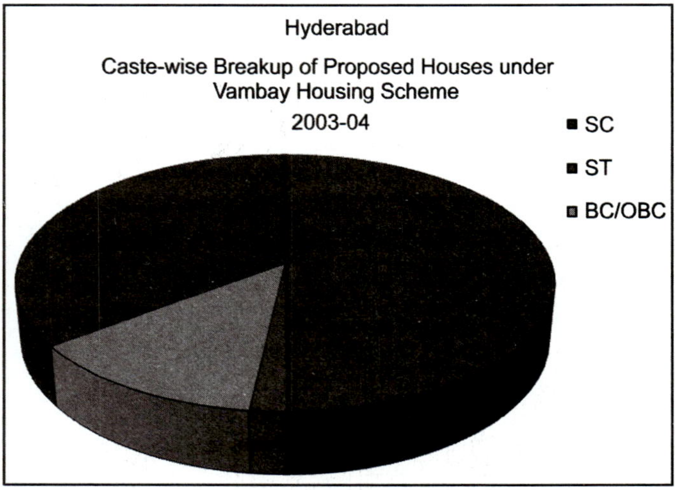

Fig. 5.7: Caste-wise Breakup of Proposed Houses Under VAMBAY Housing Scheme, Hyderabad, 2003-04 (Pie Graph)

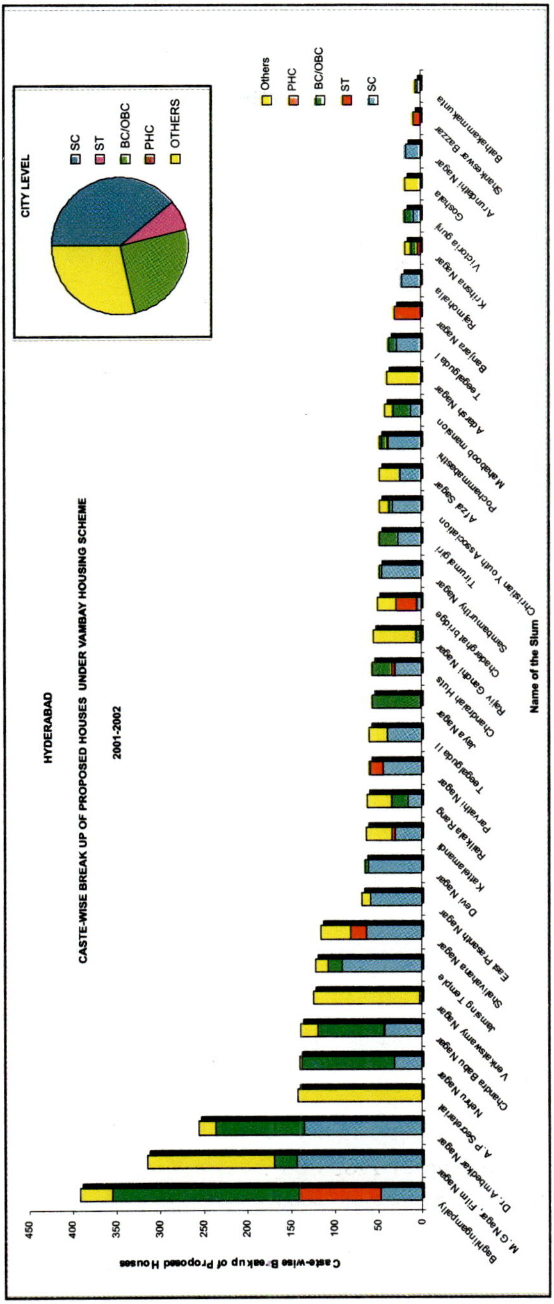

Fig. 5.8: Caste-wise Breakup of Proposed Houses Under VAMBAY Housing Scheme, Hyderabad, 2001-02 (Bar Graph)

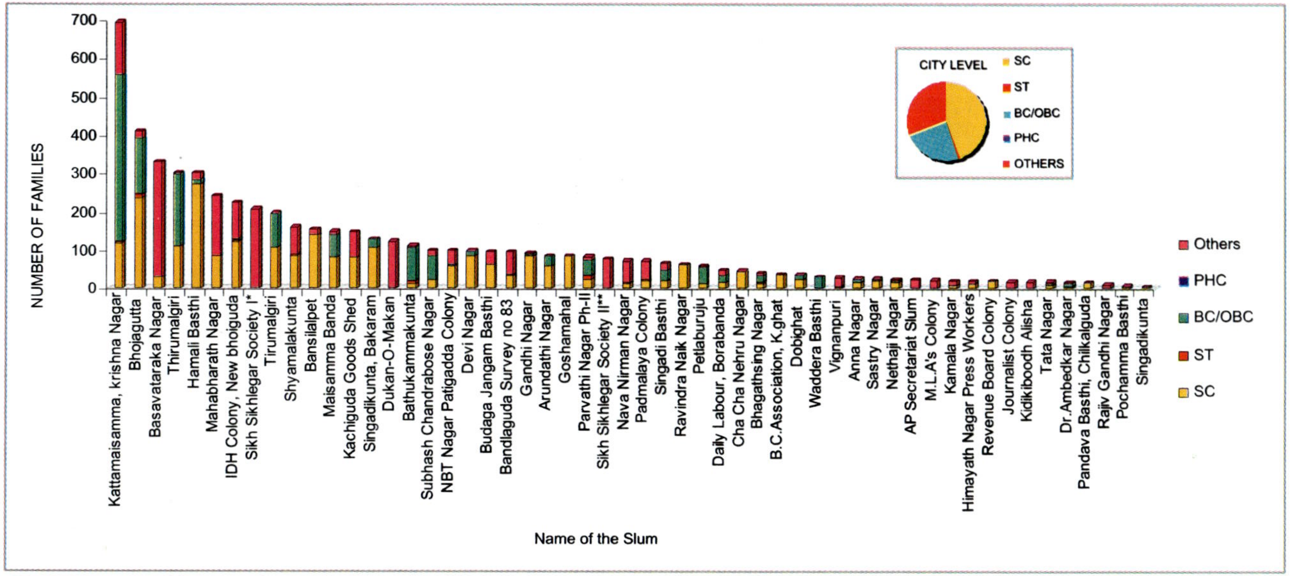

* Includes Chintal, Rasoolpurs, Erragadda, ESI Sanathnagar Roadmostnagar, IDA. Shamshabad, BCM pally area, Kotlapur area, Balanagar, Kothapet, Patlapur, Lingam pally Nagole

** Includes Subhashnagar, Hasnatipet, Bollaram & Khairtabad.

Fig. 5.9: Caste-wise Breakup of Proposed Houses Under VAMBAY Housing Scheme, Hyderabad, 2002-2003 (Bar Graph)

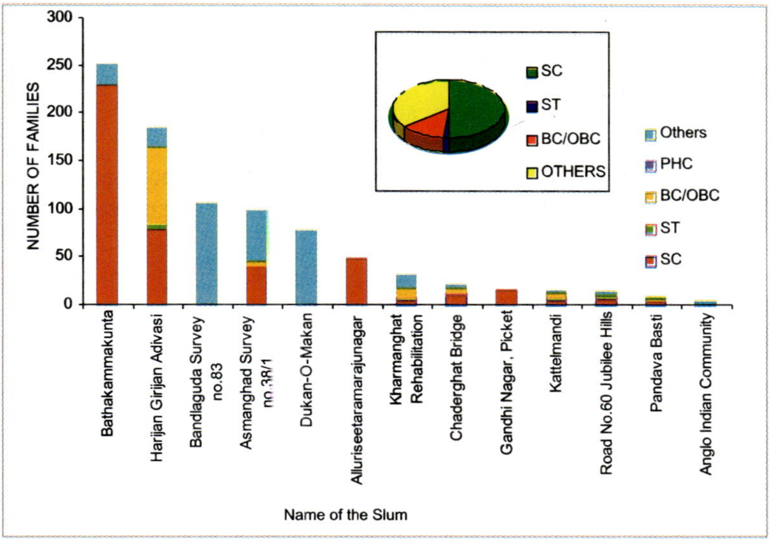

Fig. 5.10: Caste-wise Breakup of Proposed Houses Under VAMBAY Housing Scheme, Hyderabad, 2003-04 (Bar Graph)

Indira Awas Yojana

The Indira Awas Yojana also seeks to provide subsidized housing to the underprivileged. In an attempt to lessen the financial burden on beneficiaries of the 'Indiramma Housing Scheme', the state government is planning to introduce an interest-free loan system. A monthly rental of Rs. 300 in rural areas and Rs. 500 in urban centres for the repayment of principal amount has also been planned for a maximum period of 7 years.The state government has decided to pay beneficiaries of Indiramma housing through banks to curb irregularities. (*Deccan Chronicle*, August 3, 2009)

A proposal was being considered wherein no interest will be availed for constructing houses. This amount will be collected and paid to banks by the government. The beneficiaries will be given the facility of affordable repayments, subject to prompt repayment of instalments to clear the loan. (*Deccan Chronicle*, August 22, 2008)

The government has also been criticized for fixing a target to construct 30 lakh houses under the Indiramma housing scheme when the government had not been able to complete the first and second phase targets. It is alleged that it failed to implement quality control in construction of houses and allotted houses to undeserving people. While opposition parties and experts said the budget was pro-rich and anti-poor; the government made all efforts to project it as welfare-oriented budget. (*Times News Network*, 2008)

A survey conducted across 200 villages by a political party revealed that 45 per cent of eligible people did not get houses in the Indiramma scheme alongwith other irregularities like corruption and low-quality work. They demanded that the state government appoint an ombudsman to address grievances related to the Indiramma housing program. (October16, Hyderabad)

3.5 lakh houses under the Indiramma scheme are yet to be grounded in first phase due to financial constraints. (*Deccan Chronicle*, February 6) The Government has to release funds in 3 instalments facilitating construction, if organisations are willing to take up work in their respective villages.

Rajiv Swagruha Scheme

It is aimed at providing affordable independent houses or flats to the middle-income group. The scheme got a fillip with the State Government identifying more than 9,000 acres out of the 10,000 acres required to implement the scheme. Rajiv Swagruha Corporation Limited (RSCL), a Special Purpose Vehicle (SPV), has been incorporated to implement the programme.

Under the Rajiv Swagruha Scheme for middle class the government has decided to construct 69,400 houses costing Rs. 12,800 crores; 32,144 flats proposed in 16 locations in Hyderabad and its environs. It is also planned to provide housing loans at lower interest rates through nationalised banks. The Government is keen to ensure that the beneficiaries get loans at interest rates cheaper by 1 to 1.5 per cent than the existing market price. In case of lower-income range, flexible equated monthly instalment is planned. 6,500 flats are completed and handed over to allotees at Mylardevpally, Kuntlur, Annojiguda, Vikarabad and Tandur. While the former three locations are in Hyderabad and the occupancy rate of these flats is 50-60 per cent, the latter two locations are in neighbouring Rangareddy District and have an occupancy rate of 90 per cent. In all only 3000 owners have occupied the flats. The Rajiv Gruhakalpa flats have not been found upto the mark as there is a lack of basic amenities; hence, the beneficiaries are not ready to occupy the flats. (*Sunday Times of India*, October 12, 2008)

Rajiv Gruhakalpa flats are also proposed at Mylardevulapally, Laxmiguda I, Laxmiguda II, Almasguda, Torrur, Turkayamjal Kuntlur, Annojiguda, Ahmedguda, Kaukur, Nizampet, Qutbullapur, Chandanagar, Suraram (all on the periphery of Hyderabad), Vikarabad and Tandur (in Rangareddy District). At Ahmedguda 4512 flats are being constructed, at Nizampet 3296 and at Qutbullapur 3648. However, these are rar flung places with no shops, schools, hospitals, transport facilities and internal roads, water and street lighting have yet to be put in place.

Thousands of applicants of the Rajiv Swagruha Scheme may not get houses until 2011. Unable to find the houses, the government is hinting at returning the money deposited by applicants. The scheme was designed to provide houses to the middle class living in cities and towns and to build 2 lakh flats and individual residential dwellings costing 25 per cent less than the market price. The government has collected Rs. 3000 from each applicant in March 2007.

Rajiv Swagruha Corporation Limited (RSCL) however, joined the race to provide flats at attractive prices in the period of recession and downslide in the property market. They have accosted the private builders with a big cost advantage that they are offering to the customers in places like Bandlaguda, Bachupally, Kondapur and Jawaharnagar. The flats are in the range of Rs. 10 to 31 lakhs depending on quality and size. (*Deccan Chronicle*, November 21, 2009)

The RSCL has so far launched only 4 projects while others are on the anvil. Construction of multi-storied buildings has begun around the state capital at Chandanagar—1140 flats, Pocharam—2604 flats and Bandlaguda—3048 flats. The government is now proposing to acquire land even from private persons to accomplish the dream project. This may push the costs further up. Though RSS is meant to provide housing for the moderate income group at an affordable rate, the cost increases and the hesitation of the RSCL to fix clear rates is scaring many buyers away and the dream houses are remaining a dream for many. (D. Surya, *The Hindu*, July 16, 2008)

The AP Housing Board has become a hardcore realtor and has forgotten the noble aim for which it was set-up i.e. to provide low cost housing to the people. It is actively engaged in land auction and construction of profitable projects, but is not seriously looking for land to provide for the Rajiv Swagruha Scheme, which is meant for providing affordable housing to the middle class. While it had enough land to provide for the Rajiv Swagruha Scheme in most places, it did not do so and created the Rajiv Swagruha Corporation to which it neither provided land nor did the Corporation have any of its own. Hence, it failed in many places and to add to this the APHB coaxed the buyers to purchase flats built by it. This profit motivation has gone counter to the schemes meant for the not so well off.

Most of these houses are being constructed in the peripheral municipalities rather than the core city. From L.B.Nagar Municipality was upgraded into selection grade municipality from a second grade municipality in 2001. Construction of 6165 houses under Rajiv Gruha Kalpa and 1891 houses under Urban Housing Scheme are in progress. In Kapra construction of 2464 houses under Rajiv Gruha Kalpa, 2203 houses under urban poor housing scheme and 288 houses in INDIRAMMA wards was started.

Unprecedented demand, cost of construction shooting up, non-availability of land in urban areas, did not allow the government with going ahead with the scheme. According to sources APHB could acquire land for construction of 20,000 houses against the planned 2 lakh. Moreover, applicants who were allocated houses in Hyderabad are not keen on purchasing the flats as APHB has fixed Rs. 24 lakh for 2BHK on outskirts as against private realtors who were offering a better rate. (K.Srinivasa Rao, *The Hindu*, September 1, 2008)

A house committee of the State Assembly has faulted the APHB for the avowed objective of providing affordable housing. According to the report, the APHB was allotting lands at less than the market price but the private companies who got the lands at low price were reselling those at exorbitant rates. These promoters were making huge profits at the cost of common man as it had been given freedom to fix the cost of houses. Eventually, the APHB was getting only meagre revenue share of 3 to 5 per cent from these projects. The committee felt that both the common people and the board itself would have benefitted if the projects were taken up by APHB. (*Deccan Chronicle*, September 2, 2008)

The State High Court directed that AP Housing Board should not confirm the sale of its lands in Hyderabad without the permission of the court. However, while dealing with a petition challenging e-auctions of land by APHB, the court said the auctions may go on. APHB issued a notification to sell its land in Marredpally, Alwal,

Bowenpally, Thogutta, Girimapur and other places through electronic auction between August 25 and 27. Counsel for petitioners told the court that the APHB was established to provide shelter to common man at a reasonable cost. He alleged that the lands meant for housing to the common man and weaker sections were being disposed off to large companies and real estate firms. He told to court that the board had earned Rs. 784 crore in 2007-08 by selling out about 41 acres of its land in the city. (*Deccan Chronicle*, August 22, 2008)

Though the state government had plans to allot over 42000 flats to the poor before the GHMC polls, it has been able to complete only 17000 flats. However, of these 12000 were allotted before the Assembly elections to beneficiaries mostly from Ranga Reddy district. The remaining 5000 flats will be allotted to families from Hyderabad. The state government had initially wanted to allot these houses before the Assembly elections. The corporation had even received a financial sanction for these flats from JNNURM. Project was moving slow due to litigations over the sites selected for building housing colonies. Due to delay, the construction cost of each flat increased. While the JNNURM sanctioned Rs. 1 lakh per unit, the cost per unit has increased to Rs. 2 lakh. Works on the remaining 25000 flats were yet to begin. Due to increase in unit cost, GHMC are planning to execute this project under a different scheme. (*Deccan Chronicle*, July 8)

Developers are up in arms against the State Government directive to allot space in private layouts and apartments to LIGs and MIGs and economically weaker sections. The government had issued a GO on 20 per cent allotment of space to these sections in properties developed on 1 acre or more in HUDA limits. Builders say social responsibility cannot be enforced on them in such a manner and the reservation proposal was not feasible. APBF President says "when we are paying crores of rupees every year to the government in the form of taxes and other charges and government does not provide any concessions on any of these charges, it has no right to demand concessions from us." Builders say the government proposal lacked sincerity since HUDA, APHB as real estate agents were raising crores of rupees through auction of government land. The 'quota for poor' directive was given in the guidelines issued recently in the revised HUDA master plan.

"As per guidelines, 10 per cent space should be allotted to weaker sections with a maximum plinth area of 220 square feet for each unit. Likewise, 5 per cent of the total built-up area should be developed for LIGs with maximum plinth area of 440 square feet for each unit and another 5 per cent for MIGs with 660 square feet plinth area for each unit. For layout development schemes in 10 acres and more, the builders have to reserve 5 per cent of the total area and give it "free of cost" to HUDA. Another 5 per cent land has to be reserved for housing accommodation to economically weaker sections, 10 per cent to LIG and 10 per cent for MIG. In case of land pooling schemes or townships in 50 acres and more, the developers have to surrender 5 per cent of the land to HUDA and allot space to other sections."

According to Manbhum Constructions, housing projects in 1 acre or more within HUDA limits would come to a standstill due to these regulations. The builders pointed out that the directive to sell flats in such complexes to the poor and middle class did not make sense since they would not be able to afford them. However, HUDA official says "the state government is only implementing the Centre's guidelines under JNNURM as private sector also has to share social responsibility." (M.Roushan Ali, *Deccan Chronicle*, May 9)

The vigilance department probe points out that the housing board directors passed a resolution to sell some flats in the Singapore City at 20 per cent discount to the board directors (IAS Officials) and APHB employees. As many as 194 flats were sold. (*Deccan Chronicle*, August 3, 2009)

It is found in this chapter, that there is a yawning gap between the demand and supply of houses for the lower income groups. It is found that the economically and socially marginalized groups covering certain specific occupational categories form the target groups for the governmental housing schemes. Houses are being constructed under the VAMBAY (Valmiki Ambedkar Awaas Yojana) scheme for select marginalized social groups and some of them are also being made friendly to the old and the disabled. The scheme aims as relocation of houses of the beneficiaries or regularization. Most of the beneficiaries are from the Scheduled Castes, Scheduled Tribes and Backward Castes. Indira Awas Yojana (IAY) is another scheme aimed at addressing the housing needs of the underprivileged. However, irregularities have been found in identifying the beneficiaries and corruption and low quality work have tarnished the image of this scheme. The Rajiv Swagruha Scheme which is aimed at providing affordable housing to the middle class people had gained momentum during the recession.

6

Inclusivity in Urban Environment

The problem of houselessness in the shadow of affluence is not new to the urban areas, but the city of Hyderabad has witnessed an unprecedented increase of the housing stock of the rich in the past twenty years, which stands in contradistinction to housing shortage in general. The present study seeks to analyze the housing situation in Hyderabad in order to see what are the factors prompting the disproportionate growth in the housing stock of one type and an increase in unfulfilled demand at another level. Housing situation in Hyderabad displays aberrations which manifest themselves in the form of 'exclusivity'. There is an inordinate growth in the housing stock of high income groups and there is an increase in unfulfilled demand from middle and lower income groups.

The rate of increase of housing stock has not kept pace with the rate of increase of demand and the gap has been widening with the passage of time. Factors on the demand front include—(a) first generation migrants. They seek accommodation in various places depending on their educational level, placement in society as manifested in their occupations, etc., (b) Demand could also be created due to obsolescence. For every addition in the housing stock at a given point in time, there is also a deletion consequent on dilapidation and ageing. Fresh demand for housing is thus created by people who already had housing earlier, (c) Demand is also created by people who move up vertically in the socio-economic ladder, though this might be a nominal figure, and (d) All this is notwithstanding the existing compounded shortage.

Supply could be generated (a) out of the people's own resources, (b) own resources supplemented by loan or assistance (from banks, LIC, Housing boards etc), (c) for want of own resources or credibility to raise loans, supply can be generated by external assistance. It is a combined mix of the above factors that are responsible for the present housing situation in Hyderabad, which has brought in more of 'Exclusivity' on the urban front.

India will face shortage of over 26 million houses by 2012, which would lead to spurt in housing prices as demand-supply gap widens amid rising purchasing power of the middle class people, a consultancy firm has said.

'With India back on a high growth trajectory, demand for commercial and residential space is likely to witness an upward trend,' consultancy firm Ernst and Young said in a report.

Demand for residential property is rising sharply because of growing young working population, increasing urbanisation, declining household size resulting in more nuclear families with growing household income and improved availability of loans.

Co-chairman of FICCI Real Estate Committee Pranay Vakil said over $1.2 trillion investment was needed to meet the rising demand for urban development.

He said that the urban population in India would nearly double to 600 million in the next 15 years from nearly 350 million now, and this would put massive pressure on urban infrastructure, including roads, power and water supply.

Dean Hodcroft, partner-head of real estate for Europe, Middle East, India and Africa at Ernst and Young, said India needed institutional reforms to attract more investments in infrastructure development projects.

He said the country's macro-economic fundamentals were in great shape and it was poised to reap huge benefits of growth. 'India needs to fix the institutions to attract more private investments, including foreign investments,' he said.

'Comparing the investment climates in India and China, Hodcroft said: 'While it is easy for investors to get into China, it is extremely difficult to get out. In contrast, it took time for foreign companies to enter India, but exiting is comparatively much easier.'

He noted that India was lower ranked in areas that were easy to fix.

http://economictimes.indiatimes.com/markets/real-estate/news-/India-may-face-shortage-of-26-mn-houses-by-2012/articleshow/6566686.cms

Housing Shortage and Demand 2020 in HUDA Area

Census 2001 did not publish housing data till November 2002. An insight into the problem, therefore, may be made based on 1991 Data. In 1991, the HUDA area had 8.22 lakh Census Houses and 8.39 lakhs households. While the population of HUDA increased from 29,93,587 in 1981 to 46,65,950 in 1991, the ratio of population and houses also slightly improved.

Table 6.1: HUDA Area: Housing Data: 1981-1991

Parameter	*1981*	*1991*	*Rate of change*
Occupied Residential Houses	4,91,713	8,21,508	+67%
Households	51,727	8,39,421	+62%
Population	29,93,587	46,65,950	+55.86%
Persons per house	6.09	5.68	0.41
Persons per household	5.79	5.56	0.23 .

The 1991 demand for good housing was considered as: about 1 lakh slum and squatter housing, about 10 per cent of existing stock needing replacement and about 18000 'shortfall households' needing independent houses. With those assumptions the 1991 housing shortage was estimated at about 2 lakhs. (HUDA Draft Master Plan, 1994)

In 2001 the estimated population for the HUDA area is 63.83 lakhs. This is an addition of approximately 17 lakhs from 1991 population. By 2021 the population is expected to be 136.43 lakhs which is another 73 lakhs over the 2001 population. Over the next 20 years the demand for houses in the HUDA area will be approximately 80 thousand houses per year to cater to wiping out the past backlog, replacement of old and unusable houses and the provision for additional population. House construction activity in Hyderabad is mainly confined to the private sector. With the recognition to housing and construction industry and with the reduction in interest rates and other policy measures at national and state level, it is expected that investment in house construction will become more attractive for the private sector.

Source: HUDA, 2003

Land markets are in a state of flux in most cities of the developing world and Hyderabad is no exception, after the initial upward draft in the 1990s and beyond, they tumbled slightly in the 2008-2009 recession period (Table 6.2), but are again looking upwards. Short term fluctuations notwithstanding, the general tendency is for strengthening the gains attained. The stability on this count seems to stay (Table 6.3).

Table 6.2: Hyderabad: Mid End Residential Property Prices: 2008-2009

Region	March '08 (Rs./sq ft)	March '09 (Rs./sq ft)
Central	2700-4500	2600-4100
North East	2700-3100	2400-2800
West	2600-3000	2400-3000
North West	2300-2700	2300-2800

The realty scene in Hyderabad is booming again, after a brief slump. The Table 6.3 gives an approximation guide to property prices in the city.

Table 6.3: Property Prices in Hyderabad, 2008

Locality	Capital Value (Rs. sqft)	Plot unit value (Rs./sqyd
Central	2200-4500	25000-60000
East	1300-2500	20000-30000
North	1900-4500	18000-90000
South	2000-6000	20000-50000
Suburb	1600-4000	12000-30000

Source: Deccan Chronicle, July 25, 2008.

Table 6.4: Property Prices in Select Localities of Hyderabad, 2008

Location	Plot (Rs. per sq. yard)	Built up Area (Rs. per sq. foot)
Madhapur	35000-55000	3500-5000
Banjara Hills	75000-100000	5000-7000
Bengaluru Highway	2000-8000	2300-4000
Himayathnagar	30000-45000	3500-4500
DD Colony	40000-55000	4000-4500
Sri Nagar Colony	40000-60000	4000-5000

Source: Deccan Chronicle, August 8, 2008.

The realtors, however, are adopting a 'realistic approach' following economic slowdown. Instead of a range of flats at Rs. 50,00,000 to Rs. 80,00,000 which are now harder to sell, they are looking for smaller functional flats for middle income groups of 800 to 900 sft @ Rs. 25,00,000. There has been a switch over from luxury flats with

Table 6.5: Residential Prices in Hyderabad, 3Q, 2009

Location	*Achievable Price INR/sq.ft.*	*Capital Values as of 3Q 2009* *% Change from (Local Currency)*		*Short Term Outlook*
		3 mth ago	*1 year ago*	
High End Segment				
Banjara Hills	5,500-6,100	0%	-11%	→
Jubilee Hills	5,300-5,700	0%	-15%	→
Himayathnagar	3,100-3,800	-1%	-19%	→
West & East Marredpally	3,200-3,700	0%	-16%	→
Begumpet, Somajiguda	3,700-4,200	-1%	-7%	→
Madhapur, Gachilbowli	3,500-4,100	0%	-16%	→
Kukatpally	3,100-3,600	0%	-21%	→
Mid Segment				
Banjara Hills	3,300-3,900	0%	-10%	→
Jubilee Hills	3,300-3,900	0%	-10%	→
Himayathnagar	2,600-2,800	0%	-7%	→
West & East Marredpally	2,400-2,800	0%	-9%	→
Begumpet, Somajiguda	2,400-3,000	0%	-4%	→
Madhapur, Gachibowli	2,400-3,000	0%	-10%	→
Kukatpally	2,300-2,600	-4%	-13%	→

Note:

Values are average price for the respective areas. Pricing will differ based on the construction quality, developer profile and amenities available.
The above values for high end segment typically include units of 1,600 sq.ft. to 3,200 sq.ft.
The above values for mid segment typically include units of 1,200 sq.ft. to 1,600 sq. ft.

Legend

Market Rising ↑ Market Stable → Market Falling ↘

Source: Cushman and Wakefield, 2009.

costly interiors to budget flats. Construction firms are accordingly altering plans in future projects (*Deccan Chronicle* Oct.11, 2008).

In an attempt at a multi-pronged view to expand the housing market, builders in Hyderabad are also increasingly targeting non-residential Indians in the US as most of them are not keen on purchasing properties there with the recession in American economy. NRIs fear they will not get good returns since the slump is likely to continue even in the American real estate sector. Volatility in the stock market and frequent fluctuation in gold prices are prompting them to look at Hyderabad real estate, which is considered to be the safe zone for long term investment plans. Builders too feel that it is the right time to showcase them the investment opportunities in Hyderabad and surrounding areas. Most of them decided to participate in Indian Property Exhibitions, which was organised in California, Seattle and Dallas between May 10-18, 2008. Apart from Hyderabad, other cities developers also showcase investment opportunities in respective cities and it anticipates at least 5,000 prospective homebuyers to participate. (K. Srinivasa Rao, *Deccan Chronicle*, April 11, 2008)

Middle Income Group Housing is also being provided by HUDA at 5 locations—presently in Jawahar Nagar, Saheb Nagar, Nallagandla, Rampally and Shamshabad on the Private Public Partnership Model, the allotment of houses will be as per Assembly Constituencies and in the first Phase 1500 houses have been notified at Jawahar Nagar. The state government sponsored Rajiv Swagruha Scheme is aimed at providing affordable independent houses/flats to the middle-income group. However, they lack basic amenities; hence beneficiaries are not ready to occupy the flats, 32,144 flats are proposed in 16 locations in Hyderabad and environs of which 6,500 are completed and handed over to allotees. Only 3000 owners have occupied the houses (*Sunday Times of India*, October 12, 2008). The main reasons for this non occupancy are that they are in far flung places with no shops, schools, hospitals, transport facilities, internal roads, water supply, street lighting etc.

Despite efforts by the government to ameliorate the living and housing conditions of the people, who may not have the wherewithal to do it all by themselves, a large segment of the urban population of Hyderabad looks askance when the question of housing is popped at them. There are complaints galore, including those pertaining to the house, need for repair, over-crowding, environment—both physical and social besides a whole array of other issues. A majority of the people (54%) said that there has to be a change in order to give them a feeling of inclusivity in the urban environment that they inhabit.

Table 6.6: Hyderabad: Peoples' Perception of Change in the Way One Experiences Life in the Community and Society: 2007-2008

Suggestions for improvement	787	54
No response for improvement	672	46
Total Sample	**1459**	**100**

Source: Field Survey 2007-2008.

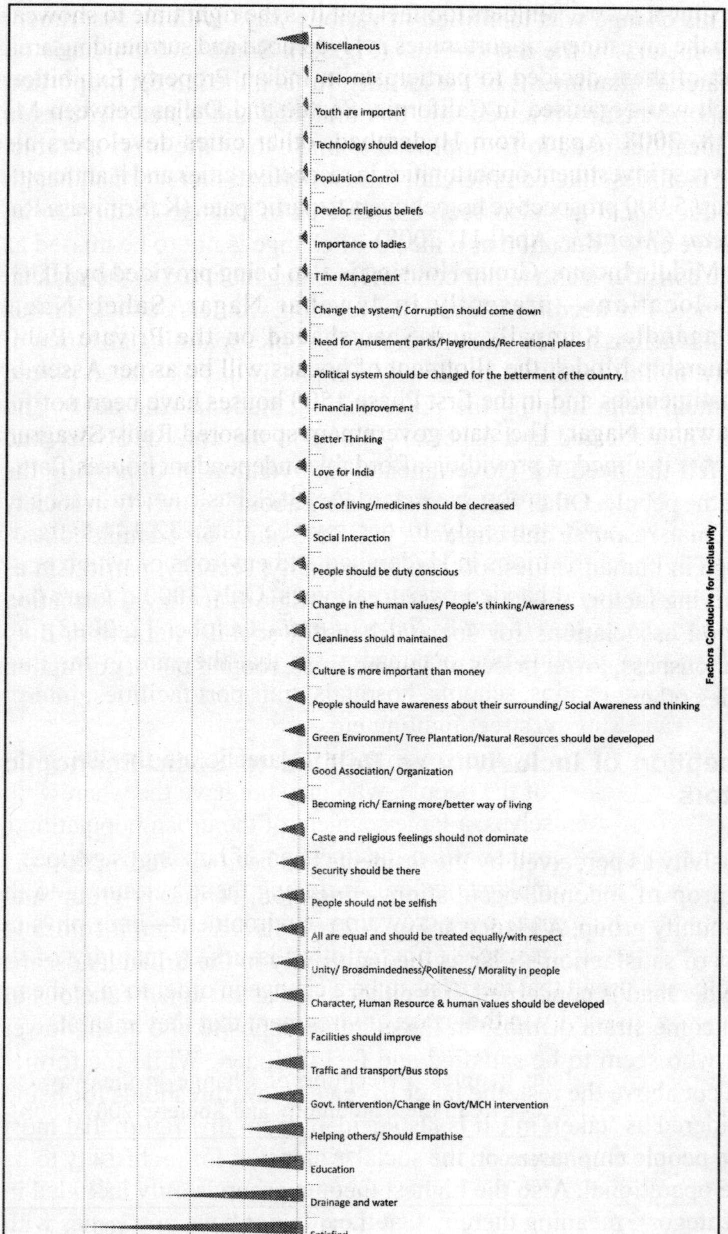

Source: Field Survey

Fig. 6.1: People's Perception of Inclusivity, Hyderabad, 2007-2008

This change was identified in various ways with an assortment of parameters by the respondents (Fig.6.5). Some laid emphasis on the material attainments of the locality. In fact, the largest proportion of respondents interviewed said that drainage and water facilities in their localities need to be improved to make their life more liveable. Other facilities, like commercial, infrastructural, recreational, health and educational are also seen as vehicles of change leading to an inclusive city. Education as a means of change is not to be missed as people consider it as a major conduit for being included in the societal ambience. The need for education, including women's education has been felt across a wide cross section of people, spanning all strata of society and all localities in the city. Emphasis has also been placed on mutual help, helping the poor, helping students, the needy and poor. The educated and especially those in the core of Hyderabad have felt the need for Governmental intervention in improving the lot of the people. Other factor cited to bring about inclusivity in society are human resource and character building, unity, broad mindedness, change in human values, politeness, equality, security, patriotism as a unifying factor, absence of caste and religious feelings, formation of good associations for societal benefit, social interaction, duty consciousness, lower prices of commodities, rooting out of corruption besides others.

Perception of Inclusivity as Related to Socio-Economic Factors

Inclusivity as perceived by the residents has been viewed against the backdrop of income, occupation, education, religious group and community group. A glance at Fig. 6.2 reveals that when it comes to levels of satisfaction so far as the inclusivity in the urban landscape of Hyderabad is concerned, it is either those at the upper echelons of the income strata or those at the extreme opposite end at the lower level who seem to be satisfied and feel included. While the former are a cut above the rest, the latter have very low thresholds for being considered as 'taken in'. It is also evident from this figure that most of the people emphasize on the social dimension for inclusivity to be made operational. Also the highest income group is only included in this category, meaning thereby that they do not have any issues with environment, amenities/facilities, economic factors and educational factors besides others. For them inclusivity has only a social

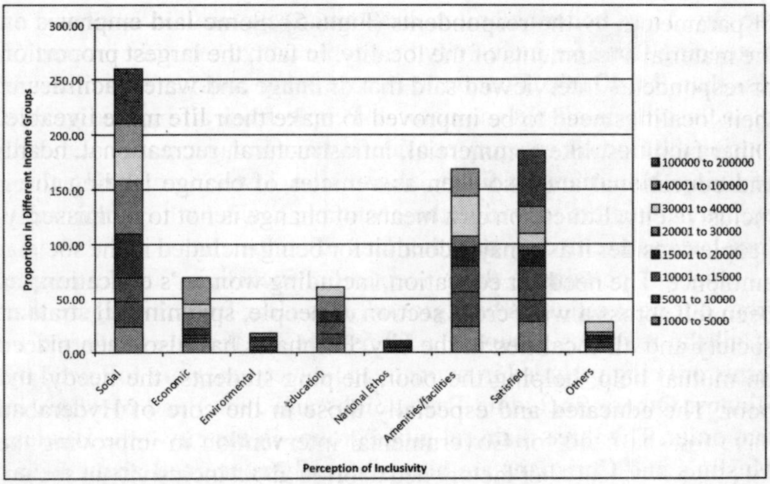

Source: Field Survey, 2008.

Fig. 6.2: Perception of Inclusivity by Residents, Hyderabad: 2008 (Bar Graph)

connotation. Specificities within this category for different income groups include a wide gamut of factors like social empathy, obliteration of caste and religious feelings in some instances and at times assigning pride of place to religious feelings in certain other instances, unity, equality, broadmindedness, politeness, strengthening of the moral fabric of society, development of human values, social awareness, social interaction and preservation of tradition and culture among others. Amenities and facilities follow as a close second as issues which have to be remedied for inclusivity to become operational, but interestingly the uppermost income group does not figure among those distressed on this front. The focus of this factor centres on the resolution of problems pertaining to drainage and water supply apart from traffic, lighting and ventilation, etc. An assortment of economic and educational factors is also referred to in order to induce inclusivity in the city population. While people citing the lack of some of the amenities and facilities, and hence a greater need for them, figure highly in the peripheral parts of the city, those vouching for educational inclusivity or extension of educational facilities to all, especially the women, cut across all localities of the city. Interestingly, they are not present in the top two income categories in the city. Thus, better and more disseminative education is viewed as a stepping stone for inclusivity by people with a monthly income of less than Rs. 40,000. Economic factors being considered a measure of inclusivity is all but too natural. People from all income groups barring the topmost category consider better earning capacity, standard of living, betterment of financial situation, lowering of land values etc. as parameters to bridge the economic divide, which ultimately translates as exclusivity or rather lack of inclusivity.

Fig. 6.3 pertains to the perception of inclusivity among people from different religious background. It is clear from this figure that of all the religious groups, the Christians are the most satisfied in terms or being included in mainstream society, they are followed by Hindus, Others (including Pasis, Sikhs and Jains) and Muslims in that order. The three main religious groups in the city—the Hindus, Muslims and Christians are almost equally concerned about social inclusivity, though the Muslims rate it a tad bit higher. Muslims also view inclusivity from the economic and the national ethos angle to a large extent. However, it is 'other' religious groups that are concerned about environmental issues. Most expressions on environmental inclusivity concern maintaining a clean environment, preservation of trees, greenery, natural resources, besides elimination of pollution and an environmental awareness.

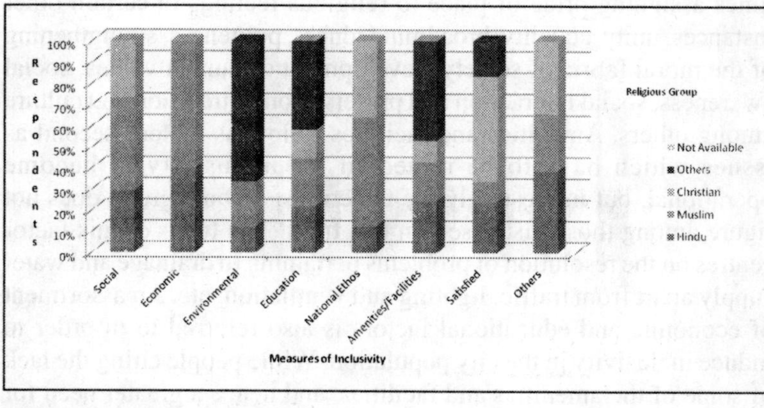

Source: Field Survey, 2008.

Fig. 6.3: Perception of Inclusivity by Religious Groups, Hyderabad: 2008 (Bar Graph)

The 'other religious' groups also feel the need for education and provision of better amenities and facilities in bringing about inclusivity in society.

Figure 6.4 pertaining to the caste and community of people conveys that while the Scheduled Tribe people in the city seem be the most satisfied on various counts of inclusivity, the minorities seem to be the least bit so. Among the prominent requirements cited by people from different communities are the need for social inclusivity among the forward class and minorities, of economic inclusivity among the Scheduled Caste and Scheduled Tribe, of environmental inclusion among the minorities, forward class and scheduled caste in that order. Among other things that emerge are the need for education among the backward castes, minorities and forward class in that order. The expression of national ethos as a measure of inclusivity is highest among the scheduled tribes followed by scheduled caste and minorities. The need for better amenities and facilities is felt to a large extent by the scheduled castes followed by the backward castes and minorities. Thus different groups exhibit varying levels of consciousness with regard to inclusivity, depending on their specific experiences and aspects of deprivation that they are confronted with.

A glimpse of Fig. 6.5 reveals very clearly that all educational categories barring Ph.D. figure on the 'satisfied' category, most groups amongst them except those with Professional and Post-Graduate

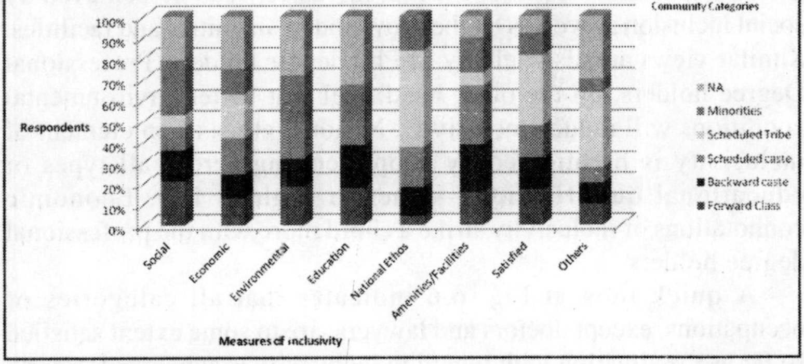

Source: Field Survey, 2008.

Fig. 6.4: Perception of Inclusivity by Caste, Hyderabad: 2008 (Bar Graph)

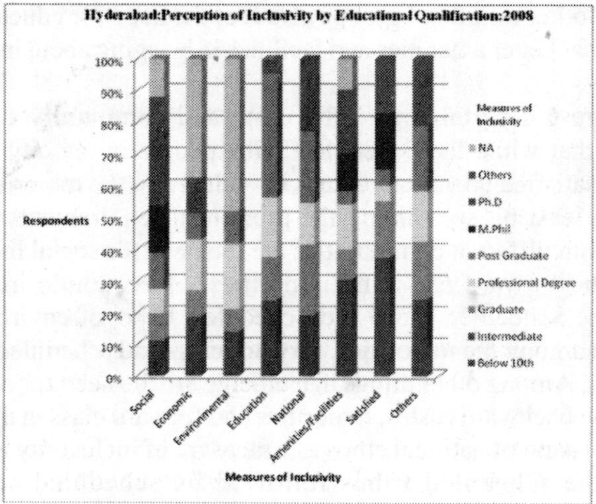

Source: Field Survey, 2008.

Fig. 6.5: Perception of Inclusivity by Educational Qualification, Hyderabad, 2008 (Bar Graph)

degrees have an equal representation. Those with Professional and Post-Graduate degrees figure low meaning that they believe there is a lot to be desired if inclusivity is to be achieved. Most of them express the need for education for all in order to achieve inclusivity. Those with Ph. D. Degree feel that inclusivity can be achieved by social inclusion as well as by the provision of amenities and facilities. Similar views are also held by M.Phil degree holders. Professional Degree holders, on the other hand, feel that better environmental conditions will induce inclusivity. National ethos as an element of inclusivity is highlighted by people cutting across all types of educational qualifications—whether high or low. Economic connotations of inclusivity strike a chord more with the professional degree holders.

A quick look at Fig. 6.6 indicates that all categories of occupations, except doctors and lawyers, are to some extent satisfied so far as the situation with regard to inclusivity is concerned. Nearly all occupational categories of people feel that the social and the amenities-facilities dimension require consideration in order to have a sense of inclusivity. The self-employed and bank employees feel that the economic factors and national ethos bring about inclusivity,

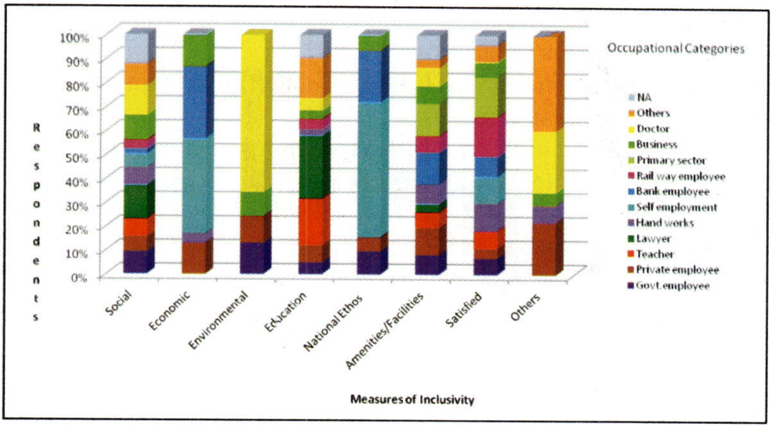

Source: *Field Survey,* 2008.

Fig. 6.6: Perception of Inclusivity by Occupational Category, Hyderabad: 2008 (Bar Graph)

while for the doctors it is inordinately a better environment. Lawyers and teachers cite education as a means of inclusivity. Here, again one finds that the specific level of understanding of each group and aspects of scarcity or plenty that they are confronted with guide their perceptions and rightly so about inclusivity.

An analysis of the socio-economic factors that are related with the perception of inclusivity among the people conveys the following broad facts:

- It is either those at the upper echelons of the income strata or those at the extreme opposite end at the lower level who seem to be satisfied and feel included in society.
- Most of the people emphasize on the social dimension for inclusivity and this category cuts across income and occupational groups.
- Factors like social compassion, annihilation of caste and religious feelings, unity, equality, broadmindedness, politeness, strengthening of the moral fabric of society, development of human values, social awareness, social interaction and preservation of tradition and culture are cited as motivations for a better and more inclusive life in the city.
- The felt need for educational inclusivity or extension of

educational facilities to all, especially the women, cuts across all localities of the city.

- Christians are the most satisfied in terms or being included in mainstream society.
- Muslims cite the need for economic and social inclusivity while people from other religions (Parsis, Sikhs and Jains) feel the need for a better environment, education and commitment to national ethos as the guiding factors for bringing about inclusivity.
- Scheduled Tribe people in the city seem be the most satisfied among the different social categories.
- The need for social inclusivity is felt among the forward class and minorities; that for economic inclusivity among the Scheduled Caste and Scheduled Tribe and for environmental inclusion among the minorities, forward class and scheduled caste population.
- National ethos as an element of inclusivity is highlighted by people cutting across all types of educational qualifications—whether high or low.
- All educational categories barring Ph.D. figure on the 'satisfied' category, highlighting the sensitivity and lack of adaptability of the highly educated to any and every situation.
- Similarly among the occupational categories all except doctors and lawyers, are to some extent satisfied so far as the percieved prevalence of inclusivity is concerned.
- All occupational categories of people feel that the better amenities and facilities would bring in a better sense of inclusivity.

A study of inclusivity within the framework of the rights and empowerment of women will not be out of place. An attempt has been made to examine the right to inheritance and ownership of land by women, ownership of property other than land by women, status of the women so far as the feasibility to acquire credit is concerned, to security of tenure and right to enter into contracts by women and availability of appropriate technology to women. Fig 6.7 reveals the spatial pattern with regard to the right to inheritance and ownership of land by women in Hyderabad is such that most locations in the core city display a low. Generally, the core city has traditional population groups while peripheral areas have more of migrants. The lowest of low are found in the central

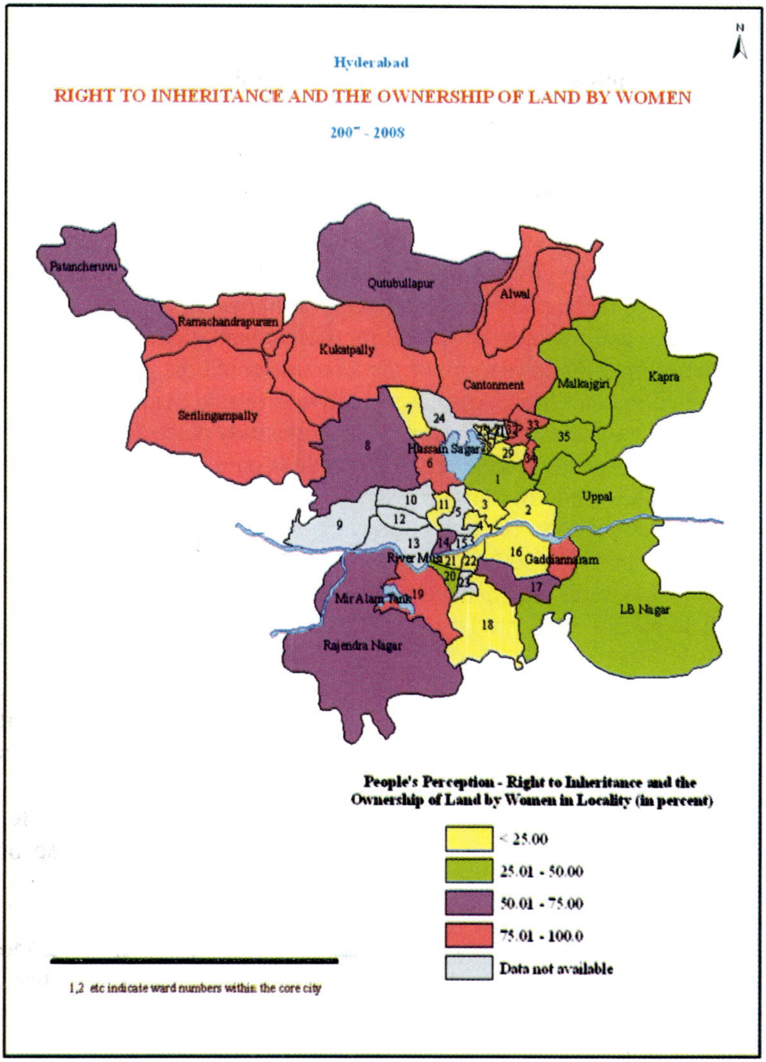

Source: field Survey.

Fig. 6.7: Right to Inheritance and the Ownership of Land by Women, Hyderabad, 2007-2008

part comprising the twin CBDs of Hyderabad and Secunderabad and substantial portions in South Hyderabad. The peripheral municipalities in the eastern part are relatively moderately placed so far as the right to inheritance and ownership of land by the women is concerned. These also are the areas that figure on the middle income category. The peripheral municipalities in the Northern and Western part rank high so far as the right to inheritance and ownership of land by women are concerned. While some of these areas have people from the IT sector others are industrial enclaves and one of them is the Military Cantonment area. Some of these areas are quite high on the socio-economic scale. So is also the case with the adjacent Banjara-Jubilee hills area in the western part of the city but which lies in the core of the city. It can thus be inferred that there are core-periphery variations so far as the right to inheritance and ownership of land by the women is concerned, while the central part displays more of lows on this count the peripheral part displays a distinct high. An east-west divide is also evidenced, where the eastern parts have relative lows and moderately placed values, those in the western part are relatively high on this count. While this has a lot to do with the standards of living which are relatively high in the western pockets, compared to the preponderance of middle class residences in the eastern part, it also has to do with the mores of the people which may be more traditional in the eastern pockets compared to the western.

The picture presented by Fig. 6.8 which shows the ownership of property other than land by women is not much at variance from that presented above in an overall sense. Barring few isolated pockets in the core city most of the wards and peripheral municipalities show that women do own property. This could be in the form of savings, jewellery or other consumer durables. There is again a spatial pattern to this picture where generally women in the western, northern and some of the central parts are perceived to posses property other than inherited property in a fairly large measure. The eastern part displays that women posses "other" property on a relatively medium scale, as mentioned earlier this is also a continuously large belt in the medium income groups.

Figure 6.9 shows that the status of the women so far as their viability to acquire credit is concerned. This figure again shows that women in the western part as well as quite a large area of Secunderbad as also in central and south Hyderabad seem to have higher credibility so far as acquiring credit is concerned. This is notwithstanding the fact that there is a lower incidence of women acquiring credit in a number of pockets in central and also south Hyderabad. The tradition versus modernity syndrome in a core-periphery context is again evident here apart from its semblance in an east- west zonation terms.

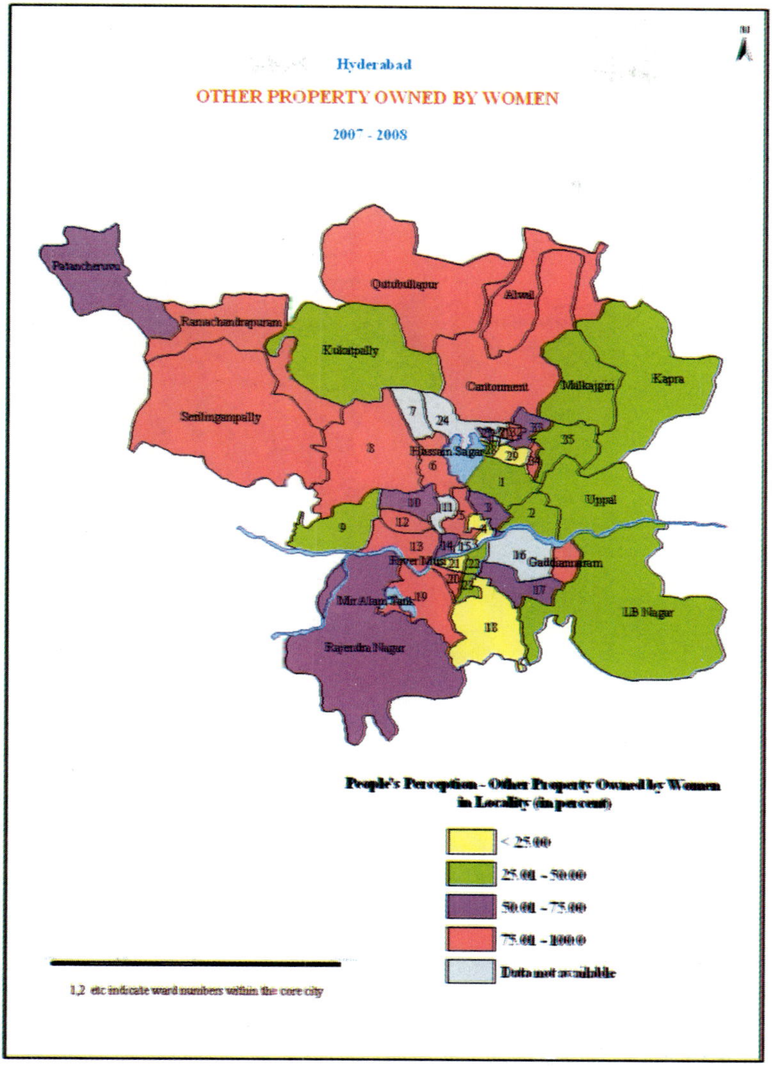

Source: Field Survey

Fig. 6.8: Other Property Owned by Women, Hyderabad, 2007-2008

Figure 6.10 pertaining to right to security of tenure and right to enter into contracts by women shows that the ranking of localities in the northern part of the city is definitely higher, the western part

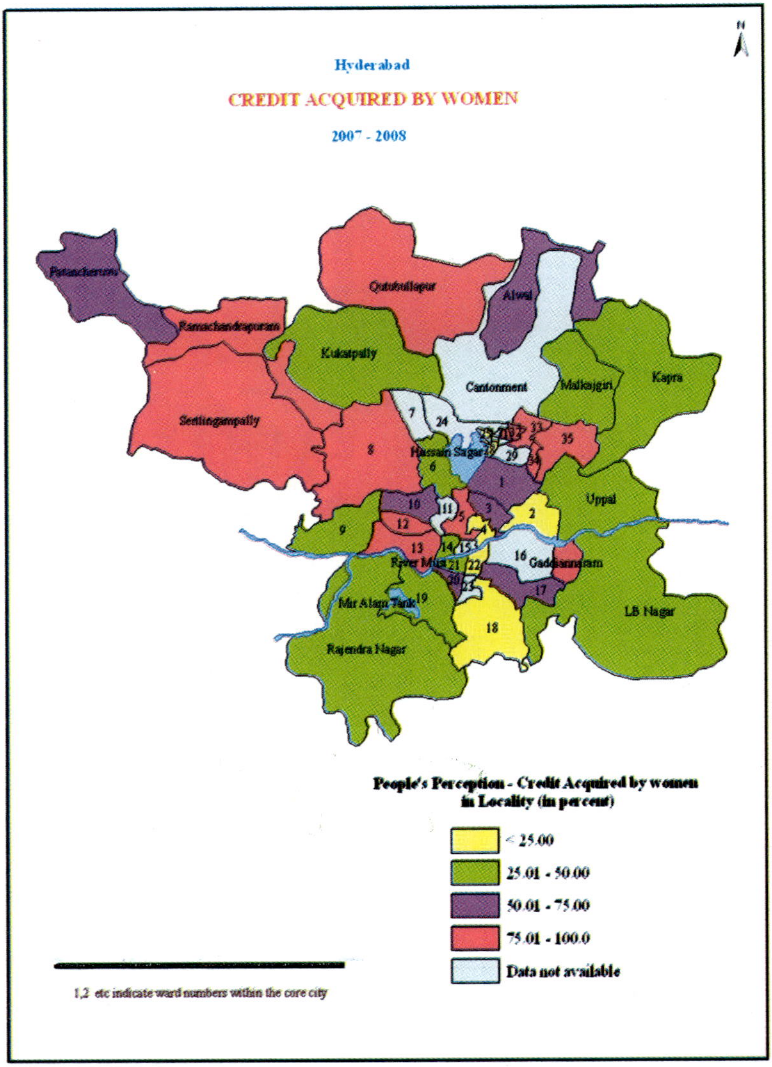

Source: Field Survey

Fig. 6.9: Credit Acquired by Women, Hyderabad, 2007-2008

displays a medium to high ranking and pockets in the core city display a low. The eastern part of the city gives an impression of a medium ranking. Thus the Tradition vs. Modernity syndrome holds good in

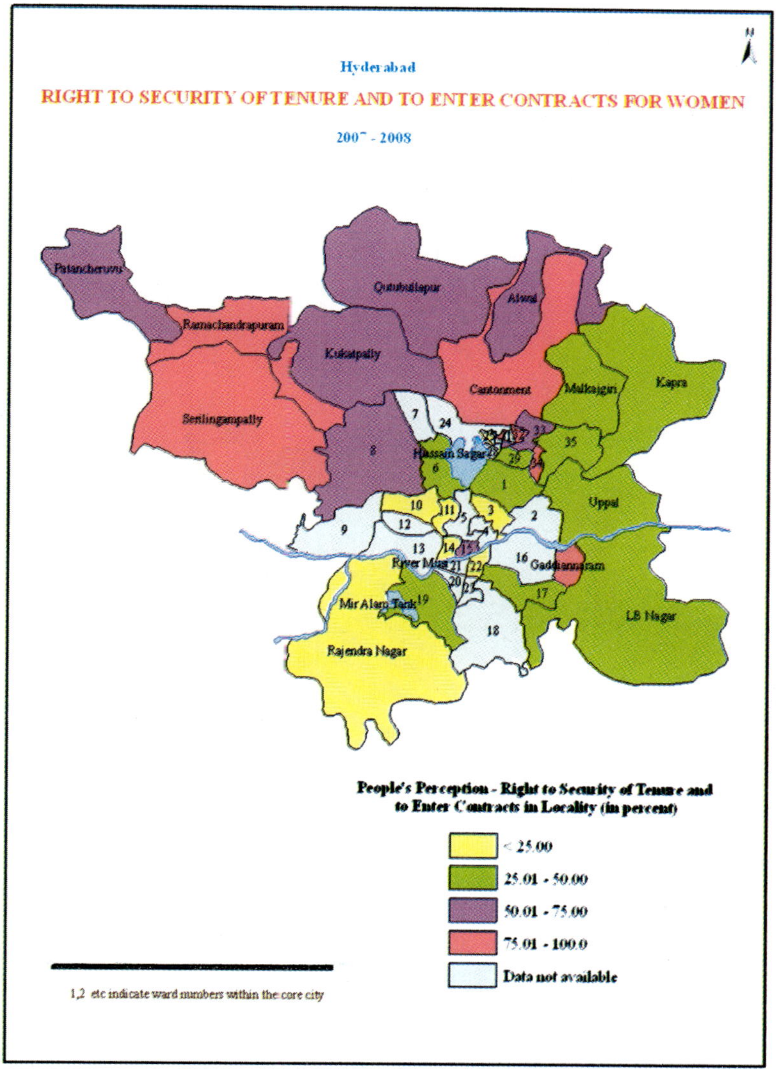

Source: Field Survey

Fig. 6.10: Right to Security of Tenure and to Enter Contracts for Women, Hyderabad, 2007-2008

the context of this variable also, where the central part appears more tradition bound compared to the periphery and the eastern part more so compared to the western part.

Figure 6.11 pertaining to the availability of appropriate technology to women reveals that the lows are again confined to the core portion of the city and that without exception all peripheral municipalities are relatively better placed on this count. The Core-periphery variations are yet again highlighted. In the traditional groups in select pockets in the core of the city and there are a large number

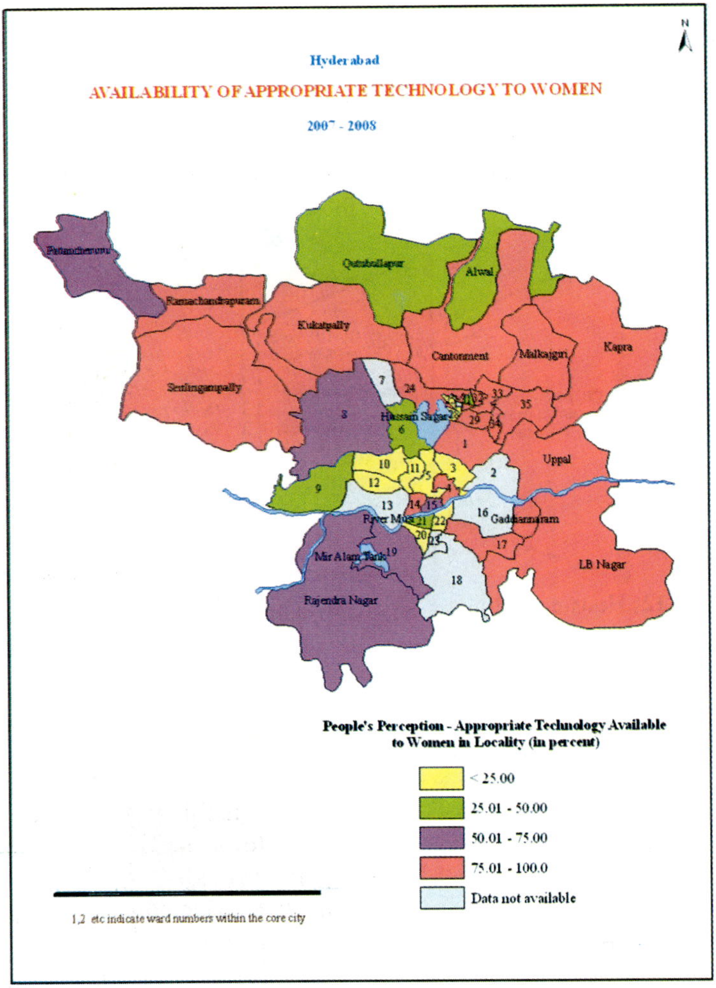

Source: Field Survey

Fig. 6.11: Availability of Appropriate Technology, to Women Hyderabad, 2007-2008

of them, women have limited access to technology, while this is not so in the peripheral municipalities.

Critique on Inclusivity in Hyderabad

An evaluation of the situation pertaining to housing and inclusivity in Hyderabad leads one to infer that the government is launching LIGH and MIGH projects on the periphery of the city. These are 'soft' state techniques for facilitating the marginal sections of the people to be part of the mainstream developmental process and reject a large chunk of people from being an integral part of the city (Fig.6.12). The colonies set up are devoid of infrastructure and hence a feeling of being left out by the people is well echoed.

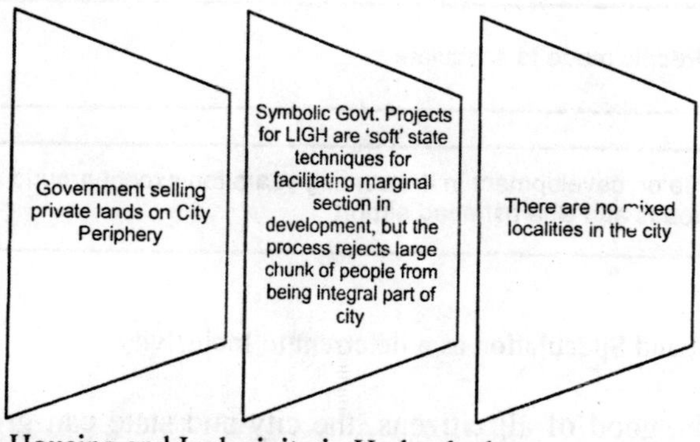

Fig. 6.12: Housing and Inclusivity in Hyderabad

It could be said in summarizing this study that while the upper income group has easy access to housing, the middle and lower income groups are at a disadvantage. Despite the various programmes initiated by the government, there is still a yawning gap between demand and supply and also an absence of amenities and facilities in the localities newly set up by the government for the lower and middle income groups. Thus, there is a lot that remains to be done keeping in view the fact that well established localities themselves are not inclusive enough from the peoples' point of view. Moreover, mixed localities are lacking in the city and certain areas become islands of affluence in a sea of poverty.

Inclusiveness in housing can be brought about by creating direct benefits like eliminating houselessness, by providing reasonably priced housing and also by protecting rental housing and ensuring that people are not displaced due to reasons beyond their control. This is apart from providing a well knit society, more so that which is heterogeneous from the religious, cultural and caste point of view, giving a multi-cultural touch to the society, which will be healthy, tolerant and nationalistic.

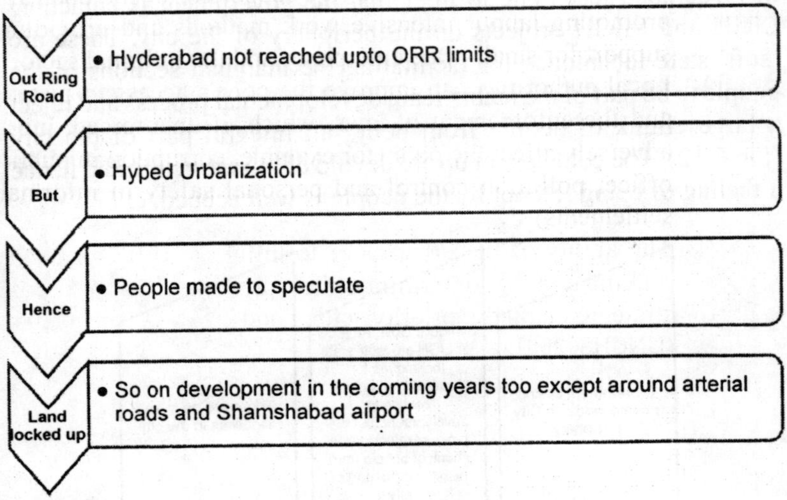

Fig. 6.13: Land Speculation as a deterrent to Inclusivity

For the good of all citizens, the city and state can grow to be partners. As inequality invalidates the efforts aimed at scrapping poverty, reducing inequality can catalyse the efforts intended towards reducing poverty and escalating economic growth. More equal cities will have a greater impact on poverty reduction than more unequal cities because the distribution of wealth will more effectively reach the urban poor.The role of local governments in promoting social inclusion, poverty reduction and economic growth has been envisioned as follows:

I. Most local authorities control access to land and are responsible for land-use planning and regulation. The ease of access, the cost and the location of land available to the poor have a significant impact on their livelihoods.

II. Access to infrastructure and basic services highlights the linkages between the health costs incurred by the poor due to unsafe water supply and inadequate health care.

III. The degree of success in local economic development determines the resources available for capital investments in such things as improved access to land, infrastructure and services.

IV. Local economic policies can be supportive of the poor, by promoting labour intensive work methods and providing support for small-scale enterprises and the informal sector.

V. Local authorities can improve the poor's access to justice and the enforcement of laws, which, if unenforced, most adversely affect the poor (for example, corruption in public office, pollution control and personal safety in informal settlements)

VI. The ability of the urban poor to influence local decision-making greatly determines the "pro-poorness" of local strategic planning, priority setting and capital investments. (UNCHS, 2001)

7

Summary and Conclusions

This is an application-oriented study of the Housing situation in Hyderabad, where use is made of traditional tools of Geographers as well as modern Geoinformatic tools. A Cartographic portyal of housing situation in Hyderabad is done using primary and secondary data and employing different techniques. An effort is made towards chalking out a theoretical and practical frame of reference of the housing needs and housing situation in the context of the 'Inclusive City' concept. An attempt is made to provide Policy inputs for the planners at the local, regional and national level.

The present study is an effort to delve into the housing market in Hyderabad, where a hiatus between the demand and supply is very evident. As a prelude to this study a comparison is drawn between Hyderabad and other emerging International cities, the population growth trends of Hyderabad are studied as also the land rates. It is found that while the houses of the upper and upper middle class continue to thrive, the middle class is left in the lurch for want of housing; the lower echelons of the socio-economic strata again have some amount of assistance by way of governmental schemes to provide housing. The shift from independent houses to multistoried complexes is also very much evident in Hyderabad over a period of time.

The spillover effect of this ever-expanding city is felt in an immense measure in the area beyond Hyderabad. Demand and now (with creation of HMDA) supply of low income housing extends beyond city limits. Far Flung suburban areas with relatively low-priced land are becoming the focus for aggressively priced housing projects. Leapfrogging of growth is thus witnessed. Though in the absence of an adequate population threshold these nodes lack infrastructure and public services; yet if planned with a long term vision, they can serve as sensitive shock absorbers for the burgeoning city population.

In this study, the economic cycles have been related to the housing market. The commercial property has been compared to the residential and the ups and downs have been registered. It is found that the owning a house is still a remote dream as the majority of the ongoing residential projects in the city cater to only upper-middle and higher income segments. The passion for Gated Communities found in the western and northern part of the city. Concepts in living like 'Service Apartments' 'Boutique Homes' 'Designer Villas' and 'Luxury Apartments' are also now trite. The gated communities have a reasonable blend of caste and religious groups. It is inclusive in terms of caste and religious groups. Exclusivity of these communities is tied up to income, educational attainment and occupation of the people. It appears that it is difficult for lower middle and middle classes to move upwards. The crisis of affordability is widening the gap between groups of people.

The high inflation on one hand and the continuous rise of interest rates on the other hand has led to a strange situation. Also the increase in tax rates, etc., is consigning the middle class to the background in the housing market. Moreover, it is also found that people from other states of India are buying property in a big way as property in Hyderabad comes at a more competitive rate when compared to the other metros. Hyderabad also has a large number of International players in the real estate market. However, the global economic meltdown has to some extent facilitated in placing housing within the reach of the common man. Real estate majors are taking up low-budget housing projects, using modern technologies and affordable housing seems to be the catchword. There is also an increasing demand for old flats in the city. The indecisive nature of builders owing to rising costs of building material has also led to a demand for old flats. Most of the localities on the periphery of the core city have witnessed an increasing spurt of building activity. A flight of the city population to the suburbs which are low on the pollution and traffic radar is also expected and hence they need proper planning so as not to repeat the blunders of the core city. Skyscrapers are also seen as a solution to the space limitation in the city and these are coming up in plenty on the city outskirts, of course at an astonishing price, keeping the employees in the IT sector in view. The core city is also witnessing renewed vitality in some places. All this has led to an appreciation of property prices.

The residents of Hyderabad display an inclination for own houses rather than rented houses, yet the preponderance of rented houses in the city core speaks of a relatively mobile population in that part. These areas also have high rents and people seem generally less satisfied with them. It is also found that most of the people living in ancestral houses are confined to central city locations. Most of the constructions in the central part of the city date back to the years prior to 1967, while the peripheral municipalities have seen building activity in a major way only in the 1980s and after. Most of the people seem to have made use of their savings for building the house. Localities which have more of government employees depend on formal sources of funding like bank loans and so on. Some in the CBDs of Hyderabad and Secunderabad depend on informal sources of credit. Most of rental house search is done with the help of friends and relatives—a rather traditional mode. Most of the houses are changed for reasons of larger accommodation; better locality and occupational mobility. While 'better localities' are generally those in the centre of the city and people shift their residences to these areas for this specific reason, those who move to the peripheral parts cite larger accommodation and occupational mobility as the reasons for shift of residence. It is also found that apart from the finer points, most people want to stay lifelong in the locality of their residence and most of them are satisfied with their accommodation. People on the eastern part are quite satisfied with accommodation size compared to those in the eastern part of the city. The relative sensitivity of the better off making for a lack of satiation and adaptability of the not so well off; making for better levels of satiation are the explanatory factors. Most people in the city are generally happy with their neighbourhoods. Most people also seem satisfied with the dispensation of social justice, human dignity and prevalence of equity, solidarity and free choice in residential location apart from free movement. Civic participation seems to be more in the northern, western, central and southern parts of the city compared to the eastern part in general. The preponderantly middle class population in the eastern part engages in more economically paying propositions.

Most people in the city rate their locality as high on the physical surroundings scale; this phenomenon is more manifest in central city locations than peripheral locations. This variable is followed by ranking on the scale of Amenities and Infrastructure, Social Environment and Security. So far as specific amenities and facilities in the house and locality are concerned, most people in the city seem to be satisfied with ventilation in the house. Also more than 50 per cent of the people seem to be satisfied with garbage disposal. This is not so in the case of drainage facility where most people in the Hyderabad part of the twin cities and the peripheral localities are not satisfied with this facility. A core-periphery scenario seems to be apparent so far as sanitation and even other variables like water supply situation, street lighting, roads, traffic movement, accessibility, satisfaction with regard to health facilities, etc. are concerned. While the core areas display a relative contentment, the peripheral areas are not so content. Primary and High Schools seem to be present in most of the localities of the city. Colleges are also present in an ample measure in most parts of the city. However, the utilization pattern of these facilities shows that they are underutilized in the central and southern part of the city, speaking for the need to increase the awareness among the parents for education. Private doctors are also present in almost all localities and at times their services are accessed from other localities also. Cinema theatres and eating places are present in an adequate measure in most parts of the city, though there is an element of underutilization so far as their use is concerned. Parks seem to be present in select central city localities, but their use is dismally low. Open spaces are more on the periphery of the city and by implication also utilized in those areas in a greater measure. Banks are present in all parts of the city though their use is slightly restricted in the Muslim dominated southern part of the city. Though ATM facility is present in most parts of the city it is utilized more along the main roads. Post and telegraph facilities are also adequately present all over the city, though their use pattern is less in comparison to its presence, owing to for one the digital revolution and secondly the low level of interaction of some of the localities with the rest of the world. It is also found that while not all people utilize super markets in the measure in which they are quoted to exist, yet all sections of the people are satisfied with commercial facilities present in their localities. An element of inclusivity so far as the basic services in the localities are concerned is witnessed; their presence and use patterns vouch for this fact.

It is found that there is a huge gap between the demand and supply of houses for the lower income groups. So far as housing finance and governmental housing schemes are concerned, it is found that the economically and socially marginalized groups covering certain specific occupational categories form the target groups for the governmental housing schemes. Houses are being constructed under the VAMBAY (Valmiki Ambedkar Awas Yojana) scheme for select marginalized social groups and some of them are also being made friendly to the old and the disabled. The scheme aims as relocation of houses of the beneficiaries or regularization. Most of the beneficiaries are from the Scheduled Castes, Scheduled Tribes and Backward Castes. Indira Awas Yojana (IAY) is another scheme aimed at addressing the housing needs of the underprivileged. However, irregularities have been found in identifying the beneficiaries and corruption and low quality work have blotched this scheme. The Rajiv Swagruha Scheme is aimed at providing affordable housing to the middle class people. This scheme had gained momentum during the recession.

Most people feel that drainage and water facilities in their localities need and uplift. A majority have felt that education is a vehicle for change and can bring about a betterment of fortunes. The perception of people with regard to inclusivity has been viewed against a backdrop of income, occupation, education, religious group and community group. It is felt that people either at the upper or lower levels of the income strata feel included in society, the middle class by implication seems left out. Certain groups of people like Christians, Scheduled Tribes feel an innate sense of inclusivity in the city. The highly educated and well placed people feel a lack of inclusivity as they have high expectations and if these are not met, they feel a sense of inadequacy. A study of the right to inheritance and ownership of land by women, ownership of property other than land by women, status of the women so far as the feasibility to acquire credit is concerned, to security of tenure and right to enter into contracts by women and availability of appropriate technology to women points to a general east-west divide in the city where the eastern part with traditional ethos is less accommodative of change on these counts This is not so with the western part of the city. The core-periphery variations where the core area is more traditional and the periphery more modern in outlook is also witnessed.

Lack of mixed localities in the city has also been found to be a reason for lack of inclusivity.

The recommendations that flow out from this study are that land meant for housing the underprivileged should be subsidized and funds at low rates of interest should be provided for construction purpose. Home loan rates should be lowered as also the Income Tax exemption limit on home loan interest repayment.

Development of integrated township in the area which can also house information technology firms can be taken up. The development of the township can be undertaken, in the private public partnership. The poor can be provided access to safe drinking water and drainage. Also pollution control and personal safety in slums can help the poor. This will cut down the health costs of the less privileged. They can also be given a sense of belongingness by encouraging labour intensive work routines and providing support for small-scale family enterprises and the informal sector. Inclusiveness in housing can be brought about by providing reasonably priced housing and also by guarding rental housing and ensuring that people are not displaced due to reasons beyond their control. This is apart from providing a well knit society, more so that which is assorted from the religious, cultural and caste point of view, giving a multi-cultural touch to the society, which will be healthy, tolerant and nationalistic.

Annexure I

Household Survey Questionnaire for UGC Major Research Project Inclusive Cities in an Era of Globalization*:* A Case for a Shelter Programme for Hyderabad

I General Information

(1) House Number ______________________________
(2) Name of Locality____________________________
(3) Circle in which located ________________________
(4) Ward and Block in which located ________________

II Household Information

(1) Name of the Respondent
(2) Religion: Hindu/Muslim/Christian/Others (Specify)
(3) Caste or Sub-Caste
(4) Native Place
(5) Duration of stay in Hyderabad
(6) Mother Tongue
(7) Gross Monthly Income (of Family)
  (a) Today
  (b) 10 years back
  (c) 20 years back
(8) Educational Level
(9) Occupation

III Particulars of Residential Accommodation

(1) Own/Rented/Rent Free (if Rent Free give details)
(2) Year of Construction

(3) Year of moving in
(4) Number of Rooms________(Exclude Kitchen and Bath/WC)
(5) Reason for moving
(6) Estimated market value of house:
    (a) Today
    (b) 10 years back (for this or similar sized house)
    (c) 20 years back (for this or similar sized house)
(7) Area of House (in square feet)
(8) Land value in the locality
(9) Tax amount for the house
(10) **If own house** furnish the following information:
    (a) Ancestral House
    (b) Built by self
        (i) If built or purchased, source of finance:
            (1) Savings
            (2) Loans from local credit sources
            (3) Loans from Govt./LIC/Bank/Housing Finance Corporations/Others (Specify)
    (c) Purchased from Housing projects/Schemes (Specify)
        (i) UPH,
        (ii) VAMBAY,
        (iii) RAJIV GRUHA KALPA,
        (iv) JNNURM,
        (v) Indira Awas Yojana,
        (vi) Dukan-O-Makan
    (d) Monthly owner cost (of maintenance)
(11) If Rented House
    (a) Private House/Institutional house
    (b) Monthly Rent in Rs.
    (c) Mode of Renting the House
        (i) Through friends/Relatives
        (ii) Press Advertisements
        (iii) Real Estate Agents, if yes
            (1) Are you satisfied with the services Yes/No
            (2) Commission Paid (Rs.——)
            (3) Do you think the charges are reasonable Yes/No
        (iv) On your own
(12) If you changed your house during the last five years give reasons:

(a) Built or purchased own house
(b) Allotted official accommodation
(c) Large Space
(d) Better Locality
(e) Occupational Mobility
(f) Others Specify

(13) Does your house need repair?
If Yes, of what type?

(14) How long do you plan to stay in this locality?
(a) < 1 year
(b) 1-2 years
(c) 3-5 years
(d) 5-10 years
(e) 10-20 years
(f) ≥ 20 years
(g) Life long

IV Work Place—Residence Relationship

Sl.No.	*Place of Work*	*Distance*	*Travel Time*	*Mode of Transport*
1. Self				
2. Others				
a.				
b.				
c.				
d.				

V Locational Amenities in the Neighbourhood

	Amenity/Facility	*Present*	*Utilized*
1.	Private Doctor		
2.	Hospital: Govt./Private/Corporate/Others (Specify)		
3.	Post/Telegraph Office		
4.	Bank: Specify Number and Name		
5.	ATM		
6.	Cinema House		
7.	Eating Place: Specify Number		
8.	Primary School		
9.	High School		
10.	College		
11.	Park		

(Contd.)

(*Contd.*)

	Amenity/Facility	*Present*	*Utilized*
12.	Playground		
13.	Open Space		
14.	Supermarket		
15.	Motor Mechanic Service		
16.	Religious Place: Temple/Church/Mosque/Others (Specify)		
17.	Bus Stops		
18.	Main roads		
19.	Arterial Roads		

VI Perception of Neighbourhood

Neighbourhood Condition	*Satisfied*	*Dissatisfied*	*Indifferent*	*No Opinion*
Location				
Accommodation				
Neighbourhood				
Sanitary facilities				
Water Supply				
Shopping Facilities				
Recreational Facilities				
Educational Facilities				
Health Facilities				
Accessibility				
Street Lighting				
Traffic Movement				

VII Perception of Housing

Housing Condition	*Satisfied*	*Dissatisfied*	*Indifferent*	*No Opinion*
Drainage				
Garbage Disposal				
Ventilation				
Water Supply				
Rent (if Applicable)				
Accomodation (Size)				

VIII. Rate Your Locality on a 7 Point Scale of Preferences in Terms of:

(1) Physical Surroundings
(2) Social Environment
(3) Amenities and Infrastructure
(4) Security

IX. Rate Your Residence on a 7 Point Scale of Preferences in Terms of Constituent Elements of the Human Right to Housing,

(a) Security of tenure/freedom from dispossession
  (i) Did the landlord ever ask you to vacate the house?
  (ii) Is the house rented for a fixed period?
(b) Public goods and services
(c) Environmental goods and services
  (i) Water, what is the quality of tap water? Is it used for:
    1. Drinking
    2. Bathing
    3. Cleaning/washing
    4. Gardening
    5. Others
  (ii) sanitation
  (iii) waste collection
  (iv) health
  (v) education
(d) Affordability
  (i) Is the rent/cost price of the house suitable? If not, what should it be?
(e) Habitability
  (i) Is the house good to live in, in terms of
    1. built structure
    2. number of rooms
    3. hygiene
(f) Accessibility
  (i) Are the following nearby:
    1. Workplace
    2. Shopping area for daily requirements

3. Place for recreation
4. Children's School/College

(g) Location
- (i) Is the site good? If not, what are the reasons/problems?

(h) Cultural appropriateness and cohesion
- (i) Is the neighbouring community homogenous in terms of—
  1. Caste
  2. Education
  3. Occupation
  4. Income
  5. Lifestyle
- (ii) With how many people in the neighbourhood do you have regular contact? Write Number

(i) Information, capacity and capacity-building
- (i) Have you been involved in neighbourhood organizing and governance initiatives? Specify
- (ii) Do you take part in neighbourhood/Housing Society Meetings? If not, why?
- (iii) What are the latest developments taking place in this locality with regard to—
  1. House building
  2. Laying of roads
  3. Development of parks
  4. Other infrastructure

(j) Participation and self-expression

(k) Resettlement
- (i) When you moved in from the previous locality, was it easy to adjust here in terms of:
  1. Neighbours
  2. Purchase of household items
  3. Daily travel

(l) Safe environment
- (i) Do thefts take place in this locality?
- (ii) Are children safe while travelling to school or playing in the neighbourhood?
- (iii) Are women safe in this locality if they go out in the evening?

(m) Privacy
- (i) Does the house have an independent gate?

(ii) How many persons are there in the house?
(iii) How many persons are there per room?

X. Does This Locality Display the Following with Regard to Housing? Yes or No

(a Equity
(b. Social justice
(c. Solidarity
(d. Human dignity
(e. Free choice
(f. Free movement
(g. Civic participation

XI. Do Women in Your Family Have:

1. Right to inheritance and the ownership of land
2. Right to other property
3. Acquired credit
4. Access to appropriate technology
5. Right to security of tenure and to enter into contracts

XII. Do NGOs and Local Elected Representatives Address Local Housing and Environmental Issues?

If yes, how often do they visit the locality?

XII.

(a) Do you feel left out or put at a distance from others in the community?
(b) What is the cause of exclusion? Caste/Income/Status/Region/Religion
(c) What are the problems associated with exclusion?
(d) How would you feel that you are part of the community?
(e) What would give you a sense of belonging and recognition?
(f) What should change in life in the community and larger society?

Annexure II

Questionnaire for the Study of Gated Communities in Hyderabad

(1) General Information
  (a) Name
  (b) Age
  (c) Gender
  (d) Qualification
  (e) Occupation
  (f) Caste
  (g) Income
(2) What do you own among the following?
  (a) land
  (b) building
  (c) vehicles
  (d) others (specify)
(3) Particulars of Residential Accommodation
  (a) Since how long have you been in this locality?
  (b) Where did you stay before coming here?
  (c) Why was this place chosen for residence?
  (d) Is it own or rented residence?
  (e) How many rooms are there in the residence?
(4) Is this locality better than the previous one in terms of following ? (Yes or No)
If yes how often do you visit them?
(a) Security
(b) Friendliness of people
(c) Helpful nature of neighbours
(d) Social relation and interaction among neighbours
(e) Physical surroundings
(f) Social set-up
(g) Amenities

(h) Drinking water
(i) Garbage
(j) Sewerage
(k) Garbage disposal
(l) Infrastructure
(m) Common halls
(n) Gym
(o) Swimming pool
(p) Roads
(q) Religious place
(r) Golf courses
(s) Horse-riding trails
(t) Linkage to the rest of the city
(u) Private parks

Bibliography

Aditya Verma, "Smart End Users", *Deccan Chronicle*, Nov. 27, 2009.

Aromer Ravi, *Shelter in India*, Vikas Publishing House, New Delhi, 1990.

Arya, D.S., S.A. Abbasi, *Urbanization and it's Environmental Impacts*, Discovery Publishing Home, New Delhi, 1905.

Asha Sachdeva 'What is the Definition of Affordable Houses? *Deccan Chronicle*, December. 3, 2009.

Census of India 2001, Series 29 A.P. Provisional Population Totals, Paper 2 of 2001, *Rural and urban Distribution of Population*, Controller of Publications, New Delhi, 2001.

Corbley, K.P., Image Processing and Analysis Empowering Users with New Tools, http://www.imagingnotes. com/mayjun00/mayjun1/htm

Dial, Gene and Grodecki, Jacek, Applications of IKONOS Imagery, ASPRS 2003 Annual Conference Proceedings, Anchorage, Alaska, May 2003.

Dutt, Ashok K., Mittra Chandreyee and Halder Animesh, 1997. "Slum Location and Cycle of Poverty: Calcutta Case", *Asian Profile*, Vol. 25, 5.

Dutt, Ashok K., Tripathi, Suprabha., and Mukhopadhyay Anupa. 1994. "Spatial Spread of Daily Activity Patterns of Slum Dwellers in Calcutta and Delhi". *The Asian City: Processes of Development, Characteristics and Planning*. Dutt, Ashok K., Costa, Frank J., Aggarwal, Surinder and Noble, Allen, G., Editors. Dordrech/Boston/London: Kluwer Academic Publishers, 309-326.

Dwit, Micheal, and Shenck, Hans, *Shelter for the Poor in India*. Delhi: Manohar Publications, 1989.

Fakhruddin, *Quality of Urban Life*, Rawat Publications, 1991.

Gallion, B., *The Urban Pattern*, East-West Press Private Ltd., New Delhi 1965.

Gopi, K.N., *Process of Urban Fringe Development: A Model*, Concept Publishing Company Pvt. Ltd., New Delhi, 1980.

Gopi, K.N., *Urban Growth and Industrial Locations*, Oxford and IBH Publishing Co., New Delhi, 1990.

Hafeez Contractor, Mass Need vs Vote Greed, *Sunday Times of India*, April 19, 2009.

Hagget, P., R.J. Johnston, D.R. Stoddart, D.M. Stoddart, D.M. Smith and D. Gregory; *Blackwell Dictionary of Human Geography*, Basil Blackwell, Oxford 1981.http://www.censusindia.net/results/slumnote.html

Homes for an Inclusive City: A Comprehensive Housing Strategy for Washington, D.C., The Final Report of the Comprehensive Housing Strategy Task Force, DRAFT Revised September 7, 2005.

Howard, P., Chudacoff, *The Evolution of American Urban Society*. Prentice Hall Inc., New Jersy, 1975.

http://htaindex.cnt.org/

http://htaindex.cnt.org/mapping_tool.php?theme_menu=0

http://in.news.yahoo.com/43/20100802/818/tnl-india-cannot-be-made-slum-free-in-fi.html

http://www.business-standard.com/india/news/outer-ring-road-phase-ii-to-be-ready-by-2012/387113/

http://www.censusindia.gov.in/towns/ap_towns.pdf

http://www.worldchanging.com/archives/004732.html

Hyderabad 2020, A Plan for Sustainable Development, Hyderabad Urban Development Authority, 2003.

Hyderabad Urban Development Authority, A Plan for Sustainable Development, Hyderabad India, 2002.

Jack, Harvey and Ernie Jowsey, *Urban Land Economics*, Palgrave MacMillian Houndmills, Basinstroke, Hampshire 2004.

Jacob, Z. Thudipara, *Urban Community Development*, Second Edition, Rawat Publications, India, 2007.

Jan, Hasseberg, *Issues in Urbanization Study of Ahmedabad City*, Rawat Publications, India, 2007.

Kamal, Deo Narain Singh, *Urban Development in India*. Abhinav Publications, New Delhi, 1978.

Kopardekar, H.D., *Social Aspects of Urban Environment*, Bombay Popular Prakashan,1986.

Lohmann, P., *et. al*, *Land Cover Classification using IKONOS Data*, http://www.geo.ucl.ac.be

Mahesh, K., "Reality Twist to Telangana Tale", *Sunday Times of India*, December, 27, 2009.

Manjula Dave, *Urban Ecology and Levels of Development*, Rawat Publications, Jaipur, 1990.

Market Beat, *Hyderabad Residential Report*, A Cushman and Wakefield Research Publication, 3Q, 2009.

Market Beat, *Hyderabad Retail Report*, A Cushman and Wakefield Research Publication, 3Q, 2009.

Michael, J. Dear, *The Post Modern Urban Condition*. Blackwell Publishers Inc, Massachusetts, U.S.A., 2000.

Michael, Pacione, *Urban Geography a Global Perspective*, Routledge, London, 2001.

Mukhopadhyay, Anupa, *Spatial Analysis of Daily Activity Pattern of a City Slum in Calcutta*. Master of Arts Thesis. University of Akron, 1990.

Nangia, Sudesh. "Slums of Urban India". *Asian Urbanization Problems and Processes*. (Ed) by Costa, Frank, J., Dutt, Ashok K., Ma, Lawrence J., and Noble, Allen G. Berlin: Gebruder Borntreager, 1988, 131-142.

Narle, G., Ashok K., Dutt, *Indian Urbanization and Planning: Vehicles of Allen Modernization*, Tata McGraw-Hill Publishing Company Ltd., New Delhi, 1977.

Nath, V., 1994. "Poverty in Metropolitan Cities in India". *The Asian City: Processes of Development, Characteristics and Planning*. Ed by Dutt, Ashok, K., Costa, Frank J., Aggarwal, Surinder and Noble, Allen, G. Dordrech/Boston/London: Kluwer Academic Publishers, 1994, pp. 295-308.

Peer Smets, *Housing Finance and the Urban Poor*, Rawat Publications, Jaipur, 2004.

Peter, Haggett, Andrew D. Cliff and Alan Frey. *Locational Models*, Edward Arnold Publishers Ltd, London U.S.A, 1996.

Prabhakar Sinha 'Housing and Dry?', *Sunday Times of India*, April 19, 2009.

Prasada Raju PVSP *et al*, "The Role of Satellite Derived Maps in National Spatial Data Infrastructure" in *http://www.gisdevelopment.net/policy/India/Technology/mi03157.htm*

Prodipto Roy, Shagun Das Gupta, Har-Anand Publications, New Delhi, 1995.

Ram Mohan Rao, R. and S.Simhadri, *Indian Cities, Towards Next Millenium*, Rawat Publications.

Ran Lake, David S.Burggraf, Milan Trninic Laurie Rae, *Geography Mark-up Language* (GMC), John Wiley and Sons Ltd, England, U.K., 2004.

Ratna Reddy, V., B.Saresh Reddy, Land Alienation and Local Communities: Case Studies in Hyderabad and Secunderabad. *Economical and Political Weekly*, Vol. XLII, No. 31, Sameeksha Trust Publication.

Ravinder, S., Sandhu and Jasmeet Sandhu, *Globalizing Cities, Inequality and Segregation in Developing Countries*, Rawat Publications, India, 2002.

Satish Sabarwal, *Process and Institution in Urban India*, Vikas Publishing House, New Delhi, 1978.

Siddhartha, K., S. Mukherjee, *Cities Urbanization and Urban Systems*, Kisabeya Publications, 2000.

Simhadri, S., Changing Pattern of Land Pricing in Urban Fringe (unpublished), Hyderabad, 1993.

Simhadri, S., Urban Land Development in Relation to Urban Land Policy (unpublished), Hyderabad, 1993.

Singh, J.P., *Urban Land Used, Planning in Hill Areas*, Inter-India Publications, New Delhi, 1979.

Singh, Tara and Misra, "*Girishwar, Human Response to Population Growth and Environmental Challenges, The Indian Experience*", Newsletter of the International Human Dimensions Programme on Global Environmental Change, 04/2004.

Sita, K., "The Cityscape of Mumbai: Continuity and Change in Baleshwar Thakur, George Pomeroy, Chris Cusack and Sudhir K. Thakur, Editors, *City, Society and Planning: Essays in Honour of Professor A.K. Dutt*, Vol. 1, City, New Delhi Concept Publishing Company Pvt. Ltd., 2007, 419-438.

Sunday Chronicle, August, 9, 2009.

Susan, S.Fainstein and Scott Campbell, *Readings in Urban Theory* Second Edition, Blackwell Publishers Ltd., Malden U.S.A, 1996.

United Nations Human Settlements Programme, Financing Urban Shelter, Global Report Human Settlements 2005, Earthscan Publishers in London U.K., 2005.

United Nations Human Settlements Programme, Meeting Development Goals In Small Urban Centers, Water and Sanitation in the World: s Cities 2006, Earthscan Publishers in London U.K 2005.

Vijaya Bhole, *Housing and Urban Development in India*, Classical Publishing Company, New Delhi,1988.

Vithal Reddy, K., R. Ram Mohan Rao, *Urban Crises in India*, Hyderabad Publishers 1985.

Wilson, A.G., P.H. Rees and C.M Leigh, *Models of Cities and Regions: Theoretical and Empirical Developments*, John Wiley and Sons Ltd, Britain, 1977.

Yadav, C.S., Migration and Urbanization in India: A Case Study of Delhi. *Urbanization in Asia*, Ed. By Frank J. Costa, Ashok K. Dutt, Lawrence J.C. Mar and Allen G. Noble. Honolulu: University of Hawaii Press, 1989, pp. 227-244.

Yeates, M.H. and Garner, P.J. *The North American City*, Harper and Row, New York, 1971. www.gdrc.org/uem/squatters/define-squatter.html

Bibliography—Archival Data on Housing, Real Estate in Hyderabad from 2006 to 2010.

2006

Anushya Rajagopalan, *The Times of India*, November 11, 2006.
Anushya Rajagopalan, *The Times of India*, September 16, 2006.
D.M.Mathew, *The Hindu*, November 4, 2006.
D.M.Mathew, *The Hindu*, October 21, 2006.
D.M.Mathew, *The Hindu*, October 28, 2006.
Deccan Chronicle, November 11, 2006.
Deccan Chronicle, November 11, 2006.
Deccan Chronicle, November 2, 2006.
Deccan Chronicle, November 23, 2006.

Deccan Chronicle, November 5, 2006.
Deccan Chronicle, October 25, 2006.
Jayesh Ranjan, *The Hindu*, April 15, 2006.
K.Srinivas Reddy, *The Hindu*, April 15, 2006.
M. Sai Gopal, *The Hindu*, December 16, 2006.
M. Sai Gopal, *The Hindu*, October 21, 2006.
M.L.M. Maitreyi, *The Hindu*, November 25, 2006.
M.L.M.Maitreyi, *The Hindu*, December 16, 2006.
M.L.M.Maitreyi, *The Hindu*, November 18, 2006.
M.L.M.Maitreyi, *The Hindu*, November 4, 2006.
M.L.Maitreyi, *The Hindu*, October 28, 2006.
M.L.Melly Maitreyi, *The Hindu*, September 30, 2006.
M.Sai Gopal, *The Hindu*, December 2, 2006.
M.Sai Gopal, *The Hindu*, October 28, 2006.
M.Srinivas, *The Hindu*, September 30, 2006.
N.Vamsi Srinivas, *Deccan Chronicle*, November 11, 2006.
N.Venkateswarlu, *The Hindu*, September 30, 2006.
Nirmala Govindarajan, *The Times of India*, December 16, 2006.
S. Bachan Jeet Singh, *The New Indian Express*, December 5, 2006.
T.Lalith Singh, *The Hindu*, December 16, 2006.
T.Lalith Singh, *The Hindu*, December 26, 2006.
T.Lalith Singh, *The Hindu*, December 9, 2006.
T.Lalith Singh, *The Hindu*, November 11, 2006.
T.Lalith Singh, *The Hindu*, November 4, 2006.
T.Lalith Singh, *The Hindu*, October 14, 2006.
The Hindu, April 15, 2006.
The Hindu, December 9, 2006.
The Hindu, November 25, 2006.
The Hindu, November 25, 2006.
The Hindu, November 4, 2006.
The New Indian Express, December 26, 2006.
The New Indian Express, December 26, 2006.
The Times of India, December 16, 2006.
The Times of India, December 31, 2006.
The Times of India, December 31, 2006.
The Times of India, November 11, 2006.
The Times of India, November 11, 2006.
V.Geetanath, *The Hindu*, December 16, 2006.
VGN, *The Hindu*, September 16, 2006.

2007

Deccan Chronicle, December 29, 2007.
K. Srinivasa Rao, *Deccan Chronicle*, October 20, 2007.
K.V. Kurmnath, *The Hindu*, Feburary 24, 2007.
M.L.M. Maitreyi, *The Hindu*, Feburary 10, 2007.
M.L.M. Maitreyi, *The Hindu*, March 17, 2007.
M. Sai Gopal, *The Hindu*, January 27, 2007.
M. Srinivas, *The Hindu*, July 7, 2007.
Seth Sutel, *Deccan Chronicle*, August 7, 2007.
T. Lalith Singh, *The Hindu*, Feburary 24, 2007.
T. Lalith Singh, *The Hindu*, January 6, 2007.
The Cyberabad Times, Sunday, April 22, 2007.
The Hindu, Feburary 10, 2007.
The Hindu, Feburary 24, 2007.
V. Geetanath, *The Hindu*, July 14, 2007.
V.Geetanath, *The Hindu*, July 7, 2007.

2008

Aditya Verma, *Deccan Chronicle*, December 12, 2008.
Ajit Nair, *Times of India*, March 16, 2008.
Anshuman Magazine, *Deccan Chronicle*, December 5, 2008.
Anuj Puri, *Deccan Chronicle*, November 21, 2008.
Surya, D., *Deccan Chronicle*, April 18, 2008.
Surya, D., *The Hindu*, July 16, 2008.
Deccan Chronicle October 11, 2008.
Deccan Chronicle, April 17, 2008.
Deccan Chronicle, April 25, 2008.
Deccan Chronicle, August 22, 2008.
Deccan Chronicle, August 22, 2008.
Deccan Chronicle, August 22, 2008.
Deccan Chronicle, August 22, 2008.
Deccan Chronicle, August 22, 2008.
Deccan Chronicle, August 3, 2008.
Deccan Chronicle, August 8, 2008.
Deccan Chronicle, December 16, 2008.
Deccan Chronicle, December 19, 2008.
Deccan Chronicle, February 1, 2008.
Deccan Chronicle, February 1, 2008.

Deccan Chronicle, February 1, 2008.
Deccan Chronicle, February 17, 2008.
Deccan Chronicle, July 18, 2008.
Deccan Chronicle, July 25, 2008.
Deccan Chronicle, July 4, 2008.
Deccan Chronicle, June 6, 2008.
Deccan Chronicle, November 4, 2008.
Deccan Chronicle, November 11, 2008.
Deccan Chronicle, November 21, 2008.
Deccan Chronicle, November 21, 2008.
Deccan Chronicle, November 4, 2008.
Deccan Chronicle, September 2, 2008.
Deccan Chronicle, September 2, 2008.
Deccan Chronicle, September 25, 2008.
Indrani Rajadurai, *Deccan Chronicle*, July 29, 2008.
Jyoti Verma, *Deccan Chronicle*, December 19, 2008.
K. Srinivasa Rao, *Deccan Chronicle*, April 11, 2008.
K. Srinivasa Rao, *Deccan Chronicle*, February 15, 2008.
K. Srinivasa Rao, *Deccan Chronicle*, February 22, 2008.
K. Srinivasa Rao, *Deccan Chronicle*, February 29, 2008.
K. Srinivasa Rao, *Deccan Chronicle*, March 21, 2008.
K.Srinivasa Rao, *Deccan Chronicle*, April 25, 2008.
K.Srinivasa Rao, *Deccan Chronicle*, August 1, 2008.
K.Srinivasa Rao, *Deccan Chronicle*, August 8, 2008.
K.Srinivasa Rao, *Deccan Chronicle*, December 12, 2008.
K.Srinivasa Rao, *Deccan Chronicle*, December 19, 2008.
K.Srinivasa Rao, *Deccan Chronicle*, December 26, 2008.
K.Srinivasa Rao, *Deccan Chronicle*, December 5; 2008.
K.Srinivasa Rao, *Deccan Chronicle*, July 25, 2008.
K.Srinivasa Rao, *Deccan Chronicle*, July 4, 2008.
K.Srinivasa Rao, *Deccan Chronicle*, June 13, 2008.
K.Srinivasa Rao, *Deccan Chronicle*, June 27, 2008 (part)
K.Srinivasa Rao, *Deccan Chronicle*, March 14, 2008.
K.Srinivasa Rao, *Deccan Chronicle*, May 23, 2008.
K.Srinivasa Rao, *Deccan Chronicle*, May 9, 2008.
K.Srinivasa Rao, *Deccan Chronicle*, November 14, 2008.
K.Srinivasa Rao, *Deccan Chronicle*, November 21, 2008.
K.Srinivasa Rao, *Deccan Chronicle*, November 7, 2008.
K.Srinivasa Rao, *Deccan Chronicle*, October 17, 2008.
K.Srinivasa Rao, *Deccan Chronicle*, October 3, 2008.

K.Srinivasa rao, *Deccan Chronicle*, October 31, 2008.
K.Srinivasa Rao, *Deccan Chronicle*, September 1, 2008.
Reddy, L.V., *Deccan Chronicle*, February 15, 2008.
Reddy, L.V., *Deccan Chronicle*, January 25, 2008.
Reddy, L.V., *Deccan Chronicle*, April 4, 2008.
Reddy, L.V., *Deccan Chronicle*, August 1, 2008.
Reddy, L.V., *Deccan Chronicle*, August 15, 2008.
Reddy, L.V., *Deccan Chronicle*, August 8, 2008.
Reddy, L.V., *Deccan Chronicle*, December 12, 2008.
Reddy, L.V., *Deccan Chronicle*, December 19, 2008.
Reddy, L.V., *Deccan Chronicle*, December 26, 2008.
Reddy, L.V., *Deccan Chronicle*, December 5, 2008.
Reddy, L.V., *Deccan Chronicle*, February 15, 2008.
Reddy, L.V., *Deccan Chronicle*, July 11, 2008.
Reddy, L.V., *Deccan Chronicle*, July 18, 2008.
Reddy, L.V., *Deccan Chronicle*, July 25, 2008.
Reddy, L.V., *Deccan Chronicle*, July 4, 2008.
Reddy, L.V., *Deccan Chronicle*, June 20, 2008.
Reddy, L.V., *Deccan Chronicle*, June 27, 2008 (part)
Reddy, L.V., *Deccan Chronicle*, March 14, 2008.
Reddy, L.V., *Deccan Chronicle*, March 28, 2008.
Reddy, L.V., *Deccan Chronicle*, May 16, 2008.
Reddy, L.V., *Deccan Chronicle*, May 23, 2008.
Reddy, L.V., *Deccan Chronicle*, May 9, 2008.
Reddy, L.V., *Deccan Chronicle*, November 14, 2008.
Reddy, L.V., *Deccan Chronicle*, November 21, 2008.
Reddy, L.V., *Deccan Chronicle*, October 31, 2008.
Reddy, L.V., *Deccan Chronicle*, September 12, 2008.
Ministry of Commerce & Industry, *Deccan Chronicle*, March 7, 2008.
Vamsi Srinivas, N., *Deccan Chronicle*, September 24, 2008.
Vamsi Srinivas, N., *The Hindu*, November 11, 2008.
Rai Umraopati Ray, *Deccan Chronicle*, August 22, 2008.
Rai Umraopati Ray, *Deccan Chronicle*, December 5, 2008.
Rai Umraopati Ray, *Deccan Chronicle*, September 19, 2008.
Umamaheshwar, S., *Deccan Chronicle*, September 26, 2008.
Sunday Times of India, October 12, 2008.
The Hindu, November 11, 2008.
Times News Network, 2008.
Times News Network, March 4, 2008.
Times of India, March 16, 2008.

Yogesh Mehendale, *The Hindu*, November 11, 2008.

2009

Contractor. H, 2009.
Deccan Chronicle, January 10, 2009.
Deccan Chronicle, January 10, 2009.
Deccan Chronicle, January 5, 2009.
Deccan Chronicle, January 10, 2009.
Deccan Chronicle, March 27, 2009.
Deccan Chronicle, April 10, 2009.
Deccan Chronicle, August 3, 2009.
Deccan Chronicle, August 3, 2009.
Deccan Chronicle, August 5, 2009.
Deccan Chronicle, August 9, 2009.
Deccan Chronicle, September, 2009.
Deccan Chronicle, November 21, 2009.
Deccan Chronicle, November 21, 2009.
Deccan Chronicle, November 26, 2009.
Deccan Chronicle, December 9, 2009.
Reddy, L.V., *Deccan Chronicle*, January 9, 2009.
Raminder Grover, *Deccan Chronicle*, November 20, 2009.
Samir Chopra, *Deccan Chronicle*, October 21, 2009.
Sunday Chronicle, August 9, 2009.
Sunday Chronicle, September 26, 2009.
Verma A, 2009.

2010

Deccan Chronicle, February 2, 2010
Deccan Chronicle, February 10, 2010 (part)
Deccan Chronicle, May 12, 2010.
N. Vamsi Srinivas, *Deccan Chronicle*, April 10, 2010.
Times of India, October 6, 2010.

2011

Times of India, January, 23, 2011.

Index